Film
Review
2013-2014

Film Review

2013-2014

Michael Darvell and **Mansel Stimpson**

EXECUTIVE EDITOR:
JAMES CAMERON-WILSON

SIGNUM BOOKS

For Anwar Brett
(23 July 1966-24 November 2013)

Michael Darvell and Mansel Stimpson dedicate this edition of Film Review *to the memory of their friend and colleague, the late, lamented Anwar Brett who died on 24 November 2013, aged 47. He was a former contributor to* Film Review *as well as many other publications including the* Guardian, What's On In London, Total Film, Flicks *and a number of regional publications. Living in Dorset he was a very active member of the Guild of Regional Film Writers and in 2011 published a book,* Dorset in Film, *about the many films that have been shot in the county. Much admired in the UK film business, Anwar was an active member of BAFTA, for whom he chaired audience Q&A sessions; he also wrote obituaries for the BAFTA website. He is sorely missed at all the press conferences and other events he always and so ably supported. Our heartfelt condolences go to his wife Tracey and their daughters Sian and Livvy.*

Acknowledgements

The editors of *Film Review 2013-2014* would like to thank the following, without whose invaluable help this book might not have appeared:

Charles Bacon, Alex Buchan, Jeremy Clarke, Peri Godbold, Marcus Hearn, Marshall Julius, Penny Lucas, Jonathan Rigby, George Savvides, Paul Taylor and Derek Winnert.

Frontispiece: Brad Pitt in *World War Z*.

First published in Great Britain in 2014 by Signum Books, an imprint of
Flashpoint Media Ltd
173 Mill Road
Cambridge
CB1 3AN

© Michael Darvell and Mansel Stimpson 2014

A CIP catalogue record for this book is available from the British Library.

ISBN 978 0 957648 11 1

Designer: Peri Godbold
Managing editor: Marcus Hearn

Printed and bound in China by 1010 Printing International Ltd.

Contents

Introduction

by **Michael Darvell**

Above:
In 1969, the late Peter O'Toole – pictured with Petula Clark in the musical remake of *Goodbye, Mr Chips* – was cover star of the 25th *Film Review* annual. (See our In Memoriam feature, page 180.)

Seven years ago, when Mansel Stimpson and I assumed the editorship of *Film Review*, there were some 400 films to cover. The following year saw that number increase by 50 or more titles. By 2009 there was a slight diminution with just 440 releases. Volume 66 was a catch-up issue while we changed publishers, covering the 700 films released over the 18 months between July 2009 and December 2010. By Volume 67 we were reviewing about 470 of the 500 films released from January to December 2011. Last year the figure of film releases for 2012 was 525, of which we managed to cover all but about 40. This current volume surveys the film output of 2013, which comprised 555 releases of which we have covered around 480.

The shortfall in our film reviews is due to the fact that the year 2013 saw a lot of very odd releases. Apart from the Bollywood quota (which, because we still experience difficulty in actually previewing them, accounts for around 60 of the missing titles), there were other foreign films that didn't appear to have been seen by anybody, least of all our reviewers. They may have appeared at film festivals, at club screenings, specialist cinemas or may have just gone straight to television or DVD. Still, nearly 500 reviews is not bad going considering that the total output of 555 comes out at an average of over ten releases a week.

Whether many of the films shown were worth seeing or even worth making in the first place, you will discover when you read the individual opinions of our band of ten critics. We are very fair-minded in giving credit where it is due and yet not above sharpening our quills should the occasion arise. Yes, at times we all wonder whatever possessed this producer to employ that director who cast these actors or actresses in that terrible screenplay which should have been rejected long before it reached the camera stage.

It's true that there are far too many films being made and released on an unsuspecting public – who, given the high price they have to pay to see a film these days, are probably more discerning now than they have ever been. Cinema admissions have generally been increasing year on year at a rate of knots, but the old adage about fooling some of the people only some of the time still holds sway. Whatever the critics say – good or bad – about a film, the general public will always make up its own mind.

Cinema admissions in the UK rose every year from the mid-1930s (912 million) to a peak of 1,635 million in 1946, since when they dwindled year on year until the all-time low of 54 million in 1984, following the widespread closure of many unprofitable cinemas. However, with the introduction of the multiplex from 1985, admissions rose again to reach 175 million in 2002. Since then there have been minor fluctuations both up and down, but the annual totals have never topped the 2002 figure. Between 2006 and 2009 annual admissions have ranged from 156 million to 173 million. From 2010 the numbers rose steadily again from 169 million in 2010, 171 million in 2011 to 172 million in 2012. For some reason the figures for 2013 are down again, with admissions hitting only 165 million.

With more films being released every week you might think that audience figures wouldn't fluctuate in this way, given such a wide choice of movies. No doubt it depends on how many blockbusters are released in any one year, because those big, popular films that everybody wants to see do make a difference to the figures. Still, it's not every year that can produce an *Iron Man* or a *Hobbit*, or a *Gravity* or a *Star Trek* or a *Fast & Furious* or a *Les Misérables*, or even a *Hangover* (he said gratefully). Audiences will flock to the films they really want to see; the trouble is that not enough good films are being made. Most weeks of the year there are one or two films worth pursuing, but the rest of the releases are, generally speaking, not worth the bother. They open, play for a week or two and then vanish again, only to resurface on DVD or Blu-ray.

At a time when going to the cinema is becoming an increasingly expensive form of entertainment, it's no wonder that audiences will cherry-pick their choice of films. Gone are the days when just 'going to the pictures' was an everyday occurrence for which you didn't have to book or plan ahead. It was a cheap and satisfying way of passing the time, if you didn't wish to support other forms of public entertainment such as horseracing, football matches, theatre, music, opera, dancing or clubs. Apart from television and radio, some forms of entertainment are now quite beyond the pockets of many punters. Consequently the cinema seems to be pricing itself out of the market and indeed live theatre (excluding London's West End) frequently offers better value than some of our major cinema chains.

That said, it is encouraging that new cinemas are still being opened. The independent chains, as opposed to the big multiplex companies (Odeon, Cineworld, Vue, Empire etc) are flourishing, providing a more intimate personal service than the mighty multiplexes can offer. When the Hampstead Everyman, an independent cinema since 1933, was threatened with closure in 1999 because it was running at a loss, the Everyman Cinema Group took over and began an expansion policy that included the purchase of the Screen cinemas from Mainline Pictures, thus instigating a strong and fiercely independent chain that now comprises the London Everyman cinemas in Baker Street, Belsize Park, Maida Vale, Islington's Screen on the Green and the original Everyman in Hampstead. It also has cinemas out of town in Oxted, Reigate, Walton-on-Thames and Winchester. The new Everyman Leeds opened in 2013 and Birmingham is scheduled for 2014. An Everyman cinema will be part of the new Canary Wharf Crossrail development in London Docklands from May 2015.

The Picturehouse group of cinemas (formerly City Screen and now owned by Cineworld) has also grown over the years since they acquired their first cinema in Oxford in 1989. Specialising in showing independent and foreign language films, they now have 21 sites in the network. London is well represented by Picturehouses in Brixton, Clapham, Notting Hill Gate, Greenwich, Hackney and Stratford East, while the rest of the UK has sites in Oxford, Cambridge, Bath, Brighton, Bury St Edmunds, Edinburgh, Exeter, Henley-on-Thames, Liverpool, Norwich, Southampton, Stratford-upon-Avon and York. Plans are in hand to refurbish the London Trocadero site in Shaftesbury Avenue as a Picturehouse cinema. At present it's run by Cineworld, the company that bought the Picturehouse network in 2012. However, the two companies remain separate entities and Picturehouse continues to be independent of the other cinema chains and multiplexes by offering a different programming policy.

Below:
The Desolation of Smaug was the latest instalment in Peter Jackson's *Hobbit* franchise.

Similarly Curzon cinemas have gradually built up their London operation from their original Mayfair showcase, by creating Curzons in Soho, Chelsea and Richmond, plus the Renoir in Brunswick Square. Additionally they now have cinemas outside London in Ripon, Yorkshire, and Knutsford in Cheshire. Curzon are also in partnership with other organisations including HMV at the Curzon in Wimbledon, the Cinema at Pinewood Studios, the Bridport Arts Centre, the Watermark in Ivybridge, Devon, the Hawth at Crawley in West Sussex, Woodend Barn at Banchory, Aberdeenshire, and the Screen @ RADA, the Royal Academy of Dramatic Art, in London. Their latest opening is the newly built five-screen Curzon at Victoria, part of the redevelopment of Victoria Street in south London. A three-screen Curzon cinema forms part of the plans for redeveloping the site of the former Regal (ABC) in Kingston-upon-Thames.

It has to be said, however, that it is not only the independent cinemas that are expanding. All the major multiplex companies have future plans. Cineworld has 14 scheduled openings, Vue has 12 more cinemas in the pipeline, while Odeon has another half-dozen new sites planned. It is encouraging that film distributors are still so positive about the future of the cinema as a place of entertainment, given that operations such as Lovefilm, Netflix and all the other home-streaming movie facilities continue to burgeon.

The one fly in the ointment is the spiralling cost of going to the cinema. I don't know what sort of audience the new Curzon at Victoria is expecting to attract, but it will have to be a well-heeled one to afford the £18 top admission price plus £1 booking fee. There are some concessions for off-peak performances including an Early Bird matinée at £9. Victoria used to have a wealth of cinemas, with the Metropole, the New Victoria, the Cameo, the Biograph and the Classic News & Cartoon Cinema on Victoria station. It has had nothing for decades, so a new cinema is very welcome. But it's a pity that locals will have to pay such a high price to see a film. Compare this with the nearby, recently opened St James Theatre where, for some shows, you can get in for just £5, or the Picturehouse at Stratford East where seniors can gain weekday afternoon admission for just £5 – and that includes tea or coffee with biscuits!

Obviously inner London is going to be more expensive than outside the capital. For example, the most famous single-screen London cinema and survivor of the multiplex cull, the Odeon Leicester Square, charges between £11 and £22 for standard tickets, dependent on whereabouts you sit and on status (child, teen, student, senior or adult). The off-peak prices for certain matinées are £9-£18. However, if you go to a local London cinema such as the Odeon at Muswell Hill, the price range is £8.10 to £9.95 at evening peak times, with an off-peak rate of £6 across the board, regardless of status. At the Odeon Swiss Cottage, however, matters become a mite more complicated: tickets are £7-£10.45 (weekday peak time), £8.50-£11.95 (weekend peak time), and £6.50-£8.95 (at weekday Super Saver matinées). There are also Club Seats at £10-£13 (weekday peak), £12.50-£16 (weekend peak) and £6.50-£8.95 (weekday super saver matinées). Of course, for 3D films there are supplements of £2 (plus £1 for 3D specs) and an extra £4.50 for IMAX films, while the really big blockbusters also incur a surcharge of £2.70 – plus booking fee.

For sheer luxury at a luxurious price, the Electric Cinema in Portobello Road, Notting Hill (formerly part of the Screen chain) takes the biscuit – which at their prices must be millionaire's shortbread. There's a choice of single armchair seating at £18, front-row double beds for two people at £30, and back-row sofas at the rear for two at £45. There are slight reductions on Sundays and Mondays (£15.50, £25 and £40) and for children it's £10, £16 and £45. There are also savings for members and the kids club screenings, but it all seems a long way away from those heady days when prices were 1/6, 2/3 or 2/9 at your local ABC, Essoldo or Granada, and the Automaticket machine issued your pass at the mere click of a button.

Going back even further, we reach an era of films all too many of which have been lost. However, every so often news comes that some film previously thought to be missing has suddenly resurfaced in the most unlikely of places. The British Film Institute has a list of the 75 'Most Wanted' films that are not in their National Archive. They include many early silent films from 1913, including *A Study in Scarlet* (1914), the first Sherlock Holmes feature; *The First Men in the Moon* (1919), the first HG Wells film adaptation; *The Adventures of Mr Pickwick* (1921), based on Dickens' book; *Who is the Man?* (1924), notable for John Gielgud's first film appearance; and *Too Many Crooks* (1930), which marked Laurence Olivier's movie debut. Other lost movies include three early Michael Powells: *Two Crowded Hours* (1931), *The Price of a Song* (1935) and *The Man Behind the Mask* (1936); Errol Flynn's first film, *Murder at Monte Carlo* (1935), and *The Diamond* (1954), the first-ever British 3D film.

Below: Cover of the campaign booklet for *Love, Life and Laughter* (1923) starring Betty Balfour.

Above left:
Joseph Cotten
in Orson Welles'
previously lost film
Too Much Johnson
(1938).

Above:
Orson Welles as
Klingsor, king of the
gypsies, in *Where is
Parsifal?* (1983).

For a long time there were several lost Hitchcock movies but now the BFI is only missing one of the great British director's films, *The Mountain Eagle*, made in 1928. Hitchcock himself described it as "awful" but the BFI is still resolute in trying to locate a copy. One recent discovery was that of George Pearson's *Love, Life and Laughter* (1923) starring Betty Balfour, the most successful British film actress of the 1920s; known as Britain's answer to Mary Pickford, she appeared as a character called Squibs in many popular films of the day. It was discovered at EYE, the Dutch Film Museum, having been sent as part of a collection of film cans found in a disused cinema when the building was about to be redeveloped in 2012.

Sometimes old films turn up that hardly anybody knew existed. Such was the case with a collection of films made from 1900 to 1913 by Sagar Mitchell and James Kenyon, two early pioneers of cinematography from Blackburn, Lancashire. They were commissioned by touring showmen and fairground operators around the UK to film the everyday lives of ordinary people at work and at leisure, which they would then show to their customers. Some 800 rolls of film were discovered in sealed barrels in the basement of a shop in Blackburn. The BFI subsequently restored the films and in conjunction with the BBC made three programmes out of them, called *The Lost World of Mitchell and Kenyon*. The series showed how the films were unearthed and restored, how people at the turn of the century entertained themselves with football matches, riding on buses and holidaying in Blackpool, plus the first-ever crime reconstruction film and, finally, how Mitchell and Kenyon fared in the USA before they parted and went their own ways. This uniquely fascinating BBC series is available to buy on DVD through the BFI.

One film that was on the BFI's 'Most Wanted' list was *Where is Parsifal?* (1983), starring Orson Welles, Tony Curtis and Peter Lawford. It appeared at the Cannes Festival in 1984 but was never released. The good news about this one is that the director, Henri Helman, donated his own personal 35mm print to the BFI for their archives.

Welles was notorious for starting projects but never finishing them. These included Joseph Conrad's *Heart of Darkness* (Coppola eventually made it as *Apocalypse Now*), *The Life of Christ*, *Cyrano de Bergerac*, *King Lear*, *Around the World in 80 Days* and *The Big Brass Ring*. This last was eventually made in 1999, based on Welles' original screenplay. One film that was made but not edited or screened is *Too Much Johnson*, a 1938 comedy written and directed by Welles. It was considered lost until it was found in a warehouse in Pordenone, Italy, by a local film society. The print has been restored by the George Eastman House and the National Film Preservation Foundation and, having been shown in New York City in November 2013, is scheduled for a Los Angeles screening in 2014.

Other recent archaeological finds involve the missing short films of Peter Sellers.

Back in the 1950s Sellers appeared in a series of spoof Government public information shorts for Park Lane Films. Titled 'Best Sellers', there were supposed to be a dozen 30-minute films in the series in which Sellers played a character called Hector Dimwittie, but only three were made, *Cold Comfort*, *Dearth of a Salesman* and *Insomnia is Good for You*, before the company went out of business. Although *Cold Comfort* survived, the last two were thought to be completely lost until they were discovered lying in cans in a skip by the building manager at the film company's office. Not really knowing what they were, he kept them in his garage for 17 years before approaching the Southend Film Festival. The films were subsequently digitally restored and all three (including *Cold Comfort*) were shown at the 2014 festival.

Perhaps the BFI should endeavour to acquire these shorts for distribution on their own DVD label. The BFI's National Archive has already

Above:
Fritz Lang's
1933 classic
*The Testament
of Dr Mabuse*,
back among us
courtesy of Eureka
Entertainment.

restored the early Sellers films *Penny Points to Paradise* and *Let's Go Crazy* and, out of historical interest, has released them on DVD and Blu-ray. The BFI catalogue of releases contains over 300 films and it issues up to 40 titles a year. These films might otherwise not be available to view in any form. The list includes classics of the cinema as well as cult movies that have by and large been overlooked by other distributors. Here you will find Buñuel's *L'Age d'Or*, Cocteau's *La Belle et la Bête*, Dreyer's *Day of Wrath*, Demy's *Les Demoiselles de Rochefort*, film noir classics, films from the Children's Film Foundation, a huge collection of British Transport films, many volumes of Chaplin's short films, the Terence Davies Trilogy, the works of Ozu and Jacques Tati, and Pasolini's *Salò* as well as good old British rubbish such as *Miss Tulip Stays the Night* and *Fun at St Fanny's*. These last and the previously mentioned Peter Sellers movies are from the library of Adelphi Films whose collections are now preserved in the BFI's National Archive.

When it comes to acquiring DVDs of vintage films, we're quite spoilt at the moment. Whereas BBC2 used to show vintage black-and-white films late at night, this type of programming is now usually restricted to early mornings on Saturday or Sunday. However, Film Four has a good reputation for screening a wide variety of old movies, as well as some foreign titles that may be unfamiliar to most viewers. The Movies 4 Men TV channel specialises in vintage black-and-white films which are usually screened in the mornings, with minor British thrillers from the 1950s and '60s interspersed with even more ancient 1930s and '40s Westerns starring the likes of Tom Mix, Buster Crabbe and Tex Ritter, while the rest of the day is often devoted to Italian action epics, war and police documentaries and mild erotica.

Movies 4 Men shows a lot of films from the Renown catalogue (motto: "rare, unseen, B-movies, must-see movies and more"), which has the pick of the film libraries of now-defunct second-feature specialists such as Butchers, New Realm, Eros, Grand National and many more. All the releases from Renown are digitally remastered and they cover every possible genre, including crime, war, SF, comedy, horror, Westerns etc, and many are issued as double-bills. They've even got Betty Balfour in a talkie version of *Squibs*, dating

from 1935, and Freddie and The Dreamers in *Cuckoo Patrol* from 1967.

For the collector of vintage movies, the choice is mind-boggling. Network DVD reissues films that no one has seen for decades. Apart from their ever-burgeoning collection of rarities from the Ealing Studios archives (*Autumn Crocus*, *Birds of Prey*, *The House of the Spaniard*, *The Fortunate Fool* etc – ever heard of them? neither had I), there are literally thousands of titles including a preponderance of British oldies, not only from Ealing but also from Gainsborough, Gaumont-British, London Films, British Lion, Rank and EMI etc. Much of the material may seem run-of-the-mill to us now, but it's good to have access to these popular movies of another era.

The Odeon Entertainment Group offers a real mixed bag of films on DVD, from the innocent pleasures of Fred Astaire and Ginger Rogers, *The Old Dark House*, *The Arsenal Stadium Mystery* and *The History of Mr Polly*, through Charlie Chan and The Saint, *Song Without End*, *The Thief of Bagdad* and *They Shoot Horses, Don't They?* to the more sensational *No Orchids for Miss Blandish*, *House of Whipcord*, *Venus in Furs* and *Justine's Hot Nights*. You could say that a whole panoply of genre movies ends up in the Odeon catalogue.

Eureka Entertainment specialises in reviving recognised film classics in their Masters of Cinema series, going right back to the silent era. William Wellman's *Wings* (1927) was the first film to win an Academy Award for Best Picture and the only silent film to do so. It's a thrilling story of romance set against spectacular and realistically staged flying action scenes of the First World War. With Clara Bow, Richard Arlen and Gary Cooper (in his screen debut), the film has been fully restored and is now available on two discs in the dual format of DVD and Blu-ray, with video documentaries on the film and its restoration and a 40-page booklet including a vintage interview with the director. Other classics given the Eureka treatment include DW Griffith's *The Birth of a Nation*, Sternberg's *The Blue Angel*, Fritz Lang's *The Testament of Doctor Mabuse*, Cecil B DeMille's 1934 *Cleopatra*, Billy Wilder's *Ace in the Hole* and *The Lost Weekend*, Orson Welles' *Touch of Evil* and *F for Fake*, Fellini's *Il Bidone*, Pasolini's *The Gospel According to Matthew*, John Cassavetes' *Too Late Blues* and Samuel Fuller's *White Dog*.

Criterion is top of the class when it comes to reissues of classic films. They're all given the new 2K digital restoration treatment, with full documentation on the films' history in printed booklets, plus video interviews, audio excerpts etc. For example, the reissue of Howard Hawks' *Red River* has the restored original theatrical release print (the one preferred by the director), plus a longer pre-release version, several interviews with critics and with the director too, a radio adaptation of the film with John Wayne, Joanne Dru and Walter Brennan, the film's trailer and a copy of the original Borden Chase novel.

For the Essential Jacques Demy box-set there are six films (*Lola, Bay of Angels, The Umbrellas of Cherbourg, Les Demoiselles de Rochefort, Donkey Skin* and *Une Chambre en ville*) plus two documentaries by Demy's wife Agnès Varda, four other short films by Demy himself, archival interviews with Demy and composer Michel Legrand, TV programmes, documentaries, video conversations, audio recordings, trailers, and a booklet of essays. Criterion truly is the definitive reissue label.

Further to my mentioning *The Lost World of Mitchell and Kenyon* (see above), I note that the two pioneers have now had their work transferred to the stage. The Dukes Theatre in Lancaster and the Oldham Coliseum collaborated on a theatre version of their story, depicting what they did and how they did it, and presented it as a kind of Music Hall show with the two cinematographers as the stars. Their short films were also part of the action, projected onto the scenery to illustrate exactly how these two unlikely men became part of cinematic history.

Turning films into theatre shows is no new idea. In volume 63 of *Film Review* (2007-2008) I wrote a feature on the films that were then currently appearing in stage versions. In the seven years since then, the idea has flourished and at the time of writing there are up to a dozen shows in the West End based on films. The long-runners are *The Bodyguard, The Lion King, The 39 Steps, Once* and *Billy Elliot*, which were more recently joined by *Charlie and the Chocolate Factory, Shrek, The Full Monty, The Commitments, From Here to Eternity, Fatal Attraction, Dirty Rotten Scoundrels* and *Twelve Angry Men*. This last is a slight anomaly in that it was originally a television play by Reginald Rose, who then adapted it for the stage prior to writing Sidney Lumet's 1957 film version. It was then remade for television in 1997 by William Friedkin. The London theatre production opened in November 2013 with a cast headed by film and TV star Robert Vaughn.

Let the Right One In has already been made as two films, the original Swedish one and an English-language version by Hammer Films called *Let Me In*, but it is now also a stage play. Hitchcock's *Strangers on a Train* ran briefly in the West End of London, *Calendar Girls* opened at Chichester Theatre and then transferred to the West End, while *American Psycho* on the London stage starred *Doctor Who*'s Matt Smith. Since 2007 the UK has also seen stage musical versions of *Sweet Smell of Success, Miracle on 34th Street, The Color Purple, Legally Blonde, Love Story, Ghost, Sister Act, White Christmas* and *Spamalot,* an adaptation of *Monty Python and the Holy Grail.*

Over in the US the latest film-to-stage transformation has been a musical version of Woody Allen's 1994 film *Bullets Over Broadway,* about a playwright who has to employ a gangster's moll to get his show produced. Allen adapted his own screenplay for the theatre show with American actor, director and screenwriter Zach Braff in the part played by John Cusack

in the film. *Act One*, the famous theatrical autobiography by American playwright and theatre director Moss Hart, was filmed in 1963 with George Hamilton as Hart. The theatre version had a brief two-month run on Broadway during 2014 with Tony Shalhoub (noted for his role in the TV series *Monk*).

Other films that have made it to the stage include Tom Stoppard's *Shakespeare in Love*, the Bette Davis film *A Catered Affair* (called *Wedding Breakfast* in the UK), Julian Jarrold's *Kinky Boots*, a huge hit on Broadway with music by Cyndi Lauper, Clint Eastwood's *The Bridges of Madison County*, John Ford's *The Man Who Shot Liberty Valance,* the Maysles Brothers' documentary *Grey Gardens*, the John Travolta film *Urban Cowboy* with music by Jason Robert Brown, Sam Raimi's *Evil Dead: The Musical,* FW Murnau's *Nosferatu: The Vampyre*, the James Stewart Western *Shenandoah*, Disney's *Newsies, Tarzan, Aladdin* and *The Jungle Book*, the Will Ferrell *Elf* film and the ultimate in movie heroes, *Spider-Man* and *Star Wars*. Me? I would rather just go and see the films again... except for *Star Wars*, of course.

On the horizon watch out for *Back to the Future*, which will return as a musical in London during 2015 to mark the 30th anniversary of the original film, and – wait for it – there are plans to bring *Harry Potter* to the stage. It will be a sort of prequel to the films, concentrating on, as the producers say, "the previously untold story of Harry's early years as an orphan and outcast." Well, at least it won't be a musical!

Getting back to the pictures, you can find further details about which movies you can expect to see at your local cinema during the rest of 2014, and which we hope to be reviewing in the next volume of *Film Review*, by turning to Mansel Stimpson's Afterword at the end of this volume.

Below:
Woody Allen's 1994 film *Bullets Over Broadway* itself became a Broadway show, opening in March 2014.

Bottom:
Rebecca Benson and Martin Quinn in *Let the Right One In*, which reached the West End the same month.

Top 20 UK *Box-Office Hits*

1 January – 31 December 2013

1. Despicable Me 2
2. The Hobbit: The Desolation of Smaug
3. Frozen
4. Les Misérables
5. Iron Man 3
6. The Hunger Games: Catching Fire
7. Gravity
8. Monsters University
9. Man of Steel
10. The Croods

11. Star Trek Into Darkness
12. Fast & Furious 6
13. Wreck-It Ralph
14. Thor: The Dark World
15. The Hangover Part III
16. Captain Phillips
17. Django Unchained
18. The Great Gatsby
19. Anchorman 2: The Legend Continues
20. Oz The Great and Powerful

Top 10 Box-Office Stars

Star of the Year: *Jennifer Lawrence*

2. **Bradley Cooper**
3. **Sandra Bullock**
4. **Tom Hanks**
5. **George Clooney**
6. **Vin Diesel**
7. **Leonardo DiCaprio**
8. **Will Ferrell**
9. **Brad Pitt**
10. **Hugh Jackman**

It's getting worse. At least, for actors it is. Of the Top 20 highest-grossing films this year (2013) in the United Kingdom, five were cartoons. Another nine were CGI-driven. At least *Gravity* – which won an Oscar for its visual effects – gave its actors a chance to deliver decent performances, netting Sandra Bullock another, much deserved, Oscar nomination.

So, who were the bona-fide movie stars attracting audiences to the cinema in 2013?

Les Misérables was a huge draw but then cinemagoers probably would have gone to see it if Greg Hicks had played Jean Valjean. (Hicks, incidentally, is a well-respected stage actor.) Such thinking would also rule out Henry Cavill as a contender, even though his *Man of Steel* amassed a massive $668 million worldwide. Thus, based on genuine pulling power and box-office precedence, the above are the true attractions of 2013.

Of course, the amazing success story is Jennifer Lawrence, who not only earned herself an Oscar in 2013 for *Silver Linings Playbook* but also confirmed that her central role in the first *Hunger Games* was no fluke. The sequel, *Catching Fire*, grossed a whopping $865m globally, while *American Hustle* knocked up $251m and earned Lawrence a BAFTA and a Golden Globe.

Incidentally, those hovering beneath the Top 10 include, in order, Judi Dench, Robert Downey Jr, Christian Bale, Russell Crowe and James Franco.

James Cameron-Wilson

Faces of the Year

by **James Cameron-Wilson**

Lily Collins in *Mirror Mirror*.

LILY COLLINS
Born: 18 March 1989 in Guildford, Surrey, England

Starring opposite Warren Beatty didn't harm the likes of Natalie Wood, Jean Seberg, Faye Dunaway, Julie Christie, Diane Keaton or Madonna. Now that the septuagenarian filmmaker (he's 77) has finally got his long-awaited project about Howard Hughes off the ground, he's chosen Lily Collins to play the female lead. And she's not a bad choice.

The daughter of the English musician (and sometime film actor) Phil Collins, Lily was born in Surrey before emigrating to Los Angeles, aged five, with her mother. But even before then she had been cutting her thespian teeth, aged two, in the BBC drama series *Growing Pains*. However, in her teens she was more interested in writing. She had her own column ('NY Confidential') in the British magazine *Elle Girl* and also contributed to *Seventeen*, *Teen Vogue* and the *Los Angeles Times*. Majoring in broadcast journalism at the University of Southern California, she dabbled in broadcasting and made her film debut in the Oscar-winning *The Blind Side*, playing Sandra Bullock's daughter.

She followed this with *Priest*, in which she was kidnapped by vampires, and then starred opposite Taylor Lautner in the action-thriller *Abduction*.

However, it was her role as Snow White in the enormously successful *Mirror Mirror* that cemented her popularity. She was wonderful – and wonderfully feisty. She was even better in *Stuck in Love* (as a gifted author who feeds her material by sleeping with as many boys as possible), supported Julianne Moore in *The English Teacher* and then landed the lead role of Clary Fray in the $60m *The Mortal Instruments: City of Bones*, the first chapter of Cassandra Clare's literary franchise. Although it was a financial disappointment (it grossed little over $90m), a follow-up, *The Mortal Instruments: City of Ashes*, has been announced.

However, before that happens, Lily Collins will be seen as Rosie Dunne in the Anglo-American romcom *Love, Rosie* and is being directed by Warren Beatty in the as-yet-untitled Howard Hughes project. She's also lined up for the lead in Jane Austen's *Pride and Prejudice and Zombies* (well, Jane Austen was an inspiration) and *How To Be Single*, in which she plays another writer.

DANE DeHAAN
Born: 6 February 1986 in Allentown, Pennsylvania, USA

Josh Trank's *Chronicle* (2012) didn't look very promising – it was another 'found footage' thriller with an unknown cast. But Dane DeHaan was in it. He had a certain look that recalled a young Leonardo DiCaprio, with an intensity above and beyond the call of the genre. As it happens, *Chronicle* was a whopping great success and, thanks largely to DeHaan's presence, was a thrilling diary involving dysfunctional family life, institutionalised bullying and telekinesis. As a socially awkward teenager with a camcorder, DeHaan brought a credibility and danger to his role that brought the whole thing alive.

Jump forward a year and the actor was being photographed by Annie Leibovitz, painted by James Franco and posing as the face of Prada. He was the hottest new thing since the iPad Air. He had supporting roles in *Lawless*, Steven Spielberg's *Lincoln* and *The Place Beyond the Pines*, playing Ryan Gosling's avenging son in the last-named. In *Kill Your Darlings* he was Lucien Carr, the lynchpin of the Beat Generation, and landed star billing opposite Daniel Radcliffe. It was a turning point.

A self-confessed "comic-book junkie", he was cast as the villainous Green Goblin in *The Amazing Spider-Man 2* and had the lead in the zombie comedy *Life After Beth* with Anna Kendrick. Perhaps even more exciting, Dane is now Dean. In the biography *Life*, directed by Anton Corbijn, DeHaan plays James Dean prior to the

Dane DeHaan in *Life*.

Armie Hammer
in *The Lone Ranger*.

release of *East of Eden*, with Robert Pattinson as Dennis Stock, the *Life* photographer who befriended him. It's an iconic role and one that is bound to cement DeHaan's own iconic status. He was then announced as the star of Justin Chadwick's *Tulip Fever*, taking the role earmarked for Jude Law a decade earlier.

ARMIE HAMMER
Born (as Armand Hammer): 28 August 1986 in Los Angeles, California, USA

His list of credits speaks for itself: *The Social Network*, Prince Charming in *Mirror Mirror* and the title role in *The Lone Ranger*. And we'll soon see him as Illya Kuryakin in Guy Ritchie's *The Man from U.N.C.L.E.*

Even if his name conjures up the image of a military weapon, Armie Hammer is in touch with his Christianity, noting "I have my own spiritual life, and I value it very much." Appropriately, then, he landed his first break when he was cast as the evangelist Billy Graham in Robby Benson's *Billy: The Early Years* (2008). The film was not a great success and his next, *Spring Breakdown*, a comedy with Amy Poehler, went straight to video. But then came David Fincher.

Cast as the twins Cameron and Tyler Winklevoss in Fincher's *The Social Network*, Hammer not only had to act opposite Jesse Eisenberg (*The Double*) but had to act opposite himself. At 6'5" he was the perfect height to play the Harvard rowers and Internet entrepreneurs who started the social networking site ConnectU, a concept adapted – or "stolen", in the words of the twins – by Mark Zuckerberg. In the event, Zuckerberg agreed to a settlement of $65 million. The film itself went on to gross $225m and garnered eight Oscar nominations.

Hammer was then snapped up by Clint Eastwood for *J. Edgar* to play Clyde Tolson, the associate director of the FBI and 'companion' of J Edgar Hoover (Leonardo DiCaprio). It was a daring role and the film was a success, although not as successful as Hammer's next outing, *Mirror Mirror*. The latter grossed a hearty $166m and Hammer proved he was not only a hunk but a convivial screen presence. Indeed, he revealed both an engaging comic ability and a facility to send himself up.

This reaped dividends in *The Lone Ranger*, a film eviscerated by the critics but not a total dud: it grossed over $260m worldwide, making it Hammer's most successful film to date. And while Johnny Depp played the fool as the Lone Ranger's sidekick, Tonto, Hammer was amusingly self-deprecatory as the man in the mask. It was a big, overblown, derivative and uneven mess, but not without a number of humorous highlights, most of them revealing Hammer as a deft comic talent. His turn in *The Man from U.N.C.L.E.* will definitely be something worth waiting for.

Melissa McCarthy in *The Heat*.

Kevin Hart in *Ride Along*.

KEVIN HART
Born: 6 July 1979 in Philadelphia, Pennsylvania, USA

In the early part of 2014, Kevin Hart proved to be a box-office Titan. He was the star of not one but *two* box-office smashes. Indeed, at the time of writing (April), *Ride Along* was the second highest-grossing film of the year. So who *is* Kevin Hart?

Like many African-American comedy actors (Bill Cosby, Richard Pryor, Eddie Murphy, Jamie Foxx), Hart started out as a stand-up comedian, using humour as a coping mechanism. And he needed laughter. His father was a cocaine addict and spent most of Kevin's childhood behind bars. So, after winning a series of comedy competitions in New England, Kevin was cast as a regular in the Judd Apatow sitcom *Undeclared* and moved into bit parts in movies (*Scary Movie 4, Drillbit Taylor, Little Fockers*). Then, when his stand-up album *I'm a Grown Little Man* was released in 2008, Hollywood took note and bigger movie roles rolled along.

He was a major player in the ensemble comedy *Think Like a Man*, a romantic comedy that turned into a sizeable hit. He played himself in the major box-office performer *This is the End* and was the glue that brought Robert De Niro and Sylvester Stallone together in *Grudge Match*. His rapid-fire delivery, recalling the shtick of Chris Rock, was certainly funnier than anything his co-stars could muster. He was then teamed opposite Ice Cube in *Ride Along*, an action-comedy that played off the two stars' contrasting personalities and proved box-office gold. By the time you read this, the sequel should already be in production. And then there was the remake of the Rob Lowe-Demi Moore romcom *About Last Night*. Another hit.

Next came the sequel to *Think Like a Man*, er *Think Like a Man Too*, and then the lead role of a nuptial wrangler in *The Wedding Ringer*, with Josh Gad as the unfortunate groom. After that Hart teamed up with Will Ferrell in *Get Hard*, the story of a convicted businessman who hires a tough guy to prime him for the dangers of prison.

MELISSA McCARTHY
Born: 26 August 1970 in Plainfield, Illinois, USA

In box-office terms, Melissa McCarthy is huge. Physically, she is also a larger-than-life figure. And it all happened so fast. There she was, a jobbing actress with roles in the sitcoms *Gilmore Girls*, *Samantha Who?* and *Mike & Molly* – and then she was in the world's second hottest comedy of 2011 with an Oscar nomination under her belt. And since then there's been no letting up.

Of course, there's no such thing as overnight fame, but it can seem overnight to the greater public. Cousin of the comedy actress (and 1994 Playmate of the Year) Jenny McCarthy, Melissa made her television debut in the latter's eponymous *Jenny* and then popped up in a series of films including *Charlie's Angels* and *The Life of David Gale*. She had the lead in the CBS sitcom *Mike & Molly*, the tale of a couple who meet in a Chicago Overeaters Anonymous group, and the show, at the time of going to press, is still on air. It also earned her an Emmy. In between, she was cast as Megan in Paul Feig's *Bridesmaids* and, being the outrageous, vulgar one, got most of the attention. The film went on to gross $288 million and gross-out the more faint-hearted filmgoers. It also got McCarthy that Academy Award nomination.

Before moving on to starring roles, she had a supporting part in Judd Apatow's *This is 40* (Apatow had produced *Bridesmaids*) and then landed the lead in *Identity Thief*. She played a ruthless, obnoxious crook who steals the identity of Jason Bateman and the movie ended up in the Top 20 highest-grossing movies of 2013 (in the US). In the same year she played a ruthless, obnoxious cop in Paul Feig's *The Heat*, opposite Sandra Bullock, and that movie made even more money than *Identity Thief*. A sequel is already in the works.

Since then she's taken the title role in *Tammy* (with solo billing above the title), about a woman experiencing a particularly bad day. Her co-stars include Susan Sarandon, Toni Collette and Dan Aykroyd. After that she was paired with Bill Murray in *St. Vincent* and then took the title role in Paul Feig's *Spy*, with Jason Statham, Jude Law and Rose Byrne in support.

AARON PAUL

Born (as Aaron Paul Sturtevant): 27 August 1979 in Emmett, Idaho, USA

Aaron Paul was not your typical leading man. In spite of a pair of piercing blue eyes, he was a little short (5'8"), sort of shifty-looking and his hairline was definitely on the ebb. Even so, one could take a measure of his stardom when he was cast as the lead in the high-octane, fast and furious *Need for Speed*. He played the strong, silent type (think Steve McQueen), growled a lot in a deep voice and ran the rubber off some pretty impressive wheels. The film was a $66m adaptation of the video game of the same name and one could sniff 'franchise' off the poster. And, luckily for Aaron, it grossed north of $200m. He's not against a sequel.

He should be happy. He went on record as saying, at the age of 34, that "My career is downhill from here." 'Here' was the role he played in the seven-year run of the cult TV series *Breaking Bad*, in which he was meth dealer Jesse Pinkman. It was a performance that made him world-famous, won him two Emmy awards and established his catchphrases "Yeah, science!" and "Yeah, bitch!" as viral YouTube fodder. Even as Hollywood was beckoning, Aaron noted that "I'm so unbelievably lucky. If it's downhill from here, fine. At least I had *Breaking Bad*!"

He also had a string of TV and film appearances. In 2012 he starred in the low-budget *Smashed*, playing the alcoholic husband of Mary Elizabeth Winstead – and it was a film and performance he should be proud of. He then starred opposite Samantha Morton and Helen Hunt in the award-winning *Decoding Annie Parker* (he was nominated Best Supporting Actor at the 2014 Milan International Film Festival) and was co-producer and star of the critically acclaimed thriller *Hellion*, with Juliette Lewis. And before *Need for Speed*, he slipped in the black comedy *A Long Way Down*, based on the novel by Nick Hornby – although the less said about that the better.

Still, the future looks all uphill. He stars opposite Christian Bale in Ridley Scott's Biblical epic *Exodus* (playing the Hebrew prophet Joshua), is paired with

Russell Crowe in the drama *Fathers and Daughters* and is lined up to star in John Hillcoat's crime thriller *Triple Nine* alongside Kate Winslet, Woody Harrelson, Chiwetel Ejiofor and Casey Affleck. He was also announced as the star of Gavin Hood's thriller *Eye in the Sky*, co-starring Colin Firth and Helen Mirren. And there's the prequel to *Breaking Bad*, called *Better Call Saul*, which airs at the end of 2014.

WILL POULTER

Born: 28 January 1993 in Hammersmith, London, UK

Will Poulter was 14 (but looked much younger) when he played the engagingly mischievous Lee Carter in *Son of Rambow*. The film, directed by Garth Jennings, was a wildly inventive and hugely funny piece about two kids – Bill Milner being the other – who join forces to make a home video inspired by Sylvester Stallone's *Rambo: First Blood*. To promote a cliché – Will Poulter was a natural.

However, three years were to pass before he popped up in his second film, albeit quite a major production: *The Chronicles of Narnia: The Voyage of the Dawn Treader*. And, as the arrogant, egotistical Eustace Scrubb, he had a starring role. It was an enormous success (grossing over $415m worldwide) and Poulter himself won enormous praise; he was nominated 'Young Performer of the Year' by the London Film Critics' Circle.

But Poulter, bless him, had a problem. He had dramatically arched eyebrows that gave his face a perpetually angry look. Inevitably, he would be cast as hard cases. This served him well in Dexter Fletcher's gripping, funny *Wild Bill*, as an abandoned kid forced to play the paterfamilias for his younger brother. Again, he was a revelation – and only three films into his career.

Poulter changed gear again and was another revelation in what looked like yet another smut-fest

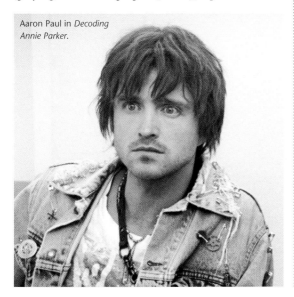

Aaron Paul in *Decoding Annie Parker*.

Will Poulter in *We're the Millers*.

from the Hollywood school of adolescent-arrested humour. But *We're the Millers* was actually very, very funny and as a miscreant – adopted by Jennifer Aniston for illegal reasons – he was not only streetwise but also surprisingly sweet and engaging. While, inevitably, the film had its share of adult/juvenile humour (Poulter's testicles come in for much ridicule), the film had a heart and a plot and Poulter's magnificent rap rendition of TLC's 'Waterfalls' was a high point. His American accent, too, was flawless.

Having won BAFTA's Rising Star award for 2013, the actor found his career in overdrive. He had a good role in Julian Gilbey's action-comedy *Plastic* (a sort of teenage *Lock, Stock…*), was in the Hollywood sci-fi thriller *The Maze Runner* and had the lead (as a gap-year student in London) in *Kids in Love* from Ealing Studios. He then joined Toni Collette in *Grassland*, a story of human trafficking in Dublin, landed a starring role in the Denver-set *Shoplifters of the World* (based on a true story about an unhinged Smiths fan) and had the title role in *iBoy*, the strange story of a young lad mentally connected to his smart phone.

LÉA SEYDOUX
Born (as Léa Hélène Seydoux-Fornier de Clausonne): 1 July 1985 in Paris, France

Anybody who saw Léa Seydoux in *Blue is the Warmest Colour* could not but be amazed by the commitment she gave to her role. Despite parts in *Inglourious Basterds*, *Robin Hood*, *Midnight in Paris* and *Mission: Impossible – Ghost Protocol*, Seydoux was as good as unknown to English-speaking audiences. In France she was nominated for a César as 'most promising actress' for her role in Christophe Honoré's *La Belle personne* and, less officially, she was given the Trophée Chopard Award for 'Female Revelation of the Year' at Cannes (for the same part).

Considering that she played one so young in *Blue is the Warmest Colour*, many were surprised that Seydoux was actually 28 – and such an experienced performer. In fact, she was a veteran of 21 films before taking the role of the coquettish art student Emma. With her pixyish

Léa Seydoux in *Blue is the Warmest Colour*.

countenance and cropped blue hair, student airs and sang-froid, she was perfect – and totally credible as the free spirit who lures Adèle Exarchopoulos' innocent schoolgirl into her bed. But Seydoux was called on to deliver much more than the film's early scenes might have suggested: playfulness, sophistication, unbridled lust, confidence, fury, disappointment and eventually forbearance. She was a hot contender for an Oscar nomination but the film's sexual frankness was hardly Academy fare. Even so, she won a mantelpiece of prestigious prizes, not least the Palme d'Or (shared with Exarchopoulos), along with a César nomination. She was also shortlisted for BAFTA's Rising Star award.

Since then Seydoux has played the lover of Tahar Rahim in *Grand Central*, snatched a cameo in *The Grand Budapest Hotel*, starred opposite Vincent Cassel in *Beauty and the Beast*, was in the fashion biopic *Saint Laurent* and appeared alongside Colin Farrell and Rachel Weisz in the SF thriller *The Lobster*. She was then announced to play Célestine R in Benoît Jacquot's adaptation of Octave Mirbeau's classic 1900 novel *The Diary of a Chambermaid*.

ALICIA VIKANDER
Born: 3 October 1988 in Gothenburg, Sweden

Alicia Vikander emanates a porcelain fragility and class that would have given Hitchcock sleepless nights. Yet beneath that regal exterior beats the heart of an accessible and normal creature who just happens to be a fantastic actress. Her poise she acquired from the Royal Swedish Ballet School in Stockholm; her perspicacity, perhaps, from her father, a psychiatrist. Her regality was put to good use when she was cast as Princess Caroline Matilda in Nikolaj Arcel's *A Royal Affair*, one of the finest films, Scandinavian or otherwise, of 2012. And although the picture was a Danish-Swedish co-production, Vikander's Caroline was actually a British subject, married off to the mad king of Denmark for bureaucratic leverage.

A Royal Affair was nominated for an Oscar in the Best Foreign-Language category and Vikander herself was shortlisted for BAFTA's Rising Star award. However, she had already attracted attention in her film debut in the Swedish drama *Pure*, which had her earmarked as a 'Shooting Star' at the 2011 Berlin Film Festival, the jury noting that "from tomboy to temptress, from street kid to secretary, Vikander shows a sheer range in her big-screen debut that is utterly hypnotic."

Pure, incidentally, was also the name of a 2002 movie starring Keira Knightley, with whom Vikander teamed up in Joe Wright's *Anna Karenina*. Vikander played another Princess, 'Kitty', and pretty much stole the film from Knightley. This was just as well as the Swedish actress had pestered Wright for the part and convinced him that not only was she good enough to play Kitty – both her resolve and her immaturity – but that she could also act in English. For the part of Caroline in *A Royal Affair* she underwent a crash course in Danish. Vikander is one determined talent.

Lisa Langseth, the director of *Pure*, is a fan: "I think Alicia has something which is very uncommon. Maybe

Alicia Vikanda in *Anna Karenina*.

it's a cliché but I think it's true that some people have faces that the camera loves. You can look at her face and you can see so many different levels of her soul at the same time."

Vikander and Langseth were reunited for the Swedish drama *Hotell* and then Vikander was off to Hollywood and beyond. She played the wife of Daniel Brühl in *The Fifth Estate* and then popped Down Under to star opposite Ewan McGregor in the crime thriller *Son of a Gun*. More interestingly, she played a robot in Alex Garland's *Ex Machina* with Domhnall Gleeson and Oscar Isaac, joined Jeff Bridges in the large-scale fantasy *Seventh Son* and was then the female lead in Guy Ritchie's *The Man from U.N.C.L.E.* Better still, she was cast as the very British Vera Brittain in *Testament of Youth* and was then announced to play Sophia in the long-awaited film version of Deborah Moggach's *Tulip Fever*, in the part originally intended for Kate Winslet.

SHAILENE WOODLEY
Born: 15 November 1991 in Simi Valley, California, USA

It's a familiar, well-trodden path. You start out in commercial modelling, land a lead in a TV show, get a good role in a high-profile film – and snare a Golden Globe nomination – and then star in a dystopian franchise based on a best-selling literary phenomenon. And no, we're not talking about Jennifer Lawrence. Although we could be.

Her name is Shailene Woodley and she started modelling at four, breaking into TV four years later in the Joyce Chopra movie *Replacing Dad*, with Mary McDonnell. However, it was the TV film *A Place Called Home* that got her nominated for a Young Artist Award, while a recurring role (as Kaitlin Cooper) in *The O.C.* didn't hurt either. She was the star of the series *The Secret Life of the American Teenager* and she clocked up 121 episodes as the sweet and smart high school

student Amy Juergens. Before leaving the show, she was cast as the daughter of George Clooney in Alexander Payne's *The Descendants* and received a slew of awards, along with a Golden Globe nomination. The film itself won an Oscar for best adapted screenplay and made Shailene a genuine contender for Hollywood stardom.

She was the female lead in the comedy-drama *The Spectacular Now*, an indie that received rave reviews if not a British release (although it was shown at the London Film Festival). For her part as the cute and clever sci-fi buff Aimee Finecky she, alongside co-star Miles Teller, won the Special Jury Award at Sundance. If her part as Peter Parker's love interest (Mary Jane) in *The Amazing Spider-Man 2* ended up on the cutting-room floor, she made up for it by starring in the Franco-American thriller *White Bird in a Blizzard* – for Gregg Araki – and landing the lead in the *Divergent* franchise.

Spider-Man director Marc Webb had nothing but praise for his jettisoned star, explaining that the Mary Jane subplot would have been one narrative thread too far for an already congested film. Indeed, he called Shailene "a fucking great actress – so cool and magical," which pretty much sums things up. Meanwhile, *Divergent* went on to gross over $264m (at the time of writing) and its three sequels are already in pre-production, while the likes of the *Los Angeles Times* paid homage to Shailene's "strong presence." In between rebelling against authority, Shailene also landed the lead in Josh Boone's adaptation of John Green's critically acclaimed novel *The Fault in Our Stars*.

Shailene Woodley in *Divergent*.

Releases *of the* Year

This section contains details of films released in the UK between 1 January and 31 December 2013.

Each film review is followed by the main credits for the film, beginning with names of the leading actors, then the Director, Producer(s), Screenplay Writer, Cinematographer, Production Designer or Art Director, Editor, Soundtrack Composer and Costume Designer.

For technical credits the normal abbreviations operate and are as follows:

Dir – for Director; *Pro* – for Producer; *Ph* – for Cinematographer; *Pro Des* – for Production Designer; *Art Dir* – for Art Director; *M* – for Composer; and *Cos* – for Costume Designer.

The production companies involved are listed, with the final name in the list being the distributor. The credits end with the film's running time, the country or countries of origin, the year of production, the UK release date and the British Board of Film Classification certificate.

Reviewers: Charles Bacon (CB), James Cameron-Wilson (JC-W), Jeremy Clarke (JC), Michael Darvell (MHD), Marshall Julius (MJ), Penny Lucas (PL), Jonathan Rigby (JR), George Savvides (GS), Mansel Stimpson (MS) and Derek Winnert (DW).

Star ratings

★★★★★   **Exceptional**
★★★★   **Very Good**
★★★   **Good**
★★   **Mediocre**
★   **Poor**

009 Re: Cyborg ★★½

This Japanese anime feature begins in 1964 when nine regular humans are abducted and transformed into cyborgs with super powers. Years later when suicide bombers begin to blow up dozens of skyscrapers across the world, it's time for these cyborgs to come back from early retirement and save the day... The plot is confusing but the superb animation and special set-pieces in 3D are very effective. Still, it's strictly for the genre's aficionados. GS

‣ Voices of Hisao Egawa, Toshiko Fujika, Hiroshi Kamya, Houko Kuwashima, Hikaru Midorikawa, Kazuya Nakai, Ryotaro Okiayu, Masaya Onosaka, Naok Tatsuta.
‣ *Dir* Kenji Kamiyama, *Pro* Tomohiko Ishii and Mitsuhisa Ishikawa, *Screenplay* Shotaro Ishinomori, *Ph* Takahiro Uezono, *Art Dir* Yusuke Takeda, *Ed* Atsuki Sato, *M* Kenji Kawai.
Ishinomori Productions/Amazon Laterna/NTV/ Panasonic etc-T-Joy Distributors.
103 mins. Japan. 2012. Rel: 7 June 2013. Cert. 12A.

2 Guns ★★★★

This is a real fun movie which pairs Mark Wahlberg and Denzel Washington to good effect. Moving from Mexico to Texas, it's a highly unlikely but engaging and energetic thriller with plenty of twists and turns as it deals with undercover agents, drug dealers and other criminals. Sensibly it is only 102 minutes in length and Iceland's arthouse director Baltasar Kormákur proves here that he can handle mainstream material with aplomb. Go along for the ride. MS

‣ Denzel Washington, Mark Wahlberg, Paula Patton, Bill Paxton, Fred J Ward, James Marsden, Edward James Olmos.
‣ *Dir* Baltasar Kormákur, *Pro* Marc Platt, Randall Emmett and others, *Screenplay* Blake Masters from the BOOM! Studios graphic novels by Steven Grant, *Ph* Oliver Wood, *Pro Des* Beth Mickle, *Ed* Michael

Opposite: Leonardo diCaprio and Carey Mulligan in *The Great Gatsby.*

The defiant ones: Harrison Ford and Chadwick Boseman shift the colour dynamic in Brian Helgeland's *42*.

Tronick, *M* Clinton Shorter, *Cos* Laura Jean Shannon.

Universal Pictures/Emmett/Furla Films/Oasis Ventures Entertainment Ltd. etc.-E1 Films. 109 mins. USA/United Arab Emirates. 2013. Rel: 16 Aug 2013. Cert. 15.

9.79* ★★★★

*9.79** is a documentary tackling the issue of illegal substance abuse among athletes. There's particular emphasis on the 1988 Summer Olympics in Seoul when Canada's winner Ben Johnson was stripped of his title after subsequently testing positive. The film is not exceptional – indeed, it has weaknesses such as a banal use of music – but it is succinct, informative and well assembled, and that's what counts. MS

▶ With Ben Johnson, Carl Lewis, Don Catlin.
▶ *Dir* and *Pro* Daniel Gordon, *Written by* Gordon and Nicholas Packer, *Ph* Charlie Grainger and Nick Bennett, *Ed* Packer, *M* Tim Atack.

ESPN Films/a Very Much So and Terra Vermelha Filmes production/BBC Films etc.-Kaleidoscope Entertainment. 83 mins. USA/UK/Brazil/Australia/The Netherlands. 2012. Rel: 20 Sep 2013. Cert. PG.

12 in a Box ★½

Although it was made in 2007, this comedy wasn't released until 2013, presumably to cash in on the current popularity of Miranda Hart. However, the actress-comedian is barely in the film for more than a few minutes and even then it fails to show her at her best. The story concerns a school reunion at a country estate where, whatever

happens, the guests have to stay put for at least four days if they're to have a chance of obtaining a million pounds each, left by the owner in his will. The screenplay is appallingly unfunny, the acting execrable and the whole thing is a thorough waste of time and talent. MHD

▶ Robert Cargill, Lucy Chalkley, Miranda Hart, Kenneth Collard, Gareth Clarke, Robert Hines, Belle Hithersay, Anjella Mackintosh.
▶ *Dir* and *Screenplay* John McKenzie, from a story by McKenzie and Bruce Windwood, *Pro* Windwood, *Ph* Nicholas Wise, *Art Dir* Sarah Massey, *Ed* Lewis Albrow, *M* Mark Revell, *Cos* Clare Harries.

Masses Entertainment-Kaleidoscope Entertainment. 96 mins. USA. 2007. Rel: 25 Mar 2013. Cert. 12.

21 and Over ★★½

The night before Jeff Chang (Justin Chon) is due to be interviewed for medical school, he decides on turning 21 to have a final fling and do all the crazy things he should do before settling down. With closest pals Miller (Miles Teller) and Casey (Skylar Astin) they hit the town running, drinking, fighting, chasing girls etc until Justin is totally smashed. The story really starts as the other two try to get him back home. It's rude, crude, dangerous to watch, with more f-words than necessary, but not always that funny, which is just what you would expect from the writers of *The Hangover* series. Avoid unless you're about 16. MHD

▶ Miles Teller, Justin Chon, Skylar Astin, Jonathan Keltz, Sarah Wright, François Chou, Russell Mercado, Samantha Futerman, Josie Loren.

▶ *Dir* and *Screenplay* Jon Lucas and Scott Moore, *Pro* David Hoberman, Ryan Kavanaugh, Todd Lieberman and Hugo Shong, *Ph* Terry Stacey, *Pro Des* Jerry Fleming, *Ed* John Refoua, *M* Lyle Workman, *Cos* Christine Wada.

Relativity Media/Sky Land Entertainment/Virgin Produced/Mandeville Films-Entertainment One. 93 mins. USA. 2013. Rel: 3 May 2013. Cert. 15.

42 ★★★★

As Hollywood spins out an ineffable number of remakes and sequels, it's astonishing that a story this strong hasn't been committed to film before. '42' is the number worn on the shirt of Jackie Robinson (Chadwick Boseman), the first African-American to play Major League baseball. Impeccably crafted and deftly executed, the film tells a story of racial discrimination that elicits the same gut-churning response as 2011's *The Help*. Written and directed by Brian Helgeland, who won an Oscar for scripting *L.A. Confidential*, *42* is one of those films that reminds us of cinema's ability to shock, to move and to inspire. JC-W

▶ Chadwick Boseman, Harrison Ford, Nicole Beharie, Christopher Meloni, Andre Holland, Lucas Black, Hamish Linklater, John C McGinley, Alan Tudyk, Max Gail.
▶ *Dir* and *Screenplay* Brian Helgeland, *Pro* Thomas Tull and Kurt Russell, *Ph* Don Burgess, *Pro Des* Richard Hoover, *Ed* Kevin Stitt and Peter McNulty, *M* Mark Isham, *Cos* Caroline Harris.

Warner Bros/Legendary Pictures-Warner Bros. 128 mins. USA. 2013. Rel: 13 Sep 2013. Cert. 12A.

47 Ronin ★★½

In ancient Japan halfbreed Kai (Keanu Reeves) joins Oishi (Hiroyuki Sanada) and his outcast samurai in their quest for revenge on the treacherous warlord who killed their master and banished them. Carl Rinsch's lavish but hollow project boasts strong production values with some really good 3D effects. However, the story's fantasy elements are way over the top and Reeves, although well cast, struggles, along with an impressive cast of Japanese actors, with the stilted dialogue and thinly sketched characterisations. GS

▶ Keanu Reeves, Hiroyuki Sanada, Ko Shibasaki, Tadanobu Asano, Min Taaka, Jin Akanshi.
▶ *Dir* Carl Rinsch, *Pro* Pamela Abdy, Scott Stuber and Eric McLeod, *Screenplay* Chris Morgan and Hossein Amini, based on a screen story by Morgan and Walter Hamada, *Ph* John Mathieson, *Pro Des* Jan Roelfs, *Ed* Stuart Baird, *M* Ilan Eshkeri, *Cos* Penny Rose.

Stuber Productions/Origo Film Group/Moving Picture Company/Mid Atlantic Films/H2F Entertainment-United International Pictures. 118 mins. USA. 2013. Rel: 26 Dec 2013. Cert. 12A.

The ABCs of Death ★★½

For this anthology of short films about death, 26 directors have each been assigned a letter from the alphabet. With films from all over the world this is a mixed bag including titles such as *Apocalypse*, *Fart* and *Orgasm*. Curiously the animation films *Klutz* and *Toilet* both deal with human excrement that causes death in the most bizarre ways. Some of these shorts are too silly to take seriously, but overall this is a diverse and unpredictable selection. GS

▶ Kaare Andrews, Angela Bettis, Bruno Forzani, Jason Eisener, Adrián Garcia Bogliano, Ernesto Diaz Espinoza, Xavier Gens, Lee Hardcastle, Noboru Iguchi, Thomas Cappelen Malling, Jorge Michael Grau, Anders Morenthaler etc.
▶ *Dir* Simon Rumley, Lee Hardcastle, Jon Schnepp, Ti West, Ben Wheatley, Adam Wingard and 21 others, *Pro* Ant Timpson, Simon Boswell, Claire Jones, Tim League, Julie Lind-Holm, Peter Lindblad, Douglas Nabors and eight others, *Screenplay* Ti West and 16 other segment writers, based on a nightmare by Ant Timpson, *Ph* Magnus Flato, Ernesto Herrera, Chris Hilleke, Chayse Irvin, Milton Kam and ten other cinematographers, *Pro Des* Nori Fukuda, Alejandro Garcia, Eric Norlin, Lorry O'Toole, *Ed* Phillip Blackford, Robert Hall, Greg Ng, Martin Wichman and seven others, *M* Simon Boswell, Phillip Blackford and nine other composers, *Cos* Kathi Moore.

Drafthouse Films/Timpson Films/Magnet Releasing-Monster Pictures. 129 mins. USA/New Zealand. 2012. Rel: 26 Apr 2013 Cert. 18.

About Time ★★

There are some wonderful moments in Richard Curtis' third outing as a director. It's just a shame they're all in the first half hour. Here, he's taken his traditional ingredients (eccentric families, fumbled romantic overtures, an American star, love, death, a wedding, a funeral – you know the sort of thing) and added a twist. The 'high concept' is that young Tim (Domhnall Gleeson)

Toilet humour: a scene from Lee Hardcastle's segment of bizarre anthology *The ABCs of Death*.

can travel back in time and change the outcome of events. So, what should have been a funny, charming short film rambles on for over two hours without any real rhyme or reason. JC-W

❱ Domhnall Gleeson, Rachel McAdams, Bill Nighy, Tom Hollander, Lindsay Duncan, Margot Robbie, Richard Cordery, Lydia Wilson, Tom Hughes.
❱ *Dir* and *Screenplay* Richard Curtis, *Pro* Tim Bevan, Eric Fellner and Nicky Kentish Barnes, *Ph* John Guleserian, *Pro Des* John Paul Kelly, *Ed* Mark Day, *M* Nick Laird-Clowes, *Cos* Verity Hawkes.
Translux/Working Title Films-Univeral Pictures.
123 mins. UK. 2013. Rel: 4 Sep 2013. Cert. 12A.

Acoustic Routes ★★★★

This 20-year-old documentary celebrates the life of legendary guitarist Bert Jansch, a pioneer of the new acoustic guitar movement and one of the world's most influential musicians. Billy Connolly is the enthusiastic presenter whose sheer enjoyment and admiration for his subject is highly infectious. Many folk and blues musicians including Davey Graham, Anne Briggs and Martin Carthy are keen to talk about their work and share their experiences. A real collector's item – very informative and highly enjoyable. GS

❱ With Bert Jansch, Billy Connolly, Davey Graham, Martin Carthy, Anne Briggs, Brownie McGhee, Ralph McTell, Al Stewart.
❱ *Dir, Ed* and *Written by* Jan Leman, *Pro* Maureen White.
Leman Productions-MusicFilmNetwork.
102 mins. UK. 1992. Rel: 1 Mar 2013. Cert. 12A.

The Act of Killing ★★★½

Gangster act: a scene from Joshua Oppenheimer's surreal The Act of Killing.

This much-discussed film is certainly striking. It's a documentary in which Joshua Oppenheimer filming in Northern Sumatra eventually persuaded two gangsters to re-enact killings which they had proudly carried out in the 1960s,

aimed at ridding the country of Communists. The film is fanciful enough to include surreal touches and a rendering of the song 'Born Free' while allowing these men to condemn themselves out of their own mouths. However, the film becomes repetitive and overblown even in this two-hour version which is substantially shorter than the director's cut. MS

❱ With Anwar Congo, Herman Koto.
❱ *Dir* Joshua Oppenheimer with Christine Cynn and others, *Pro* Signe Byrge Sørensen, Oppenheimer, Cynn and others, *Ph* Carlos Arango de Montis, Lars Skree and others, *Ed* Niels Pagh Andersen, Janus Billeskov Jansen and others.
Final Cut for Real/Piraya Film/Novaya Zemlya Ltd. etc.-Dogwoof.
122 mins. Denmark/UK/Norway/Germany/Finland/ Sweden/The Netherlands/Poland. 2012. Rel: 28 June 2013. Cert. 15.

Admission ★★★

One might be led to think that admission to a top university was the most important thing in the world. Per the title, Portia Nathan (Tina Fey) is an admissions officer at Princeton and so the lid is lifted on the politics, heartache and sheer luck that make up the battlefield of academic aspiration. It's a subject ripe for satirical appraisal and, although the film has a number of belly laughs, it's steered too far into romcom territory to be especially distinctive. Still, the Ivy League setting intrigues and there are some terrific lines and a glorious supporting turn from Lily Tomlin. JC-W

❱ Tina Fey, Paul Rudd, Michael Sheen, Wallace Shawn, Nat Wolff, Gloria Reuben, Lily Tomlin, Olek Krupa, Sonya Walger, Sarita Choudhury.
❱ *Dir* Paul Weitz, *Pro* Weitz, Scott Stuber, Ron Howard and Brian Grazer, *Screenplay* Karen Croner, *Ph* Declan Quinn, *Pro Des* Sarah Knowles, *Ed* Joan Sobel, *M* Stephen Trask, *Cos* Aude Bronson-Howard.
Imagine Entertainment/Relativity Media/Stuber Productions/Focus Features/Depth of Field-Universal Pictures.
107 mins. USA. 2013. Rel: 14 June 2013. 12A.

After Earth ★

This dull sci-fi sinks the once promising career of M Night Shyamalan even further into oblivion. After a crash landing teenager Kitai (Jaden Smith) and his father Cypher (Will Smith) are stranded on Earth, a now deserted planet following catastrophic events that happened a thousand years earlier. The cinematography shot with the Sony 4K camera looks splendid, but the thin storyline and zero chemistry between the Smiths make this a very insipid experience indeed. GS

▷ Will Smith, Jaden Smith, Sophie Okonedo, Jaden Martin, Glenn Morshower, Zore Isabella Kravitz.
▷ *Dir* M. Night Shyamalan, *Pro* Will Smith, Caleeb Pinkett, Jada Pinkett Smith and James Lassiter, *Screenplay* Shyamalan and Gary Witta, based on a story by Will Smith, *Ph* Peter Suschitzky, *Pro Des* Tom Sanders, *Ed* Steven Rosenblum, *M* James Newton Howard, *Cos* Amy Westcott.
Columbia Pictures/Overbrook/Blinding Edge Pictures-Sony Pictures Releasing.
100 mins. USA. 2013. Rel: 7 June 2013. Cert. 12A.

Aftershock ★★★

A nerdy American (Eli Roth) and two Chileans (Ariel Levy, Nicolás Martínez) are travelling around Chile. They pick up three hot women and dance the night away in Valparaiso till an earthquake strikes. The sextet must try to survive looters, escaped convicts, constant aftershocks and a possible tsunami. Starting as a character- and atmosphere-driven disaster movie, this switches half way to a full-on horror film with killers rampaging through the streets in search of women and blood. After a long, slow build-up there are surprises, shocks, gore and nasty deaths galore. It's busily and convincingly written and directed by Nicolás López (with Roth as co-writer), using both story and location backgrounds of the 2010 Chile earthquake. DW

▷ Eli Roth, Andrea Osvárt, Ariel Levy, Natasha Yarovenko, Nicolás Martínez, Lorenza Izzo, Marcia Tagle.
▷ *Dir* Nicolás López, *Pro* Roth, Brian Oliver and Miguel Asensio, *Screenplay* López, Guillermo Amoedo and Eli Roth, *Ph* Antonio Quercia, *Pro Des* Nelson Daniel, *Ed* Diego Macho Gómez, *M* Manuel Riveiro, *Cos* Elisa Hormazábal.
Cross Creek Pictures/Dragonfly Entertainment/Sobbras.com Producciones/Vertebra Films Company-Film Nation Entertainment.
89 mins. USA/Chile. 2012. Rel: 16 Aug 2013. Cert. 18.

Ain't Them Bodies Saints ★★★★

Here's a chance to encounter an unfamiliar writer-director, David Lowery, who could go far judging by his treatment of this tale set in Texas in the

1970s. It's a piece that deals with crime, death and a prison escape, but it's also a love story with a dark undertow reminiscent of such films as Nicholas Ray's *They Live By Night* (1948). Some late plot developments are less clear than they should be, but it's a memorable film with fine work from Casey Affleck and Rooney Mara. MS

Ego-centric: the industrious Steve Coogan as the eponymous *Alan Partridge: Alpha Papa.*

▷ Casey Affleck, Rooney Mara, Ben Foster, Nate Parker, Keith Carradine, Rami Malek.
▷ *Dir* and *Screenplay* David Lowery, *Pro* Toby Halbrooks, James M. Johnston, Jay Van Hoy and others, *Ph* Bradford Young, *Pro Des* Jade Healy, *Ed* Craig McKay and Jane Rizzo, *M* Daniel Hart, *Cos* Malgosia Turzanska.
IFC Films/The Weinstein Company/a Sailor Bear, Primary Productions and Parts & Labor film etc.-The Works UK Distribution Ltd.
96 mins. USA. 2013. Rel: 6 Sep 2013. Cert. 15.

Alan Partridge: Alpha Papa ★★★½

From TV sitcom to cinema idol, the talentless DJ Alan Partridge (Steve Coogan) manages to get by and, despite his blind egomania, to win through. When North Norfolk Digital is bought out and re-branded, his fellow DJ Pat (Colm Meaney) is sacked but, as a parting shot, takes the radio station personnel hostage. Pat will only negotiate with the police through Partridge. During the ensuing siege Partridge shows his mettle but his heroics are short-lived in this inspired bout of British lunacy. If you liked Partridge on the box, you'll love him to death on the big screen. MHD

▷ Steve Coogan, Colm Meaney, Anna Maxwell Martin, Nigel Lindsay, Phil Cornwell, Elizabeth Berrington, Simon Delaney, Felicity Montagu.
▷ *Dir* Declan Lowney, *Pro* Kevin Loader and Henry Normal, *Screenplay* Steve Coogan, Peter Baynham, Neil Gibbons, Rob Gibbons and Armando Iannucci, *Ph* Ben Smithard, *Pro Des* Dick Lunn, *Ed* Mark Everson, *M* Martin Coogan etc, *Cos* Julian Day.
Baby Cow Films/Baby Cow Productions-StudioCanal.
90 mins. UK/France. 2013. Rel: 7 Aug 2013. Cert. 15.

Criminal:
Jennifer Lawrence
and Amy Adams
in David
O Russell's
American Hustle.

All is Lost ★★★

There's no compromise in JC Chandor's second feature which vividly depicts the struggle of a lone sailor (Robert Redford) to survive when his yacht is holed while in the Indian Ocean. With no flashbacks and virtually wordless, it is a film easier to respect than to enjoy despite Redford's remarkable commitment. It seems like a stripped-down adventure tale rather than an allegory until its unexpected conclusion which disconcertingly comes out of nowhere. With 3D it might have been an immersive experience like *Gravity* [qv], but without that we just observe. MS

▸ Robert Redford.
▸ *Dir* and *Screenplay* JC Chandor, *Pro* Justin Nappi, Neal Dodson and others, *Ph* Frank G. DeMarco and Peter Zuccarini, *Pro Des* John P Goldsmith, *Ed* Pete Beaudreau, *M* Alex Ebert, *Cos* Van Broughton Ramsey.

Lionsgate/Roadside Attractions/Black Bear Pictures/ Treehouse Pictures etc.-Universal. 106 mins. USA/Canada. 2013. Rel: 26 Dec 2013. Cert. 12A.

All Stars ★★½

Dance-loving kid Jaden (Akai Osei-Mansfield) joins forces with Ethan (Theo Stevenson) in order to save a youth club from closure. They want to raise money by putting on a dance show but Jaden has been banned from dancing by his parents, while Ethan has two left feet. There is only one solution – to select the most talented from their school... The children deliver much more credible and energetic performances than

the adults who act as if they are in a totally different film altogether. GS

▸ Theo Stevenson, Akai Osei-Mansfield, Ashley Jensen, Kimberley Walsh, Ashley Walters, Kevin Bishop, Mark Heap, Hugh Dennis, John Barrowman, Simon Woodgate.
▸ *Dir* Ben Gregor, *Pro* Allan Niblo, Louise Killin and James Richardson, *Screenplay* Paul Gerstenberger, *Ph* Ben Wheeler, *Pro Des* Matthew Button, *Ed* Jono Griffith, *M* Simon Woodgate, *Cos* Andrew Cox.

Vertigo Films-Vertigo Films. 106 mins. UK. 2013. Rel: 3 May 2013. Cert. U.

All Things to All Men ★★

Producer turned director George Isaac makes a showy debut in this stylish but almost incomprehensible crime thriller set in London. Professional thief Riley (Toby Stephens) finds himself in the middle of a cat and mouse game that involves ruthless police officer Parker (Rufus Sewell) and notorious criminal Joseph Corso (Gabriel Byrne). As it has strong production values, it's a shame that more time wasn't invested in making the script and overcomplicated plot much clearer. GS

▸ Toby Stephens, Rufus Sewell, Mark Badham, Gabriel Byrne, Elsa Pataky, David Schofield, Julian Sands, Rob Knighton, MC Harvey, Leo Gregory, Tom Davis.
▸ *Dir* and *Screenplay* George Isaac, *Pro* Isaac and Pierre Mascolo, *Ph* Howard Atherton, *Pro Des* Matthew Button, *Ed* Eddie Hamilton,

M Thomas Wanker, *Cos* Hayley Nebauer.

Cipher Films-Cipher Films.
84 mins. UK. 2013. Rel: 5 Apr 2013. Cert. 15.

American Hustle ★★★★

Believe it or not, this is the true (ish) story of Irving Rosenfeld (based on Melvin Weinberg of the famous 'Abscam' sting), a conman conscripted by the FBI to use his 'professional' acumen to ensnare top politicians on corruption charges...With its horrendous hairstyles, massive collars and medallions, *American Hustle* is a borderline spoof and has enormous fun in the process. The dialogue crackles and pops, mixing dark truths with sudden and outrageous bursts of humour. But it's the thespian pyrotechnics one will remember, from Christian Bale's grotesque hustler to Robert De Niro's very scary mobster. But the true revelation is Jennifer Lawrence, who provides a fully fleshed, spellbinding, funny and frightening turn as a woman whose intelligence is constantly misplaced. JC-W

❥ Christian Bale, Bradley Cooper, Amy Adams, Jeremy Renner, Jennifer Lawrence, Robert De Niro, Louis CK, Jack Huston, Michael Peña, Alessandro Nivola, Paul Herman, Saïd Taghmaoui, Barry Primus.
❥ *Dir* David O. Russell, *Pro* Charles Roven, Richard Suckle and Megan Ellison, *Screenplay* Russell and Eric Warren Singer, *Ph* Linus Sandgren, *Pro Des* Judy Becker, *Ed* Alan Baumgarten, Jay Cassidy and Crispin Struthers, *M* Danny Elfman, *Cos* Michael Wilkinson.

Columbia Pictures/Annapurna Pictures/Atlas Entertainment-Entertainment Film Distributors.
137 mins. USA. 2013. Rel: 20 Dec 2013 (London; 1 January 2014 elsewhere). Cert. 15.

American Mary ★★★★

Medical student Mary (Katharine Isabelle) is in desperate need of cash in order to support her studies. The promise of "easy money" soon lures her into the dark world of illegal surgeries and mummification... Isabelle is absolutely brilliant in the title role whose journey into a world of violence and depravation soon has a strong effect on her life. The Soska sisters direct with flair and style and also make a delicious cameo appearance as the identical twins obsessed with surgery. GS

❥ Katharine Isabelle, Tristan Risk, David Lovgren, Paul Lindberg, Clay St Thomas, Nelson Wong, Jen and Sylvia Soska.
❥ *Dir* and *Screenplay* Jen Soska and Sylvia Soska, *Pro* John Curtis and Evan Tylor, *Ph* Brian Pearson, *Pro Des* Tony Devenyl, *Ed* Bruce MacKinnon, *M* Peter Allen, *Cos* Jayne Mabott.

American Mary Productions/Evolution Pictures/430 Productions/Twisted Twins Productions etc-IndustryWorks Pictures.
103 mins. Canada. 2012. Rel: 11 Jan 2013. Cert. 18.

Anchorman 2: The Legend Continues ★★★½

Ten years after the original film Ron Burgundy (Will Ferrell) appears to be happily married to Veronica (Christina Applegate) until he loses his job and is replaced by her as the nation's number one anchor. However, he gets the perfect opportunity to recruit his old team when he's offered a job on the world's first 24-hour global cable news network... This is silly, preposterous but enjoyable fun and surprisingly an improvement on the original, with the characters given the opportunity to develop even further their madcap personas. GS

❥ Will Ferrell, Steve Carell, Paul Rudd, Harrison Ford, Will Smith, Kirsten Dunst, Sasha Baron Cohen, Marion Cotillard, David Koechner, Greg Kinnear, Kristen Wiig, Christina Applegate, Dylan Baker, Meagan Good.
❥ *Dir* Adam McKay, *Pro* McKay, Ferrell and Judd Apatow, *Screenplay* McKay and Ferrell, *Ph* Oliver Wood, *Pro Des* Clayton Hartley, *Ed* Melissa Bretherton and Brent White, *M* John Nau and Andrew Feltenstein, *Cos* Susan Matheson.

Paramount Pictures/Apatow Productions/Gary Sanchez Productions-Paramount Pictures.
119 mins. USA. 2013. Rel: 18 Dec 2013. Cert. 15.

Antiviral ★★★½

Now that David Cronenberg has moved on to more 'tasteful' and rather static pictures, he's left the arena of forensic, visceral horror to his son. With his first film, Brandon Cronenberg has taken the cult of celebrity and advanced it to a whole new level. Set in an antiseptic establishment of the future, the film stars the pale, emaciated Caleb Landry Jones as Syd March. His job is to inject live, copyrighted viruses of the famous into the eager veins of their fans... It's a film of big and brazen ideas and startling imagery – a worthy complement to the body of cinematic Cronenberg horror. JC-W

Grisly detail: Katherine Isabelle in Jen Soska and Sylvia Soska's *American Mary.*

➤ Caleb Landry Jones, Sarah Gadon, Malcolm McDowell, Nicholas Campbell, Sheila McCarthy, Wendy Crewson.
➤ *Dir* and *Screenplay* Brandon Cronenberg, *Pro* Niv Fichman, *Ph* Karim Hussain, *Pro Des* Arvinder Grewal, *Ed* Matthew Hannam, *M* EC Woodley, *Cos* Patrick Antosh.

Alliance Films/TF1 International/Téléfilm Canada-Momentum Pictures.
103 mins. Canada/USA. 2012. Rel: 1 Feb 2013. Cert. 15.

Any Day Now ★★

This is that rarity, a gay film that has to be classified as a weepie. Dealing with a gay couple in 1979 who seek to adopt a child with Down's Syndrome, it might have been a compelling social drama but, instead, it comes across as a self-indulgent showcase for Alan Cumming (he's allowed to sing) and its assault on the tear ducts is as unremitting as it is contrived. Some viewers may nevertheless succumb, but I did not. MS

➤ Alan Cumming, Garret Dillahunt, Isaac Leyva, Gregg Henry, Jamie Anne Allman.
➤ *Dir* Travis Fine, *Pro* Fine, Kristine Hostetter Fine, Chip Hourihan and Liam Finn, *Screenplay* Travis Fine and George Arthur Bloom, *Ph* Rachel Morrison, *Pro Des* Elizabeth Garner, *Ed* Tom Cross, *M* Joey Newman, *Cos* Samantha Kuester.

PFM Pictures/a Famleefilm production-Peccadillo Pictures Ltd.
98 mins. USA. 2012. Rel: 6 Sep 2013. Cert. 15.

Arbitrage ★★★★

Money matters: Susan Sarandon and Richard Gere in Nicholas Jarecki's *Arbitrage.*

Richard Gere is on great form in this New York tale about a hedge fund magnate who gambles twice over: that his fraudulent juggling of accounts will not be discovered and that his family will remain unaware that he has a young mistress. When the latter dies in a car crash, he tries to conceal his presence but will his secrets be exposed? The contemporary aspects don't hide the fact that the considerable pleasures here are largely traditional, with sharpness and irony bringing to mind dramas made in the 1950s. MS

➤ Richard Gere, Susan Sarandon, Tim Roth, Brit Marling, Laetitia Casta, Nate Parker.
➤ *Dir* and *Screenplay* Nicholas Jarecki, *Pro* Laura Bickford, Kevin Turen, Justin Nappi and Robert Salerno, *Ph* Yorick Le Saux, *Pro Des* Beth Mickle, *Ed* Douglas Crise, *M* Cliff Martinez, *Cos* Joseph G. Aulisi.

Green Room Films/Treehouse Pictures/Parlay Films/LB Productions etc.-Koch Media Entertainment.
107 mins. USA/Poland. 2012. Rel: 1 Mar 2013. Cert. 15.

The Artist and the Model ★★★½

As in *Renoir* [qv] we have here a period piece about an aged artist in wartime inspired afresh by a young female model, but in Fernando Trueba's film the artist is a sculptor and fictional and played by the admirable Jean Rochefort. More austere than *Renoir* and shot in black and white, this is the superior piece, yet it is also ultimately elusive as regards what it wants to say. Rivette's *La Belle noiseuse* (1991) remains in a class of its own in portraying what it means to be a serious artist. (Original title: *El artista y la modelo*). MS

➤ Jean Rochefort, Aida Folch, Claudia Cardinale, Chus Lampreave, Götz Otto.
➤ *Dir* Fernando Trueba, *Pro* Cristina Huete, *Screenplay* Trueba and Jean-Claude Carrière, *Ph* Daniel Vilar, *Pro Des* Pilar Revuelta, *Ed* Marta Velasco, *Cos* Lala Huete.

A Fernando Trueba P.C.S.A. production. TVE, Gobierno de España etc.-Axiom Films Limited.
105 mins. Spain. 2012. Rel: 13 Sep 2013. Cert. 12A.

Austenland ★

Theme parks can be awful places but none so dire as this abysmal romcom. The story of a thirty-something American (Keri Russell) obsessed with all things Jane Austen, the film supposes that a country estate the size of West Wycombe Park with a large staff and a cast of actors could be funded by the visit of two American tourists. Bedroom farce ensues but to call this amateur would be an insult to many passionate, talented and non-professional actors. 'Embarrassing' seems an appropriate adjective. JC-W

➤ Keri Russell, JJ Feild, Bret McKenzie, Jennifer Coolidge, James Callis, Jane Seymour, Georgia King.
➤ *Dir* Jerusha Hess, *Pro* Stephenie Meyer and Gina Mingacci, *Screenplay* Hess and Shannon Hale, *Ph* Larry Smith, *Pro Des* James Merifield, *Ed* Nick Fenton, *M* Ilan Eshkeri, *Cos* Annie Hardinge.

Fickle Fish Films/Moxie Pictures-Sony Pictures Releasing.
96 mins. USA. 2013. Rel: 27 Sep 2013. Cert. 12A.

Babeldom ★

Paul Bush's experimental film defies description. In a futuristic city it's the first time since Noah that the living outnumber the dead. The past and the future are united with the present in this elegy to modern life. Animator Bush's debut feature references the Tower of Babel and combines animated data visualisation from recent scientific research of nanotechnology. Does it sound pretentious? You bet it is! Is it of any interest to anyone? I doubt it! GS

▶ With the voices of Youla Boudall and Mark Caven.
▶ *Dir, Pro, Ph* and *Written by* Paul Bush, *Ed* Lawrence Huck, *M* Andy Cowton and Stuart Earl.

Ancient Mariner Productions-Independent Cinema Office. 84 mins. UK. 2012. Rel: 8 Mar 2013. Cert. 15.

Bachelorette ★★½

When Regan (Kirsten Dunst) learns that her old schoolfriend Becky (Rebel Wilson) is about to get married, she can't wait to tell her other college mates Gena (Lizzy Caplan) and Katie (Isla Fisher), who all hated Becky at school where she was known as Pigface. As they prepare for Becky's pre-wedding party, the girls get high on drugs and booze and manage to ruin the bride's wedding dress. Their adventures in trying to repair the damage before the Big Day are played out in the feeblest and crudest comic manner imaginable. This is certainly no *Bridesmaids* – you have been warned. MHD

▶ Kirsten Dunst, Rebel Wilson, Lizzy Caplan, Paul Corning, Isla Fisher, Andrew Rannells, Anna Rose Hopkins, Adam Scott.
▶ *Dir* and *Screenplay* Leslye Headland, based on her own play, *Pro* Will Ferrell, Adam McKay, Lauren Munsch, Jessica Elbaum, Brice Dal Farra and Claude Dal Fara, *Ph* Doug Emmett, *Pro Des* Richard Hoover, *Ed* Jeffrey Wolf, *M* John Nau and Andrew Feltenstein, *Cos* Anna Bingemann.

Gary Sanchez Productions/BCDF Pictures-Lionsgate. 87 mins. USA. 2012. Rel: 16 Aug 2013. Cert. 15.

Baggage Claim ★★

Paula Patton stars as an ageing flight attendant whose mom (Jennifer Lewis) points out that she'll be the oldest unwed woman in her family. So she needs to get engaged before her youngest sister (Lauren London) gets married, but has only 30 days to find Mr Right. Using her airline spy network, she bumps into eligible ex-boyfriends and potential suitors, racking up 30,000 miles and nearly as many encounters… It's harmless, but a bunch of very nice actors are stranded in a contrived and lazy romcom that's as short on laughs and charm as it is on credibility. Writer-director David E Talbert goes for lame humour, cliché and predictability every time. DW

▶ Paula Patton, Derek Luke, Lauren London, Taye Diggs, Boris Kodjoe, Ned Beatty, Trey Songz, Jill Scott, Adam Brody, Jennifer Lewis.

Artistic licence: Aida Folch and Jean Rochefort in Fernando Trueba's *The Artist and the Model*, nominated for 13 Goya Awards.

Shark effect: Xavier Samuel holds his breath in Kimble Rendall's *Bait*.

▷ *Dir* and *Screenplay* David E Talbert, based on his own novel, *Pro* Talbert and Steven J Wolfe, *Ph* Anastas M. Michos, *Pro Des* Dina Lipton, *Ed* Troy Takaki, *M* Aaron J Zigman, *Cos* Maya Lieberman.
Sneak Preview Productions-Fox Searchlight Pictures. 96 mins. USA. 2013. Rel: 11 Oct 2013. Cert. 12A.

Bait ★★★½

If you find films like *Snakes on a Plane* entertaining, then this silly but fun Australian shark adventure is for you. After a tsunami, a group of survivors find themselves trapped in a flooded supermarket before they inevitably become bait for a starving Great White shark. The dialogue is corny and the characterisation thin, but decent 3D effects and witty direction make up for it. GS

▷ Richard Brancatisano, Xavier Samuel, Chris Betts, Sharni Vinson, Julian McMahon.
▷ *Dir* Kimble Rendall, *Pro* Peter Barber, Todd Fellman and Gary Hamilton, *Screenplay* John Kim and Russell Mulcahy, with additional writing by Shayne Armstrong, Justin Monjo, Shane Krause and Duncan Kennedy, *Ph* Ros Emery, *Pro Des* Nicholas McCallum, *Ed* Rodrigo Balart, *M* Jo Ng and Alex Oh, *Cos* Phil Eagles.
Bait Productions/Media Development Authority/ Pictures in Paradise/Black Magic Design Films/Story Bridge Films etc-Anchor Bay Films. 93 mins. Australia/Singapore. 2012. Rel: 19 Apr 2013. Cert. 15.

Ballroom Dancer ★★★½

This Danish documentary invites us to follow the efforts of a former Russian dance champion of world class to work with a new partner and regain his status. We travel with them around the world (from Moscow to Hong Kong by way of Bournemouth and Blackpool). Slavik, as he is known, can be difficult, but Anna Melnikova is his partner both on and off the floor which makes this interesting both as a personal tale and in the context of dance. At times, though, one wonders if without acknowledgment certain scenes were staged (or restaged) for the camera. MS

▷ With Slavik Kryklyvyy, Anna Melnikova, Joanna Leunis, Michael Malitowski.
▷ *Dir* and *Ph* Andreas Koefoed and Christian H Bonke, *Pro* Jakob Nordenhof Jonck, *Ed* Asa Mossberg and Marion Tudor, *M* Magnus Jarlbo.
Danish Documentary Productions/New Danish Screen etc.-Dogwoof. 84 mins. Denmark. 2012. Rel: 18 Jan 2013. Cert. PG.

The Battle of the Sexes ★★★★

You don't have to be a tennis fan to find this documentary about the game absorbing. It shows women fighting for equal rights in this context and it's adroitly built around the 1973 match in Houston when Billie Jean King accepted a challenge from the misogynistic Bobby Riggs, a former Wimbledon champion. The coda may seem self-congratulatory (King is an executive producer here) but otherwise it's a very well judged work. MS

▷ With Billie Jean King, Alexandra Jones, Lyndall Grant, Peter Russell.
▷ *Dir* and *Written by* James Erskine and Zara Hayes, *Pro* Victoria Gregory and Erskine, *Ph* Joel Devlin, *Pro Des* Toby Stevens, *Ed* Adam Recht, *M* Christopher Nicolas Bangs, *Cos* Francisco Rodriguez-Weil.
Kaleidoscope Entertainment/a New Black Films and

Media Squared Films PLC production-Kaleidoscope Film Distribution.
83 mins. UK. 2013. Rel: 28 June 2013. Cert. PG.

Battle of the Year ★★★

The title refers to a real-life Olympics-style competition for breakdancing. Here it's based in the US and attracts teams from all over the world – but America hasn't won for 15 years. LA hip-hop merchant and former breakdancer B-Boy Dante (Laz Alonso) hopes to change all that. He takes on down-on-his-luck ex-basketball coach Blake (Josh Holloway) to coach a team as potential champions, the idea being that what he did for basketball, he could also do for breakdancing. An all-American crew is assembled in the hope that the US can be dance champions again. This one is really only for dyed in the wool breakdancing nuts – *Strictly Come Dancing* it ain't! PL

▶ Josh Holloway, Laz Alonso, Josh Peck, Caity Lotz, Chris Brown, Ivan 'Fliz' Velez, Jo 'Do Knock' Cruz.
▶ *Dir* Benson Lee, *Pro* Beau Flynn, Amy Lo and Tripp Vinson, *Screenplay* Brin Hill and Chris Parker, based on Benson Lee's documentary *Planet B-Boy*, *Ph* Michael Barrett, *Pro Des* Chris Cornwell, *Ed* Alessandro Carlino and Peter S. Elliot, *M* Christopher Lennertz, *Cos* Soyon An.

Contrafilm-Sony Pictures Releasing.
110 mins. USA. 2013. Rel: 15 Nov 2013. Cert. 12.

The Bay ★★★★

Barry Levinson's mock-documentary takes place in the coastal town of Claridge, Maryland on Independence Day. The annual celebrations are interrupted when the waters of Chesapeake Bay are found to be infected by flesh-eating bacteria which begin to devour the fish as well as the residents... Levinson's eco-horror comes from the heart and is delivered with some excellent set-pieces that will make you think again before you go back into the water! GS

▶ Will Rogers, Christopher Denham, Nansi Aluka, Stephen Kunken, Frank Deal, Kether Donohue, Kristen Connolly.
▶ *Dir* Barry Levinson, *Pro* Levinson, Oren Peli, Steven Schneider and Jason Blum, *Screenplay* Michael Wallach, based on a story by Levinson and Wallach, *Ph* Josh Nussbaum, *Pro Des* Lee Bonner, *Ed* Aaron Yanes, *M* Marcelo Zarvos, *Cos* Emmie Holmes.

Automatik Entertainment/Hydraulx/Baltimore Pictures/ Alliance Films/IM Global-Lionsgate.
84 mins. USA. 2012. Rel: 1 Mar 2013. Cert. 15.

Beautiful Creatures ★★

This lavish adaptation of a popular 'Young Adult' novel reverses the *Twilight* formula in elementary style: 'natural' male teen falls for supernatural female teen, rather than the other way round. It pulls off a more surprising reversal, too. We're used to teen films being rescued by the welcome arrival of seasoned old hands; here, the teens (Alden Ehrenreich and Alice Englert) are genuinely engaging and things only begin to fall apart with the arrival of Jeremy Irons, employing a phoney Southern twang calculated to make your ears bleed. Then old hand # 2, Emma Thompson, pitches up and the film collapses irretrievably. No amount of risibly self-conscious quotes from Charles Bukowski (!) can save it. JR

▶ Alden Ehrenreich, Alice Englert, Jeremy Irons, Viola Davis, Emma Thompson, Eileen Atkins, Emmy Rossum, Thomas Mann, Margo Martindale, Tiffany Boone.
▶ *Dir* and *Screenplay* Richard LaGravenese, based on the novel by Kami Garcia and Margaret Stohl, *Pro* David Valdesa, Erwin Stoff, Molly Mickler Smith, Andrew A Kosove and Broderick Johnson, *Ph* Philippe Rousselot, *Pro Des* Richard Sherman, *Ed* David Moritz, *M* Thenewno2, *Cos* Jeffrey Kurland.

Alcon Entertainment/Belle Pictures/Warner Bros-Entertainment Films Distributors.
124 mins. USA. 2013. Rel: 13 Apr 2013. Cert. 12A.

Before Dawn ★★★

Hardly noted for their intelligence, zombies have obstinately failed to notice their sell-by date (long since past). Very occasionally, however, a film comes along that makes their omnipresence more bearable. *Before Dawn*, a tiny Brit horror made around Hebden Bridge in West Yorkshire, is one such. *Emmerdale* regular Dominic Brunt is director-editor, his wife Joanne Mitchell conceived the story, and they also star as a sundered couple attempting a rural reconciliation. Thirty-five minutes of nicely observed marital implosion are followed by some bracing zombie action, notably a ferocious sustained battle in a cramped garage. The film also boasts a nihilistic, dreamlike ending, making Brunt's vision of the "end of the bastard world" a surprisingly powerful one. JR

Dead again: Alex Baldacci shows up for Dominic Brunt's *Before Dawn*.

Schlock horror: Michael Douglas expands his sartorial range in Steven Soderbergh's *Behind the Candelabra*.

▶ Dominic Brunt, Joanne Mitchell, Eileen O'Brien, Nicky Evans, Alex Baldacci, Alan French, Holly Illis, David Nolan and the voices of Mark Charnock and Tony Earnshaw.

▶ *Dir* and *Ed* Dominic Brunt, *Pro* Brunt, Mitchell and Helen Grace, *Screenplay* Mark Illis and Joanne Mitchell, *Ph* Alex Neville, *Special Effects* Darren Grassby and Ian Jowett, *M* Thomas Ragsdale, *Cos* One True Saxon.

Mitchell-Brunt Films/Left Films-Metrodome Distribution. 82 mins. UK. 2012. Rel: 22 Feb 2013. Cert. 18.

Before Midnight ★★★½

Newcomers may not be lured in so readily, but those who understandably love Richard Linklater's *Before Sunrise* and *Before Sunset* cannot fail to be enthralled by this continuation of the story of Jesse (Ethan Hawke) and Celine (Julie Delpy) almost a decade on. Sadly I wasn't entirely convinced by the open ending, but there are stunning sequences here, not least the one in which the couple when talking through their tensions only make matters worse. This rings so true that it's painful, yet it's so well realised that it's wonderful. MS

▶ Ethan Hawke, Julie Delpy, Seamus Davey-Fitzpatrick, Walter Lassally, Ariane Labed.
▶ *Dir* Richard Linklater, *Pro* Linklater, Christos V Konstantakopoulos and Sara Woodhatch, *Screenplay* Linklater, Delpy and Hawke, based on characters created by Linklater and Kim Krizan, *Ph* Christos Voudouris, *Set Des* Anna Georgiadou, *Ed* Sandra Adair, *M* Graham Reynolds, *Cos* Vassilia Rozana.

Faliro House/Venture Forth/Castle Rock Entertainment/ a Detour Filmproduction-Sony Pictures Releasing. 109 mins. USA/Greece. 2013. Rel: 21 June 2013. Cert. 15.

Behind the Candelabra ★★★½

Made for television because no film studio would touch it (but released theatrically outside the US), Steven Soderbergh's movie is a strangely moving, albeit farcical, account of the gay relationship between celebrity pianist and closet-case (Lee) Liberace and his partner Scott Thorson. Based on Thorson's own book, it shows not only the evil side of Liberace's controlling character but also the genuine love that Thorson had for his partner. Michael Douglas is eerily real as the monstrous Lee and Matt Damon is quite brilliant as the idolising Scott. Fine support comes from Debbie Reynolds as Lee's mother and Rob Lowe as a maniacal plastic surgeon. Scriptwriter Richard LaGravenese's pen cuts just as deep as Lowe's scalpel. It's all great, grisly fun. MHD

▶ Michael Douglas, Matt Damon, Scott Bakula, Rob Lowe, Debbie Reynolds, Pat Asanti, Cheyenne Jackson, Dan Aykroyd, Josh Meyers, Paul Reiser.
▶ *Dir* Steven Soderbergh, *Pro* Susan Elkins, Gregory Jacobs and Michael Polaire, *Screenplay* Richard LaGravenese, based on the book by Scott Thorson and Alex Thorleifson, *Ph* Peter Andrews (Soderbergh), *Pro Des* Howard Cummings, *Ed* Mary Ann Bernard (Soderbergh), *M* Marvin Hamlisch, *Cos* Ellen Mirojnick.

HBO Films-Entertainment One. 118 mins. USA. 2013. Rel: 7 June 2013. Cert. 15.

A Belfast Story ★

This is clearly a personal project for Nathan Todd but the story unfortunately feels totally outdated. There is now peace in Belfast following years of bomb explosions and deep hatred amongst the community. But sadly a series of gruesome murders bring back past horrific memories... The pacing is painfully slow while Colm Meaney, usually a strong presence, looks uncomfortable here as the grumpy detective determined to solve the murders. GS

❯ Colm Meaney, Malcolm Sinclair, Tommy O'Neill, Paddy Rocks, Damien Hasson, Susan Davey, Maggie Cronin.
❯ *Dir* and *Screenplay* Nathan Todd, *Pro* John Todd, *Ph* Peter Holland, *Pro Des* Nigel David Pollock, *Ed* John Wright, *M* Nick Glennie-Smith and Mac Quayle, *Cos* Tiziana Corvisieri.

Adnuco Pictures-Kaleidoscope Entertainment.
99 mins. Ireland. 2013. Rel: 25 Oct 2013. Cert. 15.

Benjamin Britten Peace and Conflict ★★★

The originality of this film for the composer's centenary lies in its exploration of Britten's beliefs including his pacifism. Doubtless sincere and not without interest, the film is nevertheless very much a mish-mash with too much emphasis on re-enactments of Britten's schooldays at Gresham's. Vocal extracts from his music lack subtitles which would have helped the uninitiated. The *War Requiem* is central here yet the Owen settings within it are barely touched upon, the significance of the nationalities represented by the original soloists goes unmentioned and the recording of it on the soundtrack is not Britten's own. MS

❯ Alex Lawther, Mykola Allen, Bradley Hall, John Hurt (narrator).
❯ *Dir* and *Written by* Tony Britten, *Pro* Britten, Katja Mordaunt and Anwen Rees-Myers, *Ph* Roger Bonnici, *Pro Des* Emma Davis, *Ed* Ray Gotts, *Cos* Andrew Joslin.

Capriol Films/SBS-TV Australia/YLE Finland/NRK Norway etc.-Capriol Films Ltd.
109 mins. UK/Australia/Finland/Norway. 2013. Rel: 24 May 2013. Cert. PG.

Bernie ★★★

Claiming to be based on fact (but so did *Fargo*, so who knows?), this is a dark comedy set in Texas. It shows how a funeral home assistant, Bernie (Jack Black giving a pitch perfect performance) befriended the town's ancient and most hated inhabitant, Mrs Nugent (Shirley MacLaine). In time she became so overbearing that he shot her – four times. That the town likes Bernie so much that it supports him while turning a blind

eye to his homosexuality is an additional theme, but the film seems broken-backed as it uneasily transforms into a serious character study. MS

❯ Jack Black, Shirley MacLaine, Matthew McConaughey, Brady Coleman, Rick Dial.
❯ *Dir* Richard Linklater, *Pro* Ginger Sledge, Linklater and others, *Screenplay* Linklater and Skip Hollandsworth, from the latter's article in *Texas Monthly*, *Ph* Dick Pope, *Pro Des* Bruce Curtis, *Ed* Sandra Adair, *M* Graham Reynolds, *Cos* Kari Perkins.

Mandalay Vision/Wind Dancer Films/a Detour Filmproduction etc.-The Works UK Distribution Ltd.
99 mins. USA. 2011. Rel: 26 Apr 2013. Cert. 12A.

The Best Man Holiday ★★★½

Fifteen years after *The Best Man*, the cast and characters return for this belated sequel. The excuse writer-director Malcolm D Lee comes up with is that Morris Chestnut's Lance and Monica Calhoun's Mia are bringing together their group of old college friends to celebrate Christmas. It comes as a surprise only to them that all the old rivalries and romances are easily re-ignited. Lee redeems himself for *Undercover Brother* (2002) and *Scary Movie 5* [qv] with this surprisingly pleasing, fresh and charming romantic comedy-drama. Laughs and wit mix with sentimentality, religion and tears. But it's an effective package, with alternately funny and poignant dialogue and skilled performances from a group of winning actors. DW

❯ Morris Chestnut, Taye Diggs, Regina Hall, Terrence Howard, Sanaa Lathan, Nia Long, Harold Perrineau, Monica Calhoun, Melissa De Sousa.
❯ *Dir* and *Screenplay* Malcolm D Lee, *Pro* Lee and Sean Daniel, *Ph* Greg Gardiner, *Pro Des* Keith Brian Burns, *Ed* Paul Millspaugh, *M* Stanley Clarke, *Cos* Danielle Hollowell.

Universal Pictures/Blackmaled Productions/Sean Daniel Company-Universal Pictures.
123 mins. USA. 2013. Rel: 29 Nov. Cert. 15.

Black Christmas: Taye Diggs, Harold Perrineau, Eddie Cibrian and Morris Chestnut fail to find the festive spirit in Malcolm D Lee's *The Best Man Holiday*.

Drum attack: a vintage performance in Jay Bulger's alarming Beware of Mr Baker.

Dir, *Pro* and *Screenplay* (inspired by the novels of Tatiana Niculescu Bran) Cristian Mungiu, *Ph* Oleg Mutu, *Pro Des* Calin Papura and Mihaela Poenaru, *Ed* Mircea Olteanu, *Cos* Dana Paparuz.

Mobra Films/Why Not Productions/Les Films de Fleuve/ France 3 Cinéma etc.-Artificial Eye
152 mins. Romania/France/Belgium. 2012. Rel: 15 Mar 2013. Cert. 12A.

Big Bad Wolves ★★★★

This gripping thriller from Israel tells the revenge story of a desperate father who kidnaps the main suspect for his daughter's brutal murder and begins to torture him in the basement of his new country home. He also abducts the cop who first began to use unorthodox methods in order to elicit the truth from the suspect... A compelling thriller told with style and dark humour – see it before Hollywood remakes it! GS

Lior Askenazi, Rotem Keinan, Tzahi Gfrad, Doval'e Glickman, Menashe Noy, Dvir Benedek, Kais Nashif.
Dir and *Screenplay* Aharon Keshales and Navot Papushado, *Pro* Roby Star, Avraham Pirchi, Chilik Michaeli, Tami Leon and Leon & Moshe Edery, *Ph* Gloria Bejach, *Art Dir* Arad Sawat, *Ed* Asaf Korman, *M* Haim Frank Ilfman, *Cos* Michal Dor.

United Channel Movies-Metrodome Distribution.
110 mins. Israel. 2013. Rel: 6 Dec 2013. Cert. 18.

The Big Wedding ★★½

US remakes of continental films continue with *The Big Wedding* in which Robert De Niro does little to enhance his career in comedy, playing Don who, with ex-wife Ellie (Diane Keaton), has to pretend they're still married in order to please the birth mother of their Colombian adopted son Alejandro (Ben Barnes) when she arrives for her son's wedding. Sounds funny? Maybe, but it's mostly devoid of laughs, having lost something in translation from its Swiss original. Apart from the waste of talent already mentioned, the likes of Katherine Heigl, Susan Sarandon, Topher Grace, Robin Williams and Christine Ebersole are left stranded with little to do. Writer-director Justin Zackham must take full blame for the travesty. MHD

Robert De Niro, Katherine Heigl, Diane Keaton, Amanda Seyfried, Topher Grace, Susan Sarandon, Robin Williams, Ben Barnes, Christine Ebersole.
Dir and *Screenplay* Justin Zackham, based on the screenplay by Jean-Stephane Bron and Karine Sudan for *Mon frère se marie*, *Pro* Justin Zackham, Harry J Ufland, Richard Salvatore, Clay Pecorin and Anthony Katagas, *Ph* Jonathan Brown, *Pro Des* Andrew Jackness, *Ed* Jon Corn, *M* Nathan Barr, *Cos* Aude Bronson-Howard.

Two Ton Films/Millennium Films-Lionsgate.
89 mins. USA. 2013. Rel: 29 May 2013. Cert. 15.

Beware of Mr Baker ★★★★★

The year's biggest surprise is this superb documentary about the drummer Ginger Baker. A brilliant artist and an impossible man (egocentric and often cruel as in his treatment of his son), he is centre screen here. His forthright manner makes him compelling company regardless, yet this revealing film achieves a rounded, fascinating portrait. Jay Bulger's admirably crafted directorial debut becomes sublime when editor Abhay Sofsky matches images to the beat of Baker's drums. MS

With Ginger Baker, Eric Clapton, Stewart Copeland, Chad Smith, Jay Bulger.
Dir and *Written by* Jay Bulger, *Pro* Andrew Karsch, Fisher Stevens, Erik H Gordon and Bulger, *Ph* Eric Robbins, *Ed* Abhay Sofsky, *M Supervisor* Susan Jacobs.

Insurgent Media/a Pugilist At Rest production/ IFP-Artificial Eye.
92 mins. USA. 2012. Rel: 17 May 2013. Cert. 15.

Beyond the Hills ★★★

The respected Romanian director Cristian Mungiu who made *4 Months, 3 weeks and 2 Days* here brings us a story of two young women who first met in an orphanage. One has found a religious vocation regardless of the fact that they had shared a lesbian relationship, but the other now returns from abroad to draw her back into the world. Visually impressive, well acted and serious this may be, but nothing in the tale warrants a running length of 152 minutes and it lacks the detailed character development that might have justified the slow pace. (Original title: *Dupa dealuri*) MS

Cosmina Stratan, Cristina Flutur, Valeriu Andriuta, Dana Tapalaga, Dionisie Vitcu.

Blackfish ★★★★

This deeply committed documentary is concerned with centres such as Sea World which feature orca whales. The film attacks the rejection of evidence indicating that fatalities involving the whales turning savage are caused by the conditions in which they are placed. *Blackfish* is properly informative and well assembled and it's all the stronger for allowing the facts to speak for themselves. MS

‣ With John Hargrove, Samantha Berg, Dean Gomersall, Kim Ashdown.
‣ *Dir* Gabriela Cowperthwaite, *Pro* Manuel V Oteyza and Cowperthwaite, *Written by* Cowperthwaite, Eli Despres and Tim Zimmermann, *Ph* Jonathan Ingalls and Christopher Towey, *Ed* Despres, *M* Jeff Beal.

Our Turn Productions/Manny O Productions-Dogwoof.
83 mins. USA. 2013. Rel: 26 July 2013. Cert. 15.

Black Nativity ★★★

Baltimore teenager Langston (Jacob Latimore) is sent against his will to spend Christmas in New York with his estranged relatives Reverend Cornell (Forest Whitaker) and Aretha Cobbs (Angela Bassett). But as soon as Langston arrives in the city he falls victim to a street thief. He resents his grandfather's strict rules and is desperate to return home to his struggling single mother Naima (Jennifer Hudson)… The story based on Langston Hughes' stage libretto is sentimentally predictable, but Kasi Lemmons' efficient direction along with the soulful sounds of gospel music make this a surprisingly satisfying experience. GS

‣ Forest Whitaker, Angela Bassett, Jennifer Hudson, Tyrese Gibson, Jacob Latimore, Mary J Blige, Nasir Jones.
‣ *Dir* and *Screenplay* Kasi Lemmons, *Pro* Trudie Styler, Celine Rattray, Galt Niederhoffer, TD Jakes and William Horberg, *Libretto* Langston Hughes, *Ph* Anastas N Michos, *Pro Des* Kristi Zea, *Ed* Terilyn A Shropshire, *M* Laura Karpman and Raphael Saadiq, *Cos* Gersha Phillips.

Maven Pictures-20th Century Fox.
93 mins. USA. 2013. Rel: 6 Dec 2013. Cert. PG.

Black Rock ★★★

When three longtime girlfriends meet up, they decide to sort out their boyfriend issues by going to a remote island off the coast of Maine. However, they are not alone and, when they meet three ex-soldiers, the weekend really starts. One of them is attacked and so begins a chase to see who can get off the island first, the predators or the prey. Not exactly original but reasonably well executed, *Black Rock* has three decent performances (Kate Bosworth, Lake Bell and Katie Aselton, who directs her own story) but is really not savage enough to make it an outstanding addition to the independent horror genre. MHD

‣ Katie Aselton, Lake Bell, Kate Bosworth, Will Bouvier, Jay Paulson, Anslem Richardson.
‣ *Dir* Katie Aselton, *Pro* Adele Romanski, *Screenplay* Mark Duplass, based on a story by Aselton, *Ph* Hilary Spera, *Pro Des* and *Cos* Erin Staub, *Ed* Jacob Vaughan, *M* Ben Lovett.

Submarine Entertainment-Metrodome Distribution.
83 mins. USA. 2012. Rel: 21 June 2013. Cert. 15.

That Orca Moment: killer whales show off in Gabriela Cowperthwaite's *Blackfish*.

Blancanieves ★★★★

Pablo Berger's notion of making a film in silent cinema style with captions replacing dialogue and the sound limited to music originated some time ago, but *The Artist* (which I thought overrated) got into cinemas first. Berger's piece is a variation on the Snow White story adapted to Seville in the 1920s with bullfighting becoming a key element in the drama. Arguably the choice of material makes for a limited appeal but, aided by a first-class music score, it is carried off with style and panache. MS

❥ Maribel Verdú, Daniel Giménez Cacho, Sofía Oria, Macarena Garcia, Angela Molina.
❥ *Dir* and *Screenplay* Pablo Berger, *Pro* Ibon Cormenzana, Jérôme Vidal and Berger, *Ph* Kiko de la Rica, *Pro Des* Alain Bainée, *Ed* Fernando Franco, *M* Alfonso de Villalonga, *Cos* Paco Delgado.

Arcadia Motion Pictures/Mama Film/Nix Films/Sisifo Films/The Kraken Films/ ARTE France Cinéma etc.-StudioCanal Limited.
105 mins. Spain/France/Belgium. 2011. Rel: 12 July 2013. Cert. 12A.

The Bling Ring ★★★½

It's apt that Sofia Coppola's film has been acclaimed as a cool movie if, by that, one means that she is a non-judgmental observer and recorder. She has taken a real-life situation in which LA teenagers burgled the houses of absent celebrities. This obsession with celebrities makes this very much a film of today, but the distanced attitude adopted leaves it to the audience to take from it what they will. Leslie Mann in a comic supporting role runs with it divertingly. MS

❥ Emma Watson, Taissa Farmiga, Israel Broussard, Katie Chang, Claire Julien, Leslie Mann.
❥ *Dir* and *Screenplay* (based on the *Vanity Fair* article by Nancy Jo Sales) Sofia Coppola, *Pro* Roman Coppola, Sofia Coppola and Youree Henley, *Ph* Harris Savides and Christopher Blauvelt, *Pro Des* Anne Ross, *Ed* Sarah Flack, *M* Brian Reitzell, *Cos* Stacey Battat.

An American Zoetrope/NALA Films production/Pathé Distribution/FilmNation Entertainment etc.-StudioCanal Limited.
90 mins. USA/UK/Japan/Germany. 2013. Rel: 5 July 2013. Cert. 15.

Blood ★★★½

This reworking of a TV original starts out as a standard police procedural set in Liverpool but builds into something more ambitious. The central cop (Paul Bettany) takes the law into his own hands like Hank Quinlan in *Touch of Evil* when there's too little evidence to arrest the suspected killer of a teenager. In addition the cop's outlook has been shaped by his macho father (Brian Cox), himself a retired policeman. Bill Gallagher's screenplay needed more depth and detail to realise the tale's potential, but it's a good cast. MS

❥ Paul Bettany, Stephen Graham, Mark Strong, Brian Cox, Ben Crompton.

Dressed to kill: Maribel Verdú in Pablo Berger's *Blancanieves*, winner of ten Goya Awards.

Curious Blue: Adèle Exarchopoulos and Léa Seydoux in Abdellatif Kechiche's excellent *Blue is the Warmest Colour.*

❯ *Dir* Nick Murphy, *Pro* Pippa Harris, Nicola Shindler and Nick Laws, *Screenplay* Bill Gallagher from his TV series *Conviction*, *Ph* George Richmond, *Pro Des* Cristina Casali, *Ed* Victoria Boydell, *M* Daniel Pemberton, *Cos* Michele Clapton.

BBC Films/BFI/IM Global/Quickfire Films/a Neal Street/ Red production etc.-E1 Films.
92 mins. UK/USA. 2012. Rel: 31 May 2013. Cert. 15.

The Blue Black Hussar ★★★½

Jack Bond's lovingly created documentary captures Adam Ant's remarkable comeback after years of mental health problems. There is no doubt that Ant is a true survivor and Bond follows this unique artist as he prepares for his long overdue live performances at London's 100 Club as well as Hyde Park. It's always fascinating, especially when he goes to Paris to meet Charlotte Rampling, the *Night Porter* star, who inspired his first album. GS

❯ With Adam Ant, John Robb, Allen Jones, Georgina Leahy, Charlotte Rampling, Jamie Reynolds, Mark Ronson.
❯ *Dir* Jack Bond, *Pro* Bond and Mary-Rose Storey, *Ph* Mary-Rose Storey etc, *Ed* Joanna Apps and Gabriela Miranda Rodriguez, *Animation* Kevin Baldwin.

Sunrise Pictures-Sunrise Pictures.
98 mins. UK. 2013. Rel: 17 Sep 2013. No Cert.

Blue is the Warmest Colour ★★★½

Brilliant in parts and superbly acted, this French drama from the *Cous-cous* director Abdellatif Kechiche traces the realisation of a 17-year-old that she is a lesbian. Despite the controversy over its explicit sex scenes and how the actresses may have been treated, it is no exploitation movie but a serious and convincing study of a bond that grows but then breaks down. Unfortunately it's an exhaustingly over-long film (virtually three hours) and it becomes much less compelling in its second half, with scenes that lead nowhere while information that we do want is not always supplied. But at its best it is outstanding even so. (Original title: *La Vie d'Adèle Chapitres 1 et 2*). MS

❯ Léa Seydoux, Adèle Exarchopoulos, Salim Kechiouche, Jérémie Laheurte.
❯ *Dir* Abdellatif Kechiche, *Pro* Barhim Chioua, Vincent Maraval and Kechiche, *Screenplay* Kechiche and Ghalya Lacroix from the graphic novel *Le Bleu est une couleur chaude* by Julie Maroh, *Ph* Sofian El Fani, *Art Dir* Bahijja El Amrani, Michel Gionti and others, *Ed* Camille Toubkis. Albertine Lastera, Lacroix and others, *Cos* Paloma Garcia Martens, Dorothée Lissac and others.

A Wild Bunch, Quat'sous Films production/France 2 Cinéma/RTBF/Vertigo Films etc.-Artificial Eye.
180 mins. France/Belgium/Spain. 2013. Rel: 22 Nov 2013. Cert. 18.

Blue Jasmine ★★★★

To his great advantage Woody Allen is back in America with this splendidly acted piece that has as its focal point a self-centred sister losing her way. This role rightly won Cate Blanchett an Oscar and, despite the film's many comic moments, it is at heart a drama – which is only natural given the intriguing echoes here of Tennessee Williams' *A Streetcar Named Desire*. Unexpectedly Allen uses the 'Scope format which proves well-suited to the movie. MS

❯ Cate Blanchett, Alec Baldwin, Bobby Cannavale, Sally Hawkins, Peter Sarsgaard.
❯ *Dir* and *Screenplay* Woody Allen, *Pro* Letty Aronson, Stephen Tenenbaum and Edward Watson, *Ph* Javier Aguirresarobe, *Pro Des* Santo Loquasto, *Ed*

Alisa Lepsetter, *Cos* Suzy Benzinger.

Sony Pictures Classics/Gravier Productions/a Perdido production-Warner Bros.
98 mins. USA. 2013. Rel: 27 Sep 2013. Cert. 12A.

Borrowed Time ★★★

Gangly, put-upon Kevin tries a spot of burglary and is faced with an irascible OAP descending in his stairlift while levelling a blunderbuss at him. Setting up the 'odd couple' dynamic that motors the entire film, this delightfully quirky scene is typical of the way Jules Bishop's micro-budgeted debut subverts the urban clichés of recent Brit flicks. He doesn't shrink, however, from more time-honoured ones. Inevitably, the crusty old so-and-so finally mellows; just as inevitably, Kevin proves himself more than just "a basic bog-standard waste of space." Excellent though he is, Phil Davis (57 during production) is about 20 years too young for his role, and there are a few misjudgments here and there. But otherwise *Borrowed Time* scores as an engaging curio. JR

❧ Phil Davis, Theo Barklem-Biggs, Juliet Oldfield, Warren Brown, Perry Benson, Neil Cole.
❧ *Dir* and *Screenplay* Jules Bishop, *Pro* Oliver Kaempfer, *Ph* David Rom, *Pro Des* Miren Marañón, *Ed* Fiona DeSouza, *M* Christopher Barnett *Cos* Sophie Howard.

BBC Films/Film London-Parkville Pictures.
88 mins. USA. 2012. Rel: 13 Sep 2013. Cert. 15.

Breakfast with Jonny Wilkinson ★½

The action takes place at the Greyhawks Rugby Club in 2003 – the day of the Rugby World Cup Final between Australia and England – where a few loyal supporters have gathered in order to watch the game... It's a simple premise that worked well for Chris England's play *An Evening with Gary Lineker*. Unfortunately the loud and theatrical

Golden oldie: Phil Davis and Theo Barklem-Biggs in Jules Bishop's *Borrowed Time*.

acting doesn't sit comfortably in this disappointing film. The characters are verging on the stereotypical but thankfully there is the strong presence of George MacKay, as Jake, the first team prodigy. GS

❧ George MacKay, Chris England, Nigel Lindsay, Beth Cordingly, Michael Beckley, Norman Pace, Gina Varela.
❧ *Dir* Simon Sprackling, *Pro* Robb Perren, *Screenplay* Chris England, *Ph* Jonathan Iles, *Ed* Ian Baigent, *M* Andy Coles.

Future Leisure Films-Miracle Communications.
95 mins. UK. 2013. Rel: 22 Nov 2013. Cert. 15.

Breath of the Gods ★★★

This documentary about Indian savant T Krishnamacharya, widely considered the father of modern yoga, is highly accessible for those who know nothing about the origins, practice and history of this discipline. Blending interviews featuring several current yoga masters with footage of physique-defying physical exercises, it certainly holds the attention throughout. Solidly researched, it delivers a wealth of fascinating material, making it a useful introduction to its chosen subject. JC

❧ *Dir* Jan Schmidt-Garre, *Pro* Schmidt-Garre and Marieke Schroeder, *Ph* Diethard Prengel, *Pro Des* Irina Kromayer, *Ed* Gaby Kull-Neujahr.

PARS Media/FilmFernsehFonds Bayern/German Federal Film Fund/MEDIA-Blue Dolphin Film Distributors.
105 mins. Germany/India 2013. Rel: 22 Feb 2013. Cert. U.

Breathe In ★★★

Felicity Jones, who previously appeared for Drake Doremus in *Like Crazy*, here plays an English exchange student attending an American high school and causing havoc in the home of the married music teacher (Guy Pearce) who puts her up and falls in love with her. The players are fine, but the film sets out in a highly naturalistic tone and then self-consciously uses music to play up the drama while also allowing the story to slide from credible tale to unconvincing melodrama. MS

❧ Guy Pearce, Felicity Jones, Amy Ryan, Mackenzie Davis, Matthew Daddario.
❧ *Dir* Drake Doremus, *Pro* Jonathan Schwartz, Andrea Sperling and others, *Screenplay* Doremus and Ben York Jones, *Ph* John Guleserian, *Pro Des* Katie Byron, *Ed* Jonathan Alberts, *M* Dustin O'Halloran, *Cos* Emma Potter.

Indian Paintbrush/a Super Crispy Entertainment production etc.-Curzon Film World.
97 mins. USA. 2012. Rel: 19 July 2013. Cert. 15.

Bring Me the Head of the Machine Gun Woman ★★

This silly but fun Chilean adventure is a cross between Sam Peckinpah's 1974 classic *Bring Me*

the Head of Alfredo Garcia and a video game. A powerful gangster offers a lot of money to anyone who will stop the sexy mercenary known as Machine Gun Woman (Fernanda Urrejola) from killing him. Accidentally a naïve young man named Santiago (Matias Oviedo) finds himself in the middle of this crazy vendetta... It's way over the top and totally mad but thankfully its 73-minute running time doesn't outstay its welcome. (Original title: *Tráiganme la cabeza de la mujer metralleta*) GS

❯ Fernanda Urrejola, Matias Oviedo, Jorge Alis, Sofia Garcia, Alex Rivera, Felipe Avelo, Patricio Pimienta, Francisca Castillo.
❯ *Dir* and *Screenplay* Ernesto Díaz Espinoza, *Pro* and *Pho* Nicolás Ibieta, *Pro Des* Nicolás Oyarce, *Ed* Ernesto Díaz Espinoza and Nicolás Ibieta, *M* Rocco, *Cos* Caro de Maria and Gabriela Calvete.
LatinXploitation-Ronoc Entertainment. 73 mins. Chile. 2012. Rel: 27 Sep 2013. Cert. 18.

Broken ★★★★

Think of it as this year's *Tyrannosaur*. Like Paddy Considine's film this view of modern Britain is far too bleak to be considered entertainment. Unfortunately the last scenes prove contrived and unconvincing, but I have to give it a high rating because this look at three neighbouring households is otherwise so authentic. The acting is superb, theatre director Rufus Norris takes to cinema with real authority and, despite its late misjudgments, the film although largely overlooked by critics is nothing less than extraordinary. MS

❯ Tim Roth, Cillian Murphy, Rory Kinnear, Robert Emms, Bill Milner, Denis Lawson, Eloise Laurence, George Sargeant.
❯ *Dir* Rufus Norris, *Pro* Dixie Linder, Tally Garner, Nick Marston and Bill Kenwright, *Screenplay* Mark O'Rowe from the novel by Daniel Clay, *Ph* Rob Hardy, *Pro Des* Kave Quinn, *Ed* Victoria Boydell, *M* Electric Wave Bureau, *Cos* Jane Petrie.
BBC Films/BFI/LipSync Productions/Bill Kenwright Films/ a Cuba Pictures production etc.-StudioCanal Limited. 91 mins. UK. 2012. Rel: 8 Mar 2013. Cert. 15.

The Broken Circle Breakdown
★★

In this Belgian film a married couple who sing country and western songs have a young daughter diagnosed with cancer, a situation that brings out conflicts between the atheist father and the religious mother. Music and sex are used to spice up the weepie aspect although it eventually goes maudlin. Meanwhile, to hide the piece's stage origin the film incorporates not only flashbacks but scenes that confuse until revealed as being flashforwards! Some people appear to like this film, but I'll take *In Your Hands* (2003) every time. MS

❯ Johan Heldenbergh, Veerle Baetens, Nell Cattrysse, Geert Van Rampelberg, Nils de Caster.
❯ *Dir* Felix van Groeningen, *Pro* Dirk Impens, *Screenplay* Carl Joos and van Groeningen with Charlotte Vandermeersch based on *The Broken Circle Breakdown Featuring the Cover-ups of Alabama* by Johan Heldenbergh and Mieke Dobbels, *Ph* Ruben

Dysfunctional Britain: the brilliant Eloise Laurence and Tim Roth in Rufus Norris' *Broken*.

Impens, *Art Dir* Kurt Rigolle, *Ed* Nico Leunen, *M* Bjorn Eriksson, *Cos* Ann Lauwerys.

Menuet & Topkapi Films/Eurimages/Kinepolis Film Distribution etc.-StudioCanal Limited.
112 mins. Belgium/The Netherlands. 2012. Rel: 18 Oct 2013. Cert. 15.

Broken City ★★★★

Efficient rather than memorable but without any of the banalities of *Gangster Squad* [qv], this is a New York thriller in which ex-cop turned private investigator Billy Taggert (Mark Wahlberg) tangles with the corrupt mayor (Russell Crowe). There are echoes of the clearly superior *Chinatown* (1974) and of earlier films too, but those in the mood for this kind of movie will find *Broken City* watchable enough if hardly distinctive. MS

❧ Mark Wahlberg, Russell Crowe, Catherine Zeta-Jones, Barry Pepper, Jeffrey Wright.
❧ *Dir* Allen Hughes, *Pro* Randall Emmett, Mark Wahlberg, Hughes and others, *Screenplay* Brian Tucker, *Ph* Ben Seresin, *Pro Des* Tom Duffield, *Ed* Cindy Mollo, *M* Atticus Ross, Claudia Sarne and Leopold Ross, *Cos* Betsy Heimann.

An Emmett/Furla Films and New Regency production/Inferno International etc.-StudioCanal Limited.
109 mins. USA. 2012. Rel: 1 Mar 2013. Cert. 15.

Bula Quo! ★

Perhaps the temptation to make an utterly redundant film on the beautiful island of Fiji was irresistible for the legendary group Status Quo. Otherwise it's difficult to find anything positive to say about this silly film which takes place during the finale of the Status Quo 50 Year Celebration Tour. Francis Rossi and Rick Parfitt want to party after a concert but find themselves playing Russian roulette with a gang of ruthless gamblers... This charmless effort aspires to be like The Beatles' *Help* but fails miserably. GS

❧ Jon Lovitz, Craig Fairbrass, Laura Aikman, Francis Rossi, Rick Parfitt, Mat Kennard, Jean Heard, Andrew Bown.
❧ *Dir* Stuart St Paul, *Pro* Tim Major, *Screenplay* St Paul and Jean Heard, *Ph* Chas Bain, *Pro Des* Felix Coles, *Ed* Lewis Albrow, *M* Andrew Bown, Rick Parfitt, John Rhino Edwards, Francis Rossi, *Cos* Georgina Harper.

INDY UK Films Ltd/Status Quo Films-Miracle Communications.
90 mins. UK/Fiji. 2013. Rel: 5 July 2013. Cert. PG.

Bullet to the Head ★★★

Sylvester Stallone returns to his iconic action star roots as Jimmy Bobo, a jaded New Orleans hitman who reluctantly teams up with a New York City cop (Sung Kang) to bring down the killers of their respective partners. Thoroughly reprehensible but totally and richly enjoyable, it's an exciting old-style buddy-buddy action thriller enthusiastically, even stylishly filmed by a one-time master, the 71-year-old Walter Hill, after a decade away from the big screen. Basically a Western in disguise, it's full of non-stop explosive action, thrilling fight scenes and classic one-liners. Based on French author Alexis ('Matz') Nolent's popular graphic novel, it's set in some weird parallel universe, where guns and killing are essential, frequent and 'fun'. DW

❧ Sylvester Stallone, Christian Slater, Jon Seda, Sung Kang, Sarah Shahi, Jason Momoa.
❧ *Dir* Walter Hill, *Pro* Alfred Gough, Miles Millar and Alexandra Milchan, *Screenplay* Alessandro Camon, based on *Du plomb dans la tête*, the graphic novel by Alexis Nolent and Colin Wilson, *Ph* Lloyd Ahern II, *Pro Des* Tony Corbett, *Ed* Tim Alverson, *M* Steve Mazzaro, *Cos* Ha Nguyen.

Dark Castle Entertainment/IM Global/After Dark Films/Automatik Entertainment/EMJAG Productions/Headshot Films/Millar Gough Inc/Silver Reel-Entertainment One.
92 mins. USA. 2012. Rel: 1 Feb 2013. Cert. 15.

Bullhead ★★★½

Nominated for an Oscar, this debut by the Belgian director Michaël R Roskam, made in 2010, gave a leading role to the impressive Matthias Schoenaerts who later made *Rust and Bone*. It's a very tough drama, overlong but often compelling and visually distinguished. Described as a personal drama set against the backdrop of the Belgian bovine hormone mafia, its tale of criminals and rival groups goes into flashback as part of a story of bullying and genital mutilation. If it too often seems over-complex, it is also impressive. (Original title: *Rundskop*). MS

The axemen cometh: Sylvester Stallone and Jason Momoa in Walter Hill's *Bullet to the Head.*

> Matthias Schoenaerts, Jean-Marie Lesuisse, Jeroen Perceval, Jeanne Dandoy.
> *Dir* and *Screenplay* Michaël R Roskam, *Pro* Bart Van Langendonck, *Ph* Nicolas Karakatanis, *Pro Des* Walter Brugmans, *Ed* Alain Dessauvage, *M* Raf Keunen, *Cos* Margriet Procee.

Savage Film/Eyeworks/Artémis Productions/Waterland Film etc.-Soda Pictures.
129 mins. Belgium/The Netherlands. 2011. Rel: 1 Feb 2013. Cert. 15.

The Butler ★★½

An African American worked in the White House for many years and served many presidents. However, while derived from that fact, this is a largely fictional tale and, although the butler is central, his rebel son is far more sympathetic, so it is perhaps understandable that Forest Whitaker is dull in the title role. The film touches but without much subtlety on the more important racial crises of America in the 20th century, but it ends up as a weepie that also suggests a commercial for Obama. Well meant, doubtless, but puerile. MS

> Forest Whitaker, Oprah Winfrey, David Oyelowo, John Cusack, Jane Fonda, Cuba Gooding Jr, Terrence Howard, Lenny Kravitz, James Marsden, Vanessa Redgrave, Alan Rickman, Liev Schreiber, Robin Williams, Mariah Carey, Alex Pettyfer.
> *Dir* Lee Daniels, *Pro* Pamela Oas Williams, Laura Ziskin, Daniels and others, *Screenplay* Danny Strong, inspired by the article *A Butler Well Served by This Election* by Wil Haygood, *Ph* Andrew Dunn, *Pro Des*

Tim Galvin, *Ed* Joe Klotz, *M* Rodrigo Leão, *Cos* Ruth E Carter.

The Weinstein Company/Windy Hill Pictures/
Follow Through Productions/Salamander Pictures etc.-Entertainment Film Distributors Ltd.
132 mins. USA. 2013. Rel: 15 Nov 2013. Cert. 12A.

The Butterfly's Dream ★★½

Yilmaz Erdoğan's highly ambitious epic takes place in the Black Sea city of Zonguldak during World War II. All the men are forced to work in the mines and inevitably most of them develop consumption. Two poets, Rustu and Muzzafer, fall for the same woman and their only weapon to win her heart is their poetry. Impressive production values offer stunning cinematography and breathtaking locations. The story is decent, but it's far too long and eventually falls into melodrama. GS

> Kivanç Tatlitug, Mert Firat, Belçim Bilgin, Farah Zeynep Abdullah, Yilmaz Erdogan, Mert Firat.
> *Dir* and *Screenplay* Yilmaz Erdoğan, *Pro* Necati Akpinar, *Ph* Gökhan Tiryaki, *Pro Des* Kivanc Baruonu, *Ed* Bora Göksingol, *M* Rahman Altin, *Cos* Gülümser Gürtunca.

BKM Film/Bocek Yapim-Turkish Films International.
138 mins. Turkey. 2013. Rel: 22 Feb 2013. Cert. 12A.

Byzantium ★★★★

A feminist slant colours this sadly underrated vampire film from Neil Jordan. With a contemporary seaside setting (Hastings was a

Epic poetry: Mert Firat in Yilmaz Erdoğan's *The Butterfly's Dream.*

location), it tells of two female vampires, mother and daughter, who have both survived for over 200 years despite their very contrasted outlooks but now face an uncertain future. That we feel emotionally involved is down to the wonderful Saoirse Ronan as the younger vampire yearning for love. The film is also technically adroit and there's great photography from Sean Bobbitt. MS

▶ Saoirse Ronan, Gemma Arterton, Sam Riley, Jonny Lee Miller, Caleb Landry Jones.
▶ *Dir* Neil Jordan, *Pro* Stephen Woolley, Elizabeth Karlsen and others, *Screenplay* Moira Buffini, from her play *A Vampire Story*, *Ph* Sean Bobbitt, *Pro Des* Simon Elliott, *Ed* Tony Lawson, *M* Javier Navarette, *Cos* Consolata Boyle.

A Number 9 Films, Parallel Films, Demarest Films production/Irish Film Board/Lipsync Productions etc.-StudioCanal Limited.
118 mins. Ireland/UK/USA. 2012. Rel: 31 May 2013. Cert. 15.

Caesar Must Die ★★★★★

Impossible to categorise, this exceptional Italian work from the veteran Taviani brothers features prisoners who, while incarcerated, perform plays. We see them engaged on Shakespeare's *Julius Caesar* and, if the film is a documentary about art and rehabilitation, it is also a remarkably powerful albeit abridged version of the play. It's an intriguing one-off that at times prompts comparisons with the Orson Welles *Othello*

Dogs of war: Salvatore Striano and Giovanni Arcuri in Paolo and Vittorio Taviani's Caesar Must Die.

(1951). There's an effective use of black-and-white photography by Simone Zampagni, but it begins and ends in colour. Although short, it's richly resonant. (Original title: *Cesare deve morire*). MS

▶ Cosimo Rega, Salvatore Striano, Giovanni Arcuri, Antonio Frasca.
▶ *Dir* Paolo and Vittorio Taviani, *Pro* Grazia Volpi, *Screenplay* The Taviani brothers in collaboration with Fabio Cavalli, based on Shakespeare's *The Tragedy of Julius Caesar*, *Ph* Simone Zampagni, *Ed* Roberto Perpignani, *M* Giuliano Taviani and Carmelo Travia.

A Kaos Cinematografica production/Stemal Entertainment/Le Talee/RAI Cinema etc.-New Wave Films.
77 mins. Italy. 2011. Rel: 1 Mar 2013. Cert. 12A.

The Call ★★½

Jordan (Halle Berry) is an experienced 911 Emergency Call Centre operator who gets a second chance after a young woman gets killed while talking to her on the phone. Now she receives a desperate call from teenager Casey (Abigail Breslin), who has just been kidnapped... Berry delivers her best performance for years. The action is suitably claustrophobic, especially in the early parts of the film, but unfortunately as the climax develops it becomes increasingly silly and loses credibility. GS

▶ Halle Berry, Abigail Breslin, Morris Chestnut, Michael Eklund, David Otunga, José Zuniga, Roma Maffia
▶ *Dir* Brad Anderson, *Pro* Bradley Gallo, Jeff Graup, Michael A. Helfant and Robert L Stein, *Screenplay*

Terms of internment: Marc Wiese's harrowing *Camp 14: Total Control Zone.*

Richard D'Ovidio from a story by him, Nicole D'Ovidio and Jon Bokenkamp, *Ph* Tom Yatsko, *Pro Des* Franco-Giacomo Carbone, *Ed* Avi Youabian, *M* John Debney, *Cos* Magali Guidasci.

Tri-Star Pictures/Stage 6 Films/Troika Pictures/WWE Studios/Amasia Entertainment/Apotheosis Media Group-Warner Bros.
94 mins. USA. 2013. Rel: 20 Sep 2013. Cert. 15.

Call Girl ★★★

Sweden, the 1970s. Claiming a factual basis, this feature debut by Mikael Marcimain has at its centre a 14-year-old problem girl. It shows how this girl Iris, already in a juvenile care home, is drawn into prostitution. This long but not inefficient film becomes a rather generalised portrayal of how corruption makes it more difficult to bring down the call girl ring in which Iris becomes involved. Furthermore, the film is less a searing exposé than a rather tacky take on events that doesn't stint on naked nymphettes. MS

▶ Sofia Karemyr, Simon J Berger, Pernilla August, David Dencik, Sven Nordin.
▶ *Dir* Mikael Marcimain, *Pro* Mimmi Spång, *Screenplay* Marietta von Hausswolff von Baumgarten, *Ph* Hoyte van Hoytema, *Pro Des* Lina Nordqvist, *Ed* Kristofer Nordin, *M* Mattias Bärjed, *Cos* Cilla Rörby.

Garagefilm International/Friland Produksjon/
Newgrange Pictures etc.-Curzon Film World.
140 mins. Sweden/Norway/Finland/Ireland. 2012.
Rel: 16 Aug 2013. Cert. 18.

Camp 14: Total Control Zone
★★★★★

Utterly devastating documentary built around interviews with (mainly) a man who was born into and as an adult escaped from a North Korean Death Camp and (with less material) a former guard at one such camp. It being impossible to film inside these institutions, the filmmakers brilliantly deploy bleak, grey-toned animation to put images of camp life (classrooms, public executions) on the screen. Be horrified as humans grow up in an environment devoid of moral goodness. One of the most unsettling films you'll ever see. JC

▶ With Shin Dong-hyuk, Hyuk Kwon, Oh Yangnam.
▶ *Dir* Marc Wiese, *Exec Pro* Axel Engstfeld, *Ph* Jörg Adams, *Ed* Jean-Marc Lesguillons.

Engstfeld Filmproduktion GmBh/Arte/Bayerischer Rundfunk/Westdeutscher Rundfunk-Kaleidoscope Entertainment.
106 mins. Germany/South Korea. 2012. Rel: 4 Oct 2013. Cert. 12A.

Captain Phillips ★★★★

This real-life maritime tale from 2009 dramatises the hijacking by Somali pirates of an American container ship captained by Richard Phillips. Tom Hanks plays the captain and award-winning newcomer Barkhad Abdi is the leading pirate and both are excellent, with the first two-thirds of the film gaining from the documentary style direction by Paul Greengrass, he of *United 93* (2006). The last third takes place on a lifeboat and is rather less interesting, the film itself being overlong. But at its best *Captain Phillips* is very impressive. MS

▶ Tom Hanks, Barkhad Abdi, Barkhad Abdirahman, Faysal Ahmed, Mahat M Ali, Catherine Keener.
▶ *Dir* Paul Greengrass, *Pro* Scott Rudin, Dana Brunetti and Michael De Luca, *Screenplay* Billy Ray, based on the book *A Captain's Duty: Somali Pirates, Navy SEALs and Dangerous Days at Sea* by Richard Phillips with Stephan Talty, *Ph* Barry Ackroyd, *Pro Des* Paul Kirby, *Ed* Christopher Rouse, *M* Henry Jackman, *Cos* Mark Bridges.

Columbia Pictures/a Scott Rudin, Michael De Luca, Trigger Street production-Sony Pictures Releasing.
134 mins. USA. 2013. Rel: 18 Oct 2013. Cert. 12A.

Carrie ★★

Brian De Palma's 1976 classic based on Stephen King's first novel gets an unnecessary remake here under Kimberley Peirce's efficient but uninspired direction. It's a decent attempt but Chloë Grace Moretz lacks Sissy Spacek's vulnerability, especially in the scene when she arrives at the prom. Julianne Moore is strong as Carrie's deeply religious mother but not as fierce as Piper Laurie in the original. Overall, a pointless film – just see the original instead! GS

❯ Julianne Moore, Chloë Grace Moritz, Gabriella Wilde, Portia Doubleday, Zoë Belkin, Judy Greer, Samantha Weinstein.
❯ Dir Kimberly Peirce, Pro Kevin Misher, Screenplay Laurence D Cohen and Robert Aguirre-Sacasa, based on the novel by Stephen King, Ph Steve Yedlin, Pro Des Carol Speer, Ed Lee Percy and Nancy Richardson, M Marco Beltrami, Cos Luis Sequeira.

Metro-Goldwyn-Mayer/Screen Gems/Misher Films-Sony Pictures Releasing
100 mins. USA. 2013. Rel: 29 Nov 2013. Cert. 15.

Ten years a slave: Eamon Farren in Jennifer Lynch's *Chained.*

Chained ★★★

Listen out for the odd phrase "In one ear and out the window" and you'll have a clue to the pulpy but pleasurable twist ending applied to this otherwise grimly realistic drama. Vincent D'Onofrio is Bob, a hulking serial killer who imprisons and enslaves the nine-year-old son of one of his victims; the main action takes place ten years later, with the waif-like 'Rabbit' (Eamon Farren) by now tragically acclimatised to D'Onofrio's sordid serial-killing routine. With one exception – a graphic throat-slashing that earned the film an NC-17 rating in America – the murders take place off screen, though Jennifer Lynch's film is no less gruelling an experience for that. To her credit, she also makes it queasily compelling. JR

❯ Vincent D'Onofrio, Eamon Farren, Evan Bird, Julia Ormond, Conor Leslie, Jake Weber, Gina Philips.
❯ Dir and Screenplay Jennifer Lynch, based on a screenplay by Damian O'Donnell, Pro Lee Nelson, Rhonda Baker and David Buelow, Ph Shane Daly, Pro Des Sarah McCudden, Ed Daryl K Davis and Chris A Peterson, M Climax Golden Twins, Cos Brenda Shenher.

RGB Productions/Envision Media Arts/Apothecary Films-Anchor Bay Entertainment.
94 mins. Canada. 2012. Rel: 1 Feb 2013. Cert. 18.

Chasing Mavericks ★★½

This is the true story of Jay Moriarty (Jonny Weston), a young surfing protégé who manages to break the mountainous Mavericks, one of the biggest waves on Earth, not far from his Santa Cruz home. This is a likable but average film with a surprisingly restrained performance from Gerard Butler as Jay's trainer. It would have been better suited to afternoon television if it weren't for the spectacular climactic sequence. GS

❯ Gerard Butler, Jonny Weston, Elisabeth Shue, Abgail Spencer, Leven Rambin, Greg Long, Peter Mel.
❯ Dir Michael Apted and Curtis Hanson, Pro Hanson, Brandon Hooper, Jim Meenaghan and Mark Johnson, Screenplay Kario Salem, from a story by Hooper and Meenaghan, Ph Oliver Euclid, Pro Des Ida Random, Ed John Gilbert, M Chad Fischer, Cos Sophie De Rakoff.

Fox 2000 Pictures/Walden Media/Gran Via/Deuce Three Productions/Dune Entertainment-20th Century Fox Film Corporation.
116 mins. USA. 2012. Rel: 5 July 2013. Cert. PG.

Cherry ★

From working in a Long Beach launderette 18-year-old Angelina (Ashley Hinshaw) plunges into the world of hardcore porn in San Francisco. Actually, 'plunges' is far too emphatic a word, for, like this fatally enervated film, Angelina is bizarrely passive and listless. "I like to try new things," she says, and the film's insight into her motivation goes no deeper than that. Things, new or otherwise, just seem to happen to her. Trouble is, they never rise above soap opera level and the film ekes out its running time with the kind of improvised (or seemingly improvised) duologues that go absolutely nowhere. *Cherry* puts a positive spin on the porn industry but ends up seeming timid, giving some good actors absolutely nothing dramatic to chew on. (Original title: *About Cherry*) JR

❧ Ashley Hinshaw, Lili Taylor, Dev Patel, Dianne Farr, Jonny Weston, James Franco, Heather Graham, Maya Raines.
❧ *Dir* Stephen Elliott, *Pro* Gordon Bijelonic, Datari Turner, Taylor Phillips, Elana Krausz, Jordan Kesler, Rick Dugdale and Elizabeth Destro, *Screenplay* Elliott and Lorelei Lee, *Ph* Darren Genet, *Pro Des* Michael Grasley, *Ed* Michelle Boticelli, *M* Jeff Russo, *Cos* Daniella Turner.

Enderby Entertainment/Gordon Bijelonic/ Datari Turner Films-Rézo Films.
98 mins. USA. 2013. Rel: 2 Sep 2013. Cert. 18.

Child's Pose ★★★★½

Centre screen in this remarkable Romanian drama is Luminita Gheorghiu giving one of the year's best performances. She plays an admirably strong-minded woman but one willing to go to extreme lengths to aid her married son when, while driving at speed, he causes the death of a child. If it is clear that her strength also involves dominance, it is for the viewer to ponder the extent to which she is knowingly ruthless or is, perhaps, a self-deceiver. The ending which invites speculation may be too abrupt for some, but this is an outstanding, thought-provoking piece. (Original title: *Pozitia copilului*). MS

❧ Luminita Gheorghiu, Bogan Dumitrache, Ilinca Gola, Natasha Raab, Vlad Ivanov.
❧ *Dir* Calin Peter Netzer, *Pro* Netzer and Ada Solomon, *Screenplay* Razvan Radulescu and Netzer, *Ph* Andrei Butica, *Pro Des* Malina Ionescu, *Ed* Dana Lucretia Bunescu, *Cos* Irina Marinescu.

A Parada Film production/Hai-Hui Entertainment/HBO Romania-StudioCanal Limited.
112 mins. Romania. 2012. Rel: 1 Nov 2013. Cert. 15.

Chimpanzee ★★★★

This sweet film is superbly photographed in the deep forests of Africa and follows the True Life Adventure of an adorable young chimpanzee named Oscar. He's very curious about life and soon learns how to crack even the most stubborn nut, but his innocent existence takes an unexpected turn when a rival group of chimpanzees attacks his family... Alastair Fothergill and his patient crew deliver perfect family entertainment and

inevitably, as this is a Disney film, the violent scenes take place off screen. GS

❧ Narrated by Tim Allen.
❧ *Dir* Alastair Fothergill and Mark Linfield, *Pro* Fothergill, Linfield and Alix Tidmarsh, *Screenplay* Fothergill, Linfield and Don Hahn, based on an original concept by Fothergill and Linfield, *Ph* Martyn Colbeck and Bill Wallauer, *Ed* Andy Netley, *M* Nicholas Hooper.

Great Ape Productions-Walt Disney Studios Motion Pictures.
78 mins. Tanzania/USA. 2012. Rel: 3May 2013. Cert. U.

The Christmas Candle ★★½

Films like this don't come along very often. Based on the 2013 novel by Max Lucado, the film tells the story of a village called Gladbury where, every 25 years, an angel descends to bless a candle, bestowing a miracle on whosoever lights it. But, this being 1890, the advent of electricity and the appearance of a progressive new vicar (Hans Matheson) threaten to overturn the legend... As is to be expected from such fare, there is a good deal of cheesiness and Dickensian stereotyping, but the film has a sincerity and message of community that should appeal to less demanding viewers. Incidentally, the film provides a historic footnote of sorts, being the acting debut of Susan Boyle as the churchwarden's wife. CB

❧ Hans Matheson, Samantha Barks, Lesley Manville, Sylvester McCoy, James Cosmo, Susan Boyle, Barbara Flynn, John Hannah.
❧ *Dir* John Stephenson, *Pro* Tom Newman and Hannah Leader, *Screenplay* Candace Lee and Eric Newman, based on the novel by Max Lucado, *Ph* Mike Brewster, *Pro Des* Tony Noble, *Ed* Emma E Hickox, *M* Tim Atack, *Cos* Hannah Summers.

Pinewood Studios/Big Book Media/Impact Productions-Pinewood Pictures.
100 mins. UK/USA. 2013. Rel: 13 Dec 2013. Cert. U.

Cirque du Soleil: Worlds Away ★★★★

This celebratory journey into magical realism features some of the best elements of seven Cirque du Soleil live shows in Las Vegas. It has

Mother courage: the superb Luminita Gheorghiu in Calin Peter Netzer's *Child's Pose.*

a dreamlike quality with a thin narrative that interlinks the acts. A young girl visits the circus in order to escape life and falls instantly in love with the aerialist who sadly slips and falls into another world. It's an imaginative and melancholy journey into the unknown, superbly shot in 3D. GS

▶ Erica Linz, Igor Zarippov, John Clarke, Lutz Halbhubner, Dallas Barnett etc.
▶ *Dir* and *Screenplay* Andrew Adamson, *Pro* Adamson, Martin Bolduc and Aron Warner, *Ph* Brett Turnbull, *Art Dir* Guy Barnes, *Ed* Sim Evan-Jones and Dirk Westervelt, *M* Benoit Jutras, *Cos* Josalene Ginn and Jenny Rushton.

Paramount Pictures/Cirque du Soleil/Reel FX/Strange Weather/Cameron I Pace Group-Paramount Pictures. 91 mins. USA. 2012. Rel: 1 Feb 2013. Cert. PG.

Citadel ★★★★

In writer-director Ciaran Foy's first feature Tommy lives in a derelict block with pregnant wife Joanne. As she is about to give birth, she is attacked by a gang of feral hooded kids. She dies and Tommy is left with the baby. He becomes agoraphobic and dare not leave his flat because he thinks the gang are out to kill his child. This is a very disturbing film, based on the director's own experience of violence. Shot in the dark and in grey light, there is a constant air of dread. Terrific performances by Aneurin Barnard as Tommy and James Cosmo as the disturbed priest who rids Tommy of the wild kids make this a gripping psychological horror story. MHD

▶ Aneurin Barnard, James Cosmo, Amy Shiels, Wunmi Mosaku, Ingrid Craigie, Jake Wilson.
▶ *Dir* and *Screenplay* Ciaran Foy, *Pro* Brian Coffey and Katie Holly, *Ph* Tim Fleming, *Pro Des* Tom Sayer, *Ed* Tony Kearns and Jake Roberts, *M* tomandandy, *Cos* Anna Robbins.

Blinder Films/Sigma Films/Irish Film Board-Revolver Entertainment. 84 mins. Ireland/UK. 2012. Rel: 1 Mar 2013. Cert. 15.

One man and a baby: Aneurin Barnard in Ciaran Foy's chilling *Citadel.*

Cleopatra (reissue) ★★★½

One of the most famous films ever made, if only because of the publicity surrounding it in 1963 and the fact that it took ages to complete and cost a fortune. The new print looks magnificent but it might have been better to release it as the full, two-part, six-hour epic which director Joseph L Mankiewicz really wanted. A great performance by Rex Harrison as Caesar and an OK one by Richard Burton as Antony are offset by the rather mundane acting of Miss Taylor as the Queen of Egypt. Beautiful she was, but vocally she sounded like a Hollywood housewife. The documentary *Cleopatra: the Film That Changed Hollywood* is actually far more interesting than its subject. MHD

▶ Elizabeth Taylor, Richard Burton, Rex Harrison, Pamela Brown, George Cole, Hume Cronyn, Cesare Danova, Kenneth Haigh, Martin Landau, Roddy McDowall.
▶ *Dir* Joseph L Mankiewicz, *Pro* Walter Wanger, *Screenplay* Mankiewicz, Ranald MacDougall and Sidney Buchman, based on histories by Plutarch, Suetonius and Appian, and Carlo Mario Franzero's book *The Life and Times of Cleopatra*, *Ph* Leon Shamroy, *Pro Des* John DeCuir, *Ed* Dorothy Spencer, *M* Alex North, *Cos* Vittorio Nino Novarese and Renié.

20th Century-Fox/Producers Pictures Corporation/MCL Films S.A./Walwa Films S.A.-20th Century Fox. 192 mins. UK/USA/Switzerland. 1963. Rel: 31 July 1963. Reissued: 12 July 2013. Cert. PG.

Closed Circuit ★★★½

The explosion of a terrorist bomb in London starts off this thriller which sadly sidesteps the opportunity to comment tellingly on such issues as cover-ups achieved by using state security as a pretext to keep evidence out of court. Instead *Closed Circuit* is simply akin to unexceptional Rank releases of the 1950s which found an audience because cinema-going was close to its peak. As such it passes the time and is not boring – and you do get Rebecca Hall and some nice shots of London. MS

▶ Eric Bana, Rebecca Hall, Ciarán Hinds, Riz Ahmed, Anne-Marie Duff, Kenneth Cranham, Julia Stiles, Jim Broadbent, Denis Moschitto.
▶ *Dir* John Crowley, *Pro* Tim Bevan, Eric Fellner and Chris Clark, *Screenplay* Steve Knight, *Ph* Adriano Goldman, *Pro Des* Jim Clay, *Ed* Lucia Zucchetti, *M* Joby Talbot, *Cos* Natalie Ward.

Focus Features/ a Working Title production-Universal. 96 mins. USA/UK. 2013. Rel: 25 Oct 2013. Cert. 15.

Cloud Atlas ★★★★

This take on David Mitchell's epic novel by Tom Tykwer and the Wachowskis ranges across six time zones from 1849 to the 23rd century,

with the likes of Tom Hanks, Halle Berry, Jim Broadbent, Hugo Weaving, Hugh Grant, Ben Whishaw and Susan Sarandon playing multiple parts as the six stories cover 19th century slavery, a 1930s gay composer, a nuclear reactor in the 1970s, a murderous 21st century novelist, the year 2144 in which slaves are exploited as a source of food, and a final apocalyptic vision where most of humanity are tribesmen. Brilliantly filmed without meaningful explanations, *Cloud Atlas*, like its inspiration, *2001: A Space Odyssey*, takes you on a journey to you know not where. A fascinating epic of movie-making. MHD

▷ Tom Hanks, Halle Berry, Jim Broadbent, Hugo Weaver, Jim Sturgess, Susan Sarandon, Hugh Grant, Robert Fyfe, Doona Bae, Ben Whishaw, Sylvestra Le Touzel.
▷ *Dir* and *Screenplay* Tom Tykwer, Andy Wachowski and Lana Wachowski, based on David Mitchell's novel, *Pro* Tykwer, the Wachowskis, Stefan Arndt, Alex Boden, Grant Hill, *Ph* Frank Griebe and John Toll, *Pro Des* Hugh Bateup and Uli Hanisch, *Ed* Alexander Berner and Claus Wehlisch, *M* Tykwer, Johnny Klimek and Reinhold Hell, *Cos* Kym Barrett and Pierre-Yves Gayraud.

Cloud Atlas Productions/Anarchos Pictures/X-Films Creative Pool/Ascension Pictures/Dreams of Dragon Picture/Five Drops/Media Asia Group etc-Warner Bros. 172 mins. USA/Germany/Hong Kong/Singapore. 2012. Rel: 22 Feb 2013. Cert. 15.

Cloudy with a Chance of Meatballs 2 ★★★

This sees the return of well-intentioned inventor Flint, his romantic interest and nerdy weather girl Sam and other ensemble characters on their island home besieged by food. This sequel follows the food-as-weather subject matter of the original with a 'food as living creatures' conceit (eg, one species is made of cheese burgers, another of tacos). A sometimes nonsensical riot of movement and colour, it moves along at a breathless pace and is very much its own film. One of this year's better new CG animated children's offerings; quite possibly its most oddball one. JC

▷ Voices of Bill Hader, Anna Faris, James Caan, Will Forte, Andy Samberg, Benjamin Bratt, Neil Patrick Harris.
▷ *Dir* Cody Cameron and Kris Pearn, *Pro* Kirk Bodyfelt and Pam Marsden, *Screenplay* Jonathan Goldstein, John Francis Daley and Erica Rivinoja, from a story by Rivinoja, Christopher Miller and Phil Lord, based on characters created by Judi and Ron Barrett, *Pro Des* Justin Thompson, *Ed* Robert Fisher Jr and Stan Webb, *M* Mark Mothersbaugh.

Columbia Pictures/Sony Pictures Animation/Sony Pictures Imageworks-Columbia Pictures. 95 mins. USA. 2013. Rel: 25 Oct 2013. Cert. U.

Oxbridge son: Ben Whishaw in Lana Wachowski, Tom Tykwer and Andy Wachowski's *Cloud Atlas.*

Cold Comes the Night ★★★

Alice Eve and Bryan Cranston play deadly cat and mouse as a struggling motel owner and near-blind crook who forces her to help him retrieve his stash of cash from a bent cop. There are edge-of-seat thrills aplenty in this good, strong, solid noir-ish thriller, decently written and tensely directed by Tze Chun. It motors on the excellent star turns by the feisty Eve as the young mother in peril and a very tough, compelling Cranston as the Russian villain on the run who makes the mistake of staying at her motel. Chun co-wrote the script with Anthony Perkins' son Osgood and Nick Simon. DW

‣ Alice Eve, Logan Marshall-Green, Bryan Cranston, Leo Fitzpatrick, Erin Cummings, Ursula Parker.
‣ *Dir* Tze Chun, *Pro* Mynette Louis and Trevor Sagan, *Screenplay* Chun, Osgood Perkins and Nick Simon, *Ph* Noah Rosenthal, *Pro Des* Laurie Hicks, *Ed* Paul Frank, *M* Jeff Grace, *Cos* Anney Perrine.

Sasquatch Films/Whitewater Films/Venture Forth/ Syncopated Films/Three Point Capital-Sony Pictures Releasing.
90 mins. USA. 2013. Rel: 20 Sep 2013. Cert. 15.

Come As You Are ★★★

Three young Belgians journey to Spain planning to lose their virginity in a brothel. There is humour here and the film is adept when it comes to sending up the trio over their initial hostility to the unglamorous nurse with whom they travel (the splendid Isabelle De Hertogh). Yet the piece is essentially serious since the trio are victims (hence the nurse): one is blind, another quadriplegic and the third in a wheelchair. Unfortunately this leads to material that is ultimately both romanticised and sentimentalised: starting out warm-hearted, the film ends up manipulative. (Original title: *Hasta la vista*) MS

‣ Robrecht Vanden Thoren, Gilles De Schryver, Tom Audenaert, Isabelle De Hertogh.
‣ *Dir* Geoffrey Enthoven, *Pro* Mariano Vanhoof, *Screenplay* Pierre de Clercq, from a story by Vanhoof based on the experiences of Asta Philpot and friends, *Ph* Gerd Schelfhout, *Art Dir* Kurt Rigolle, *Ed* Philippe Ravoet, *M* Meuris Papermouth, *Cos* Joëlle Meerbergen.

Fobic Films/a Mariano Vanhoof production etc.-Eureka Entertainment Ltd.
114 mins. Belgium/The Netherlands. 2011. Rel: 7 June 2013. Cert. 15.

The Comedian ★★

Edward Hogg is a talented actor waiting for a great part but the eponymous figure here, a 32-year-old gay man seeking work in stand-up comedy and sharing London rooms with a French singer (female), is not it. Unwisely encouraging improvisation, writer-director Tom Shkolnik aimed for everyday realism and the first edit came in at four hours! Cut down to 79 minutes it's atmospheric but fatally undramatic and inept at exploring in detail the issues around sexuality that it raises. MS

‣ Edward Hogg, Elisa Lasowski, Nathan Stewart-Jarrett, Steven Robertson.
‣ *Dir* and *Screenplay* Tom Shkolnik, *Pro* Bertrand Faivre and Dan McCulloch, *Ph* Benjamin Kracun, *Pro Des* Marie Lanna, *Ed* Pierre Haberer.

BFI/a The Bureau production/Celluloid Dreams etc.-Trinity Filmed Entertainment.
79 mins. UK/France/Russia. 2012. Rel: 31 May 2013. Cert. 15.

Blind date: Bryan Cranston and Alice Eve in Tze Chun's *Cold Comes the Night.*

Come Out and Play ★★

This Mexican horror concerns a young couple's visit to the island of Punta Hueca, where it gradually dawns on them that all the adults have been slaughtered by the children. Horror connoisseurs will identify it at once as a remake of the 1976 Spanish classic *Would You Kill a Child?* Among the tiny handful of credits given on screen, great emphasis is reserved for the author of the source novel, yet the original's writer-director, Narciso Ibáñez Serrador, goes unmentioned. This is disingenuous in the extreme, since this new version, concocted by jack-of-all-trades Makinov, is a carbon copy almost as 'shot for shot' slavish as Gus Van Sant's *Psycho*. There are extra body parts but not a trace of the original's sun-drenched eeriness. At least it's shorter. JR

❧ Vinessa Shaw, Ebon Moss-Bachrach, Daniel Giménez Cacho, Gerardo Taracena, Alejandro Alvarez.
❧ *Dir, Pro, Pho, Ed* and *Screenplay* Makinov, based on Juan José Plans' novel *El juego de los niños*.
Canana in association with Videocine S.A. de C.V.-Metrodome Distribution.
105 mins. Mexico. 2013. Rel: 3 May 2013. Cert. 18.

Compliance ★★★½

The excellent Ann Dowd steps into the lead role here for a drama derived from real-life incidents including one in Kentucky in 2004. She plays the manager of a fast food joint deceived by a telephone call from a bogus policeman accusing a waitress of theft. The disturbing issue that arises is just how far the manager and others will go in humiliating the suspect when requested to do so by someone who claims to have authority. What would we do in this situation? It's an intriguing question, but it loses its force in the film's second half when plot developments prove less persuasive. MS

❧ Ann Dowd, Dreama Walker, Pat Healy, Bill Camp, Philip Ettinger.
❧ *Dir* and *Screenplay* Craig Zobel, *Pro* Sophia Lin, Lisa Muskat, Zobel and others, *Ph* Adam Stone, *Pro Des* Matthew Munn, *Ed* Jane Rizzo, *M* Heather McIntosh, *Cos* Karen Malecki.
Dogfish Pictures/Muskat Filmed Properties/a Bad Cop/ Bad Cop production etc.-Soda Pictures.
90 mins. USA. 2012. Rel: 22 Mar 2013. Cert. 15.

Computer Chess ★★½

There should be various names for spoof documentaries: mockumentary for send-ups (*Best in Show*); rockumentary, if music is involved (*This is Spinal Tap*); shlocku-mentary for anything nasty or salacious (*Jackass*); perhaps faux-mentary for a mixture of truth and fiction (*The Imposter*); ficto-mentary for films masquerading as

Her master's voice: Dreama Walker in Craig Zobel's *Compliance*.

documentary (*The Blair Witch Project*), to which category can now be added *Computer Chess*, although it ought to be labelled crockumentary or something similar. Andrew Bujalski sets his imaginary docu-comedy in a 1980s convention where real people play chess with computers, perhaps because nobody else will. This black-and-white recreation of a bygone era is faithful enough but having actors play computer-chess nerds doesn't make them interesting, just irritating. MHD

❧ Kriss Schludermann, Wiley Wiggins, Tom Fletcher, Patrick Riester, Kevin Brewersdorf, Gene Williams.
❧ *Dir, Ed* and *Screenplay* Andrew Bujalski, *Pro* Houston King and Alex Lipschultz, *Ph* Matthias Grunsky, *Pro Des* Michael Bricker, *Cos* Colin Wilkes.
Computer Chess-Eureka Entertainment.
92 mins. USA. 2013. Rel: 22 Nov 2013. Cert. 15.

Confine ★★½

British fashion model Daisy Lowe enjoys her first star role as the troubled former model Pippa who, because of psychological trauma, hasn't dared leave her London apartment for the past four years. The well-cast Lowe proves a capable performer in writer-director Tobias Tobbell's tense, tautly handled psychological thriller. Eliza Bennett co-stars as an armed thief who breaks in and takes Pippa hostage, while Alfie Allen (Theon Greyjoy in TV's *Game of Thrones*) plays Bennett's troubled partner-in-crime. The story stretches credibility and ends limply but the actors make it work, and the director takes it at a good, gripping pace, delivering some powerful moments in a short running time. DW

❧ Daisy Lowe, Eliza Bennett, Alfie Allen, Richard Wellings-Thomas, Adam Leese, Emily Corcoran.
❧ *Dir and Screenplay* Tobias Tobbell, *Pro* Emily Corcoran, *Ph* Eben Bolter, *Pro Des* Luke Hull,

Sheets happen:
Vera Farmiga
and spooky
co-star in James
Wan's fearsome
The Conjuring.

Ed Simon J Brooks, *M* Paul Lawler, *Cos* Lisa Mitton.

Two Bells Productions/Cork Films-Koch Media.
81 mins. UK. 2013. Rel: 1 July 2013. Cert. 15.

The Conjuring ★★★★

A chilling haunted-houser with a fiendish
sensibility, focused on creeping you out and
making you jump out of your seat and out of
your skin over and over again, *The Conjuring*
is a masterpiece of audience manipulation.
Deliciously dark and consistently fearsome with
a game trio of stars (Vera Farmiga, Patrick Wilson
and Lili Taylor), it's first-rate movie magic from
Master of the Spooky Arts James Wan. MJ

▶ Patrick Wilson, Vera Farmiga, Ron Livingstone,
Lili Taylor, Shanley Caswell.
▶ *Dir* James Wan, *Pro* Peter Safran, Tony DeRosa-Grund
and Rob Cowan, *Screenplay* Chad Hayes and Carey
W Hayes, *Ph* John R Leonetti, *Pro Des* Julie Berghoff,
Ed Kirk Morri, *M* Joseph Bishara, *Cos* Kristin M. Burke.

New Line Cinema/The Safran Company/Evergreen
Media Group-Warner Bros.
112 mins. USA. 2013. Rel: 2 Aug 2013. Cert. 15.

The Counsellor ★★

Veteran director Ridley Scott is working here with
an all-star cast and the production values are fine
but the result is so dull that the film is dead in
the water. A tale of drug-dealing, sex and revenge
is bogged down by dialogue – by novelist Cormac
McCarthy, no less – which veers between the

banal and the pretentious while the characters are
either unappealing or unconvincing. Avoid. MS

▶ Michael Fassbender, Penélope Cruz, Cameron
Diaz, Javier Bardem, Brad Pitt, Bruno Ganz.
▶ *Dir* Ridley Scott, *Pro* Scott, Nick Wechsler, Steve
Schwartz and Paula Mae Schwartz, *Screenplay* Cormac
McCarthy, *Ph* Dariusz Wolski, *Pro Des* Arthur Max,
Ed Pietro Scalia, *M* Daniel Pemberton *Cos* Janty Yates.

Fox 2000 Pictures/a Scott Free/Nick Wechsler/
Chockstone Pictures production etc.-20th Century Fox.
117 mins. USA/UK. 2013. Rel: 15 Nov 2013. Cert. 18.

The Crash Reel ★★★★

That established documentarian Lucy Walker here
gives us a long but absorbing film. It may be centred
on a professional snowboarder, Kevin Pearce, who
sustained a serious injury in 2010 at Salt Lake City
(a fact that leads to footage commenting on the
risks in the sport), but it has wider interest too. That
stems from its telling investigation of family ties
and the balance between self-fulfilment regardless
of danger and duties to those close to you. MS

▶ With Kevin Pearce, Shaun White, Jack Mitrani,
Luke Mitrani.
▶ *Dir* Lucy Walker, *Pro* Julian Cautherley and Walker,
Written by Pedro Kos and Walker, *Ph* Nick Higgins,
Ed Kos.

HBO Documentary Films/Impact Partners/a Tree Tree
Tree film etc.-Soda Pictures.
108 mins. USA/UK/Denmark/The Netherlands. 2013.
Rel: 4 Oct 2013. Cert. 12A.

Crawl ★★

Directed in 2011 by debutant Englishman Paul China, this stylish Australian thriller has a severe case of Coen brothers-itis; indeed, enumerating the 'echoes' would take too long. Viewed on its own terms, *Crawl* suffers from a dawdling concept of suspense (though it never quite slows to a – ahem – crawl) and a pervading sense of blood-spattered purposelessness. There's also a bafflingly gratuitous spanking interlude. Even so, the story, involving a Croatian hit-man terrorising a plucky waitress for no very discernible reason, is redeemed by some diverting performances, particularly George Shevtsov's camel-faced killer, Georgina Haig's beleaguered heroine, and a Robert Newton-style turn from sleazy backwoods 'entrepinour' Paul Holmes. JR

❥ George Shevtsov, Georgina Haig, Paul Holmes, Lauren Dillon, Catherine Miller, Andy Barclay, Bob Newman, Lynda Stoner.
❥ *Dir* and *Screenplay* Paul China, *Pro* Benjamin China and Brian J Breheny, *Ph* Breheny, *Pro Des* John Anderson, *Ed* Bin Li and John Scott, *M* Christopher Gordon, *Cos* Maria Tsoukas.

Crawl Productions-Arrow Film Distributors.
80 mins. Australia. 2011. Rel: 22 Feb 2013. Cert. 15.

The Croods ★★★

Animation has been drawn to prehistoric times since the very first cartoon, *Gertie the Dinosaur* (1914), through to *The Flintstones* and up to the *Ice Age* films. *The Croods* – in which a family of cave dwellers, the Croods, survive on an appetite of terror – steps somewhere in between. As Alpha Male Grug (Nicolas Cage) tells his brood, "Fear keeps us alive." It's an agreeable yarn with loads of good ideas along the way – terrestrial whales, flying piranha – and visually it's top-range. It's just a shame that the heroine, Eep (ably voiced by Emma Stone), is rather hard on the eyes. JC-W

❥ Voices of Nicolas Cage, Emma Stone, Ryan Reynolds, Catherine Keener, Cloris Leachman.
❥ *Dir* and *Screenplay* Kirk DeMicco and Chris Sanders, based on an idea by John Cleese, *Pro* Kristine Benson and Jane Hartwell, *Ph* Yong Duk Jhun, *Pro Des* Christophe Lautrette, *Ed* Eric Dapkewicz and Darren T Holmes, *M* Alan Silvestri.

DreamWorks Animation-20th Century Fox.
98 mins. USA. 2013. Rel: 22 Mar 2013. Cert. U.

Cutie and the Boxer ★★★★

This engaging documentary is a portrait of a most unlikely couple. The man is 80-year-old action painter and sculptor Ushio Shinohara and the woman, an artist in her own right, is his wife Noriko, who is over 20 years his junior. Ushio's sense of superiority may seem insufferable, but this persuasive view of two Japanese expatriates making their own lives in New York's artistic circles convinces us that they belong together. MS

❥ With Shinohara Ushio, Shinohara Noriko.
❥ *Dir* and *Ph* Zachary Heinzerling, *Pro* Patrick Burns, Sierra Pettengill and Heinzerling, *Ed* David Teague, *M* Yasuaki Shimizu.

ExLion Tamer/a Cine Mosaic production/Little Magic Films, Inc. etc.-Dogwoof.
82 mins. USA. 2013. Rel: 1 Nov 2013. Cert. 12A.

Dark Skies ★★★

An eerie little chiller with a fair few scares and a dash of sci-fi freakiness, *Dark Skies* follows the fate of a regular suburban family plagued by visits of a malicious nature. Although it plays like a supernatural tale, the menace at the heart of this mysterious, mid-budget effort is actually of extraterrestrial origin. Considering it comes from writer-director Scott Stewart, of *Priest* and *Legion* infamy, *Dark Skies* is surprisingly tense and involving, with plenty of atmosphere. MJ

❥ Keri Russell, Josh Hamilton, Dakota Goyo, Kadan Rockett, J.K. Simmons, LJ Benet, Rich Hutchman, Myndy Crist.
❥ *Dir* and *Screenplay* Scott Stewart, *Pro* Jason Blum, *Ph* David Boyd, *Pro Des* Jeff Higinbotham, *Ed* Peter Gvozdas, *M* Joseph Bishara, *Cos* Kelle Kutsugeras.

Blumhouse Productions/Alliance Films/Automatic Entertainment/Cinema Vehicle Services-Momentum Pictures.
97 mins. USA. 2013. Rel: 3 Apr 2013. Cert. 15.

Day of the Flowers ★★½

Not without echoes of *Carla's Song* (1996), this tale of two sisters leaving Glasgow for Cuba to learn

Bodywork: Ushio Shinohara and Noriko Shinohara in Zachary Heinzerling's *Cutie and the Boxer*.

Vengeance is theirs: Colin Farrell and Noomi Rapace in Niels Arden Oplev's *Dead Man Down*.

more about secrets buried there relating to their late parents has potential. Sadly, Eirene Houston's screenplay lets down the cast headed by the able Eva Birthistle. Comic touches undercut any reality while the drama that develops relies on narrative contrivances. Dancer Carlos Acosta may appear but his feet never break into dance. MS

❥ Eva Birthistle, Charity Wakefield, Carlos Acosta, Chris Simpson, Bryan Dick.
❥ *Dir* John Roberts, *Pro* Jonathan Rae, *Screenplay* Eirene Houston, *Ph* Vernon Layton, *Pro Des* Andrew Sanders, *Ed* David Freeman and John Wilson, *M* Stephen Warbeck, *Cos* Leonie Hartard.

A Roberts-Rae production/a Rogue Elephant Pictures production-Metrodome Distribution Ltd.
99 mins. UK. 2013. Rel: 29 Nov 2013. Cert. 15.

Days of Grace ★★★½

A feature from Mexico, this long film is an ambitious piece intertwining three stories set in 2002, 2006 and 2010 respectively, each one playing out against the setting of the FIFA World Cup. Differing screen sizes are used for each of these years, the sport remains in the background and the tales, each connected with a kidnapping, could be seen as an indictment of life in Mexico City. The film has energy but sometimes seems too complex and too indulgent in its own cleverness to satisfy. (Original title: *Días de gracia*) MS

❥ Tenoch Huerta, Dolores Heredia, Carlos Bardem, Kristyan Ferrer, Eileen Yañez.
❥ *Dir* and *Screenplay* Everardo Gout, *Pro* Leopoldo Gout, Everardo Gout, Luis Sansans and Ozcar Ramirez Gonzalez, *Ph* Sansans, *Pro Des* Bernardo Trujillo, *Ed* Herve Schneid, Jose Salcedo and Valerio Grautoff, *M* Nick Cave, Atticus Ross, Shigeru Umebayashi and others, *Cos* Bertha Romero.

Días de Gracia Producciones Fondo de Inversión y Estimulos al Cine (Fidecine) etc.-Artificial Eye.
132 mins. Mexico/USA/France. 2011. Rel: 26 July 2013. Cert. 15.

Deadfall ★★

Beginning with a truly spectacular car crash from which the two leading characters emerge with scarcely a scratch, this film maintains that degree of implausibility throughout. It's a thriller set in Michigan about a ruthless killer and the sister whose loyalty to him is eventually challenged. But the plotting is so contrived that it becomes ever more preposterous and not even sympathetic players like Sissy Spacek, Kris Kristofferson and young Charlie Hunnam can save it. MS

❥ Eric Bana, Olivia Wilde, Charlie Hunnam, Kate Mara, Treat Williams, Kris Kristofferson, Sissy Spacek.
❥ *Dir* Stefan Ruzowitzky, *Pro* Gary Levinsohn, Shelly Clippard, Ben Cosgrove and Todd Wagner, *Screenplay* Zach Dean, *Ph* Shane Hurlbut, *Pro Des*

Paul Denham Austerberry, *Ed* Arthur Tarnowski and Dan Zimmerman, *M* Marco Beltrami and Buck Sanders, *Cos* Odette Gadoury.

StudioCanal/2929 Productions/a Mutual Film Company production-Warner Bros.
95 mins. USA/France. 2011. Rel: 10 May 2013. Cert. 15.

Dead Man Down ★★★

Given that it marks the US debut of Niels Arden Oplev (the Danish director who, with star Noomi Rapace, created the extraordinary original version of *The Girl with the Dragon Tattoo)*, *Dead Man Down* must rank as an indifferently scripted disappointment. Preconceptions aside, it scores as a sleekly efficient revenge thriller, with Rapace out to avenge herself on the drunk driver who disfigured her while Colin Farrell seeks out the gangsters responsible for killing his wife and child. The power-cut chic of Paul Cameron's lighting gets old very quickly, and unfortunately the plot tends to be just as murky. But there are some pulverising set-pieces and a compellingly weird chemistry between Farrell and the typically excellent Rapace. JR

➤ Colin Farrell, Noomi Rapace, Terrence Howard, Dominic Cooper, Isabelle Huppert, Luis Da Silva Jr, F. Murray Abraham.
➤ *Dir* Niels Arden Oplev, *Pro* Neal H Moritz and JH Wyman, *Screenplay* Wyman, *Ph* Paul Cameron, *Pro Des* Niels Sejer, *Ed* Timothy A Good and Frédéric Thoraval, *M* Jacob Groth, *Cos* Renee Ehrlich Kalfus.

Film District/IM Global/WWE Studios/Automatik/ Original Film/Frequency Films-Entertainment One.
118 mins. USA. 2013. Rel: 3 May 2013. Cert. 15.

The Deep ★★★★★

In contrast to *2 Guns* [qv] this finds Baltasar Kormákur on home ground paying tribute to the fishermen of Iceland by recreating an incident that occurred in 1984. In that year a fishing vessel sank and only one man survived after an almost unbearable ordeal in the water lasting hours. Shot with absolute conviction in an almost documentary style, it finds Ólafur Darri Ólafsson performing this key role compellingly. This is a truly nationalistic film in the very best sense of that term. (Original title: *Djúpid*) MS

➤ Ólafur Darri Ólafsson, Jóhann G. Jóhansson, Stefán Hallur Stefánsson, Björn Thors.
➤ *Dir* Baltasar Kormákur, *Pro* Agnes Johansen and Kormákur, *Screenplay* Jón Atli Jónasson and Kormákur, *Ph* Bergsteinn Björgúlfsson, *Pro Des* Atli Geir Grétarsson, *Ed* Sverrir Kristjánsson and Elisabet Ronaldsdóttir, *M* Ben Frost and Daniel Bjarnason, *Cos* Helga I. Stefánsdóttir.

Blueeyes Productions/Filmhuset Produksjoner-Metrodome Distribution Ltd.
93 mins. Iceland/Norway. 2012. Rel: 12 July 2013. Cert. 12A.

Def Leppard: Viva! Hysteria – Live at the Joint ★★

This concert was filmed live over two nights in March 2013 at the Hard Rock Hotel and offers fans a chance to watch Def Leppard from the front seats. The rock band sing all the songs from the *Hysteria* album as well as hits from *Rock of Ages* and *Photograph*. Unlike most other music documentaries, here it's just the concert with no backstage stuff. Strictly for the fans. GS

➤ With Rick Allen, Phil Collen, Vivian Campbell, Rick Savage, Joe Elliott.
➤ *Technical Dir* Michael Minkoff, *Pro, Dir* and *M* Def Leppard.

Mercury Records-More2Screen.
87 mins. USA. 2013. Rel: 19 Sep 2013. Cert. PG.

Despicable Me 2 ★

Having failed to become the world's Greatest Villain of All Time, Gru (voiced by Steve Carell) now puts his grotesquely cute orphaned daughters first and is running a jam and jelly business. Then the Anti-Villain League calls on him to help out when someone – or something – starts turning soft, cuddly things into horrible little monsters courtesy of a stolen mutagen. Of course, Gru has a lot of soft, cuddly things at his beck and call, although more cynical viewers might find his yellow, pill-shaped 'Minions' the world's most exasperating creations. Either way, this lame follow-up is desperately wanting for wit and is a brash, ugly and cacophonous affair. JC-W

➤ Voices of Steve Carell, Kristen Wiig, Benjamin Bratt, Miranda Cosgrove, Russell Brand, Steve Coogan, Ken Jeong.
➤ *Dir* Pierre Coffin and Chris Renaud, *Pro* Chris

Waterlogged: Ólafur Darri Ólafsson in Baltasar Kormákur's *The Deep.*

Melandandri and Janet Healy, *Screenplay* Cinco Paul and Ken Daurio, *Pro Des* Yarrow Cheney and Eric Guillon, *Ed* Gregory Perier, *M* Heitor Pereira.

Universal Pictures/Illumination Entertainment-Universal Pictures International.
98 mins. USA. 2013. Rel: 28 June 2013. Cert. U.

Diana ★★★

Widely reviled yet highly competent technically, this film certainly reduces the love of Princess Diana for the surgeon Hasnat Khan to the level of Mills & Boon. But if accepted as just that, the film is serviceable and the leading players do not disgrace themselves. It could be considered somewhat tasteless to tell the story in this style but it takes a sympathetic view of Diana herself. The work of editor Hans Funck is admirable. MS

❧ Naomi Watts, Naveen Andrews, Douglas Hodge, Geraldine James, Juliet Stevenson.
❧ *Dir* Oliver Hirschbiegel, *Pro* Robert Bernstein and Douglas Rae, *Screenplay* Stephen Jeffreys from the book *Diana: Her Last Love* by Kate Snell, *Ph* Rainer Klausmann, *Pro Des* Kave Quinn, *Ed* Hans Funck, *M* David Holmes and Keefus Ciancia, *Cos* Julian Day.

An Ecosse Films production/SCOPE Pictures/Le Pacte/ Film i Väst/Filmgate Films etc.-E1 Films.
113 mins. UK/Belgium/France/Sweden. 2013. Rel: 20 Sep 2013. Cert. 12A.

Dirty Wars ★★★★½

This is a fine example of investigative journalism on film. The case made by Jeremy Scahill is complex but presented with absolute clarity as he uncovers American actions in Afghanistan, Yemen and Somalia between 2009 and 2012. The atrocities revealed make for a deeply disturbing look at a country which likes to be thought of as a bastion of freedom. John Le Carré has rightly described the film as "gripping, compelling and totally convincing". MS

❧ With Jeremy Scahill.
❧ *Dir* and *Ph* Richard Rowley, *Pro* Anthony Arnove, Brenda Coughlin and Jeremy Scahill, *Written by* Scahill and David Riker, *Ed* Rowley and Riker, *M* David Harrington.

Civic Bakery/a Big Noise film etc.-Brit Doc Films.
86 mins. USA/UK. 2013. Rel: 29 Nov 2013. Cert. 15.

Django Unchained ★★★

This extraordinarily violent Western drama with racial themes built around pre-Civil War slavery epitomises all you need to know about its creator Quentin Tarantino. The film is literate, well acted (except by Tarantino himself) and it shows his absolute mastery as a director. But no less importantly the second half increasingly wallows in its own violence and does so with such enthusiasm that it becomes disgusting. I saw it within days of a school massacre being reported and for me the film represents the sick soul of America. If you disagree with that view, you will want to increase the star rating considerably. MS

❧ Jamie Foxx, Christoph Waltz, Leonardo DiCaprio, Kerry Washington, Samuel L Jackson, Don Johnson, Quentin Tarantino, Bruce Dern, Jonah Hill.
❧ *Dir* and *Screenplay* Quentin Tarantino, *Pro* Stacey Sher, Reginald Hudlin and Pilar Savone, *Ph* Robert Richardson, *Pro Des* J Michael Riva, *Ed* Fred Raskin, *M (Django theme)* Luis Enriquez Bacalov *Cos* Sharen Davis.

The Weinstein Company/Columbia Pictures-Sony Pictures Releasing.
165 mins. USA. 2012. Rel: 18 Jan 2013. Cert. 18.

Do Elephants Pray? ★★½

Advertising man Callum Cutter (Jonnie Hurn) is on the brink of bankruptcy when he meets Malika, a free-spirited French woman (Julie Dray) at a Tai-Chi class. She persuades him to drop everything and run wild in a forest in France, in order to get a fresh view of the world. Leaving his agency staff (John Last and Marc Warren) behind, Callum goes on a spiritual journey in search of the meaning of life which leads him to the Lake of No Return where he and Malika get naked and go skinny dipping. Rarely convincing as either reality or satire, Paul Hills' film ends up as neither, although the leading players do their best to make matters halfway feasible. MHD

❧ Jonnie Hurn, Julie Dray, Marc Warren, Rosie Fellner, Grace Vallorani, John Last, Abi Titmuss.
❧ *Dir* Paul Hills, *Pro* Hills and Hurn, *Screenplay* Jonnie Hurn, *Ph* Roger Bonnici, *Pro Des* Seane Grasso, *Ed*

Slave rave: Jamie Foxx in Quentin Tarantino's Oscar-winning *Django Unchained*.

Caroline Richards, *M* Marcel Barsotti, *Cos* Jade Page.

Amaranth Film Partners/Elephant Features-Bluebell Films.
105 mins. UK. 2010. Rel: 1 Feb 2013. Cert. 15.

Dom Hemingway ★

Occasionally one wonders what possesses serious filmmakers to shoot an awful mess of a film that has no redeeming qualities. Did *Dom Hemingway* really look good on paper? It's doubtful but Richard Shepard went ahead and filmed his own screenplay anyway. A miscast Jude Law plays the title character, an East End thug fresh out of jail after 12 years and on the prowl to collect some big dosh from crime boss Mr Fontaine (Demian Bichir). Law, playing against type, overacts abominably, although Richard E Grant as Dom's sidekick Dickie polishes up his *Withnail* performance again. This one is strictly for true fans of the gangsterati genre. MHD

▶ Jude Law, Richard E Grant, Kerry Condon, Demian Bichir, Larissa Jones.
▶ *Dir* and *Screenplay* Richard Shepard, *Pro* Jeremy Thomas, *Ph* Giles Nutgens, *Pro Des* Laurence Dorman, *Ed* Dana Congdon, *M* Rolfe Kent, *Cos* Julian Day.

Pinewood Studios/Recorded Picture Company/BBC Films/Isle of Man Film-Lionsgate.
93 mins. UK. 2013. Rel: 15 Nov 2013. Cert. 15.

Don Jon ★★★

Here that talented actor Joseph Gordon-Levitt turns both writer and director in addition to taking the leading role. He plays a womaniser whose obsession with internet pornography threatens to dominate his actual relationships even when they start to become serious. It's an ambitious piece moving from comedy to tragedy but still aiming at a happy ending. Too often the result is heavy-handed and I was never convinced that this Don Jon would become serious about a woman 20 years his senior. MS

▶ Joseph Gordon-Levitt, Scarlett Johansson, Julianne Moore, Glenne Headly, Brie Larson.
▶ *Dir* and *Screenplay* Joseph Gordon-Levitt, *Pro* Ram Bergman, *Ph* Thomas Kloss, *Pro Des* Meghan C Rogers, *Ed* Lauren Zuckerman, *M* Nathan Johnson, *Cos* Leah Katznelson.

Voltage Pictures/A HitRecord Films production-Warner Bros.
90 mins. USA. 2013. Rel: 15 Nov 2013. Cert. 18.

Dragon ★★★½

Takeshi Kaneshiro stars as a determined detective sent to investigate after bumbling paper-maker Jin-Xi (Donnie Yen) apparently accidentally kills bandits trying to rob the local store in 1917 China. But the detective believes Jin-Xi is hiding his martial arts skills and suspects him of murder,

Paper tiger: Donnie Yen in Peter Chan's quirky *Dragon*.

though he passes every painful test. Then thugs Kara Hui and Jimmy Wang Yu appear, willing to murder or maim Jin-Xi's loved ones to force him to reveal himself. Director Peter Chan keeps the drama taut and the wire-assisted fight scenes thrilling in this quirky, often brilliant actioner. Yen shows he can combine martial arts skills with subtle acting and Wei Tang impresses as his wife. (Original title: *Wu xia*) DW

▶ Donnie Yen, Takeshi Kaneshiro, Wei Tang, Jimmy Wang Yu, Kara Hui.
▶ *Dir* Peter Chan, *Pro* Jojo Yuet-Chun Hui, *Screenplay* Joyce Chan and Oi Wah Lim, *Ph* Yui-Fai Lai, *Pro Des* Li Sun, *Ed* Derek Hui, *M* Kwong Wing Chan, *Cos* Dora Ng.

Ding Sheng Cultural Industry/JSBC Eudemonia Blue Ocean TV & Movie Group/Yunnan Film Group/We Pictures/Stellar Mega Films-We Distribution.
115 mins. Hong Kong/China. 2011. Rel: 3 May 2013. Cert. 15.

Drinking Buddies ★★★★

That established purveyor of 'mumblecore' pictures, Joe Swanberg, moves on to embrace colour and the wide screen but remains true to himself. *Drinking Buddies* is an intimate comic piece set in Chicago and at its centre are two couples whose world is less stable than they imagine. Eschewing an elaborate plot and with a Rohmer-like emphasis on dialogue (much of it improvised adroitly), *Drinking Buddies* may be small-scale but it provides a persuasive account of modern relationships. MS

▶ Olivia Wilde, Jake Johnson, Anna Kendrick, Ron Livingston, Ti West, Mike Brune.
▶ *Dir*, *Screenplay* and *Ed* Joe Swanberg, *Pro* Andrea Roa, Swanberg, Alicia Van Couvering and others, *Ph* Ben Richardson, *Pro Des* Brandon Tonner-Connolly, *Cos* Amanda Ford.

Burn Later/Rise Entertainment/Dark Arts-Sony Pictures Releasing.
90 mins. USA. 2013. Rel: 1 Nov 2013. Cert. 15.

Spy game: Brit Marling in Zal Batmanglij's *The East.*

corporations. It's tensely and atmospherically directed by Zal Batmanglij and provocatively written by him and Marling. They succeed in making a modern-day social anxiety thriller nearly as good as their 1970s role models, *The Parallax View* and *All the President's Men.* DW

▶ Brit Marling, Alexander Skarsgård, Ellen Page, Toby Kebbell, Shiloh Fernandez, Patricia Clarkson.
▶ *Dir* Zal Batmanglij, *Pro* Marling, Ridley Scott, Jocelyn Hayes-Simpson, Michael Costigan etc, *Screenplay* Batmanglij and Brit Marling, *Ph* Roman Vasyanov, *Pro Des* Alex DiGerlando, *Ed* Bill Pankow and Andrew Weisblum, *M* Halli Cauthery and Harry Gregson-Williams, *Cos* Jenny Gering.

Scott Free Productions-Fox Searchlight Pictures. 116 mins. USA/UK. 2013. Rel: 28 June 2013. Cert. 15.

The Dyatlov Pass Incident ★★★½

Five American college students set off with cameras to investigate what happened to nine skiers who died in a real-life mystery from the Soviet era. Co-directors Holly King (Holly Goss) and Jensen Day (Mat Stokoe), expert climbers JP (Luke Albright) and Andy (Ryan Hawley) and sound engineer Denise (Gemma Atkinson) put themselves in peril retracing the steps of the doomed hikers. This change of pace is a good move for director Renny Harlin, who delivers a gripping and effective horror movie that manages to refresh the stale style of found footage. Basically, he makes it work, telling a good story and filming tensely and spectacularly on frozen northern Russian locations. The little-known actors do a grand, convincing job. The climax may be outlandish but it is novel and satisfying. (US title: *Devil's Pass*) DW

▶ Holly Goss, Matt Stokoe, Ryan Hawley, Luke Albright, Gemma Atkinson.
▶ *Dir* Renny Harlin, *Pro* Harlin, Sergei Bespalov, Kia Jam, Alexander Rodnyanski and Sergey Melkumov, *Screenplay* Vikram Weet, *Ph* Denis Alarkon-Ramires, *Art Dir* Fyodor Savelyev, *Ed* Steven Mirkovich, *M* Yuri Poteyenko, *Cos* Varvara Avdyushko.

Future Films/Midnight Sun Pictures/Non-Stop Productions/K. JAM Media/Aldamisa Entertainment-Anchor Bay Entertainment. 100 mins. USA/UK/Russia. 2013. Rel: 23 Aug 2013. Cert. 15.

The East ★★★★

Rare and unusual, *The East* is a particularly engrossing, suspenseful and intelligent corporate espionage thriller, with Brit Marling an intense star performer and strong acting all round. It's exciting that you never know quite where it's going or how it's going to end. Marling plays Sarah, a morally troubled agent for a private intelligence company that sends her to infiltrate and take down a radical, environmental terrorist collective executing covert attacks on major

Easy Money ★★★

Watchable but unexceptional (a follow-up movie went straight to DVD here), this Swedish-set thriller touches on corruption in high places but centres on a youth taking to crime to fund his ambitions to rise in society. Other underworld characters appear but the attempt to give weight to them is thwarted by indifferent writing, an over-emphatic music score and undistinguished acting, even if lead actor Joel Kinnaman has now found fame in Hollywood. (Original title: *Snabba cash*). MS

▶ Joel Kinnaman, Matias Padin Varela, Dragomir Mrsic, Lisa Henni, Dejan Cukic.
▶ *Dir* Daniél Espinosa, *Pro* Fredrik Wikström, *Screenplay* Maria Karlsson with Espinosa and others, from the novel *Snabba cash* by Jens Lapidus, *Ph* Aril Wretblad, *Pro Des* Roger Rosenberg, *Ed* Theis Schmidt, *M* Jon Ekstrand, *Cos* Denise Östholm.

Tre Vänner/Film i Väst/Nordisk Film/Sveriges Television etc.-Lionsgate UK. 125 mins. Sweden/Denmark/Germany/Norway/France. 2010. Rel: 19 July 2013. Cert. 15.

Eden ★★★

Sex-trafficking is the theme here and the film is based on the kidnapping in Dallas in 1994 of a South Korean girl who was forced into prostitution. Having eventually escaped, this girl, Chong Kim, has become an advocate for human and civil rights. Director Megan Griffiths, anxious to avoid sensationalism and exploitation of the subject, gives us an underpowered first half and then allows the drama to seem fictional. However, Beau Bridges brings his expertise to bear and makes an effective villain. MS

▶ Jamie Chung, Matt O'Leary, Beau Bridges, Jeanine Monterroza, Eddie Martinez.
▶ *Dir* Megan Griffiths, *Pro* Colin Harper Plank and Jacob Mosler, *Screenplay* Richard B Phillips and Griffiths, from a story by Phillips and Chong Kim

based on the latter's real-life story, *Ph* Sean Porter, *Pro Des* Ben Blankenship, *Ed* Eric Frith, *M* Joshua Morrison, Jeramy Koepping and Matthew Emerson Brown, *Cos* Rebecca Luke.

A Centripetal Films production/Washington Filmworks-Clear Vision.
98 mins. USA. 2012. Rel: 19 July 2013. Cert. 15.

Either Way ★★★½

Set in the bleak wilderness of Iceland, Hafsteinn Gunnar Sigurdsson's first film is both a visual and compassionate treat. Set in 1980, it documents the relationship between two labourers tasked to paint lines on a deserted road who could not be more different. However, through the inevitable intimacy forced on them in such remoteness, the men form a friendship that is both beguiling and perfectly credible. Although at times a little slight, the film certainly marks Sigurdsson out as a filmmaker to watch. (Original title: *Á annan veg*) CB

▶ Hilmar Guöjónsson, Sveinn Ólafur Gunnarsson, Þorsteinn Bachmann, Valgeröur Rúnarsdótirr.
▶ *Dir* and *Screenplay* Hafsteinn Gunnar Sigurdsson, from a story by Sigurösson and Sveinn Ólafur Gunnarsson, *Pro* Hreinn Beck, Tobias Munthe, Theo Youngstein etc, *Ph* Árni Filippusson, *Pro Des* Halfdan Pedersen, *Ed* Kristján Loömfjörö, *Cos* Margrét Einarsdóttir.

Mystery Island/Flickbook Films-Vanguard Cinema.
84 mins. Iceland. 2011. Rel: 18 Oct 2013. Cert. 15.

Elysium ★★★★

The second film from Neill Blomkamp, director of the Oscar-nominated *District 9*, *Elysium* is a grimly compelling, ultra-violent tale of a polluted, over-populated world overseen by a humourless robotic police force. But all is not lost, for those with an obscene amount of money can live on Elysium, a space station just 19 minutes from our planet... An authentically realised vision of hell on Earth in 2154, *Elysium* is probably the year's most credible dystopian thriller. Matt Damon fills the screen very well and there's a terrific score and some brilliant sound design. And these things really do matter. JC-W

▶ Matt Damon, Jodie Foster, Sharlto Copley, Alice Braga, Diego Luna, Wagner Moura, William Fichtner.
▶ *Dir* and *Screenplay* Neill Blomkamp, *Pro* Blomkamp, Bill Block and Simon Kinberg, *Ph* Trent Opaloch, *Pro Des* Philip Ivey, *Ed* Julian Clarke and Lee Smith, *M* Ryan Amon, *Cos* April Ferry.

TriStar Pictures/Alphacore/Media Rights Capital/QED International-Sony Pictures Releasing.
109 mins. USA. 2013. Rel: 21 Aug 2013. Cert. 15.

Emperor ★★★★

This film from Peter Webber, he who gave us *Girl with a Pearl Earring* (2003), deals with the situation in Japan at the end of the Second World War when the Americans had to decide whether or not Emperor Hirohito should be brought to trial as a war criminal. Those keen on arthouse cinema already have their version of this material in Sokorov's *The Sun* (2005). However, if one accepts this as mainstream fare, even incorporating an interracial love story, it gives a general audience some insight into the issues and is helped by a strong performance from Tommy Lee Jones as General Douglas MacArthur. MS

Future tense: Matt Damon and Sharlto Copley in Neill Blomkamp's grimly compelling *Elysium*.

After the conscious uncoupling: James Gandolfini and Julia Louis-Dreyfus in Nicole Holofcener's *Enough Said*.

❯ Matthew Fox, Tommy Lee Jones, Eriko Hatsune, Masayoshi Haneda, Colin Moy.
❯ *Dir* Peter Webber, *Pro* Yoko Narahashi, Gary Foster, Russ Krasnoff and Eugene Nomura, *Screenplay* David Klass and Vera Blasi, from the book *His Majesty's Salvation* by Shiro Okamoto, *Ph* Stuart Dryburgh, *Pro Des* Grant Major, *Ed* Chris Plummer, *M* Alex Heffes, *Cos* Ngila Dickson.

Krasnoff/Foster Entertainment/United Performers' Studio etc.-The Works UK Distribution Ltd.
105 mins. USA/Japan. 2012. Rel: 4 Oct 2013. Cert. 12A.

Ender's Game ★★

They've dumbed down and cut down Orson Scott Card's 700-page book, making it fashionably teen-friendly and in the process a bland muddle. The 16-year-old Asa Butterfield lacks star appeal as young Ender Wiggin, recruited to lead the fight against an invading alien race. So Harrison Ford and Ben Kingsley are brought in as Colonel Graff and Mazer Rackham, but neither looks very thrilled to be aboard. The visual effects are the real stars and the quality is very high, luckily so, as there are 950 effects shots. There's plenty of lively action too, but it's all standard, regulation stuff. Gavin Hood's grip on the story-telling is loose. DW

❯ Harrison Ford, Ben Kingsley, Asa Butterfield, Hailee Steinfeld, Abigail Breslin, Viola Davis.
❯ *Dir* and *Screenplay* Gavin Hood, based on the book by Orson Scott Card, *Pro* Card, Robert Cartoff, Alex Kurtzman, Lynn Hendee, Robert Orci etc, *Ph* Donald McAlpine, *Pro Des* Sean Haworth and Ben Procter, *Ed* Lee Smith and Zach Staenberg, *M* Steve Jablonsky, *Cos* Christine Bieselin Clark.

Summit Entertainment/Chartoff Productions/OddLot
Entertainment/ Taleswapper/KO Paper Products/Digital Domain-Momentum Pictures.
114 mins. USA. 2013. Rel: 25 Oct 2013. Cert. 12A.

Enough Said ★★★

Although it's a film acclaimed by some and one which offered a leading role to the late James Gandolfini, I feel that Nicole Holofcener, striking out here for something more mainstream, has created a work that seems to belong to the artificial world of television comedies. On that level this story of two divorced people finding each other until a plot twist seems to undermine their rapport may please. But if you love the depth of Holofcener's *Please Give* (2009) as I do then this is a disappointment. MS

❯ Julia Louis-Dreyfus, James Gandolfini, Catherine Keener, Toni Collette, Ben Falcone.
❯ *Dir* and *Screenplay* Nicole Holofcener, *Pro* Anthony Bregman and Stefanie Azpiazu, *Ph* Xavier Grobet, *Pro Des* Keith Cunningham, *Ed* Robert Frazen, *M* Marcelo Zarvos, *Cos* Leah Katznelson.

Fox Searchlight Pictures/a Likely Story production/ Ingenious Media etc.-20th Century Fox.
93 mins. USA/UK/Australia. 2013. Rel: 18 Oct 2013. Cert. 12A.

Epic ★★★★

In spite of parallels to *The Borrowers* and *FernGully the Last Rainforest*, Blue Sky Studios' *Epic* is a total original. Adapted from the children's book *The Leaf Men and the Brave Good Bugs* by William Joyce, *Epic* is set in another world – at our feet. It is here that the beings of the undergrowth live at a speed and in a dimension beyond our senses, yet flourish nonetheless. The story also moves at an agreeable trot, the sylvan animation is a joy to behold and there's a welcome absence of 'adult' innuendo. You may never look at a forest in the same light again. JC-W

▶ Voices of Colin Farrell, Josh Hutcherson, Amanda Seyfried, Christoph Waltz, Aziz Ansari, Chris O'Dowd, Pitbull, Jason Sudeikis, Steven Tyler, Beyoncé Knowles.
▶ *Dir* Chris Wedge, *Pro* Lori Forte and Jerry Davis, *Screenplay* William Joyce, James V Hart, Daniel Shere, Tom J Astle and Matt Ember, based on Joyce's book *The Leaf Men and the Brave Good Bugs*, *Ph* Renato Falcão, *Pro Des* Joyce and Greg Couch, *Ed* Andy Keir, *M* Danny Elfman.

Blue Sky Studios/20th Century Fox Animation-20th Century Fox.
102 mins. USA. 2013. Rel: 22 May 2013. Cert. U.

The Epic of Everest ★★★

The silent documentary of the 1924 Mallory and Irvine expedition, filmed in largely static shots on location under difficult conditions, conveys something of the majesty and elemental power of the eponymous mountain. Footage of light and shadows crossing the region are breathtaking. Effectively employing colour-tinted black-and-white footage, this restoration benefits further from a specially commissioned and hugely atmospheric score by Simon Fisher Turner. JC

▶ Restored by the British Film Institute's Archive. Supported by the Eric Anker-Petersen Charity.
▶ *Dir, Pro, Pho* and *Ed* Captain John Noel, *M* Simon Fisher Turner.

British Film Institute-BFI Distribution.
87 mins. UK. 1924. Restoration released: 18 Oct 2013. Cert. U.

Ernest & Celestine ★★★½

This sweet and cute Franco-Belgian animated comedy-drama, based on Gabrielle Vincent children's books, tells the story of an unlikely friendship between Ernest the bear (voice of Lambert Wilson) and Celestine the mouse (Pauline Brunner). (Forest Whitaker and Mackenzie Foy take over in the English version.) Simple, cosy and old-fashioned it may be, but it has plenty of heart and warmth in its story of the value of friendship wherever you find it, and charm to spare in its delightful animated images. It was Oscar-nominated for 2014's Best Animated Feature. (Original title: *Ernest et Célestine*) DW

▶ Voices of Forest Whitaker. Mackenzie Foy, Lauren Bacall, Paul Giamatti, William H Macy, Megan Mullally, Nick Offerman, Jeffrey Wright.
▶ *Dir* Stéphane Aubier, Vincent Patar and Benjamin Renner, *Pro* Eric Beckman, David Jesteadt, Michael Sinterniklaas etc, *Screenplay* Daniel Pennac, from the book by Gabrielle Vincent, *Pro Des* Zaza and Zyk, *Animation* Michael Crouzat etc, *M* Vincent Courtois.

La Parti Productions/Les Armateurs/StudioCanal/ Melusine Productions/Maybe Movies-StudioCanal.
80 mins. France/Belgium/Luxembourg. 2012. Rel: 1 May 2013. Cert. U.

Escape Plan ★★

Originally titled *The Tomb*, which makes the movie sound cooler than it actually is, *Escape Plan* is a middling prison caper starring old-school action vets Sly Stallone and Arnie Schwarzenegger. The results are rather less than magical, with little in the way of snappy dialogue, not much action to speak of, ludicrously two-dimensional characters

Celestine and Ernest in the Oscar-nominated cartoon *Ernest & Celestine*.

and let's just say it's no acting masterclass. Neither good, bad, nor good-bad, *Escape Plan* is a staunchly mediocre experience. MJ

▶ Sylvester Stallone, Arnold Schwarzenegger, Jim Caviezel, Faran Tahir, Amy Ryan, Sam Neill, Vincent D'Onofrio, Vinnie Jones, Curtis '50 Cent' Jackson.
▶ *Dir* Mikael Håfstrom, *Pro* Mark Canton, Randall Emmett, Remington Chase and Robbie Brenner, *Screenplay* Miles Chapman and Arnell Jesko, based on a story by Chapman, *Ph* Brendan Galvin, *Pro Des* Barry Chusid, *Ed* Elliot Greenberg, *M* Alex Heffes, *Cos* Lizz Wolf.

Summit Entertainment/Emmett/Furia Films/Mark Canton Productions/Envision Entertainment etc- Entertainment One.
115 mins. USA. 2013. Rel: 18 Oct 2013. Cert. 15.

Everybody Has a Plan ★★½

Viggo Mortensen plays identical twins living in Argentina where the actor himself spent part of his childhood. His desire to act in Spanish may have blinded him to the unfortunate improbabilities that mar this story of a man who overturns his conventional existence to take on the life of his now deceased brother, a criminal. The Tigre delta provides a novel setting and Sofia Gala Castiglione is a promising young actress, but slow pacing and lack of credibility make for a lacklustre piece. (Original title: *Todos tenemos un plan*) MS

▶ Viggo Mortensen, Soledad Vilamil, Daniel Fanego, Sofia Gala Castiglione, Javier Godino.
▶ *Dir* Ana Piterbarg, *Pro* Mariela Besuievsky, Gerardo Herrero, Vanessa Ragone and Viggo Mortensen, *Screenplay* Piterbarg with Ana Cohan, *Ph* Lucio Bonelli, *Pro Des* Mariela Rípodas, *Ed* Irene Blecua and Alejandro Lázaro, *M* Lucio Godoy and Federico Jusid, *Cos* Valentina Bari.

20th Century Fox/Tornasol Films/Haddock films/

Castafiore Films etc.-Metrodome Distribution Ltd.
118 mins. Spain/Argentina/Germany. 2012.
Rel: 31 May 2013. Cert. 15.

Everyday ★★★★½

Michael Winterbottom's film was made over five years so that the players would age authentically with their characters in this study of how a father's prison term affects his wife and their four young children. John Simm and Shirley Henderson play the parents admirably and the fine editing aids the flow of the story. The final scenes following release from jail are less persuasive, but until then this profound portrayal of the everyday details which make up the family's existence has a Bressonian concentration that makes it unforgettable. MS

▶ John Simm, Shirley Henderson, Shaun Kirk, Robert Kirk, Stephanie Kirk, Katrina Kirk.
▶ *Dir* Michael Winterbottom, *Pro* Melissa Parmenter, *Screenplay* Laurence Coriat and Winterbottom, *Ph* James Clarke, Sean Bobbitt, Marcel Zyskind and others, *Ed* Mags Arnold and Paul Monaghan, *M* Michael Nyman.

Revolution Films-Soda Pictures.
90 mins. UK. 2012. Rel: 18 Jan 2013. Cert. 15.

Evil Dead ★½

The American horror film has become like a gruesome virus: a mutation with increasingly disturbing symptoms. Sam Raimi's original *The Evil Dead* (1981), complete with definite article, was a micro-budgeted frightfest with genuine freshness, energy, imagination and, at the time, was genuinely unsettling stuff. Now, following two sequels, comes the $17 million remake which is everything the original wasn't. Dishing out the clichés with a CGI-heavy hand, the film is like a handbook of bad horror tropes, where a textbook score warns of

The mating habit: John Simm and Shirley Henderson in Michael Winterbottom's *Everyday.*

every 'scare' and where every shadow arrives with a bang, much like the ludicrous dialogue. JC-W

▶ Jane Levy, Shiloh Fernandez, Lou Taylor Pucci, Jessica Lucas, Elizabeth Blackmore.
▶ *Dir* Fede Alvarez, *Pro* Bruce Campbell, Robert Tapert and Sam Raimi, *Screenplay* Alvarez and Rodo Sayagues, *Ph* Aaron Morton, *Pro Des* Robert Gillies, *Ed* Bryan Shaw, *M* Roque Baños, *Cos* Sarah Voon.

TriStar Pictures/FilmDistrict/Ghost House Pictures-StudioCanal.
91 mins. USA. 2013. Rel: 18 Apr 2013. Cert. 18.

The Expatriate ★★½

"If you were a company, where would you hide?" asks surly teen Liana Liberato in this overfamiliar conspiracy thriller. Released in the US as *Erased* (a title echoing such extremely similar films as *Taken* and *Stolen*), it benefits from a queasy sequence in which former CIA hitman Aaron Eckhart reports for work in Brussels to find that his job, and even the company, have been mysteriously, yes, erased. His subsequent quest leads from a well-staged battle in an Antwerp hospital to a pleasantly reptilian appearance from Garrick Hagon as the corporate villain behind it all. Director Philipp Stölzl sprinkles discreetly stylish touches over the kind of 'give me back my daughter' action-movie material that has been done to death in recent years. (US title: *Erased*) JR

▶ Aaron Eckhart, Liana Liberato, Olga Kurylenko, Garrick Hagon, Eric Godon.

▶ *Dir* Philipp Stölzl, *Pro* Claude Leger, Karl Richards, Adrian Politowski and Jonathan Vanger, *Screenplay* Arash Amel, *Ph* Kolja Brandt, *Pro Des* Jean-François Campeau, *Ed* Dominique Fortin, *M* Jeff Danna, *Cos* Pascaline Chavanne.

E-Motion/Expatriate Films Inc./Informant Media/Smash Media/Essential Entertainment Media etc-Myriad Pictures.
100 mins. USA/UK/Belgium/Canada. 2012. Rel: 5 Apr 2013. Cert. 15.

The Eye of the Storm ★★★

This Australian adaptation of Patrick White's novel has a veteran director, Fred Schepisi, and a very talented cast. It studies family tensions at a time when a matriarch (Charlotte Rampling) is dying and does so while blending the humorous and the dramatic. Unfortunately not one of the characters is truly sympathetic and dialogue, often taken direct from the novel, has on screen an artificiality that clashes with the naturalistic look of the piece. There are, however, some memorable comic moments. MS

▶ Geoffrey Rush, Charlotte Rampling, Judy Davis, Alexandra Schepisi, Helen Morse.
▶ *Dir* Fred Schepisi, *Pro* Antony Waddington, Gregory Read and Schepisi, *Screenplay* Judy Morris, from the novel by Patrick White, *Ph* Ian Baker, *Pro Des* Melinda Doring, *Ed* Kate Williams, *M* Paul Grabowsky, *Cos* Terry Ryan.

A Paper Bark Films production/an Antony Waddington presentation/RMB Productions etc.-Munro Film Services.
119 mins. Australia/UK. 2011. Rel: 3 May 2013. Cert. 15.

Where there's a will: Charlotte Rampling, Geoffrey Rush and Judy Davis in Fred Schepisi's *The Eye of the Storm*.

The Fall of the Essex Boys ★

Some films are so risibly inept that it's a wonder they get written, read, financed and distributed. This frenzied, profane stab at the prize for Amateur Night Special is the fourth film to recount the events surrounding the homicide of three Essex men in 1995, otherwise known as the Rettendon Triple Murder. According to the production notes, "not since Jack the Ripper has a killer's identity so captivated the nation." Hmmm. Well, the triple killing has certainly gripped the interest of filmmakers. Bizarrely, there's probably room for a fifth feature on the subject – a good one. JC-W

‣ Nick Nevern, Robert Cavanah, Kierston Wareing, Kate Magowan, Peter Barrett, Jay Brown, Ewan Ross, Peter Woodward.
‣ *Dir* Paul Tanter, *Pro* Jonathan Sothcott and Simon Phillips, *Screenplay* Stephen Reynolds, *Ph* Haider Zafar, *Pro Des* Felix Coles, *Ed* Richard Colton, *Cos* Georgina Napier.
Chata Pictures-Metrodome Distribution.
87 mins. UK. 2013. Rel: 8 Feb 2013. Cert. 18.

The Family ★★★★

Fred Blake is an American informant who, with witness protection from the FBI, is living undercover in France. But even here he cannot escape the attentions of a would-be assassin hired to exact revenge for his testimony in court. This is less a comedy-thriller than a comedy that successfully metamorphoses into episodes of suspenseful action. Dismissed by many, Luc Besson's film worked for me and I found it well cast – and that includes Robert De Niro's criticised turn as Fred Blake! MS

‣ Robert De Niro, Michelle Pfeiffer, Tommy Lee Jones, Dianna Agron, John D'Leo.
‣ *Dir* Luc Besson, *Pro* Virginie Besson-Silla and Ryan Kavanaugh, *Screenplay* Besson and Michael Caleo, from the book *Malavita* by Tonino Benacquista,

Marseille magic: Victoire Bélézy and Daniel Auteuil in Auteuil's own Fanny.

Ph Thierry Arbogast, *Pro Des* Hugues Tissandier, *Ed* Julien Rey, *M* Evgueni Galperine and Sacha Galperine, *Cos* Olivier Beriot.
Europacorp/Relativity Media/Tf1 Films Production/Grive Productions etc.-E1 Films.
111 mins. France/USA. 2013. Rel: 22 Nov 2013. Cert. 15.

Fanny ★★★★½

After *The Well-Digger's Daughter*, actor-director Daniel Auteuil has lovingly remade Marcel Pagnol's 1930s trilogy of *Marius*, *Fanny* and *César* in Marseille locations that look ravishing in colour. Marius loves Fanny but the sea calls him away from the shore and he leaves Fanny with a baby due any moment. Fanny has to decide whether to wait for Marius' return, bring up the baby herself, commit suicide or marry old Panisse. It is all charmingly told and Raphaël Personnaz as Marius, Victoire Bélézy as Fanny and particularly Auteuil as César fit their parts admirably. We can now look forward to part three, the story of César himself. MHD

‣ Daniel Auteuil, Victoire Bélézy, Jean-Pierre Darroussin, Raphaël Personnaz, Marie-Anne Chazel, Nicolas Vaude.
‣ *Dir* and *Screenplay* Daniel Auteuil, from the play by Marcel Pagnol, *Pro* Alain Sarde and Jérôme Seydoux, *Ph* Jean-François Robin, *Pro Des* Christian Marti, *Ed* Joëlle Hache, *M* Alexandre Desplat, *Cos* Pierre-Yves Gayraud.
Les Films Alain Sarde/Zack Films/Indéfilms/Cofimage 24/Canal+/Ciné+/Pathé etc-Pathé Film Distribution.
102 mins. France. 2013. Rel: 6 Dec 2013. Cert. PG.

Fast and Furious 6 ★★★½

The crew are back in action for another round of mayhem and destruction. This time Diplomatic Security Service agent Hobbs (Dwayne Johnson) tracks down Dom (Vin Diesel) and his gang of professional criminals. He offers them a pardon if they can stop the activities of former British Special Forces soldier Owen Shaw (Luke Evans), who has destroyed a Russian military convoy and is about to attack a military base. Dom's crew go all out to stop Shaw's mob from escaping by aircraft in a protracted chase in which cars swoop and slide, fly and fall and bite the dust in a spectacularly well-choreographed onslaught. Never mind the plot and the yucky ending, just go for the beautiful ballet of bouncing vehicles. Roll on No 7! (Original title: *Furious 6*) MHD

‣ Vin Diesel, Paul Walker, Dwayne Johnson, Jordana Brewster, Michelle Rodriguez, Tyrese Gibson, Luke Evans, Chris 'Ludacris' Bridges.
‣ *Dir* Justin Lin, *Pro* Diesel, Neal H. Moritz and Clayton Townsend, *Screenplay* Chris Morgan, based on characters created by Gary Scott Thompson, *Ph* Stephen F Windon, *Pro Des* Jan Roelfs, *Ed* Greg

D'Auria, Christian Wagner, Leigh Folsom-Boyd, Dylan Highsmith and Kelly Matsumoto, *M* Lucas Vidal, *Cos* Sanja Milkovic Hays.

Universal Pictures/Relativity Media/Original Film/One Race Films etc.-Universal Pictures International. 130 mins. USA. 2013. Rel: 17 May 2013. Cert. 12A.

A Field in England ★★★★

Writer-director Ben Wheatley had mayhem and marriage in *Down Terrace*, a hit squad in *Kill List*, and random senseless murders in *Sightseers*. Now he comes up with a tale set during the English Civil War in which army deserters and an alchemist's assistant leave the battle to go in search of a pub. They meet an Irishman who claims there's treasure buried in the field. They start digging but in-fighting breaks out, leading to what appears to be a killing. It may sound weird (well, it is) but it has a streak of wonder running through it that makes it easy to succumb to Wheatley's oddly amoral look at life and death. MHD

❧ Julian Barratt, Peter Ferdinando, Richard Glover, Ryan Pope, Reece Shearsmith, Michael Smiley.
❧ *Dir* Ben Wheatley, *Pro* Claire Jones and Andrew Starke, *Screenplay* Amy Jump, *Ph* Laurie Rose, *Pro Des* Andy Kelly, *Ed* Jump and Wheatley, *M* Jim Williams, *Cos* Emma Fryer.

Film 4/Rook Films-Film 4 Productions. 91 mins. UK. 2013. Rel: 5 July 2013. Cert. 15.

The Fifth Estate ★★★½

Unluckily for Benedict Cumberbatch great performances in commercially unsuccessful films rarely (if ever) pick up awards. His Julian Assange in this drama about the founder of WikiLeaks is superbly realised. But with Assange's story still without any resolution, the film can add nothing to Alex Gibney's distinguished documentary *We Steal Secrets: the Story of WikiLeaks* [qv]: that film fatally overshadows this one. MS

❧ Benedict Cumberbatch, Daniel Brühl, Anthony Mackie, David Thewlis, Alicia Vikander, Peter Capaldi, Stanley Tucci, Laura Linney.
❧ *Dir* Bill Condon, *Pro* Steve Golin and Michael Sugar, *Screenplay* Josh Singer, based on the books *Inside Wikileaks* by Daniel Domscheit-Berg and *Wikileaks* by David Leigh and Luke Harding, *Ph* Tobias Schliessler, *Pro Des* Mark Tildesley, *Ed* Virginia Katz, *M* Carter Burwell, *Cos* Shay Cunliffe.

DreamWorks Pictures/Reliance Entertainment/an Anonymous Content production etc.-E1 Films. 128 mins. USA. 2013. Rel: 11 Oct 2013. Cert. 15.

Fill the Void ★★★½

Rama Burshtein, here making her feature debut, is both writer and director and may be too close to her material since at times this atmospheric tale of an Orthodox Hassidic family living in Tel Aviv is confusing in its relationships and storyline. Nevertheless, Hadas Yaron is excellent as a girl under pressure to follow tradition by marrying her former brother-in-law when he becomes a widower. Furthermore, this is a convincing portrayal of a lifestyle rarely seen in films distributed here. (Original title: *Lemale et ha'halal*) MS

❧ Hadas Yaron, Yiftach Klein, Irit Sheleg, Chaim

Having a field day: Reece Shearsmith, Michael Smiley, Richard Glover, Peter Fernandino and Ryan Pope in *A Field in England*.

The grin reaper: Dory and Marlin in Andrew Stanton and Lee Unkrich's timeless *Finding Nemo*.

Sharir, Razia Israely, Hila Feldman.
▶ *Dir* and *Screenplay* Rama Burshtein, *Pro* Assaf Amir, *Ph* Asaf Sudry, *Art Dir* Ori Aminov, *Ed* Sharon Elovic, *M* Yitzhak Azulay, *Cos* Chani Gurewitz.

Norma Productions/Sundance Institute/Israel Film Council etc.-Artificial Eye.
91 mins. Israel/USA. 2012. Rel: 13 Dec 2013. Cert. U.

Filth ★★★★

Detective Sergeant Bruce Robertson is an Edinburgh policeman addicted to drugs, alcohol, sexual abuse and bullying, who likes nothing better than to play 'games' that discredit his colleagues. He longs to be made Detective Inspector but, when investigating the murder of a Japanese student, he begins to hallucinate and gradually verges on madness. When his wife leaves him he begins dressing as a transvestite to keep the memory of her close. James McAvoy is both hilarious and appalling as Bruce, Eddie Marsan as his friend Clifford is his usual sympathetic self and Jamie Bell plays hard man as Bruce's partner in crime. Adapted from Irvine Welsh's novel, the dialogue is fairly choice and uncompromising but, despite its theme, *Filth* is a filthily splendid black comedy. MHD

▶ James McAvoy, Imogen Poots, Jamie Bell, Eddie Marsan, Joanne Froggatt, Shirley Henderson, Jim Broadbent, Martin Compston, Kate Dickie, David Soul.
▶ *Dir* and *Screenplay* Jon S Baird, from the novel by Irvine Welsh, *Pro* Baird, McAvoy, Mark Amin, Trudie Styler, Celine Rattray, Will Clarke etc, *Ph* Matthew Jensen, *Pro Des* Mike Gunn, *Ed* Mark

Eckersley, *M* Clint Mansell, *Cos* Guy Speranza.

Steel Mill Pictures/Film I Väst-Lionsgate.
97 mins. UK. 2013. Rel: 4 Oct 2013. Cert. 18.

Finding Nemo 3D ★★★★

Converted into 3D, Pixar's 2003 ocean outing has dated well; it feels as if it was made this year. The 3D process adds something to the underwater ocean scapes. Dory, the short-term memory-loss character, remains a great bit of scriptwriting. The narrative's quest structure makes it a bit episodic, but all the episodes are strong. Keep watching right to the end of the closing credits for the film's best sight gag. JC

▶ Voices of Albert Brooks, Ellen DeGeneres, Geoffrey Rush, Elizabeth Perkins, Barry Humphries, Eric Bana, Alexander Gould, Willem Dafoe, Brad Garrett, Austin Pendleton.
▶ *Dir* Andrew Stanton and Lee Unkrich, *Pro* Graham Walters, *Screenplay* Stanton, Bob Peterson and David Reynolds, based on an original story by Stanton, *Pho* Sharon Calahan and Jeremy Lasky, *Pro Des* Ralph Eggleston, *Ed* David Ian Salter, *M* Thomas Newman, *Animation Supervisor* Dylan Brown.

Walt Disney Pictures/Pixar Animation Studios/Disney Enterprises-Walt Disney Studios Motion Pictures.
100 mins. USA. 2003. Re-Released in 3D: 29 Mar 2013. Cert. U.

Fire in the Blood ★★★★

Straightforward and responsible, this is a documentary about the failure of pharmaceutical companies to respond adequately to the need for genetic antiviral drugs to combat AIDS. The chequered history is told in chronological order and across several countries. Witnesses include a judge, an economist, Bill Clinton and the remarkable Zackie Achmat, who on principle rejected drugs he could afford until such time as price reductions brought them within reach of the majority. MS

▶ With Peter Mugyenyi, Edwin Cameron, Zackie Achmat, Bill Clinton, Dr Yusuf Hamied.
▶ *Dir*, *Pro*, *Written by* and *Ed* Dylan Mohan Gray, *Ph* Jay J Odedra, *M* Ashutosh Phatak.

Dartmouth Films/Films Transit International/a Sparkwater India production-Dartmouth Films. 87 mins. India/UK/Canada. 2012. Rel: 22 Feb 2013. Cert. PG.

Fire in the Night ★★★½

Made 25 years on, this is a fitting tribute to those caught up in the fire which gutted the Piper Alpha oil rig in the North Sea on 6 July 1988 (167 men died). This worst of all oil disasters is here recalled by survivors and by others and restrained reconstructions blend well with original footage. As a critic I have to say that the film is at times too repetitive and therefore overlong, but this is nevertheless a valuable historical document marked by its humanity. MS

▶ *Dir* and *Pro* Anthony Wonke, *Based on the book by* Stephen McGinty, *Ph* Mike Eley, *Art Dir* Tayyaba Irtizaali, *Ed* Steve Ellis, *M* Andrew Phillips.

STV Productions/Berriff McGinty Films etc.-Soda Pictures. 94 mins. UK. 2013. Rel: 21 June 2013. No Cert.

Fire with Fire ★½

There can be few films on this budget ($20 million) that are quite so moronic. Josh Duhamel plays a fireman in a witness protection program(me) that resembles a sieve. Having witnessed a double murder in a convenience store – and barely escaped with his life at the hands of Vinnie Jones – Duhamel volunteers to testify against the killer David Hagan (Vincent D'Onofrio). Big mistake… Besides its laughable dialogue and preposterous plot, the film is also really, really nasty (in spite of its 15 certificate) and, mysteriously, co-stars Bruce Willis. JC-W

▶ Josh Duhamel, Bruce Willis, Rosario Dawson, Julian McMahon, Quinton 'Rampage' Jackson, Curtis '50 Cent' Jackson, Richard Schiff, Vinnie Jones, Vincent D'Onofrio, Bonnie Somerville, Kevin Dunn.
▶ *Dir* David Barrett, *Pro* Curtis '50 Cent' Jackson, Andrew Deane and Randall Emmett, *Screenplay* Tom O'Connor, *Ph* Christopher Probst, *Pro Des* Nathan Amondson, *Ed* Paul Harb, *M* Trevor Morris, *Cos* Mia Maddox.

Grindstone Entertainment Group/Cheetah Vision/Emmett/Furla Films-Warner Bros. 97 mins. USA. 2012. Rel: 8 Mar 2013. Cert. 15.

First Position ★★★½

Following competitors between the ages of ten and nineteen taking part in an American dance event leading to finals in New York, this is a film about ballet that never takes one by surprise but which in its conventional way will give pleasure to the right audience. A number of young dancers are placed in the spotlight and the film does its job well enough even if it lacks freshness. MS

▶ With Rebecca Houseknecht, Joan Sebastian Zamora, Michaela DePrince, Aran Bell.
▶ *Dir* and *Pro* Bess Kargman, *Ph* Nick Higgins, *Ed* Kate Amend and Kargman, *M* Chris Hajian.

A Bess Kargman production supported by the Manhattan Movement & Arts Center-Artficial Eye. 95 mins. USA. 2011. Rel: 12 Apr 2013. Cert. U.

Flight ★★★

Denzel Washington is impressive here playing a pilot who, despite his addiction to drink and drugs, saves the lives of his passengers when a fault in his aircraft causes it to crash. The aerial scenes at the start are great, but then the film changes tack to become the story of a back-sliding, tiresome alcoholic who eventually finds redemption. The screenplay, superficial and all too ready to embrace sentimentality, fails the material but Melissa Leo, making a late appearance that increases the dramatic temperature, does not. MS

▶ Denzel Washington, Don Cheadle, Kelly Reilly, John Goodman, Bruce Greenwood, Melissa Leo.
▶ *Dir* Robert Zemeckis, *Pro* Walter F Parkes, Laurie MacDonald, Zemeckis and others, *Screenplay* John

Plane drunk: Denzel Washington in his Oscar-nominated role as 'Whip' Whitaker in Robert Zemeckis' *Flight*.

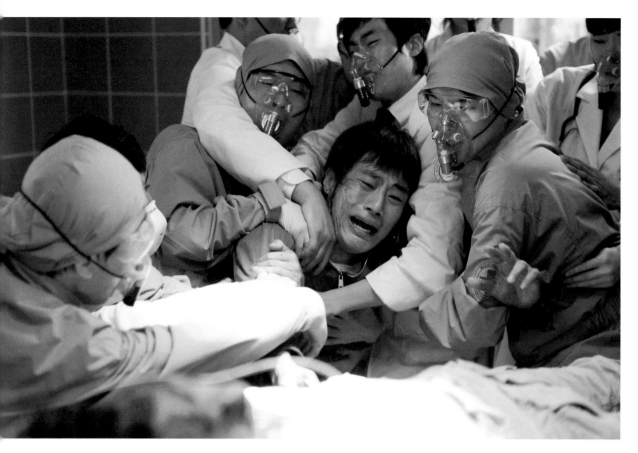

Going viral: a Seoul survivor in Kim Sung-su's thrilling and intelligent *Flu*.

Gatins, *Ph* Don Burgess, *Pro Des* Nelson Coates, *Ed* Jeremiah O'Driscoll, *M* Alan Silvestri, *Cos* Louise Frogley.

Paramount Pictures/an ImageMovers production/a Parkes + MacDonald production etc.-Paramount Pictures UK. 138 mins. USA. 2012. Rel: 1 Feb 2013. Cert. 15.

Floating Skyscrapers ★★½

Given attitudes to homosexuality in Poland, this Polish work about two contrasted youths who meet and fall in love may be a brave piece. However, the style is minimalistic and the ending is bleak while it quite lacks the emotional resonance of the Israeli film *Eyes Wide Open* (2009) which it recalls. Furthermore, as an example of Polish gay cinema Malgoska Szumowska's *In the Name of...* [qv] is decidedly superior – but that is not to deny the sincerity here or the stunningly fine visuals. (Original title: *Plynace wiezowce*) MS

▶ Mateusz Banasiuk, Marta Nieradkiewicz, Bartosz Gelner, Katarzyna Herman, Olga Frycz.
▶ *Dir* and *Screenplay* Tomasz Wasilewski, *Pro* Roman Jarosz and Izabela Igel, *Ph* Kuba Kijowski, *Pro Des* Jacek Czechowski, *Ed* Aleksansra Gowin, *M* Baasch, *Cos* Monika Kaleta.

An Alter Ego, Polski Instytut Sztuki Filmowej production/ Super Krak etc.-Matchbox Films/Verve Pictures. 93 mins. Poland. 2013. Rel: 6 Dec 2013. Cert. 18.

Flower Girl ★★★

Believe it or not, Nigerian cinema ('Nollywood') is the second largest in the world, eclipsing even the output of the United States. So it's nice to be able to sample a specimen, especially something as vibrant, genial and inoffensive as this floral romcom. Kemi (the comely Damilola Adegbite) is a shy florist with marriage on her mind, but unable to get her reluctant boyfriend to commit. Then help comes from the unexpected quarter of Nollywood itself, this when Kemi is hit by a car driven by the movie star Tunde Kulani (Chuks Chukwujekwu). Sweet. CB

▶ Damilola Adegbite, Chris Attoh, Chuks Chukwujekwu, Eku Edewor, Bikiya Graham Douglas, Patrick Doyle.
▶ *Dir* and *Pro* Michelle Bello, *Screenplay* and *Ed* Jigi Bello, *Ph* James M Costello, *Pro Des* Bola Belo, *M* Joe Hogue, *Cos* Bolaji Animashaun.

Blu Star Entertainment-Talking Drum Entertainment. 94 mins. Nigeria. 2013. Rel: 4 Oct 2013. Cert. 12A.

Flu ★★★★

Hyuk Jang and Soo Ae star in writer-director Kim Sung-su's spectacular South Korean epic disaster movie about an outbreak of deadly bird flu that throws Bundang, an affluent suburb of Seoul, into total panic and chaos. The film focuses on three key characters struggling to survive – the

Emergency Response Team worker Kang Ji-koo (Hyuk Jang), immunologist Kim In-hae (Soo Ae) and her precocious young daughter Kim Mi-reu (Min-ah Park). This helps to keep the intimate human factor high and the budget affordable in a film that can also boast thrilling large-scale action sequences. It's intelligently written and commandingly directed, and there's drama, tension, thrills and even a bit of humour throughout. (Original title: *Gamgi*) DW

‣ Hyuk Jang, Soo Ae, Min-ah Park, In-Pyo Cha, Khoi Dao, Yoo Hae-jin, Hee-joon Lee.
‣ *Dir* Kim Sung-su, *Pro* Teddy Jung and Seong-jin Kim, *Screenplay* Kim Sung-su and Lee Yeong-jong, from a story by Jae-ho Jung, *Ph* Lee Mo-gae, *Pro Des* Il-hyun Park, *Ed* Nam Na-young, *M* Kim Tae-seong, *Cos* Kim Kyeong-mi.

iLoveCinema/iFilm Co.-February Films.
122 mins. South Korea. 2013. Rel: 22 Nov 2013. Cert. 15.

Flying Blind ★★

A middle-aged English woman who is an aerospace engineer takes up with a younger man, a French-Algerian student who is an illegal immigrant and who has weapons stashed away in his bathroom. Is he genuinely drawn to her or out to extract information about her work? Security services want to know, but we may not share their interest because the actors are mainly marooned in the middle of the wide screen mouthing dialogue that sounds wholly inauthentic. Good photography though. MS

‣ Helen McCrory, Najib Oudghiri, Kenneth Cranham, Tristan Gemmill.
‣ *Dir* Katarzyna Kimkiewicz, *Pro* Alison Sterling, *Screenplay* Naomi Wallace, Bruce McLeod and Caroline Harrington, *Ph* Andrzej Wojciechowski, *Pro Des* Alison Riva, *Ed* Ewa J Lind, *M* Jon Wygens, *Cos* Saffron Webb.

South West Screen/BBC Films/an Ignition Films/
iFeatures production etc.-Soda Pictures.
93 mins. UK. 2012. Rel: 12 Apr 2013. Cert. 15.

Folie à Deux: Madness Made of Two ★★★

Filmed over five years, Kim Hopkins' *Storyville* documentary is a fascinating emotional rollercoaster and study in obsession and self-destruction, as a rich couple's plans to convert the shabby 72-room historic Gray's Court in the centre of York into a tasteful boutique hotel are scuppered by the 2008 economic crisis. "I set out to make a film about achieving a dream. It then turned into a nightmare," says Hopkins. Helen Heraty proves an incredibly feisty but frustratingly obstinate character who endlessly fights the banks for a loan for spiralling renovation, and her National Trust neighbours over rights to a

shared courtyard. Tears mix with black comedy in an entertaining and finally affecting film. DW

‣ With Helen Heraty.
‣ *Dir* and *Ph* Kim Hopkins, *Pro* and *Ed* Hopkins and Margareta Szabo, *M* Lucy Ward and Barnabás Balázs.

Labor of Love Films-Ballpark Film Distributors.
101 mins. Hungary/UK. 2012. Rel: 4 Oct 2013. Cert. 15.

For Ellen ★★★★½

Korea's So Yong Kim has an American setting for this minimalist drama about the effects of divorce on a father (Paul Dano) and his seven-year-old daughter Ellen (Shaylena Lynn Mandigo). The child actress is no less perfect than Dano and, if some scenes seem stretched out and the ending is questionable, much of the second half is magnificent. The episode in which the father is allowed to spend a couple of hours with his child is one of the most compelling sequences in any film released during the year. MS

‣ Paul Dano, Jon Heder, Jena Malone, Margarita Levieva, Shaylena Lynn Mandigo.
‣ *Dir* and *Screenplay* So Yong Kim, *Pro* Jen Gatien, Bradley Rust Gray and Kim, *Ph* Reed Morano Walker, *Pro Des* Ryan Smith, *Ed* Kim and Gray, *M* Johann Johannsson.

A Deerjen & Soandbrad production etc.-Soda Pictures.
93 mins. USA. 2011. Rel: 15 Feb 2013. Cert. 15.

For Those in Peril ★★½

Paul Wright's film finds him mistaking artiness for art. It's a drama which, despite its Scottish setting, brings to mind *Peter Grimes*. It is concerned with a youth who, having survived a fatal fishing expedition which resulted in the deaths of his brother and others, becomes a scapegoat hounded by the villagers. George MacKay in the central role and Kate Dickie as his mother are fine, but the attempt to integrate a mythical aspect into a psychological study results in a distinctly experimental and distancing work. MS

Father's day: Paul Dano in So Yong Kim's magnificent *For Ellen*.

Truffaut meets Woody Allen: Greta Gerwig as Frances in *Frances Ha*, co-written with her boyfriend Noah Baumbach.

▶ George MacKay, Kate Dickie, Nichola Burley, Michael Smiley.
▶ *Dir* and *Screenplay* Paul Wright, *Pro* Mary Burke and Polly Stokes, *Ph* Benjamin Kracun, *Pro Des* Simon Rogers, *Ed* Michael Aaglund, *M* Erik Enocksson, *Cos* Jo Thompson.

BFI/Film 4/Creative Scotland/Screen Yorkshire/A Warp X production etc.-Soda Pictures.
92 mins. UK/Sweden/Australia. 2013. Rel: 4 Oct 2013. Cert. 18.

Foxfire ★★★★

France's Laurent Cantet moves to America to adapt a novel by Joyce Carol Oates but it misleadingly bears a subtitle, *Confessions of a Girl Gang*, suggestive of a Corman movie. Confidently made albeit overlong at 143 minutes, it's the story of a rebel schoolgirl who in 1955, angry at male attitudes, forms a group with female friends. Under the name 'Foxfire' this group will become notorious. It's an interesting if predictable tale of the rise and fall of 'Foxfire' that gains immensely from a fine performance by its leading actress Raven Adamson. MS

▶ Raven Adamson, Katie Coseni, Madeleine Bisson, Claire Mazerolle, Paige Moyles.
▶ *Dir* Laurent Cantet, *Pro* Carole Scotta, Caroline Benjo, Simon Arnal and others, *Screenplay* Robin Campillo and Cantet, from the novel by Joyce Carol Oates, *Ph* Pierre Milon, *Pro Des* Franckie

Diago, *Ed* Campillo, Stéphanie Léger, Sophie Reine and Clémence Samson, *M* Timber Timbre, *Cos* Gersha Phillips.

Haut et Court/The Film Farm/Memento Films International/France 2 Cinéma etc.-Curzon Film World. 144 mins. France/Canada/Spain/UK/Switzerland. 2011. Rel: 9 Aug 2013. Cert. 15.

Frances Ha ★★★★

This is a New York movie with a voice of its own. It's a perfect fit for indie star Greta Gerwig whose Frances, having broken up with her boyfriend, hangs around with her close acquaintances, not least with Sophie (Mickey Sumner) with whom she shares a Brooklyn apartment. It absolutely invites contemporary youngsters who view it to identify with Frances and will positively encourage them to regard black-and-white photography as cool. The story may be slight but for the right age group it's a must. MS

▶ Greta Gerwig, Mickey Sumner, Adam Driver, Michael Zegen, Patrick Heusinger, Charlotte d'Amboise, Grace Gummer.
▶ *Dir* Noah Baumbach, *Pro* Baumbach, Scott Rudin, Lila Yacoub and Rodrigo Teixeira, *Screenplay* Baumbach and Greta Gerwig, *Ph* Sam Levy, *Pro Des* Sam Lisenco, *Ed* Jennifer Lame.

RT Features/a Pine District Pictures/Scott Rudin production-Metrodome Distribution Ltd.
86 mins. USA. 2012. Rel: 26 July 2013. Cert. 15.

Free Birds ★½

Reggie the turkey (Owen Wilson) has a narrow escape from becoming the main attraction at the Thanksgiving table after being adopted by the President's daughter as her pet. But his glamorous lifestyle at the White House is interrupted when Jake (Woody Harrelson), a fanatic turkey, forces him to travel back in time to save their fellow turkeys from the chop... This animation has a fun central idea but the plot becomes sillier as it develops and finally just stupid. Wilson has fun with his turkey while Harrelson is miscast as the revolutionary. The 3D animation is very basic and the product placement at the climax is outrageous. GS

❧ Voices of Owen Wilson, Woody Harrelson, Amy Poehler, George Takei, Colm Meaney, Keith David, Dan Fogler.
❧ *Dir* Jimmy Hayward, *Pro* Scott Mosier, *Screenplay* Hayward and Mosier, from a story by David I Stern and John J Strauss, *Pro Des* Kevin R Adams, *Ed* Chris Catagena, *M* Dominic Lewis.

Relativity Media/Reel FX Creative Studios-Momentum Pictures.
91 mins. USA. 2013. Rel: 29 Nov 2013. Cert. U.

From Up On Poppy Hill ★★★★

Based on a Japanese graphic novel, this is a comparatively slight but engaging piece of animation from Studio Ghibli with Goro Miyazaki taking over the directorial reins from his father, Hayao Miyazaki, whose credit here is as co-writer. Unusually for animation, this is in essence a love story and one that takes place in Yokohama in 1963. It features a strong young heroine and, despite raising a few political points and using the threat of possible incest to delay a happy ending, it is rather pleasingly old-fashioned. (Original title: *Kokurikozaka Kara*) MS

❧ With the voices of Nagasawa Masami, Okada Junichi, Takeshita Keiko, Ishida Uriko and Fubuki Jun (Japanese version)
Sarah Bolger, Anton Yelchin, Gillian Anderson, Christina Hendricks, Bruce Dern and Jamie Lee Curtis (English language version)
❧ *Dir* Goro Miyazaki, *Pro* Suzuki Toshio, *Screenplay* Hayao Miyazaki and Niwa Keiko, from the graphic novel by Takahashi Chizuru and Sayama Tetsuro, *Dir of Digital Imaging* Okui Atsushi, *M* Takebe Satoshi, *Animation Dirs* Yamashita Akihiko, Yamagata Atsushi and Kousaka Kitaro.
English language version: *Dir* Gary Rydstrom, *Pro* Geoffrey Wexler, *Screenplay* Karey Kirkpatrick and Patrick Mullen.

A Studio Ghibli production/Nippon Television Network/ Dentsu/Walt Disney Japan etc.-StudioCanal Limited. 92 mins. Japan. 2011. Rel: 2 Aug 2013. Cert. U.

Frozen ★★★

An enormous box-office success (over a billion dollars worldwide, and counting), *Frozen* is inspired by Hans Andersen's *The Snow Queen*, in which future queen Elsa has a nasty knack of freezing anything she touches. Although kept out of harm's way and under lock and key until her coronation, Elsa manages to ice the whole of her kingdom. Only sister Anna with her friend Kristoff, a reindeer called Sven, and Olaf the snowman (really?) can help save the country from, as it were, total meltdown. Frankly this kind of computer-generated animation is becoming rather too slick and artless, comfort cartoons for kids to wallow in, the soothing filmic equivalent of Calpol. It may be an Academy Award winner, but it's still Disney at its blandest and cutest. MHD

❧ Voices of Kristen Bell, Idina Menzel, Jonathan Groff, Josh Gad, Ciarán Hinds, Santino Fontana.
❧ *Dir* Chris Buck and Jennifer Lee, *Pro* Peter Del

Olympic torching: *From Up On Poppy Hill* was directed by Gorō Miyazaki, son of Hayao Miyazaki.

Venus in a burka: Maja Borg's intriguing *Future My Love*.

Vecho, *Screenplay* Lee, based on a story by Buck, Lee, Shane Morris and Dean Wellins, inspired by Hans Christian Andersen's *The Snow Queen*, *Pro Des* David Womersley, *Ed* Jeff Draheim, *M* Christophe Beck.

Walt Disney Pictures/Walt Disney Animation Studios-Walt Disney Studios Motion Pictures.
102 mins. USA. 2013. Rel: 6 Dec 2013. Cert. PG.

The Frozen Ground ★★

For those who still can't get enough of screen serial killers, *The Frozen Ground* is a competent enough thriller, enlivened by some tense face-offs between cop on the case Nicolas Cage and the hangdog killer himself, John Cusack. But the clichés are piled on right from the opening titles, with the requisite Biblical quotation followed by the legend 'Based on actual events'. The trouble is that the sleazily voyeuristic tone threatens to trivialise those events (namely, the 1971-83 Alaskan murder spree of Robert Hansen), while the police procedural aspect fails utterly because a good 50 per cent of the dialogue is incomprehensible. One eerily imaginative moment – heroine Vanessa Hudgens encountering a stray moose on a snowbound Anchorage street. JR

▶ Nicolas Cage, John Cusack, 50 Cent, Vanessa Hudgens, Radha Mitchell.
▶ *Dir* and *Screenplay* Scott Walker, *Pro* Curtis Jackson, Remington Chase, Jeff Rice, Mark Ordesky etc, *Ph* Patrick Murguia, *Pro Des* Clark Hunter, *Ed* Sarah Boyd, *M* Lorne Balfe, *Cos* Lynn Falconer.

Grindstone Entertainment Group/Emmett/Furia Films/Cheetah Vision/Envision Entertainment/Valentina Films etc-Koch Media.
105 mins. USA. 2013. Rel: 19 July 2013. Cert. 15.

F**k for Forest ★

The film's title is the name of a charity set up in Berlin to obtain money for environmental causes. The money comes from charging people to watch pornography and the group also invites members of the public to join in and be photographed having sex. Nobody has anything to say to justify any of this and a trip to South America to help border people struggling to preserve their land is seen to go wholly awry. It's a singularly unilluminating film about a group that seems merely weird. MS

▶ With Danny DeVero, Tommy Hol Ellingsen, Leona Johansson, Natty, Kaajal.
▶ *Dir* and *Ph* Michal Marczak, *Pro* Mikolaj Pokromski and Marczak, *Written by* Marczak and Lukasz Grudinski, *Ed* Dorota Wardeszkiewicz *M* Marcin Masecki.

Pokromski Studio/Kinomaton Berlin/Against Gravity etc.-Dogwoof.
86 mins. Poland/Germany. 2012. Rel: 19 Apr 2013. Cert. 18.

Future My Love ★★★★

Swedish film director Maja Borg revisits the Venus Project in Florida to meet its founder, social engineer and industrial designer Jacque Fresco, expert on such topics as sustainability, energy efficiency, automation, cybernetics and natural resource management. The Venus Project is not only a research centre for Fresco and his partner Roxanne Meadows but also an educational centre for its supporters. In the film Fresco explains to Borg his ideas for the future of mankind and a resource-based economy. This is an intriguing insight into the work of the inventor as seen through the eyes of a concerned outsider. PL

❧ With Maja Borg, Jacque Fresco, Roxanne Meadows, Daniel Bedford, Colin D Calway, John Darvill, Nadia Cazan.
❧ *Dir* and *Written by* Maja Borg, *Pro* Borg and Sonja Henrici, *Ph* Minttu Mantynen, *Animation* Andrew Buxton, *Ed* Patricia Gomes and Colin Monie, *M* Per Störby.

Lisbet Gabrielsson Film AB/Scottish Documentary Institute/Sveriges Television/ Swedish Film Institute/ Creative Scotland-Independent Cinema Office. 97 mins. UK/Sweden. 2012. Rel: 15 Nov 2013. Cert. 12A.

Gangster Squad ★★½

I regard this movie as irresponsible filmmaking. It is competently handled and boasts a talented cast but the tone is such that this tale of gangsters and a special LAPD squad that is equally ruthless emerges as an orgy of violence. It's set in 1949 and has a factual basis, but the film's message for today is that guns are good and that any amount of violence is justified provided that America wins the day. MS

❧ Josh Brolin, Ryan Gosling, Nick Nolte, Emma Stone, Sean Penn, Anthony Mackie, Giovanni Ribisi, Michael Peña, Robert Patrick.
❧ *Dir* Ruben Fleischer, *Pro* Dan Lin, Kevin McCormick and Michael Tadross, *Screenplay* Will Beal, from the book by Paul Lieberman, *Ph* Dion Beebe, *Pro Des* Maher Ahmad, *Ed* Alan Baumgarten and James Herbert, *M* Steve Jablonsky, *Cos* Mary Zophres.

A Warner Bros. Pictures presentation/A Lin Pictures/ Kevin McCormick production etc.-Warner Bros. 113 mins. USA. 2013. Rel: 10 Jan 2013. Cert. 15.

The Gatekeepers ★★★★

Pondering the Israeli-Palestinian conflict from the Six Days War of 1967 onwards, this is a remarkable documentary offering critical insights into Israel's secret service agency Shin Bet. Central to it are six former heads of that agency and all of them talk with surprising frankness. This is indeed a talking heads movie and one which is quite demanding for those not au fait with its subject matter. But, if it is challenging and on the long side, it undoubtedly provides much food for thought. MS

❧ With Avraham Shalom, Yaakov Peri, Carmi Gillon, Ami Ayalon, Avi Dichter.

❧ *Dir* Dror Moreh, *Pro* Moreh, Estelle Fialon and Philippa Kowarsky, *Ph* Avner Shahaf, *Pro Des* Doron Koren, *Ed* Oron Adar, *M* Ab Ovo, Jérôme Chassagnard and Régis Baillet.

Dror Moreh Productions/Les Films du Poisson/Wild Heart Productions etc.-Metrodome Distribution Ltd. 101 mins. Israel/France/Belgium/Germany/Canada/ Sweden/Denmark/ Norway/ Finland/The Netherlands. 2012. Rel: 12 Apr 2013. Cert. 15.

Getaway ★½

In order to save the life of his wife who has been kidnapped, former racing car driver Brent Magna (Ethan Hawke) begins a race against time driving through the streets of Sofia following the mysterious captor's absurd demands... Hawke is a strong presence but needs a better script than this and shares zero chemistry with Selina Gomez as his unwilling passenger. This action thriller isn't really boring – it simply doesn't make sense. GS

❧ Ethan Hawke, Selena Gomez, Jon Voight, Rebecca Budig, Paul Freeman, Bruce Payne.
❧ *Dir* Courtney Solomon, *Pro* Solomon, Christopher Milburn, Alan Zeman and Moshe Diamant, *Screenplay* Sean Finegan and Gregg Maxwell Parker, *Ph* Yaron Levy, *Pro Des* Michelle Jones and Nate Jones, *Ed* Ryan Dufrene, *M* Justin Caine Burnett, *Cos* Roseanne Fiedler and Irina Kotcheva.

After Dark Films/Dark Castle Entertainment/Signature Entertainment/Silver Reel/Dunulf Productions/Emmitt Productions/The Fyzz Facility etc-Warner Bros. 90 mins. USA/Bulgaria. 2013. Rel: 6 Dec 2013. Cert. 12A.

G.I. Joe: Retaliation ★

Blood spills, tyres screech and stuff explodes as the Joes return for a second round of bullet-spraying, punch-throwing, rocket-blasting, property-smashing, world-saving adventure that, although

Sofia, so fearless: Selena Gomez and Ethan Hawke on tenterhooks in *Getaway*.

it sounds terribly busy and exciting, is actually a colossal bore. Channing Tatum, Bruce Willis and Dwayne Johnson are just three of the stars going through the motions in this witless and juvenile waste of time and resources that's so very far from fun. Even worse than the first film. MJ

❯ Dwayne Johnson, Jonathan Pryce, Byung-hun Lee, Bruce Willis, Elodie Yung, Ray Stevenson, DJ Cotrona, Channing Tatum.
❯ *Dir* Jon M. Chu, *Pro* Lorenzo di Bonaventura and Brian Goldner, *Screenplay* Rhett Reese and Paul Wernick, *Ph* Stephen Windon, *Pro Des* Andrew Menzies, *Ed* Jim May and Roger Barton, *M* Henry Jackman, *Cos* Louise Mingenbach.

Paramount Pictures/Metro-Goldwyn-Mayer Pictures/ Skydance Productions/Hasbro/Di Bonaventura Pictures/ Saints LA-Paramount Pictures.
110 mins. USA. 2013. Rel: 27 Mar 2013. Cert. 12A.

Gimme the Loot ★★★

Two black kids (Ty Hickson and Tashiana Washington) are growing up in the Bronx thinking of graffiti as art works and planning to put their stamp on a local landmark even if raising the necessary funds involves stealing. It's well played and brings the streets to life in a style that recalls the movies of John Cassavetes. However, the expletive-ridden talk, the difficult accents and the film's abrupt non-ending alienate me, thus making the rating above somewhat objective. MS

❯ Tashiana Washington, Ty Hickson, Meeko, Sam Soghor, Adam Metzger, Zoë Lescaze.
❯ *Dir* and *Screenplay* Adam Leon, *Pro* Natalie Difford, Dominic Buchanan and Jamund Washington, *Ph* Jonathan Miller, *Pro Des* Sammy Lisenco and Katie Hickman, *Ed* Morgan Faust, *M* Nicholas Britell.

A Seven for Ten production/Flagstone Features/DOT Pictures etc.-Soda Pictures.
79 mins. USA. 2012. Rel: 3 May 2013. Cert. 15.

She will survive: Paulina García in Sebastián Lelio's *Gloria*, for which she won the best actress award at Berlin.

Girl Most Likely ★★½

This film seems to have been embraced by Kristen Wiig in her quest for another central role in a comedy following her hit movie *Bridesmaids*. To her credit she's found something capable of being individual but, sadly, the writing makes her character unsympathetic (be it falling for the wrong guy or giving up on her writing ambitions). Add that she has a horrendous mother (Annette Bening) and a supposedly dead father who is in fact alive (Bob Balaban) and you have an oddball family saga echoing Wes Anderson. But the characters are never real enough for us to care and, different though this is, it's essentially a misfire. MS

❯ Kristen Wiig, Annette Bening, Matt Dillon, Darren Criss, Natasha Lyonne, Bob Balaban.
❯ *Dir* Shari Springer Berman and Robert Pulcini, *Pro* Celine Rattray, Trudie Styler, Alix Madigan and Mark Amin, *Screenplay* Michelle Morgan, *Ph* Steve Yedlin, *Pro Des* Annie Spitz, *Ed* Pulcini, *M* Rob Simonsen, *Cos* Tom Broecker.

Voltage Pictures/a Maven Pictures and Anonymous Content Pictures production etc.-Lionsgate UK.
103 mins. USA. 2012. Rel: 27 Sep 2013. Cert. 12A.

Gloria ★★★

The title role, played by the acclaimed Paulina García, is a middle-aged woman in Santiago, Chile whose children have grown up and who, 12 years on from her divorce, continues to frequent a disco still hoping for a new man in her life. However, a relationship that does arise proves problematic to say the least. Feminists may be cheering by the end and many have found this a very sympathetic film, but personally I remained detached. It probably turns on how appealing you find Gloria herself. MS

> Paulina García, Sergio Hernández, Diego Fonecilla, Fabiola Zamora, Coca Guazzini.
> *Dir* Sebastián Lelio, *Pro* Juan de Dios Larrain, Pablo Larrain, Lelio and Gonzalo Maza, *Screenplay* Lelio and Maza, *Ph* Benjamin Echazarreta, *Pro Des* Marcela Urivi, *Ed* Lelio and Soledad Salfate, *Cos* Eduardo Castro.

Fabula, Nephilim Producciones-Network Releasing. 109 mins. Chile/Spain. 2012. Rel: 1 Nov 2013. Cert. 15.

A Good Day to Die Hard ★

The difference between this fifth *Die Hard* adventure and the films preceding it is that, while his 'wrong time wrong place' adventures are usually good for a laugh or indeed several, this latest John McClane effort is a witless, charmless dud. Tooling around Russia with his estranged son Jack (Jai Courtney), John causes more damage than a hurricane full of rhinos, more harm certainly than the bad guys ever could. But, while he fights for his life in every scene, Bruce Willis' hard-boiled New York cop is already dead from the neck up. MJ

> Bruce Willis, Jai Courtney, Sebastian Koch, Mary Elizabeth Winstead, Yulia Snigir.
> *Dir* John Moore, *Pro* Wyck Godfrey and Alex Young, *Screenplay* Skip Woods, based on characters created by Roderick Thorp, *Ph* Jonathan Sela, *Pro Des* Daniel P Dorrance, *Ed* Dan Zimmerman, *M* Marco Beltrami, *Cos* Bojana Nikitovic.

20th Century Fox/Big Screen Productions/Giant Pictures/Dune Entertainment/Ingenious Media etc-20th Century Fox. 98 mins. USA. 2013. Rel: 14 Feb 2013. Cert. 12A.

Good Vibrations ★★★★

The team who in 2008 gave us the underrated *Cherrybomb*, Lisa Barros D'Sa and Glenn Leyburn, now offer this piece about a record shop in Belfast in the 1970s. The owner, a real-life figure, was Terri Hooley (Robert Dormer) who fostered punk rock by recording local artists and promoting music as a bridge between Catholic and Protestant. The film's style (on occasion almost surreal) captures the irreverent spirit of the music and it's an engaging, sympathetic work. Those who enjoy this type of music should positively delight in it, but it appeals anyway. MS

> Robert Dormer, Jodie Whittaker, Michael Colgan, Karl Johnson, Liam Cunningham. Adrian Dunbar, Dylan Moran.
> *Dir* Lisa Barros D'Sa and Glenn Leyburn, *Pro* Chris Martin, Andrew Eaton, David Holmes and Bruce Charlesworth, *Screenplay* Colin Carberry and Glenn Paterson, from the true stories of Terri Hooley, *Ph* Ivan McCullough, *Pro Des* Derek Wallace, *Ed* Nick Emerson, *M* Holmes and Keefus Green, *Cos* Maggie Donnelly.

BBC Films/a Cinderblinks Film, Revolution Films and Treasure Entertainment production etc.-The Works UK Distribution Ltd. 103 mins. UK/Ireland. 2012. Rel: 29 Mar 2013. Cert. 15.

The vinyl solution: Robert Dormer (left) in Lisa Barros D'Sa and Glenn Leyburn's *Good Vibrations*.

Roman holiday: Tony Servillo in Paolo Sorrentino's *The Great Beauty*, which won the Oscar for best foreign language film.

Gravity ★★★★★

Justifiably lauded, Alfonso Cuarón's Oscar-winning space drama about two astronauts trying to get back to Earth puts the splendid Sandra Bullock centre screen. Nevertheless what counts above all is the film's technological brilliance. *Gravity* is the only film known to me which in its use of the highest quality 3D produces a unique experience for the audience who feel transported into its world. As such it demands to be seen in that form and is the one sci-fi film with sufficient imaginative power to equal Kubrick's classic *2001: A Space Odyssey*. This one should go down in cinema history. MS

❥ Sandra Bullock, George Clooney. With Ed Harris (voice only).
❥ *Dir* Alfonso Cuarón, *Pro* Cuarón and David Heyman, *Screenplay* Alfonso and Jonás Cuarón, *Ph* Emmanuel Lubezki, *Pro Des* Andy Nicholson, *Ed* Alfonso Cuarón and Mark Sanger, M Steven Price, *Cos* Jany Temime.

**Warner Bros. Pictures/an Esperanto Filmoj production/ a Heyday Films production-Warner Bros.
91 mins. USA/UK. 2013. Rel: 8 Nov 2013. Cert. 12A.**

The Great Beauty ★★★★★

Taking his cue from Fellini's *La dolce vita*, Paolo Sorrentino offers an updated guide to all the pleasures enjoyed by the small percentage of the population of Rome who can afford to indulge themselves with nary a thought for the poor of this society. Meet journalist and socialite Jep Gambardella (the Marcello Mastroianni-type part, here resurrected by Toni Servillo) as he arranges parties for the wealthiest residents while reminiscing about his long-lost first love as a teenager, a sadness that no amount of wealth can rectify. Beautifully lit and shot, *The Great Beauty* lives up to its name in spades and is true cinema on a grand scale. (Original title: *La grande bellezza*) MHD

❥ Toni Servillo, Carlo Verdone, Sabrina Ferilli, Carlo Buccirosso, Iaia Forte, Pamela Villoresi, Galatea Ranzi, Vernon Dobtcheff.
❥ *Dir* Paolo Sorrentino, *Pro* Francesca Cima and Nicola Giuliano, *Screenplay* Sorrentino and Umberto Contarello, from a story by Sorrentino, *Ph* Luca Bigazzi, *Pro Des* Stefania Cella, *Ed* Cristiano Travaglioli, *M* Lele Marchitelli, *Cos* Daniela Ciancio.

**Indigo Film/Medusa Film/Babe Film/Pathé/France 2 Cinema/Canal+/Ciné+/ Mediaset Premium etc-Artificial Eye.
142 mins. Italy/France. 2013. Rel: 6 Sep 2013. Cert. 15.**

The Great Gatsby ★★★½

Although the 3D is not helpful, this new treatment of F Scott Fitzgerald's classic of the jazz age is much better than advance reports had suggested.

Retaining much of the dialogue from the novel, the film despite some misjudgments captures the blend of social comment and love story and, if Joel Edgerton seems miscast as Daisy's husband, the two lead performances (Leonardo DiCaprio as Jay Gatsby and Carey Mulligan as Daisy) are both well judged. Imperfect then, but always interesting. MS

‣ Leonardo DiCaprio, Carey Mulligan, Tobey Maguire, Joel Edgerton, Jason Clarke, Isla Fisher, Amitabh Bachchan, Elizabeth Debicki, Jack Thompson.
‣ *Dir* Baz Luhrmann, *Pro* Luhrmann, Catherine Martin, Douglas Wick and others, *Screenplay* Luhrman and Craig Pearce, from the novel by F Scott Fitzgerald, *Ph* Simon Duggan, *Pro Des* and *Cos* Martin, *Ed* Matt Villa, Jason Ballantine and Jonathan Redmond, *M* Craig Armstrong.

Warner Bros. Pictures/Village Roadshow Pictures/a Bazmark/Red Wagon Entertainment production etc.-Warner Bros.
143 mins. Australia/USA. 2013. Rel: 16 May 2013. Cert. 12A.

The Great Hip Hop Hoax ★★★½

This intriguing documentary follows the incredible story of hip hop duo the Silibil 'n' Brains, who, although they come from Dundee in Scotland, claim at their first meeting with Sony that they are two Californian kids. Billy and his rap partner Gavin see no alternative but to lie in order to achieve their goal and hit the big time. Here they tell their story with honesty and humour, revealing how they managed to keep their secret for two amazing years. GS

‣ With Gavin Bain, Billy Boyd.
‣ *Dir* Jeanie Finlay, *Pro* Finlay and Al Morrow, *Ph* Roger Knott-Fayle, *Ed* Jim Scott.

BBC Scotland/EM Media/Glimmer Films/Met Film Production-Vertigo Films.
93 mins. UK. 2013. Rel: 6 Sep 2013. Cert. 18.

Greedy Lying Bastards ★★★½

This documentary concerned with global warming concentrates on the oil companies which have a vested interest in denigrating those espousing that cause. The film is watchable enough but could have been shorter and would be entirely at home on television. There's nothing seriously wrong here but you only have to compare it with, say, *Chasing Ice* (2012) to be aware which film offers a truly memorable and cinematic experience. MS

‣ With Enoch Adams, Kert Davies, Myron Ebell, Craig Scott Rosebraugh.
‣ *Dir* Craig Scott Rosebraugh, *Pro* Jeremy Chilvers, Patrick Gambuti Jr and Rosebraugh, *Screenplay* Gambuti and Rosebraugh, *Ph* Carl Bartels, *Ed* Gambuti, *M* Michael Brook.

One Earth Productions-Kaleidoscope Film Distribution.
90 mins. USA. 2012. Rel: 2 Sep 2013. Cert. PG.

Grown Ups 2 ★

When this opened on the same day in the States as *Pacific Rim* [qv] and bafflingly beat Guillermo del Toro's movie to the top of the box-office, we naturally assumed that was the seventh sign of the apocalypse and that all life on Earth would imminently end. In reality, it was merely an indication that America has lost its mind, flocking to a terrible sequel to an awful movie rather than an original, spirited sci-fi monsters vs robot adventure. MJ

‣ Adam Sandler, Chris Rock, Kevin James, David Spade, Selma Hayek, Maya Rudolph, Maria Bello, Steve Buscemi.
‣ *Dir* Dennis Dugan, *Pro* Adam Sandler and Jack Giaraputo, *Screenplay* Sandler, Tim Herlihy and Fred Wolf, based on characters created by Sandler and Wolf, *Ph* Theo van de Sande, *Pro Des* Aaron Osborne, *Ed* Tom Costain, *M* Rupert Gregson-Williams, *Cos* Ellen Lutter.

Columbia Pictures/Happy Madison Productions/Sony Pictures Entertainment-Columbia Pictures.
101 mins. USA. 2013. Rel: 9 Aug 2013. Cert. 12A.

The Guilt Trip ★★★

When salesman Andy Brewster (Seth Rogen) hits the road from New Jersey to San Francisco in an effort sell his new cleaning product, he decides to check out the long-ago first love of his mother Joyce (Barbra Streisand), after whom Andy was named. Without telling her his intentions, Andy invites momma along for the ride. The road trip portrays their arguments and odd adventures en route, including a meat-eating contest in which Joyce has to down an enormous steak to win $100. It's basically a comedy with romantic overtones, although at times the script stretches the fun to bursting point. It's all rather average considering the two leads' extensive previous experience in comedy. MHD

Dundee deceit: Silibil N' Brains in Jeanie Finlay's *The Great Hip Hop Hoax*.

The philosopher's tone: Barbara Sukowa in Margarethe von Trotta's *Hannah Arendt*.

❯ Barbra Streisand, Seth Rogen, Julene Renee-Preciado, Miriam Margolyes, Rose Abdoo, Tom Virtue, Colin Hanks.
❯ *Dir* Anne Fletcher, *Pro* Evan Goldberg, Lorne Michaels and John Goldwyn, *Screenplay* Dan Fogelman, *Ph* Oliver Stapleton, *Pro Des* Nelson Coates, *Ed* Dana E Glauberman and Priscilla Nedd-Friendly, *M* Christophe Beck, *Cos* Danny Glicker.

Paramount Pictures/Skydance Productions/Michaels-Goldwyn-Paramount Pictures.
95 mins. USA. 2012. Rel: 8 Mar 2013. Cert. 12A.

Hammer of the Gods ★

The most impressive thing about this movie is its title. In truth, it's a Viking epic on a budget and the armies of six and seven do little to alleviate the atrocious dialogue. The marauding Vikings speak like Oxbridge graduates (with a generous injection of the Anglo-Saxon 'f' word), while the Anglos are portrayed as a motley crew of Barbarians. The 'battle' scenes are tedious, the sound effects silly and the electronic score like something lifted from a 95-minute trailer. So, where's Dolph Lundgren when you need him? JC-W

❯ Charlie Bewley, Elliot Cowan, Clive Standen, Michael Jibson, Alexandra Dowling, Glynis Barber, James Cosmo.
❯ *Dir* Farren Blackburn, *Pro* Rupert Preston and Huberta Von Liel, *Screenplay* Matthew Read, *Ph* Stephan Pehrsson, *Pro Des* Ben Smith, *Ed* Sam Williams, *M* Benjamin Wallfisch, *Cos* Matthew Price.

Vertigo Films-Vertigo Films.
95 mins. UK. 2013. Rel: 30 Aug 2013. Cert. 18.

The Hangover Part III ★★½

Absurd, outrageous and potty-mouthed, this third and final *Hangover* may lack the surprise of the first but it is, at least, significantly better than the second. Propelled by the madness of Leslie Chow (Ken Jeong), hungover heroes Phil, Stu and Alan (Bradley Cooper, Ed Helms and Zach Galifianakis) are hurled from one insane situation to the next. Some gags work, others fall flat, but if you're amenable to tasteless nonsense you could do a lot worse. MJ

❯ Bradley Cooper, Ed Helms, Zach Galifianakis, Justin Bartha, Ken Jeong, John Goodman, Melissa McCarthy, Jeffrey Tambor, Heather Graham.
❯ *Dir* Todd Phillips, *Pro* Phillips and Daniel Goldberg, *Screenplay* Phillips and Craig Mazlin, based on characters created by Jon Lucas and Scott Moore, *Ph* Lawrence Sher, *Pro Des* Maher Ahmad, *Ed* Jeff Groth and Debra Neil-Fisher, *M* Christophe Beck, *Cos* Louise Mingenbach.

Green Hat Films/Legendary Pictures-Warner Bros.
100 mins. USA. 2013. Rel: 24 May 2013. Cert. 15.

Hannah Arendt ★★★★

In Britain Margarethe von Trotta is best known for such films as *Rosa Luxemburg* made in the 1980s so we should give her a warm welcome back for what is a characteristic piece: a study of a remarkable woman, the German-Jewish philosopher and writer Hannah Arendt played by the admirable Barbara Sukowa. Concentrating on the 1960s and on Arendt's controversial comments for the *New Yorker* on the trial of Adolf Eichmann, this is a film for thinking people which ends impressively with what is virtually a monologue, splendidly handled by Sukowa. MS

▷ Barbara Sukowa, Axel Milberg, Janet McTeer, Julia Jentsch, Nicholas Woodeson.
▷ *Dir* Margarethe von Trotta, *Pro* Bettina Brokemper and Johannes Rexin, *Screenplay* Pam Katz and von Trotta, *Ph* Caroline Champetier, *Pro Des* Volker Schaefer, *Ed* Bettina Böhler, *M* André Mergenthaler, *Cos* Frauke Firl.

A Heimatfilm production/Amour Fou Luxembourg/MACT Productions/Metro Communications etc.-Soda Pictures. 113 mins. Germany/Luxembourg/France/Israel. 2012. Rel: 27 Sep 2013. Cert. 12A.

Hansel and Gretel: Witch Hunters ★★

Following a traumatic childhood adventure, siblings Hansel and Gretel discover a penchant for killing witches. Grown up into Jeremy Renner and Gemma Arterton, they travel through period Germany tracking down and despatching them. Cue lots of action and special effects. There's nothing here to raise this above the level of the mundane, although those seeking nothing more than a mindless supernatural action movie will probably be happy with it. Indeed, a sequel is already in development. JC

▷ Jeremy Renner, Gemma Arterton, Famke Janssen, Pihla Viitala, Derek Mears, Thomas Mann.
▷ *Dir* and *Screenplay* Tommy Wirkola, *Pro* Will Ferrell, Adam McKay and Beau Flynn, *Ph* Michael Bonvillain, *Pro Des* Stephen Scott, *Ed* Jim Page, *M* Atli Örvasson, *Cos* Marlene Stewart.

Paramount Pictures/Metro-Goldwyn-Mayer Pictures/ MTV Films/Gary Sanchez Productions/Studio Babelsberg etc-Paramount Pictures. 88 mins. Germany/USA. 2013. Rel: 27 Feb 2013. Cert. 15.

Harrigan ★★½

It's the winter of 1974 and Detective Sergeant Barry Harrigan (Stephen Tompkinson) rejoins the police force in Newcastle after a short spell fighting corruption in Hong Kong. But things are even worse back home and personal events finally force Harrigan to confront a local gang against his boss's orders... Vince Woods' police drama boasts strong period details and a committed performance from Tompkinson as the eponymous hero. Arthur McKenzie has written credible characters but unfortunately this routine police thriller feels more like an episode for television. GS

▷ Stephen Tompkinson, Gillian Kearney, Ronnie Fox, Craig Conway, Mark Stobbart, Darren Morfitt, Amy Manson, Maurice Roëves.
▷ *Dir* Vince Woods, *Pro* Vince Woods, *Screenplay* Arthur McKenzie, *Ph* James McAleer, *Pro Des* Sarah Beaman, *Ed* Michael Pentney, *M* James Edward Barker, *Cos* Camille Bender.

TallTree Pictures-High Fliers Distribution. 97 mins. UK. 2013. Rel: 20 Sep 2013. Cert. 15.

The Harry Hill Movie ★½

To accommodate the requirements of big-screen feature entertainment, the surreal stylings of affable telly absurdist Harry Hill are stretched so very thin that the whole lot comes apart at the seams. Defiantly shapeless and so stream-of-consciousness silly that it quickly becomes annoying, the film sees Harry hitting the road with his nan (Julie Walters) and a talking hamster. Though a few of the gags hit home, and the songs sometimes amuse, it's mainly just incredibly stupid. MJ

▷ Harry Hill, Julie Walters, Matt Lucas, Simon Bird, Johnny Vegas, Sheridan Smith, Jim Broadbent.
▷ *Dir* Steve Bendelack, *Pro* Robert Jones, *Screenplay* Harry Hill, Jon Foster and James Lamont, from a story by Hill, *Ph* Baz Irvine, *Pro Des* Grenville Horner and Fleur Whitlock, *Ed* Michael Parker, *M* Steve Brown, *Cos* Leah Archer.

Lucky Features-Entertainment Film Distributors. 88 mins. UK. 2013. Rel: 20 Dec 2013. Cert. PG.

A Haunted House ★½

Having abandoned the *Scary Movie* franchise, Marlon Wayans starts up his own as co-writer, producer and star. He plays Malcolm, who moves into his dream home with wife Kisha (Essence Atkins) and soon finds they're sharing it with a demon. Kisha gets possessed, so Malcolm calls in a priest (Cedric the Entertainer), a psychic and, of course, ghostbusters. There are hardly any laughs to be found in this dreary, over-familiar parody of the found footage genre, such as the *Paranormal Activity*

Road to Blackpool: Harry Hill and Julie Walters in *The Harry Hill Movie.*

franchise. Wayans' idea of 'funny characters' doing 'funny things' just isn't funny, though he remains a likeable performer. On a mini-budget of $2m, it earned $60m, spawning a 2014 sequel. DW

‣ Marlon Wayans, Marlene Forte, Essence Atkins, David Koechner, Dave Sheridan, Nick Swardson, Cedric the Entertainer.
‣ *Dir* Michael Tiddes, *Pro* and *Screenplay* Marlon Wayans and Rick Alvarez, *Ph* Steve Gainer, *Pro Des* Fred Andrews, *Ed* Suzanne Hines, *M* Rick Balentine, *Cos* Ariyela Wald-Cohain.

Automatik Entertainment/Baby Way Productions/ IM Global/Endgame Entertainment/Cutting Edge-Vertigo Films.
86 mins. USA. 2013. Rel: 19 June 2013. Cert. 15.

The Haunting in Connecticut 2: Ghosts of Georgia ★★★½

Supposedly based on a true story, this surprisingly original and very creepy unrelated sequel follows the story of a young family who move into an historic new home in Georgia in 1993. Chad Michael Murray stars as Andy Wyrick and Abigail Spencer as his wife Lisa, who discover they are not the house's only inhabitants when their little daughter Heidi (Emily Alyn Lind) begins to see people in and around their home. There's a well-placed and nicely staged series of startling shocks and tingling thrills in this satisfyingly scary ghost story with a decent yarn to tell and convincing actors to play it. It's skilfully made by debut director Tom Elkins, a former film editor. DW

Phantom menace: Abigail Spencer in *The Haunting in Connecticut 2: Ghosts of Georgia*, based on a true story, apparently.

‣ Abigail Spencer, Chad Michael Murray, Katee Sackhoff, Emily Alyn Lind, Cicely Tyson.
‣ *Dir* Tom Elkins, *Pro* Paul Brooks and Scot Niemeyer, *Screenplay* David Coggeshall, *Ph* Yaron Levy, *Art Dir* Jeremy Woolsey, *Ed* Elkins and Elliot Greenberg, *M* Michael Wandmacher, *Cos* Dana

Marie Embree and Jennifer Kamrath.
Gold Circle Films-Lionsgate.
101 mins. USA. 2013. Rel: 31 Oct 2013. Cert. 15.

Hawking ★★★★

Famed as a physicist and also as the author of the best-selling book *A Brief History of Time*, Stephen Hawking has also become well known as a man, now in his seventies, who has done so much despite being diagnosed with Motor Neurone Disease while still young. This documentary film under the direction of Stephen Finnigan gives a decent impression of what Hawking describes as his journey through the world. He is a co-author here and, since he tells it his way, this is virtually an autobiography on film. MS

‣ With Professor Stephen Hawking, Jane Hawking, Buzz Aldrin, Richard Branson.
‣ *Dir* and *Pro* Stephen Finnigan, *Written by* Hawking, Finnigan and Ben Bowie, *Ph* Paul F Jenkins, *Pro Des* Sharon Katanka, *Ed* Tim Lovell, *M* Nick Powell.

Vertigo Films/a Darlow Smithson production/PBS/ Channel 4-Vertigo Films.
88 mins. UK. 2013. Rel: 20 Sep 2013. Cert. PG.

The Heat ★½

It's a formula that's worked before: two law enforcers from different departments are thrown together to track down a dangerous criminal mastermind. The twist is that these two law enforcers operate by different rules, yet against the odds somehow get the job done. It's called the buddy cop movie and there have been zillions of them. The novelty here is that the two cops are female, the real joke being that the fairer sex can be just as crude, violent and underhand as the guys. Ho ho. JC-W

‣ Sandra Bullock, Melissa McCarthy, Demián Bichir, Marlon Wayans, Michael Rapaport, Jane Curtin.
‣ *Dir* Paul Feig, *Pro* Peter Chernin and Jenno Topping, *Screenplay* Katie Dippold, *Ph* Robert Yeoman, *Pro Des* Jefferson Sage, *Ed* Jay Deuby and Brent White, *M* Mike Andrews, *Cos* Catherine Marie Thomas.

20th Century Fox/Chernin Entertainment/TSG Entertainment-20th Century Fox.
116 mins. USA. 2013. Rel: 31 July 2013. Cert. 15.

A Hijacking ★★★★

This drama from Denmark very effectively adopts an almost documentary tone in portraying what happens when a Danish cargo ship is seized by Somali pirates. The hi-jacking theme makes it comparable with *Captain Phillips* [qv], but they are very different films because here the emphasis is on the stress of the negotiations involving the CEO of the shipping company, the outsider expert advising him and the pirates themselves.

The shower scream: Jessica Biel lets rip as Vera Miles while Anthony Hopkins looks on as *Hitchcock*.

It's fascinating, powerful a...siguet Sookham, *Ed* Lee Chatametikool,
(Original title: *Kapringen*) ...u Koichi, *Cos* Cattleya Paosrijareon.

❯ Søren Malling, Pilou Asba... /Halo Productions/Pop Pix Productions
Møller, Gary Skjoldmose Po... Night
❯ *Dir* and *Screenplay* Tobias ... Thailand. 2010. Rel: 1 Mar 2013. Cert. PG.
Radoor and René Ezra, *Ph* M...
Pro Des Thomas Greve, *Ed* A... ock ★★★★
Gudnadottir, *Cos* Louise Hau... rrated film about the making of
Nordisk Film Production/The D... its faults (not the least being when it
and Nordisk Film & TV Fund-Ar... the figure of Ed Gein, the killer who
103 mins. Denmark. 2012. Rel: ... ototype for *Psycho*'s Norman Bates, to
...cock). Even so, Anthony Hopkins

Hi-so ★★★
...Mirren are highly enjoyable as Mr &
...ock and movie buffs are likely to get
Film star Ananda (Ananda Ev... ...e pleasure from this film. This, surely,
home to post-tsunami Thaila... ...nt to remember Hitch rather than as
a new film. His American girl... ...gure portrayed in the TV film released
him for a short break but fin... ...ly with this. In support James D'Arcy
to the rhythm of a small seas... ...ings Anthony Perkins back to life. MS
gentle, beautifully shot film w...
to unfold. The making of Ana... ...opkins, Helen Mirren, Scarlett
first half is far more interestin... ...i Collette, Danny Huston, Jessica Biel,
half which develops into a mo...
memories reflecting his past a... ...rvasi, *Pro* Ivan Reitman, Tom
...djuck and others, *Screenplay* John
❯ Ananda Everingham, Sajee Ap... ...ased on Stephen Rebello's book
Leang, Kongdej Jaturanrasamee, ... *and the Making of Psycho*, *Ph* Jeff
❯ *Dir* and *Screenplay* Aditya Assa... ...*o Des* Judy Becker, *Ed* Pamela Martin,
Sukhum and Aditya Assarat, *Ph* U... ...an, *Cos* Julie Weiss.

The bookmark overlay reads: "You can never get a cup of tea large enough or a book long enough to suit me." — C.S. LEWIS — Book Depository .com

Look who's Tolkien: Ian McKellen as Gandalf in Peter Jackson's *The Hobbit: The Desolation of Smaug.*

Fox Searchlight Pictures/a Montecito Picture Company/ Barnette/Thayer production etc.-20th Century Fox. 98 mins. USA/UK/Australia. 2012. Rel: 8 Feb 2013. Cert. 12A.

The Hobbit: The Desolation of Smaug ★★★★

The second in the trilogy of films adapted from JRR Tolkien's novel is a vast improvement on the first film. Bilbo Baggins (Martin Freeman), along with a group of 13 dwarves led by Thorin Oakenshield (Richard Armitage), continue their quest to reclaim the Lonely Mountain and the lost Dwarf Kingdom of Frebor... The narrative is not entirely crystal clear but the striking set-pieces are out of this world, and especially the amazing climactic sequence featuring Smaug (brilliantly voiced by Benedict Cumberbatch). GS

❯ Ian McKellen, Martin Freeman, Richard Armitage, Ken Stott, Graham McTavish, William Kircher, James Nesbitt, Orlando Bloom, Cate Blanchett, Benedict Cumberbatch, Stephen Fry.
❯ *Dir* Peter Jackson, *Pro* Jackson, Fran Walsh, Zane Weiner and Carolynne Cunningham, *Screenplay* Jackson, Walsh, Philippa Boyens and Guillermo del Toro, based on JRR Tolkien's novel *The Hobbit*, *Ph* Andrew Lesnie, *Pro Des* Dan Hennah, *Ed* Jabez Olssen, *M* Howard Shore, *Cos* Bob Buck, Richard Taylor and Ann Maskrey.

Metro-Goldwyn-Mayer/New Line Cinema/WingNut Films-Warner Bros.
161 mins. USA/New Zealand. 2013. Rel: 13 Dec 2013. Cert. 12A.

Hollow ★★★

A surprisingly satisfactory British horror film, with debut director Michael Axelgaard managing a slightly fresh take on the tired old *Blair Witch* found footage idea. Matthew Holt's story concerns the site of an old monastery in remote Suffolk. Left in ruins, the spot is marked only by a twisted, antique tree with an ominous hollow. Two holidaying young couples decide to explore the local legend and get into a mass of terror when they uncover the ancient evil of Greyfriar's Hollow. Plot, character development, acting and direction are all well taken care of, and there are some nicely executed big shocks. DW

❯ Emily Plumtree, Sam Stockman, Jessica Ellerby, Matt Stokoe, Simon Roberts, David Baukham, Ian Attfield.
❯ *Dir* Michael Axelgaard, *Pro* Axelgaard and Matthew Holt, *Screenplay* Holt, *Ph* Mark James, *Pro Des* John-Paul Frazer, *Ed* Ian Farr and Chris Gill.

Hollow Pictures-Metrodome Distribution.
91 mins. UK. 2011. Rel: 25 Jan 2013. Cert. 15.

Home (Yurt) ★★★★★

This poetic requiem for a lost Eden is an undervalued example of minimalist cinema, a debut work by the actor Muzaffer Özdemir who, turning writer and director, gives us a work in which every shot is beautifully composed. The central character retreats from Istanbul to that part of Anatolia where he spent his childhood, an area where with political support the countryside will be used for development. This set-up also resonates symbolically as a reflection of modern life in general: have we lost touch with nature or is the troubled central figure seeking to find again a world that never was? (Original title: *Yurt*) MS

❯ Kanbolat Gorkem Arslan, Pinar Ünsal, Coskun Çetinalp, Ismail Ergün.
❯ *Dir* and *Screenplay* Muzaffer Özdemir, *Pro* Sadik Incesu, *Ph* Ilker Berke, *Art Dir* Serpil Özdemir, *Ed* Ayhan Ergürsel, Muzaffer Özdemir, Selda Taskin and Derya Baser.
Tutya Film/Republic of Turkey, Ministry of Culture and Tourism etc.-Verve Pictures.
76 mins. Turkey. 2011. Rel: 5 Apr 2013. Cert. 12A.

Homefront ★★

Former drug enforcement agent Phil Broker (Jason Statham) moves with his daughter to an apparently peaceful small town in order to escape from his troubled past. But soon Broker is forced out of retirement when the local meth drug lord Gator (James Franco) begins to terrorise the town... There is nothing new in Sylvester Stallone's bottom-drawer script, especially under Gary Fleder's unimaginative direction. The best performance comes from Izabela Vidovic as Broker's feisty nine-year-old daughter. GS

❯ Jason Statham, James Franco, Izabela Vidovic, Winona Ryder, Kate Bosworth, Marcus Hester, Clancy Brown.
❯ *Dir* Gary Fleder, *Pro* Sylvester Stallone, Kevin King Templeton, John Thompson and Lee Weldon, *Screenplay* Stallone, based on the novel by Chuck Logan, *Ph* Theo van de Sande, *Pro Des* Greg Berry, *Ed* Padraic McKinley, *M* Mark Isham, *Cos* Kelli Jones.
Homefront Productions/Millennium Films/Mojo Films/Nu Image Films-Lionsgate.
100 mins. USA. 2013. Rel: 6 Dec 2013. Cert. 15.

Hors Satan ★★★½

Bruno Dumont's films never offer the audience an easy ride and this drama played out against the French countryside raises religious issues not easily fathomed. Superbly cast, the two central characters, a girl sexually abused by her stepfather and a male outsider who becomes her champion and companion, are figures in a landscape and the film's flow of images is wondrous. Yet the man, sometimes Christ-like and sometimes a lost soul capable of killing, typifies both the intriguing complexity of the film and its frustrating failure to make its point clearly. MS

❯ David Dewaele, Alexandra Lematre, Christophe Bon, Juliette Bacquet, Aurore Broutin.
❯ *Dir* and *Screenplay* Bruno Dumont, *Pro* Jean Bréhat, Rachid Bouchareb and Muriel Merlin, *Ph* Yves Cape, *Ed* Dumont and Basile Belkhiri, *Cos* Alexandra Charles.

3B Productions/Cinéimage 5/Canal+ etc.-New Wave Films.
110 mins. France/The Netherlands. 2011. Rel: 4 Jan 2013. Cert. 15.

The Host ★

Panned by critics and weak at the box-office, *The Host* has a host of problems that start with the ponderous, poorly written screenplay and flat direction by Andrew Niccol, struggling to adapt Stephenie (*Twilight*) Meyer's romantic sci-fi thriller novel. Her stale *Body Snatchers*-style idea is that the human race has been taken over by small parasitic aliens called Souls. There's plenty of fake-profound talk and the more serious *The Host* gets the more unintentionally funny it is. Alas, not funny enough to stop it from being tedious. In its favour, you have the capable performances of stars Saoirse Ronan as Wanderer and Diane Kruger as The Seeker, while Max Irons and Jake Abel provide some eye candy. DW

❯ Saoirse Ronan, Diane Kruger, Max Irons, Jake Abel, Rachel Roberts, Shyaam Karra, Brent Wendell Williams, Jalen Coleman.
❯ *Dir* and *Screenplay* Andrew Niccol, from the novel by Stephenie Meyer, *Pro* Meyer, Paula Mae Schwartz, Steve Schwartz and Nick Wechsler, *Ph* Roberto Schaefer, *Pro Des* Andy Nicholson, *Ed* Thomas J Nordberg, *M* Antonio Pinto, *Cos* Erin Benach.
Chockstone Pictures/Nick Wechsler Productions/Silver Reel-Entertainment Film Distributors.
125 mins. USA. 2013. Rel: 29 Mar 2013. Cert. 12A.

Hôtel Normandy ★★

Following the death of her husband, Alice (Héléna Noguerra) turns her back on romance. However, her friends have other ideas and ship her off to a luxurious resort where they pay a Lothario-for-rent to open her eyes and legs... Few people do romance with such élan and

Figures in a landscape: Alexandra Lematre and David Dewaele in Bruno Dumont's enigmatic *Hors Satan*.

War of the wold: Saoirse Ronan and Harley Bird hang out in the British wilderness in Kevin Macdonald's *How I Live Now*.

sophistication as the French, so it's a blistering disappointment that *Hôtel Normandy* is so bland and formulaic. Still, Noguerra brings a surprising credibility and comic skill to the proceedings – and more than a little sex appeal. CB

▶ Éric Elmosnino, Héléna Noguerra, Ary Abittan, Frédérique Bel, Anne Girouard, Annelise Hesme, Alice Belaidi, Jean-Marie Lamour.
▶ *Dir* Charles Nemes, *Pro* Alain Terzian, *Screenplay* Jean-Paul Bathany and Stéphanie Ben Lahcene, *Ph* Robert Alazraki, *Art Dir* Patrick Schmitt, *Ed* Véronique Parnet, *M* Jean-Claude Petit, *Cos* Ariane Daurat.
Alter Films/StudioCanal/Canal+/Ciné+/France 2 Cinéma/France Télévisions-StudioCanal.
97 mins. France. 2013. Rel: 6 June 2013. Cert. 12.

How I Live Now ★★★★

This undervalued piece from Kevin Macdonald stars the splendid Saoirse Ronan and is a work comparable to *The Boy in the Striped Pyjamas*, being first and foremost aimed at teenagers ready to take on board tales with serious issues. Here it's all about youngsters in England seeking to survive in a semi-futuristic world devastated by war. You might expect the ending to fail being either too escapist or alternatively just too downbeat but that trap is admirably avoided here. MS

▶ Saoirse Ronan, George MacKay, Tom Holland, Harley Bird, Anna Chancellor.
▶ *Dir* Kevin Macdonald, *Pro* Andrew Ruhemann, John Battsek, Charles Steel and Alasdair Flind, *Screenplay* Jeremy Brock, Penelope Skinner and Tony Grisoni, from the novel by Meg Rosoff,

Ph Franz Lustig, *Pro Des* Jacqueline Abrahams, *Ed* Jinx Godfrey, *M* Jon Hopkins, *Cos* Jane Petrie.
Film4/BFI/a Cowboy Films and Passion Pictures production/Protagonist Pictures etc.-E1 Films.
101 mins. UK/Canada. 2013. Rel: 4 Oct 2013. Cert. 15.

How to Make Money Selling Drugs ★★★

Very well made though this film is, I find it obnoxious since much of it comes across as a perfect commercial to encourage drug taking. Then, instead of making a case for legalising drugs, it offers a volte-face by condemning what, consciously or not, it has been promoting. Given how easily impressionable young viewers could be, the film's initial approach seems to me to be decidedly dangerous. For a serious and responsible take on this subject which allows you to think for yourself turn instead to *The House I Live In* (2012). MS

▶ With Barry Cooper, John E Harriel Jr, Bobby Carlton, Brian O'Dea, Eminem, 50 Cent. Narrated by Matthew Cooke.
▶ *Dir* and *Ph* Matthew Cooke, *Pro* Bert Marcus and Adrian Grenier, *Ed* Cooke and Jeff Cowan, *M* Spencer Nezey.
Bert Marcus Productions/Reckless Productions-Vertigo Films.
91 mins. USA. 2012. Rel: 26 Dec 2013. Cert. 18.

How to Survive a Plague ★★★½

This acclaimed and deeply sincere documentary concentrates on New York in the 1980s and 1990s and deals with brave activists who challenged the authorities and the drug companies who responded so inadequately to the AIDS crisis. One feels insensitive in not praising this able enough film more highly given its subject matter, but as a critic I have to declare that I found *We Were Here* (2011), a somewhat comparable work from San Francisco, by far the more moving film and the better piece of cinema too. MS

▶ With Peter Staley, Bob Rafsky, Larry Kramer, Ray Navarro, Ann Northrop.
▶ *Dir* David France, *Pro* Howard Gertler and France, *Written by* France, T Woody Richman and Tyler Walk, *Ph* Derek Wiesehahn, *Ed* Richman and Walk, *M* Stuart Bogie and Luke O'Malley.

Ninety Thousands Words/a France/Tomchin Film/Ford Foundation/JustFilms etc.-Dartmouth Films.
110 mins. USA/UK. 2012. Rel: 8 Nov 2013. Cert. 15.

Hummingbird ★★★★

This London-based thriller finds the writer Steven Knight making his directorial debut. Perhaps more importantly it enables Jason Statham and newcomer Agata Buzek to illustrate how strong performances can aid material that is often contrived. The story concerns a deserter traumatised by experiences in Vietnam that have nevertheless made him into a killing machine and shows the effect of his encounters with a Polish nun working in a soup kitchen. Accept the improbabilities and you get also London photographed by Chris Menges and a convincing view of the city's many faces. MS

▶ Jason Statham, Agata Buzek, Vicky McClure, Benedict Wong, Ger Ryan, Danny Webb.
▶ *Dir* and *Screenplay* Steven Knight, *Pro* Paul Webster and Guy Heeley, *Ph* Chris Menges, *Pro Des* Michael Carlin, *Ed* Valerio Bonelli, *M* Dario Marianelli, *Cos* Louise Stjernsward.

IM Global/a Shoeboxfilms production-Lionsgate UK.
100 mins. UK/USA. 2012. Rel: 28 June 2013. Cert. 15.

The Hunger Games: Catching Fire ★★★½

After winning the Games, Katniss (Jennifer Lawrence) and Peeta (Josh Hutcherson) return home triumphant but almost immediately must embark on a Victors Tour of the districts. Meanwhile President Snow (Donald Sutherland) is preparing for the 75th Annual Hunger Games (The Quarter Quell), despite the fact that there is more than a whiff of rebellion in the air... It takes a while to get going but, once the games start, this is great fun. Director Francis Lawrence keeps the action flowing, complemented by strong production values. GS

▶ Jennifer Lawrence, Liam Hemsworth, Jack Quaid, Taylor St Clair, Sandra Ellis Lafferty, Woody Harrelson, Josh Hutcherson, Donald Sutherland, Stanley Tucci, Lenny Kravitz, Philip Seymour Hoffman, Toby Jones.
▶ *Dir* Francis Lawrence, *Pro* Nina Jacobson and Jon Kilik, *Screenplay* Simon Beaufoy and Michael Arnt, based on Suzanne Collins' novel *Catching Fire*, *Ph* Jo Willems, *Pro Des* Philip Messina, *Ed* Alan Edward Bell, *M* James Newton Howard, *Cos* Trish Summerville.

Lionsgate/Color Force-Lionsgate.
146 mins. USA. 2013. Rel: 21 Nov 2013. Cert. 12A.

Hyde Park on Hudson ★★½

The title refers to Franklin D Roosevelt's country residence and shows a visit in 1939 to FDR (Bill Murray) by George VI (Samuel West) and Queen Elizabeth (Olivia Colman), who there encountered both the president's wife (Olivia Williams) and his most significant mistress, his cousin Daisy (Laura Linney). It's a great cast and there may have been hopes of duplicating the success of *The King's Speech*, but Richard Nelson's screenplay is tepid. It emerges only as a little ado about nothing, feeble in its comedy and superficial in its drama. MS

▶ Bill Murray, Laura Linney, Samuel West, Olivia Colman, Olivia Williams, Elizabeth Marvel, Elizabeth Wilson, Eleanor Bron.
▶ *Dir* Roger Michell, *Pro* Kevin Loader, Michell and David Aukin, *Screenplay* Richard Nelson, *Ph* Lol Crawley, *Pro Des* Simon Bowles, *Ed* Nicolas Gaster, *M* Jeremy Sams, *Cos* Dinah Collin.

Focus Features/Film4/a Free Range Film/Daybreak Pictures production etc.-Universal.
95 mins. USA/UK. 2012. Rel: 1 Feb 2013. Cert. 12A.

I Am Breathing ★★★½

Neil Platt lived for less than 40 years, dying of motor neurone disease in 2009. This documentary record of the last months of his life is sensitively presented and a tribute both to him and to his family. It also looks back over his life but, inevitably, it's a tough watch and not

Marching orders: Woody Harrelson, Josh Hutcherson and Jennifer Lawrence in Francis Lawrence's *The Hunger Games: Catching Fire*, the highest-grossing film of 2013 in the US.

for everybody. It will doubtless be welcomed by the families of other sufferers and it supports the need for research funds in this area. MS

▶ With Neil Platt, Louise Platt.
▶ *Dir* Emma Davie and Morag McKinnon, *Pro* Sonja Henrici, *Ph* Davie, *Ed* Peter Winther, *M* Kieran Hebden and Jim Sutherland.

SDI Productions/Scottish Documentary Institute/ Danish Documentary Production etc.-Scottish Documentary Institute.
72 mins. UK/Denmark/Finland. 2012. Rel: 21 June 2013. Cert. 12A.

I Am Nasrine ★★★

A fresh perspective on multicultural Britain is always welcome and Tina Gharavi's first feature is refreshingly authentic. Opening on the streets of Tehran in May of 2001, it places Nasrine squarely in the narrative when she is stopped by police and told to re-position her headscarf. Not long afterwards she is raped by a police officer... As Nasrine, Micsha Sadeghi is a totally believable presence and is indistinguishable from any Middle Eastern girl one might encounter on the streets of Britain. And, in its own way, this modest, low-budget feature is a humane and touching work that deserved a much wider release than it received. JC-W

▶ Micsha Sadeghi, Shiraz Haq, Christian Coulson, Steven Hooper, Nichole Hall.
▶ *Dir* and *Screenplay* Tina Gharavi, *Pro* James Richard Baillie, *Ph* David Raedeker, *Pro Des* Chryssanthy Kofidou, *Ed* Lesley Walker and Lucia Zucchetti, *M* Kamal Kamruddin and Benjamin McAvoy (Wave Media Prods), *Cos* Rachel McWha.

Bridge + Tunnel Productions/Northstar Ventures-Bridge + Tunnel Productions.
93 mins. UK. 2012. Rel: 17 June 2013. Cert. 15.

I Give It a Year ★★★

This British romcom has every appearance of being spot-on while lacking a vital element, the courage of its own convictions. It can't make up its mind whether it's a straightforward romcom or a French farce or indeed a serious commentary on young love and marriage. Falling between too many stools, it details the whirlwind romance of writer Josh (Rafe Spall) and ad agency exec Nat (Rose Byrne). Straight after the wedding, cracks appear in their relationship and they seek counselling. The leads acquit themselves with dignity and the supporting cast of familiar British faces back them up well, but director Dan Mazer's farcical screenplay is all over the place and rarely gets to the real heart of the matter. MHD

▶ Rose Byrne, Anna Faris, Rafe Spall, Simon Baker, Alex Macqueen, Stephen Merchant, Jane Asher, Terence Harvey, Minnie Driver, Jason Flemyng, Nigel Planer, Clare Higgins, Olivia Colman.
▶ *Dir* and *Screenplay* Dan Mazer, *Pro* Tim Bevan, Eric Fellner and Kris Thykier, *Ph* Ben Davis, *Pro Des* Simon Elliott, *Ed* Tony Cranstoun, *M* Ilan Eskeri, *Cos* Charlotte Walker.

StudioCanal/Paradis Films/Anton Capital Entertainment/Starcrossed Films/TFI Films Production/ Canal+/Ciné+/LOVEFILM/Working Title etc-StudioCanal.
97 mins. UK. 2013. Rel: 8 Feb 2013. Cert. 15.

I Want Your Love ★★★★

This short feature shot in San Francisco by gay director Travis Mathews was banned in Australia and it is less a story piece than a direct study of sexual relationships. What removes it from porn is the emotional truth conveyed in its highly explicit consensual sex scenes expressive of the caring and consideration involved. Porn is uninterested in feelings, but feelings are central here. MS

▶ Jesse Metzger, Ben Jasper, Keith McDonald, Ferrin Solano, Wayne Bumb, Brontez Purnell.
▶ *Dir*, *Screenplay* and *Ed* Travis Mathews, *Pro* Jack Shamama and Mathews, *Ph* Keith Wilson, *Pro Des* Jacquelyn Scott.

Naked Sword/Gduroy/Tim Valenti/Jason Buchtel/a Jack Shamama production-Peccadillo Pictures Ltd.
71 mins. USA. 2012. Rel: 28 June 2013. Cert. 18.

I Wish ★★★

If Kore-eda's splendid 2008 feature *Still Walking* was Ozu-like, this is even more so. It's about two brothers not yet in their teens living apart due to the divorce of their parents and it reminds one of the boys in Ozu's silent masterpiece of 1932, *I Was Born, But...* However the engaging children (real-life brothers) are not on that level and the fairytale notion of wishes coming true when two bullet trains pass each other is an over-stretched whimsy. (Original title: *Kiseki*) MS

▶ Maeda Koki, Maeda Oshiro, Hayashi Ryoga, Nagayoshi Seinosuke, Uchida Kyara.

Sex seen: Ben Jasper and Jesse Metzger in Travis Mathews' *I Want Your Love*.

▶ *Dir*, *Screenplay* and *Ed* Kore-eda Hirokazu,
Pro Koike Kentaro and Taguchi Hijiri, *Ph* Yamazaki
Yutaka, *Art Dir* Matsuo Ayako, *M* Quruli, *Cos*
Kobayashi Miwako.

Shirogumi Inc./Bigx-Arrow Films.
128 mins. Japan. 2011. Rel: 8 Feb 2013. Cert. PG.

The Iceman ★★★★

This underrated crime thriller which evokes
thoughts of Scorsese's work is genuinely shocking
in its telling of the true story of a contract killer.
As portayed by Michael Shannon, he is both a
ruthless criminal and a surprisingly caring family
man. It's not an edifying tale, but both acting
and direction give it intensity and drive and
there is no sense of the audience being invited to
lap up the violence. MS

▶ Michael Shannon, Winona Ryder, James Franco,
Ray Liotta, Chris Evans.
▶ *Dir* Ariel Vromen, *Pro* Avi Lerner, Vromen and
Ehud Bleiberg, *Screenplay* Morgan Land and
Vromen, based on *The Iceman: The True Story of
a Cold Blooded Killer* by Anthony Bruno and the
documentary *The Iceman Tapes: Conversations with
a Killer* by James Thebaut, *Ph* Bobby Bukowski,
Pro Des Nathan Amondson, *Ed* Danny Rafic, *M* Haim
Mazar, *Cos* Donna Zakowska.

**A Millennium Films presentation/an Ehud Bleiberg/Nu
Image production-Lionsgate UK.**
106 mins. USA. 2012. Rel: 7 June 2013. Cert. 15.

Identity Thief ★½

There is a film to be made about identity theft.
But this is not it. Once the premise has been
set up for Sandy Patterson (Jason Bateman) to
fly from Colorado to Florida to apprehend the
woman (Melissa McCarthy) who has drained his
family's bank account, the movie switches into a
mismatched buddy road movie. This is the sort
of witless farce in which consumerism is given
its own platform, in which precious objects are
destroyed in the name of humour. This is not
funny. Then to redeem the obnoxious character
played by McCarthy in a sentimental coda is just
cloying and weak. JC-W

▶ Jason Bateman, Melissa McCarthy, Jon Favreau,
Amanda Peet, Tip 'TI' Harris, Morris Chestnut,
Genesis Rodriguez, Jonathan Banks, John Cho,
Robert Patrick, Maggie Elizabeth Jones.
▶ *Dir* Seth Gordon, *Pro* Scott Stuber and
Pamela Abdy, *Screenplay* Craig Mazin, *Ph* Javier
Aguirresarobe, *Pro Des* Shepherd Frankel, *Ed* Peter
Teschner, *M* Christopher Lennertz, *Cos* Carol Ramsey.

**Aggregate Films/DumbDumb/Stuber Productions-
Universal Pictures.**
111 mins. USA. 2013. Rel: 22 Mar 2013. Cert. 15.

I'm So Excited! ★★★

Generally dismissed as a sub-standard work for
Pedro Almodóvar, it's worth recording that when
I saw it at an early press show there was much

Plane sailing:
Carlos Areces,
Raúl Arévalo and
Javier Cámara in
Pedro Almodóvar's
I'm So Excited!

Russian roulette:
Vladimir Svirski
and Vlad
Abashin in Sergei
Loznitsa's bleak
In the Fog.

laughter. Well designed, it finds Almodóvar aiming low with a camp tale which, being wholly artificial, can seek fun from a situation in which passengers are trapped on a plane that's likely to disintegrate if it tries to land. Replete with sex jokes, the film may well engage those who normally bypass foreign language films but relish Hollywood's cruder comedies. (Original title: *Los amantes pasajeros*) MS

▶ Antonio de la Torre, Hugo Silva, Javier Cámara, Cecilia Roth, Lola Dueñas, Antonio Banderas, Penélope Cruz.
▶ *Dir* and *Screenplay* Pedro Almodóvar, *Pro* Agustín Almodóvar and Esther García, *Ph* José Luis Alcaine, *Art Dir* Antxón Gómez, *Ed* José Salcedo, *M* Alberto Iglesias, *Cos* Tatiana Hernández.
El Deseo/Blue Lake Media Fund/FilmNation Entertainment etc.-Pathé Productions. 90 mins. Spain/USA. 2013. Rel: 3 May 2013. Cert. 15.

The Impossible ★★★½

This tells the real-life story of a family who, caught up in the 2004 tsunami in Thailand, survived that tragedy. It is superbly acted both by the adult players and by the youngsters in the cast and much of the recreation of the event is brilliant and horrifyingly convincing. But, against that, the film becomes pure Hollywood in its determination to manipulate the emotions. That's an approach which, apart from yielding some highly contrived scenes, cheapens what it touches. MS

▶ Naomi Watts, Ewan McGregor, Tom Holland, Samuel Joslin, Oaklee Pendergast, Geraldine Chaplin.
▶ *Dir* Juan Antonio Bayona, *Pro* Belén Atienza,

Álvaro Augustin, Enrique López-Lavigne and Ghislain Barrois, *Screenplay* Sergio G Sánchez, from a storyline by Mariá Belón, *Ph* Oscar Faura, *Pro Des* Eugenio Caballero, *Ed* Elena Ruíz and Bernat Vilaplana, *M* Fernando Velázquez, *Cos* Sparka Lee Hall, Anna Bingemann and Maria Reyes.
Summit Entertainment/Mediaset España/an Apaches Entertainment, Telecinco Cinema production etc.-E1 Films. 114 mins. Spain. 2012. Rel: 1 Jan 2013. Cert. 12A.

In a World... ★★½

The real star of this low-budget, rather esoteric sitcom is the director, writer and producer Lake Bell. A vehicle for her own talents as a comedian, the film establishes Ms Bell as a member of that rare breed of performer: an actress who is both sexy and funny. Set in the Hollywood world of voice-over rivalry, *In a World...* is a tad limited in its filmic proportions – it feels like an extended TV sitcom – but has enough goofiness and wit to keep one smiling throughout. JC-W

▶ Lake Bell, Fred Melamed, Demetri Martin, Michaela Watkins, Rob Corddry, Nick Offerman, Geena Davis, Eva Longoria, Talulah Riley, Cameron Diaz.
▶ *Dir* and *Screenplay* Lake Bell, *Pro* Bell, Eddie Vaisman, Jett Steiger and Mark Roberts, *Ph* Seamus Tierney, *Pro Des* Megan Fenton, *Ed* Tom McArdle, *M* Ryan Miller, *Cos* Lindy McMichael.
3311 Productions/In A World/Team G-Sony Pictures. 92 mins. USA. 2013. Rel: 13 Sep 2013. Cert. 15.

In Fear ★★★½

The first date for young couple Tom and Lucy (Iain De Caestecker and Alice Englert) is a trip to a music festival in a remote Scottish location. The plan is to drive there and stay at a countryside hotel but their journey soon turns into a nightmare... This is an impressive debut from Jeremy Lovering, whose assured direction creates enough tension and suspense to keep us engrossed till the end, despite the rather unconvincing finale. GS

▶ Ian De Caestecker, Allen Leech, Alice Englert.
▶ *Dir* and *Screenplay* Jeremy Lovering, *Pro* James Biddle and Nira Park, *Ph* David Katznelson, *Pro Des* Jeff Sherriff, *Ed* Jonathan Amos, *M* Daniel Pemberton and Roly Porter, *Cos* Rosa Dias.
Big Talk Productions-StudioCanal.
85 mins. UK. 2013. Rel: 15 Nov 2013. Cert. 15.

In the Fog ★★★★

Magnificently shot by the Romanian photographer Oleg Mutu, this is an astonishingly bleak work of art set in 1942 when the western frontiers of the USSR were occupied by the Germans. It centres on a Russian falsely assumed to have betrayed his comrades but contrasts his attitude with that of two other men while showing how all three of them are in effect prisoners of the war which controls their lives. It's a triumph for writer-director Sergei Loznitsa but a challenge for audiences who look for some ray of hope. (Original title: *V tumane*). MS

▶ Vladimir Svirski, Vlad Abashin, Sergei Kolesov, Nikita Peremotovs, Julia Peresild.
▶ *Dir* and *Screenplay* (based on Vasil Bykov's novel) Sergei Loznitsa, *Pro* Heino Deckert, *Ph* Oleg Mutu, *Pro Des* Kiril Shuvalov, *Ed* Danielius Kokanauskis, *Cos* Dorota Roqueplo.
Ma.ja.de fiction/GP Cinema Company/Rija Films/ Lemming Film/Belarusfilm etc.-New Wave Films.
128 mins. Germany/Russia/Latvia/The Netherlands/ Belarus. 2012. Rel: 26 Apr 2013. Cert. 12A.

In the House ★★★½

Boasting an excellent cast including Kristin Scott Thomas, this François Ozon film is his own adaptation of a stage play although that origin is skilfully hidden. A teacher (Fabrice Luchini) encourages a teenage student (Ernst Umhauer) to write and what the pupil writes is illustrated on screen. It influences the lives of those around him and, this being a post-modern comedy, what we see may be true or imagined. The film is clever but ultimately overplays its hand: it's too unreal to be touching if that is, indeed, the ultimate intention. (Original title: *Dans la maison*) MS

▶ Fabrice Luchini, Kristin Scott Thomas, Ernst Umhauer, Emmanuelle Seigner.
▶ *Dir* and *Screenplay* (freely adapted from the play *El chico de la última fila* by Juan Mayorga) François Ozon, *Pro* Eric and Nicolas Altmayer, *Ph* Jérôme Almeras, *Art Dir* Arnaud de Moleron, *Ed* Laure

Gardette, *M* Philippe Rombi, *Cos* Pascaline Chavanne.
Mandarin Cinéma/Mars Films/France 2 Cinéma/Foz/ Canal+ etc.-Momentum Pictures.
105 mins. France. 2012. Rel: 29 Mar 2013. Cert. 15.

In the Name of... ★★★★

This striking film from Poland is a brave enterprise, as director and co-writer Malgoska Szumowska approaches with great sympathy the story of a gay priest struggling with his sexuality but eventually going to bed with a young man. The story-telling could sometimes be clearer, but this well-acted drama, rather than dealing with the topical theme of paedophile priests, chooses instead to tell with approval a quite different story, one which may help to challenge attitudes to homosexuality in Poland. (Original title: *W imie...*) MS

▶ Andrzej Chyra, Mateusz Kosciukiewicz, Maja Ostaszewska, Lukasz Simlat.
▶ *Dir* Malgoska Szumowska, *Pro* Agnieszka Kurzydlo, *Screenplay* Szumowska and Michal Englert, *Ph* Englert, *Pro Des* Marek Zawierucha, *Ed* Jaciek Drosio, *M* Pawel Mykietyn and Adam Walicki, *Cos* Katarzyna Lewinska and Julia Jazra-Brataniec.
A Mental Disorder 4 production/Zentropa International Poland/Canal+ etc.- Peccadillo Pictures Ltd.
102 mins. Poland/France. 2013. Rel: 27 Sep 2013. Cert. 15.

The Incredible Burt Wonderstone ★★★★

Magician Burt Wonderstone (a comically weird Steve Carell) and his stage partner Anton Marvelton (a weirdly comic Steve Buscemi) were, in their heyday, the bee's knees in Vegas, and nobody could touch them. Now the act is old-fashioned and needs spicing up if they are to compete with the latest sensation: one Steve Gray (horribly funny Jim Carrey), an outrageous street magician who does the most incredible

Happening in Vegas: Steve Carell in Don Scardino's *The Incredible Burt Wonderstone.*

stunts. Seeking the advice of Rance Holloway (Alan Arkin at his brilliant best), a seasoned old pro magician, they plan the trick to end all tricks. Don Scardino keeps this cheerful comedy afloat and the leads all turn in cherishable performances. A nice surprise. MHD

▶ Steve Carell, Steve Buscemi, Olivia Wilde, Jim Carrey, James Gandolfini, Alan Arkin, Jay Mohr, David Copperfield.
▶ *Dir* Don Scardino, *Pro* Carell, Chris Bender, Taylor Mitchell and Jake Weiner, *Screenplay* Jonathan Goldstein and John Frances Daley, from a story by Goldstein, Daley, Mitchell and Chad Kiltgen, *Ph* Matthew Clark, *Pro Des* Keith P. Cunningham, *Ed* Lee Haxall, *M* Lyle Workman, *Cos* Dayna Pink.

New Line Cinema/Benderspink/Carousel Productions-Warner Bros.
100 mins. USA. 2013. Rel: 15 Mar 2013. Cert. 15.

InRealLife ★★★½

Beeban Kidron's documentary takes on the challenge of reflecting on the life-changing effect of the internet. Users and experts comment and the downside, including bullying and the easy availability of porn, is represented, but elsewhere the film's viewpoint is more positive. But as a result of squeezing everything into one film this suggests a useful introduction to be screened before a seminar rather than an effective investigation in its own right. MS

▶ *Dir* Beeban Kidron, *Pro* Freya Sampson and Kidron, *Ph* Neil Harvey, *Ed* David Charap.

Heavy metal: Robert Downey Jr and Gwyneth Paltrow in Shane Black's *Iron Man 3*.

Sky/BFI/a Cross Street Films and Studio Lambert production/BFI's Film Fund-Dogwoof.
89 mins. UK. 2013. Rel: 20 Sep 2013. Cert. 15.

Insidious: Chapter 2 ★★★½

Insidious 2 assembles all the familiar clichés of the horror genre: creaking hinges, muffled voices, slamming doors, the image in the mirror and that old favourite, the piano that plays itself. But director James Wan knows of what he tweaks and here he creates a sense of genuine unease within the parameters of the first film's otherworldly logic. He sets up the atmosphere with sphincter-flinching finesse and then blows the mind with a scenario that no amount of WD-40 can fix. As a piece of effective horror and 'entertainment,' *Chapter 2* sets itself up nicely for a future terrace of haunted real estate. JC-W

▶ Patrick Wilson, Rose Byrne, Ty Simpkins, Lin Shaye, Barbara Hershey.
▶ *Dir* James Wan, *Pro* Jason Blum and Oren Peli, *Screenplay* Leigh Whannell, *Ph* John R Leonetti, *Pro Des* Jennifer Spence, *Ed* Kirk M Morri, *M* Joseph Bishara, *Cos* Kristin M Burke.

FilmDistrict/Stage 6 Films/Entertainment One-E1 Films.
105 mins. USA/Canada. 2013. Rel: 13 Sep 2013. Cert. 15.

The Internship ★

The chemistry between Owen Wilson and Vince Vaughn is as effortless as ever but they need a much better script than this. Shawn Levy directed the duo with more success in *Wedding Crashers* – here they play two out-of-work salesmen who have to compete for a job at Google against a plethora of young interns. The scenario never rings true while Levy's lazy direction encourages his actors to almost sleepwalk through the action. GS

▶ Vince Vaughn, Owen Wilson, Rose Byrne, Aasif Mandvi, Max Minghella, Josh Brener, Dylan O'Brien.
▶ *Dir* Shawn Levy, *Pro* Vaughn and Levy, *Screenplay* Vince Vaughn and Jared Stern, from a story by Vaughn, *Ph* Jonathan Brown, *Pro Des* Tom Meyer, *Ed* Dean Zimmerman, *M* Christophe Beck, *Cos* Leesa Evans.

20th Century Fox/Regency Enterprises/Wild West Picture Show/21 Laps/Dune Entertainment-20th Century Fox.
110 mins. USA. 2013. Rel: 4 July 2013. Cert. 12A.

Les Invisibles ★★★

Laudable in intent, this prizewinning documentary by Sébastien Lifshitz features 11 people, now elderly gays and lesbians, whose sexuality has shaped their lives. To give them a voice is fine but the film lasts almost two hours and personally I was disappointed by its shapelessness and its failure to put telling questions to the interviewees so that their comments would be truly revealing

The daily sketch:
Don Hertzfeldt's
*It's Such a
Beautiful Day.*

of their experiences and attitudes. The people are interesting but the project could – and should – have yielded so much more. MS

❧ With Pierrot, Thérèse, Christian, Monique, Pierre, Yann, Catherine, Elisabeth, Bernard and Jacques.
❧ *Dir* Sébastien Lifshitz, *Pro* Bruno Nahon, *Ph* Antoine Parouty, *Ed* Tina Baz and Pauline Gaillard.
Zadig Films/Rhône-Alpes Cinéma/Sylicone/CNC/ Cinemage 6 etc.-Peccadillo Pictures Ltd.
115 mins. France. 2012. Rel: 12 July 2013. Cert. 15.

Iron Man 3 ★★★★

Budget: $200 million. With that sort of money at stake you better cover your bottom line. And *Iron Man 3* does so in spades. There's a chilling plot ripped from tomorrow's headlines (genetic terrorism), loads of snappy dialogue, superlative CGI, an informed imagination, plenty of surprises and a catalogue of in-jokes (*Downton Abbey* fans unite!). And holding it all together is the flip insouciance of Robert Downey Jr, as if he were delivering an intimate dialogue to a crowd of mates at some small, late-night comedy club. In short, this is superior popcorn that only flags near the end (when the special effects lose their effect through repetition). JC-W

❧ Robert Downey Jr, Gwyneth Paltrow, Don Cheadle, Guy Pearce, Ben Kingsley, Rebecca Hall, Jon Favreau, Paul Bettany (voice only), William Sadler, James Badge Dale, Miguel Ferrer, Shaun Toub, Mark Ruffalo.
❧ *Dir* Shane Black, *Pro* Kevin Feige, *Screenplay* Black and Drew Pearce, *Ph* John Toll, *Pro Des* Bill Brzeski,

Ed Jeffrey Ford and Peter S Elliot, *M* Brian Tyler, *Cos* Louise Frogley.
Marvel Studios/Paramount Pictures/DMG Entertainment-Walt Disney Studios Motion Pictures.
130 mins. USA. 2013. Rel: 25 Apr 2013. Cert. 12A.

It's a Lot ★

When Shawn (Femi Oyeniran) realises he doesn't fit into his privileged background he secretly enrols at his cousin's college. He's very keen to impress the girls so he soon organises a party at his parents' mansion while they're away on holiday... Leading actor Oyeniran lacks conviction and charm and is not helped by the fact that he is surrounded by loud and unconvincing performances. He has also co-written and co-directed this lame and unfunny comedy. GS

❧ Femi Oyeniran, Red Madrell, Roxy Sternberg, Jazzie Zonzolo, Charley Palmer Merkell, Miles McDonald, Jack Doolan.
❧ *Dir* Darwood Grace and Femi Oyeniran, *Pro* Dean Fisher, *Screenplay* Oyeniran and Nick Walker, *Ph* Richard Swingle, *Pro Des* Niina Topp, *Ed* Emanuele Giraldo, *Cos* Janine Jauvel.
Scanner-Rhodes Productions/Mirror Image-Kaleidoscope Film Distribution.
96 mins. UK. 2013. Rel: 25 Oct 2013. Cert. 15.

It's Such a Beautiful Day ★★★★½

Don Hertzfeldt is arguably the most original animator alive. For *It's Such a Beautiful Day* he has combined three of his short films, *Everything Will*

Be Okay (2006), *I Am So Proud of You* (2008) and *It's a Beautiful Day* (2012) into one. The titles are ironic, as in most lives everything is not okay, there may not be anybody who's proud of you and is it really ever a beautiful day? His hero Bill, drawn simply as an animated stickman against live-action backgrounds, trudges through life encountering its many problems, and it's only when he learns that he may be terminally ill that he appreciates the world around him. Simple but heart-warming, this is film-making of a high order. PL

▶ Narrated by Don Hertzfeldt.
▶ *Dir, Pro, Ph* and *Screenplay* Don Hertzfeldt, *Ed* Brian Hamblin.

Bitter Films-ICA Films.
62 mins. USA. 2012. Rel: 3 May 2013. No Cert.

Jack the Giant Slayer ★★★★

The vast canon of fairy tale literature is plundered again in this truly outsize (price tag: $195 million) retelling of the old pantomime favourite. But before one groans too loudly, this is a film from the writer (Christopher McQuarrie) and director (Bryan Singer) of *The Usual Suspects.* Even so, there's no cynicism here – just the larger-than-life realisation of an extraordinary tale pumped with lashings of action and humour. The visuals are truly stunning – it's like an animated epic come to life – and terms like 'rollicking,' 'rip-roaring' and 'awesome' do spring to mind. It's one helluva ride. JC-W

▶ Nicholas Hoult, Eleanor Tomlinson, Stanley Tucci, Ian McShane, Bill Nighy, Ewan McGregor, Eddie Marsan, Ewen Bremner, Ralph Brown, Christopher Fairbank, Warwick Davis, Ben Daniels.
▶ *Dir* Bryan Singer, *Pro* Singer, Neal H Moritz, David Dobkin, Patrick McCormick and Ori Marmur, *Screenplay* Darren Lemke, Christopher McQuarrie and Dan Studney, *Ph* Newton Thomas Sigel, *Pro Des* Gavin Bocquet, *Ed* John Ottman and Bob Ducsay, *M* Ottman, *Cos* Joanna Johnston.

Full of beans: Nicholas Hoult ascends the heights in Bryan Singer's rip-roaring *Jack the Giant Slayer.*

New Line Cinema/Legendary Pictures/Original Film-Warner Bros.
113 mins. USA. 2013. Rel: 22 Mar 2013. 12A.

Jackass Presents: Bad Grandpa ★★★★

The 86-year-old Irving (Johnny Knoxville) begins a long journey across America along with his eight-year-old grandson Billy (Jackson Nicoll). The mission is to deliver Billy back to his father but first Grandpa must introduce Billy to a world of bizarre situations and pranks ...This candid camera movie from the Jackass team is inevitably grotesque but is also very funny thanks to the winning chemistry between the two protagonists. However, it's the young Nicoll who threatens to steal the film from under the nose (and Oscar-nominated make-up) of Knoxville. GS

▶ Johnny Knoxville, Jackson Nicoll, Greg Harris, Georgina Cates, Kamber Hejlik, Jill Kill, Madison Davis, George Faughnan, Spike Jonze.
▶ *Dir* Jeff Tremaine, *Pro* Knoxville, Jonze, Tremaine and Derek Freda, *Screenplay* Tremaine, Johnny Knoxville and Spike Jonze, from a story by Knoxville, Jonze, Tremaine, Fax Bahr and Adam Small, *Ph* Dimitry Elyashkevich and Lance Bangs, *Art Dir* JP Blackmon, *Ed* Seth Casriel, Matt Kosinski and Matthew Probst, *M* Kool G Murder and Sam Spiegel, *Cos* Lindsay Kear.

Dickhouse Productions/MTV Films-Paramount Pictures.
92 mins. USA. 2013. Rel: 23 Oct 2013. Cert. 15.

Jadoo ★★★

Even though Amit Gupta's charming comedy was initially written as a radio play, it effortlessly transfers to the big screen. Brothers Raja (Harish Patel) and Jagi (Kulvinder Ghir), both talented chefs, used to be partners but are now rivals, with each running his own Indian restaurant opposite the other in Leicester. But Raja's daughter Shalini (Amara Karan) is determined to bring them back together... It's a sweet but predictable film featuring mouth-watering recipes. See it, but make sure you eat first! GS

▶ Harish Patel, Kulvinder Ghir, Tom Mison, Amara Karan, Ray Panthaki, Adeel Akhtar, Madhur Jaffrey.
▶ *Dir* and *Screenplay* Amit Gupta, *Pro* Nikki Parrott, Amanda Faber, Richard Holmes and Isabelle Georgeaux, *Ph* Roger Pratt, *Pro Des* Adrian Smith, *Ed* Eddie Hamilton, *M* Stephen Warbeck, *Cos* Nigel Egerton.

AIR Productions/Tigerlily Films-Intandem Films.
84 mins. UK. 2013. Rel: 8 Sep 2013. Cert. 12.

Jeune et Jolie ★★★★★

Superbly directed, this work from François Ozon ends with an intriguingly ambiguous scene but

strikes me as a brilliantly realised portrayal of our oversexualised society which has lost any sense of providing a moral compass for the young. Ozon himself might query my view of his story about a teenage girl (the excellent Marine Vacth) who, indulging in prostitution, unexpectedly stumbles on her only sexual encounter with true human feeling. At the very least this is a striking work to see and discuss. MS

▶ Marine Vacth, Géraldine Pailhas, Frédéric Pierrot, Johan Leysen, Charlotte Rampling.
▶ *Dir* and *Screenplay* François Ozon, *Pro* Eric and Nicolas Altmayer, *Ph* Pascal Marti, *Pro Des* Katia Wyszkop, *Ed* Laure Gardette, *M* Philippe Rombi, *Cos* Pascaline Chavanne.

Mandarin Cinéma/Mars Films/France 2 Cinéma/Canal+ etc.-Lionsgate UK.
94 mins. France. 2013. Rel: 29 Nov 2013. Cert. 18.

Jiro Dreams of Sushi ★★★★

An American, David Gelb, went to Tokyo to film this documentary study of 85-year-old Ono Jiro and his sushi restaurant. Situated in a subway and seating only ten, it nevertheless earned three stars in the Michelin guide. The film is a fascinating portrait not just of this establishment but also of a family, including the different responses of Jiro's two sons to a father whose self-evident love of what he does means that he is still the boss man, keeping any successor waiting. MS

▶ With Ono Jiro, Takahashi Harutaki, Yamamoto Masuhiro, Nakazama Daisuke.
▶ *Dir* and *Ph* David Gelb, *Pro* Kevin Iwashina, Tom Pellegrini and Gelb, *Ed* Brandon Driscoll-Luttringer.

Fortissimofilms/City Room Media/a Weaver/Pellegrini, Preferred Content production etc.-Soda Pictures.
82 mins. USA. 2011. Rel: 11 Jan 2013. Cert. U.

Jurassic Park 3D IMAX ★★★★½

Steven Spielberg's spectacular dinosaur adventure celebrates its 20th anniversary and looks absolutely splendid in 3D and IMAX. This exciting and deeply atmospheric epic needs no introduction and is very much worth re-discovering without any of the hype that upstaged its initial release. Miraculously it hasn't dated at all and the performances are perfectly pitched. But inevitably it's the dinosaurs that rule. GS

▶ Sam Neill, Laura Dern, Jeff Goldblum, Richard Attenborough, Bob Peck, Martin Ferrero, Joseph Mazzello, Samuel L. Jackson,
▶ *Dir* Steven Spielberg, *Pro* Kathleen Kennedy and Gerald R Molen, *Screenplay* Michael Crichton and David Koepp, from the novel by Crichton, *Ph* Dean Cundey, *Pro Des* Rick Carter, *Ed* Michael Kahn, *M* John Williams, *Cos* Mitchell Ray Kenney and Kelly Porter, *Special Effects* Stan Winston Studio etc.

Universal Pictures/Amblin Entertainment-Universal Pictures.
127 mins. USA. 1993. Rel: 16 July 1913.
Re-released in 3D: 23 Aug 2013. Cert. PG.

Emotional currency: Johan Leysen and Marine Vacth in François Ozon's brilliantly realised *Jeune et Jolie*.

Avengers assemble: Chloë Grace Moretz and Aaron Taylor-Johnson prepare for war in Jeff Wadlow's ludicrously violent *Kick-Ass 2*.

Justin and the Knights of Valour ★★½

Reginald (Alfred Molina) wants his son Justin (Freddie Highmore) to become a lawyer but Justin, inspired by his Gran (Julie Walters), embarks on a quest to become a knight... This likeable but uneven animated feature has far too many subplots and a myriad of characters that aren't always successful, especially the wizard Melquiades (David Walliams) and Sir Clorex (Antonio Banderas), both of whom belong to a different film altogether. One character nearly saves the day but Gustav the toothless crocodile isn't around for long enough. GS

▷ Voices of Antonio Banderas, James Cosmo, Julie Walters, Rupert Everett, Olivia Williams, Freddie Highmore, Barry Humphries, Alfred Molina, Mark Strong, David Walliams, Saoirse Ronan, Michael Culkin, Charles Dance.
▷ *Dir* Manuel Sicilia, *Pro* Banderas, Marcelino Almansa and Ralph Kamp, *Screenplay* Sicilia and Matthew Jacobs, *Ph* Javier Fernández, *Art Dir* Esteban Martin and Oscar J Vargas, *Ed* Claudio Hernández, *M* Ilan Eshkeri.

Allwood Mediterráneo Producciones/Kandor Graphics/ Out of the Box Features-Entertainment One. 90 mins. Spain. 2013. Rel: 13 Sep 2013. Cert. PG.

Kelly + Victor ★★★

Documentary director Kieran Evans' film of Niall Griffiths' bleak novel explores the world

of sadomasochistic sex with its pervading atmosphere of gloom and doom but ultimately leaves the audience high and dry without any real explanations. Kelly and Victor meet in a Liverpool nightclub and are instantly attracted. They have sex at Kelly's place where she immediately goes all out to almost throttle her new lover just before he climaxes. Finding that Victor enjoys the sensation, Kelly repeats the experience the next time, becoming even more extreme. The young actors, Antonia Campbell-Hughes and Julian Morris, imbue their roles with admirable excitement but the whole exercise remains a cold experiment in tragic sexual cruelty. MHD

▷ Antonia Campbell-Hughes, Julian Morris, William Ruane, Stephen Walters, Claire Keelan, Michael Ryan.
▷ *Dir* and *Screenplay* Kieran Evans, from the novel by Niall Griffiths, *Pro* Janine Marmot, *Ph* Piers McGrail, *Pro Des* Anthea Nelson, *Ed* Tony Kearns, *Music Editor* Steve Fanagan, *Cos* Orla Smyth.

Hot Property Films/Venom Films-Verve Pictures. 95 mins. Ireland/UK. 2012. Rel: 20 Sep 2013. Cert. 18.

Kevin Hart: Let Me Explain ★★★½

Kevin Hart must be the highest-paid US actor-comedian now working. Stand-up success led to his appearances in films (*Little Fockers*, *Think Like a Man*) and television series (*Modern Family*, *Real Husbands of Hollywood*), while 2014 sees him in four movies with another five in preparation. However, he claims he will never desert his stand-up fans. *Let Me Explain*, streamed to UK cinemas and the O2 Arena, is a record of his appearance at Madison Square Garden before an audience of 30,000. It's an extended monologue about dating, loving, fighting, arguing and divorce, a family day out on a horse and making up incredible lies to save face. It's a comic tour de force but, to appreciate it fully, you probably had to be there. MHD

▶ With Kevin Hart, Harry Ratchford, Will 'Spank' Horton, Joey Wells, Dwayne Brown, Na'im Lynn, Nate Smith.
▶ *Dir* Leslie Small and Tim Story, *Pro* Jeff Clanagan, *Ph* Larry Blandford, *Pro Des* Bruce Ryan, *Ed* Spencer Averick, *M* Kennard Ramsey.

Hartbeat Productions/Codeblack Entertainment-Summit Entertainment.
75 mins. USA. 2013. Rel: 30 Aug 2013. Cert. 15.

Kick-Ass 2 ★★★★

To be fair, Matthew Vaughn's *Kick-Ass* was a hard act to follow. The story of an ordinary, hormone-addled teenager attempting to be a masked superhero – and becoming a laughing stock – was original, daring, anarchic and very, very funny. Obviously, the freshness and shock of the original will be lost in the sequel and so the filmmakers have had to up the ante. The result is that the follow-up is decidedly darker, and often unpleasantly so. But there are some terrific one-liners and the teen audience for whom it's intended will lap it up. JC-W

▶ Aaron Taylor-Johnson, Christopher Mintz-Plasse, Chloë Grace Moretz, Jim Carrey, Morris Chestnut, John Leguizamo, Lindy Booth, Clark Duke, Augustus Prew, Yancy Butler, Iain Glen, Lyndsy Fonseca, Claudia Lee, Olga Kurkulina, Steven Mackintosh.
▶ *Dir* and *Screenplay* Jeff Wadlow, *Pro* Adam Bohling, Tarquin Pack, Matthew Vaughn, Brad Pitt and David Reid, *Ph* Tim Maurice-Jones, *Pro Des* Russell De Rozario, *Ed* Eddie Hamilton, *M* Henry Jackman and Matthew Margeson, *Cos* Sammy Sheldon Differ.

Universal/Marv Films/Plan B Entertainment-Universal Pictures.
102 mins. USA/UK. 2013. Rel: 14 Aug 2013. Cert. 15.

Kill Your Darlings ★★★½

Being set in the mid-1940s when Allen Ginsberg was a student in New York, this film is quite distinct from *Howl* (2010) which looked at his later life. Daniel Radcliffe is impressive as the young Ginsberg finding his way under the bohemian influence of fellow student Lucien Carr (Dane DeHaan). Admittedly such people can be irritating and the screenplay is inferior to that of *Howl*, but the narrative becomes tellingly dramatic when Carr is accused of a crime and seeks to conceal his homosexuality. However, it's

Radcliffe's immersion in his role that is the prime reason to see this. MS

▶ Daniel Radcliffe, Dane DeHaan, David Cross, Ben Foster, Michael C Hall, Jack Huston, Jennifer Jason Leigh, Elizabeth Olsen.
▶ *Dir* John Krokidas, *Pro* Michael Benaroya, Christine Vachon, Rose Ganguzza and Krokidas, *Screenplay* Krokidas and Austin Bunn, from Bunn's story, *Ph* Reed Morano, *Pro Des* Stephen Carter, *Ed* Brian A Kates, *M* Nico Muhly, *Cos* Christopher Peterson.

Benaroya Pictures/a Killer Films production/Sunny Field Entertainment-The Works UK Distribution Ltd.
104 mins. USA. 2013. Rel: 6 Dec 2013. Cert. 15.

Killing Oswald ★★★★

The commemoration industry was in full swing during 2013 marking the 50th anniversary of the killing of John F. Kennedy. Is there anything left to say on the subject? *Executive Action* (1973), *JFK* (1991) and *Parkland* (2013, qv) are probably the best 'fictional' films on the subject. The ironically titled *Killing Oswald* is a mixture of archive footage and reconstructed scenes using actors, where the focus is on Lee Harvey Oswald, his background, his history and his movements, building up a picture of a complex individual and not just a lone killer. We will never know if Kennedy's assassination was orchestrated by other hands but this is a worthy document to add to the file labelled 'Likely Possibilities'. PL

▶ With Raymond Burns, Nigel Barber, Luke Hope, Livia Sardao, Vitaly Yerenkov.
▶ *Dir* and *Ed* Shane O'Sullivan, *Ph* O'Sullivan and Baharesh Hosseini.

E2 Films-E2Films.
102 mins. UK. 2013. Rel: 22 Nov 2013. No Cert.

The King of Pigs ★★★★

This astonishing 2D animated drama from South Korea concerns two men who catch up, having

Butcher to the Beat: Daniel Radcliffe and Dane DeHaan in John Krokidas' *Kill Your Darlings*.

not seen each other since high school 15 years previously. Much of the narrative comprises flashbacks to their schooldays, when both were victims of bullying as 'Pigs' – lower-class students tormented by the better-off, self-styled, superior 'Dogs'. It's relentless, harrowing stuff... yet strangely compelling. It also ably demonstrates animation's ability to tackle dark, grown-up subject matter head on. (Original title: *Dwae-ji-ui wang*) JC

▶ Voices of Ik-june Yang, Jung-se Oh, Hye-na Kim, Kkobbi Kim, Hee-von Park.
▶ *Dir* and *Screenplay* Sang-ho Yeon, *Pro* Young-kag Cho, *Art Dir* Je-keun Woo, *Ed* Yeon-jeong Lee and Sang-ho Yeon, *M* Been Eom.

Studio Dadashow/KT & G Sangsangmadang-Terracotta Distribution.
97 mins. South Korea. 2011. Rel: 22 Jan 2013. Cert. 15.

King of the Travellers ★★

This bare-knuckle drama plays like an Irish Western, featuring as it does feuding traveller families (with only a venal landowner separating them) and a young has-been pugilist reliving the childhood trauma of seeing his noble father murdered. Anyone with a working knowledge of *Hamlet* will realise that the boy's Uncle Francis ought really to be called Claudius, while a forbidden romance furnishes some appealingly gauche *Romeo and Juliet* moments between John Connors and Carla McGlynn. Elsewhere, there's such a jumble of cinematic as well as Shakespearean quotes that the film's impact becomes strangely blunted – surprising for a story involving flaming caravans, a street stabbing, a tarring and feathering, a ghostly visitation, even a talking ladybird. JR

▶ John Connors, Peter Coonan, Michael Collins, Carla McGlynn, Mick Foran.

Danish blue: Marcuz Jess Petersen and Frank Hvarn in Mikkel Nørgaard's jaw-dropping *Klown*.

▶ *Dir* and *Screenplay* Mark O'Connor, *Pro* Cormac Fox, *Ph* David Grennan, *Pro Des* Padraig O'Neill, *Ed* John Murphy, *M* John Reynolds, *Cos* Joan O'Clery.

Vico Films-Metrodome Distribution.
80 mins. Ireland. 2012. Rel: 29 Mar 2013. Cert. 15.

The Kings of Summer ★★½

This may be about modern-day youngsters in a semi-rural American setting but it's no *Stand By Me*. These young teenagers rebelling against the adults in their life are initially engaging, however, and their attempt to escape and live off the land echoes Mark Twain's world. But the able cast lose out to plot developments that are sometimes utterly ridiculous and at other times just contrived and unlikely. The blend of comedy and drama doesn't work either. MS

▶ Nick Robinson, Gabriel Basso, Moises Arias, Nick Offerman, Erin Moriarty.
▶ *Dir* Jordan Vogt-Roberts, *Pro* Tyler Davidson, Peter Saraf and John Hodges, *Screenplay* Chris Galleta, *Ph* Ross Riege, *Pro Des* Tyler Robinson, *Ed* Terel Gibson, *M* Ryan Miller, *Cos* Lynette Meyer.

CBS Films/a Low Sparks/Big Beach production-StudioCanal Limited.
95mins. USA. 2013. Rel: 23 Aug 2013. Cert. 15.

Klown ★★★★

An outrageously crass and shocking Danish comedy. A bumbling joker whose pregnant girlfriend suspects will make a terrible dad, Frank (Frank Hvam) aims to prove himself by dragging her 12-year-old nephew (Marcuz Jess Petersen) on a weekend canoe trip with his best friend (Casper Christensen), a sex tourist less than thrilled to have a kid in tow. Your jaw will drop so often, you might as well leave it on the floor throughout. MJ

▶ Frank Hvam, Casper Christensen, Marcuz Jess Petersen, Mia Lyhne, Iben Hjej.
▶ *Dir* Mikkel Nørgaard, *Pro* Louise Vesth, *Screenplay* Casper Christensen and Frank Hvam from a story by Nørgaard, Christensen and Hvam, *Ph* Jacob Banke Olesen, *Pro Des* Rasmus Thjellesen, *Ed* Morten Egholm and Martin Schade, *M* Kristian Eidnes Andersen, *Cos* Louise Hauberg.

Zentropa Productions/TV2 Zulu/Zentropa Entertainments-Arrow Films.
93 mins. Denmark. 2010. Rel: 6 Dec 2013. Cert. 18.

Kuma ★★★

Clumsy story-telling weakens the impact of a genuinely intriguing tale about a family in Turkey marrying off a 19-year-old daughter who will start her married life in Austria. However, she finds herself marrying not the son of the family (who in any case turns out to be gay) but the father seeking a second wife. Her response,

despite hostility from some of her new relatives, is positively saintly – too much so, one feels, and, indeed, what should have worked as a most unusual drama reflecting realities leaves us asking too many questions that remain unanswered. MS

❯ Nihal Koldas, Begüm Akkaya, Vedat Erincin, Murathan Muslu, Merve Cervik.
❯ *Dir* Umut Dag, *Pro* Veit Heiduschka and Michael Katz, *Screenplay* Petra Ladnigg, from Dag's story, *Ph* Carsten Thiele, *Pro Des* Katrin Huber, *Ed* Claudia Linzer, *M* Iva Zabar, *Cos* Cinzia Cioffi.

Veit Heiduschka/Michael Katz presents a Wega Film production/Babylon etc.-Peccadillo Pictures Ltd.
93 mins. Austria. 2012. Rel: 16 Aug 2013. Cert. 12A.

The Last Exorcism Part II ★★★

Part II begins with Ashley Bell's troubled young Nell Sweetzer recovering in a care home after an exorcism. She's the sole survivor of Part I, her family and the documentary crew filming her exorcism having all been wiped out. But nightmares, voices and visions trouble her and the demon stalking her still holds great power. With the crew dead, the first film's documentary style is happily abandoned this time in favour of 'proper film-making'. The new movie tries to take us inside the heroine's head, and with some success, helped by the capable Bell's intense, strong and persuasive performance. It produces a different kind of chiller film from the first, more of a classical horror movie, so there's a built-in freshness. DW

❯ Ashley Bell, Julia Garner, Spencer Treat Clark, David Jensen, Tarra Riggs, Louis Herthum.
❯ *Dir* and *Ed* Ed Gass-Donnelly, *Pro* Eli Roth, Marc Abraham, Eric Newman and Thomas A Bliss, *Screenplay* Gass-Donnelly and Damien Chazelle, from a story by Chazelle, based on characters created by Huck Botko and Andrew Gurland, *Ph* Brendan Steacey, *Pro Des* Merideth Boswell, *M* Michael Wandmacher, *Cos* Abby O'Sullivan.

StudioCanal/Arcade Pictures/Strike Entertainment-StudioCanal.
88 mins. USA. 2013. Rel: 7 June 2013. Cert. 15.

Last Passenger ★★★

Omid Nooshin's promising feature debut is a convincingly acted, tense and enjoyable old-style Brit suspense thriller. It's set on a late-night out-of-control London commuter train as a small group of passengers desperately try to battle their crazed driver and stop his doomsday plan for everyone on board. Dougray Scott, Lindsay Duncan and David Schofield are especially excellent, bringing their stereotypes to life. The film is packed with plenty of sweaty-palm tension, and there are enough good effects to make it look convincing, despite its obvious low budget. The story's contrived but they make it credible. DW

❯ Dougray Scott, Kara Tointon, Iddo Goldberg, David Schofield, Lindsay Duncan, Joshua Kaynaa, Samuel Geker-Kawle.
❯ *Dir* Omid Nooshin, *Pro* Ado Yoshizaki Cassuto

That floating feeling: Ashley Bell in Ed Gass-Donnelly's *The Last Exorcism Part II.*

String theory: Mark Ivanir, the late Philip Seymour Hoffman, Christopher Walken and Catherine Keener in Yaron Zilberman's *A Late Quartet*.

and Michiyo Yoshizaki, *Screenplay* Nooshin, Andrew Love and Kas Graham, *Ph* Angus Hudson, *Pro Des* Jon Bunker, *Ed* Joe Walker, *M* Liam Bates, *Cos* Alison Mitchell.

Pinewood Studios/2B Pictures/NDF International/Future Films/UK Film Council-Kaleidoscope Entertainment. 97 mins. UK. 2013. Rel: 18 Oct 2013. Cert. 15.

The Last Stand ★★★½

Arnold Schwarzenegger looks pretty darned fit at 65 ("I'm old!") and slips winningly into the character of a semi-retired, Deep South, small-town sheriff. He has to assemble a rag-tag crew to stop a drugs cartel baddie (Eduardo Noriega) getting through his territory and across the border (on a makeshift metal bridge) into Mexico and freedom. Older, a bit stiffer and slower, Arnold is still credible and warm, and can do all the fights and shootouts the script chucks his way. Nobody could complain the action isn't convincing or well staged or that the movie isn't fun. Johnny Knoxville enjoys himself hugely as local arms freak Lewis Dinkum. DW

➤ Arnold Schwarzenegger, Johnny Knoxville, Eduardo Noriega, Forest Whitaker, Titos Menchaca, Richard Dillard.
➤ *Dir* Kim Je-woon, *Pro* Lorenzo di Bonaventura, *Screenplay* Andrew Knauer, *Ph* Ji-yong Kim, *Pro Des* Franco-Giacomo Carbone, *Ed* Steven Kemper, *M* Mowg, *Cos* Michele Michel.

Di Bonaventura Pictures-Lionsgate. 107 mins. USA. 2013. Rel: 25 Jan 2013. Cert. 15.

A Late Quartet ★★★★

The string quartet is a delicate bloom that needs cultivation: the right combination of players for excellence in performance with an emotional bond that binds the individuals together. Ideally each player must know intuitively what the others are going to do. In Yaron Zilberman's debut as writer-director, a famous quartet is celebrating its quarter century when the cellist (Christopher Walken) announces he has Parkinson's Disease and cannot continue. This throws the musicians into turmoil and all kinds of anger and recriminations surface. It is a gentle, warm-hearted film on a human level that both pleases and saddens. Great performances all round, in particular from Walken, the late Philip Seymour Hoffman, Catherine Keener and Mark Ivanir as the musicians. MHD

➤ Christopher Walken, Philip Seymour Hoffman, Catherine Keener, Mark Ivanir, Imogen Poots, Madhur Jaffrey, Wallace Shawn.
➤ *Dir* Yaron Zilberman, *Pro* Zilberman, Mandy Tagger Brockey, Tamar Sela, Emanuel Michael, David Faigenbaum and Vanessa Coifman, *Screenplay* Zilberman and Seth Grossman, from a story by Zilberman, *Ph* Frederick Elmes, *Pro Des* John Kasarda, *Ed* Yuval Shar, *M* Angelo Badalamenti, *Cos* Joseph G Aulisi.

RKO Pictures/Opening Night Productions/Unison Films/ Spring Pictures/ Concept Entertainment-Artificial Eye. 105 mins. USA. 2012. Rel: 5 Apr 2013. Cert. 15.

The Lebanese Rocket Society ★★★

The filmmakers, Joana Hadjithomas and Khalil Joreige, provide their own voice-over in English for this documentary about the role of Lebanon in building rockets in the early 1960s. This has become a hidden history which is interestingly resurrected in this movie using both fresh interviews and old footage. Nevertheless you probably need to be Lebanese to feel that there is enough here to sustain a feature-length film. MS

▶ With Manoug Manougian, Hampar Karageozian, Harry Koundakjian.
▶ *Dir* Joana Hadjithomas and Khalil Joreige, *Pro* Georges Schoucair and Édouard Mauriat, *Ph* Jeanne Lapoirie and Rachel Aoun, *Ed* Tina Baz Legal, *M* Nadim Mishlawi.

Abbout Productions/Mille et une Productions/Doha Film Institute etc.-Soda Pictures.
96 mins. France/Lebanon/Qatar/United Arab Emirates. 2012. Rel: 18 Oct 2013. Cert. PG.

Leviathan ★★★★★

This imaginative, exceptional, award-winning documentary was filmed among the commercial fishing industry in the North Atlantic. Directed by Lucien Castaing-Taylor and Véréna Paravel of the Sensory Ethnography Laboratory at Harvard University, their experimental work views the fishing ship as the all-devouring Biblical sea monster Leviathan. The filmmakers use natural sounds and raw images in a fresh and innovative way to expose the dangers of mass consumption and show how it shames our society, damaging the seas and the workers alike. The film's special quality was acknowledged when it won the Michael Powell Award for Best British Feature Film at the 2013 Edinburgh Film Festival, and the US Society of Critics gave it their Experimental Film Award. DW

▶ With Declan Conneely, Johnny Gatcombe, Adrian Guillete, Brian Jannelle, Clyde Lee, Arthur Smith, Christopher Swampstead.
▶ *Dir, Pro, Ph, Ed* and *Written by* Lucien Castaing-Taylor and Véréna Paravel, *Sound Composition* Ernst Karel.

Le Bureau/Arrete Ton Cinema-Dogwoof.
87 mins. France/UK/USA. 2012. Rel: 29 Nov 2013. Cert. 12A.

The Liability ★★★½

Jack O'Connell shows why he's a rising star as 19-year-old Adam, who's forced to do a day's driving for his mum's gangster boyfriend Peter (Peter Mullan). This leads the boy on a madcap tour of the wild side through murder, sex trafficking and revenge, guided by hired assassin Roy (Tim Roth). A femme fatale (Talulah Riley) soon shows up, turning the yarn into a three-way game of cat and mouse. Thrilling violent moments mix with wry humour in a satisfyingly oddball thriller, with a tense and twisty script and four good actors to make it work. Excellent though veterans Roth and Mullan are, O'Connell sure gives them a run for their money. DW

▶ Tim Roth, Jack O'Connell, Talulah Riley, Peter Mullan, Kierston Wareing, Tomi May, Jack McBride.

▶ *Dir* Craig Viveiros, *Pro* Rupert Jermyn and Richard Johns, *Screenplay* John Wrathall, *Ph* James Friend, *Pro Des* Matt Gant, *Ed* Pia Di Ciaula, *M* Vicky Wijeratne, *Cos* Alison McLaughlin.

Corona Pictures/Starchild Pictures-Metrodome Distribution.
82 mins. UK. 2012. Rel: 17 May 2013. Cert. 15.

A Liar's Autobiography: The Untrue Story of Monty Python's Graham Chapman ★★★★

Based on his autobiographical book and using sound tapes of his most bizarre comic ramblings, *Monty Python* star Graham Chapman comes eerily and poignantly back to life in this hilarious, informative and touching animated comedy. The animation is polished, witty and stylish, providing the main argument for seeing the film rather than reading the book. Highlights are his coming out to his parents, a meeting with the Queen Mother and his nightmarish struggle with alcohol withdrawal. Other than Eric Idle, all the other Pythons are involved, with John Cleese notably voicing his friend David Frost as well as himself. It's a fine, loving tribute to a lovely if troubled man. Stephen Fry voices Oscar Wilde. DW

▶ Voices of Graham Chapman, Terry Gilliam, John Cleese, Michael Palin, Terry Jones, Carol Cleveland, Stephen Fry.
▶ *Dir* Bill Jones, Jeff Simpson and Ben Timlett, *Pro* Jones and Timlett, *Screenplay* Graham Chapman and David Sherlock, based on Chapman's book *A Liar's Autobiography Volume VI*, *Ed* Bill Jones, *M* John Greswell and Christopher Murphy Taylor.

Bill and Ben Productions/Brainstorm Media/EPIX etc-Trinity Filmed Entertainment.
85 mins. UK. 2012. Rel: 8 Feb 2013. Cert. 15.

Pipe dreams: Bill Jones, Jeff Simpson and Ben Timlett's *A Liar's Autobiography: The Untrue Story of Monty Python's Graham Chapman.*

Life's a Breeze ★★★★

Fionnula Flanagan stars as a retired schoolteacher in writer-director Lance Daly's cheering Irish feelgood comedy. Her adult children decide to clean up her house as a birthday present and chuck out an old mattress that turns out to contain her life savings. The family then go on a wild chase around the streets of Dublin to hunt for the missing money. Flanagan is a knockout and newcomer Kelly Thornton shines as her teenage granddaughter. The 88 minutes rush past with plenty of breezy high spirits and laughter thanks to a funny script and a game, talented cast. DW

▷ Kelly Thornton, Fionnula Flanagan, Pat Shorrt, Eva Birthistle.
▷ *Dir, Ph* and *Screenplay* Lance Daly, *Pro* Daly and Macdara Kelleher, *Ph* Lance Daly, *Pro Des* Waldemar Kalinowski, *Ed* Shimmy Marcus, *M* Daly and Declan and Eugene Quinn, *Cos* Anna Agren.

Fastnet Films/Anagram Produktion/Film I Väst/Irish Film Board-Wildcard Distribution.
88 mins. Ireland. 2013. Rel: 29 Nov 2013. Cert. 12A.

Like Father, Like Son ★★★½

For two thirds of its length, this film finds Japan's distinguished writer-director Kore-eda Hirokazu on his best form with an involving story about two sets of contrasted parents (one well-off, the other poor) who six years on discover that their children were swapped at birth. What to do – or even not to do? It's a wholly absorbing work which seems to reach a conclusion but then meanders on without really developing further for another half-hour or so. (Original title: *Soshite chichi ni naru*) MS

▷ Fukuyama Masaharu, Ono Maschiko, Maki Yoko, Lily Franky, Shogen Whang, Keita Ninomiya.

▷ *Dir, Screenplay* and *Ed* Kore-eda Hirokazu, *Pro* Matsuzaki Kaoru and Taguchi Hijiri, *Ph* Takimoto Mikiya, *Pro Des* Mitsumatsu Keiko, *M* Matsumoto Junichi, Mori Takashi and Matsubara Takeshi, *Cos* Kurosawa Kazuko.

A Fuji Television Network, Inc., Amuse Inc. and Gaga Corporation presentation/a Film, Inc. production-Arrow Films.
121 mins. Japan. 2013. Rel: 18 Oct. 2013. Cert. PG.

Like Someone in Love ★★★½

This film may take Iran's Abbas Kiarostami to a new location – Tokyo – but it is a work with a wholly personal signature. Its oddly abrupt ending leaves one dissatisfied because until then it is an admirably subtle tale about an elderly retired professor, the girl called out by him and the girl's boyfriend who assumes that the old man is her grandfather. We see things from the viewpoint of each character in turn and there's both irony and tenderness in the falseness of appearances. It could have been a masterpiece but for its infuriatingly deliberate non-ending. MS

▷ Okuno Tadashi, Takanashi Rin, Kase Ryo, Denden.
▷ *Dir* and *Screenplay* Abbas Kiarostami, *Pro* Marin Karmitz and Horikoshi Kenzo, *Ph* Yanagijima Katsumi, *Art Dir* Isomi Toshihiro, *Ed* Bahman Kiarostami.

MK2/Eurospace/L'agence pour les Affaires culturelles, Gouvernement du Japon etc.-New Wave Films.
110 mins. France/Japan. 2012. Rel: 21 June 2013. Cert. 12A.

Lincoln ★★★★

Steven Spielberg's film about the 16th US President covers the last few months of Lincoln's life as he brought an end to both the American Civil War and slavery. Much of the action takes

Blood money: Pat Short, Kelly Thornton and Fionnula Flanagan in Lance Daly's buoyant *Life's a Breeze*.

place indoors, in Lincoln's White House office or on the floor of the House of Representatives during the slavery debate. There's very little light and Lincoln (Daniel Day-Lewis) is rarely seen full-face but sideways or in shadow. It is a remarkable performance and the actor eschews any pyrotechnics to give a controlled, thoughtful reading of the great man. Good work too from Sally Field as Mrs Lincoln, Tommy Lee Jones as Congressman Stevens and David Strathairn as Lincoln's Secretary of State. Spielberg's direction is impeccable and the production design seems totally authentic. MHD

▶ Daniel Day-Lewis, Sally Field, David Strathairn, Joseph Gordon-Levitt, James Spader, Hal Holbrook, Tommy Lee Jones, John Hawkes, Jackie Earle Haley.
▶ *Dir* Steven Spielberg, *Pro* Spielberg and Kathleen Kennedy, *Screenplay* Tony Kushner, based in part on Doris Kearns Goodwin's book *Team of Rivals: The Political Genius of Abraham Lincoln*, *Ph* Janusz Kaminski, *Pro Des* Rick Carter, *Ed* Michael Kahn, *M* John Williams, *Cos* Joanna Johnston.

DreamWorks Pictures/20th Century Fox/Participant Media/The Kennedy-Marshall Company/Amblin Entertainment/Dune Entertainment-20th Century Fox. 150 mins. USA. 2012. Rel: 25 Jan 2013. Cert. 12A.

The Lone Ranger ★

A bloated big-screen treatment of a forgotten hero from TV's distant past, this is an epic Jerry Bruckheimer misfire aimed at no one in particular.

Too long and slow for kids, too bland and nonsensical for adults, it's a shot in the dark and the bullets are blanks. Genre, content, style, pace and execution aside, the cast of Gore Verbinski's lacklustre Western adventure isn't much of a draw either – Armie Hammer, as the Ranger, is a milquetoast; Johnny Depp, as Tonto, is a costume player on autopilot. Paper-thin yet cluttered, the movie lacks wit, imagination and personality. MJ

▶ Johnny Depp, Armie Hammer, William Fichtner, Tom Wilkinson, Ruth Wilson, Helena Bonham-Carter, James Badge Dale.
▶ *Dir* Gore Verbinski, *Pro* Verbinski and Jerry Bruckheimer, *Screenplay* Justin Haythe, Terry Rossio and Ted Elliott, *Ph* Bojan Bazelli, *Pro Des* Jess Gonchor, *Ed* James Haygood and Craig Wood, *M* Hans Zimmer, *Cos* Penny Rose.

Walt Disney Pictures/Jerry Bruckheimer Films/Blind Wink/Silver Bullet Productions/Infinitum Nihil/Classic Media-Walt Disney Studios Motion Pictures. 149 mins. USA. 2013. Rel: 9 Aug 2013. Cert. 12A.

A Long Way from Home ★★★

Adapting her own short story, writer-director Virginia Gilbert's wistful romantic drama is lucky enough to have some on-form heavyweight performers to put it across. James Fox and Brenda Fricker star as Joseph and Brenda, a couple who live the dream of retiring to the rural South of France, where life's one long holiday. But their life is turned upside down when they meet a much

Theatre of war: Gloria Reuben, Sally Field and Sir Daniel Day-Lewis in Steven Spielberg's *Lincoln*.

younger holidaying couple and Joseph becomes infatuated with the arty and attractive Suzanne (Natalie Dormer), unappreciated by her dynamic but grouchy partner Mark (Paul Nicholls). The glorious sun-drenched French scenery and Fox's yearning performance are the star attractions. DW

▶ James Fox, Natalie Dormer, Paul Nicholls, Brenda Fricker, Betty Krestinsky, Brian Gilbert, Catriona McColl.
▶ *Dir* and *Screenplay* Virginia Gilbert, *Pro* Guillaume Benski and Junyoung Jang, *Ph* Ed Rutherford, *Pro Des* Thomas Laporte, *Ed* Thomas Goldser, *Music Supervisor* Christian Siddell, *Cos* Mimi Milburn-Foster.
February Films/Superbe Films-Soda Pictures.
80 mins. UK/France. 2013. Rel: 6 Dec 2013. Cert. 12A.

The Look of Love ★★★

Soho's famous entrepreneur and creator of the Revuebar, Paul Raymond, is the subject of Matt Greenhalgh's screenplay directed by Michael Winterbottom. Having made *9 Songs*, Winterbottom finds amusement in the prim attitudes that branded Raymond a threat to decent living, but this tone clashes with the downbeat side of the film centred on Raymond's daughter (Imogen Poots). Steve Coogan is adept as the anti-hero, but the film never finds the right balance. MS

▶ Steve Coogan, Anna Friel, Imogen Poots, Tamsin Egerton, Chris Addison.
▶ *Dir* Michael Winterbottom, *Pro* Melissa Parmenter, *Screenplay* Matt Greenhalgh, based on material from *Members Only: The Life and Times of Paul Raymond* by Paul Willetts, *Ph* Hubert Taczanowski, *Pro Des* Jacqueline Abrahams, *Ed* Mags Arnold, *M* Antony Genn and Martin Slattery, *Cos* Stephanie Collie.
StudioCanal/Film4/a Revolution Films production/Baby Cow Films etc.-StudioCanal Limited.
101 mins. UK/Luxembourg. 2013. Rel: 26 Apr 2013. Cert. 18.

Revue bar none: Imogen Poots in Michael Winterbottom's *The Look of Love.*

Looking for Hortense ★★★

One wonders if that excellent actress Kristin Scott Thomas is making too many films. Pascal Bonitzer's movie, part comedy and part drama, is about the breakdown of the relationship of a couple who have a young son. The man's relationship with his father (a scene-stealing performance from Claude Rich) plays a part too, as does a plea for help for a foreign girl who is an illegal immigrant. Touching uneasily on its deeper issues, the film then opts for a Hollywood-style happy ending. It's all bearable but lacks weight and balance. (Original title *Cherchez Hortense*) MS

▶ Jean-Pierre Bacri, Isabelle Carré, Kristin Scott Thomas, Claude Rich, Jackie Berroyer.
▶ *Dir* Pascal Bonitzer, *Pro* Saïd Ben Saïd, *Screenplay* Agnès de Sacy and Bonitzer, *Ph* Romain Winding, *Pro Des* Manu de Chauvigny, *Ed* Élise Fievet, *M* Alexei Aigui, *Cos* Marielle Robaut.
An SBS Productions production/Orange Cinéma Séries/Cinemage 6 etc.-Arrow Films.
100 mins. France. 2012. Rel: 9 Aug 2013. Cert. 12A.

The Lookout ★★★★

A first-rate French thriller with a sterling, dogged turn by hangdog Daniel Auteuil as Police Detective Mattei, who is about to arrest a notorious gang of bank robbers when an unknown rooftop sniper kills most of the policemen on site during a daring heist. The investigation leads Mattei onto the trail of Vincent Kaminski (Mathieu Kassovitz), the marksman who foiled his plan, digging up dark secrets along the way. The credible, intricately plotted and totally engrossing screenplay by Denis Brusseaux and Cédric Melon puts most British and American scripts to shame. And so does the ultra-tense handling of veteran Italian director Michele Placido. (Original title: *Le Guetteur*) DW

▶ Daniel Auteuil, Mathieu Kassovitz, Olivier Gourmet, Francis Renaud, Nicolas Briançon, Jérôme Pouly.
▶ *Dir* Michele Placido, *Pro* Fabio Conversi and Eric Tavitian, *Screenplay* Denis Brusseaux and Cédric Melon, *Ph* Arnaldo Catinari, *Pro Des* Jean-Jacques Gernolle, *Ed* Consuelo Catucci and Sebastien Prangere, *M* Nicolas Errèra, *Cos* Virginie Montel and Isabelle Pannetier.
Babe Film/Climax Films/StudioCanal/Ran Entertainment/France 2 Cinéma/Appaloosa Films/Ra Cinema/Canal+/Ciné+/France Télévision etc-StudioCanal.
89 mins. France/Belgium/Italy. 2012. Rel: 11 Jan 2013. Cert. 15.

The Lords of Salem ★★★★

Sheri Moon Zombie is credible and charismatic as a Salem radio DJ who's sent a wooden box with a vinyl record that plays backwards and sends

After the sneeze: Rob Zombie's *The Lords of Salem*, "an eyeball attacker."

her scary flashbacks. It comes from Manson-style hippie witches planning a bloody return at a rock gig. With Mrs Zombie turning into Jesus on a mound of naked witches at the climax, writer-director Rob Zombie's horror movie is gob-smacking stuff, taking no prisoners. Made on a low budget of $1,500,000, it still looks quite astonishing. Filming in Salem with beautifully crafted cinematography and no CGI effects, it's an eyeball attacker. Bruce Davison gives the right intense, grave turn as a troubled witch hunter; Judy Geeson, Dee Wallace and Patricia Quinn are eerily effective as wicked sisters. DW

▶ Sheri Moon Zombie, Bruce Davison, Jeff Daniel Phillips, Judy Geeson, Meg Foster, Patricia Quinn, Dee Wallace.
▶ *Dir* and *Screenplay* Rob Zombie, *Pro* Rob Zombie, Steven Schneider, Oren Pell, Andy Gould and Jason Blum, *Ph* Brandon Trost, *Pro Des* Jennifer Spence, *Ed* Glenn Garland, *M* Griffin Boice and John 5, *Cos* Leah Butler.

Alliance Films/Blumhouse Productions/Automatik Entertainment/Haunted Movies/IM Global-Momentum Pictures.
101 mins. USA/UK/Canada. 2012. Rel: 19 Apr 2013. Cert. 18.

Lore ★★½

Australia's Cate Shortland here tells a story centred on a German girl, Hannelore, living in Germany just before the end of the Second World War and of necessity taking charge of her even younger siblings. A long trek to seek out a grandmother near Hamburg involves a meeting with a Jewish youth to whom Nazi-indoctrinated Lore feels drawn regardless. It's promising material with an able German cast but, sadly, artiness including pointless camera movement together with unpersuasive story-tellling result in a film which I found hugely disappointing. MS

▶ Saskia Rosendahl, Kai Malina, Nele Trebs, Ursina Lardi, Hans Jochen-Wagner.
▶ *Dir* Cate Shortland, *Pro* Karsten Stöter, Liz Watts, Paul Welsh and Benny Drechsel, *Screenplay* Shortland and Robin Mukherjee, from Rachel Seiffert's novel *The Dark Room*, *Ph* Adam Arkapaw, *Pro Des* Silke Fischer, *Ed* Veronika Jenet, *M* Max Richter, *Cos* Stefanie Bieker.

Screen Australia/a Rohfilm, Porchlight Films, Edge City Films production etc.-Artificial Eye.
109 mins. Germany/Australia/UK. 2012. Rel: 22 Feb 2013. Cert. 15.

Love is All You Need ★★★★½

This looks like the Richard Curtis film he didn't make. Although it has similarities to the work of the British filmmaker, it in fact comes from Susanne Bier and her co-writer Anders Thomas Jensen, with whom she also wrote *Brothers*, *After the Wedding* and *In a Better World*. Pierce Brosnan plays a widower who encounters a hairdresser (Trine Dyrholm) recovering from cancer and who happens to be the mother of his son's bride-to-be. They meet en route to the wedding in Italy and so begins an off-on relationship. Far from being a sentimental romcom, Bier's film has an edge to it

that lifts it above the norm. It may be a feelgood movie but it's that for all the right reasons. MHD

▶ Trine Dyrholm, Pierce Brosnan, Stina Ekblad, Sebastian Jessen, Molly Blixt Egelind, Ciro Petrone, Marco D'Amre.
▶ *Dir* Susanne Bier, *Pro* Sisse Graum Jørgensen and Vibeke Windeløv, *Screenplay* Anders Thomas Jensen, from a story by Bier and Jensen, *Ph* Morten Søborg, *Pro Des* Peter Grant, *Ed* Pernille Bech Christensen and Morten Egholm, *M* Johan Söderqvist, *Cos* Signe Sejlund.
Zentropa Productions/Film I Väst/Lumière and Company/Todora Film/Slot Machine/Liberator Productions/ARTE/ZDF etc-Arrow Films.
116 mins. Denmark/Sweden/Italy/France/Germany. 2013. Rel: 19 Apr 2013. Cert. 15.

Love Tomorrow ★★★½

Christopher Payne's modest second film deals with a possible romance between two ballet dancers who meet in London – she's on home ground but not without problems and he's from Cuba and married. It's a slight piece undoubtedly, but there's a palpable sincerity to the project which gives the film a genuine charm. Kevin

Norma Jeane Mortenson as seen in Liz Garbus' *Love, Marilyn*.

Pollard's music score manages to be emotionally atmospheric without becoming manipulative. MS

▶ Cindy Jourdain, Arionel Vargas, Max Brown, Samuel Barnett, John McArdle.
▶ *Dir* and *Screenplay* Christopher Payne, *Pro* Stephanie Moon, *Ph* Paul Teverini, *Pro Des* Alexandra Walker, *Ed* Nick Calori and Barry Moen, *M* Kevin Pollard, *Cos* Matt Price.
Rayla Films, LaLuna Films, Manilla Productions-Soda Pictures.
79 mins. UK. 2012. Rel: 8 Nov 2013. Cert. PG.

Love, Marilyn ★★★

Marilyn Monroe has not lost her ability to fascinate us. By using her own words from notes, letters and even poems, this documentary seeks to confirm her intelligence and to reveal her inner life. In fact using a range of actresses to represent her and to speak her words feels totally artificial. (Adrien Brody speaking for Truman Capote comes off best.) Yet there are revelations and, even though the film is misjudged, Marilyn emerges as a more tragic figure than ever before, her on-screen triumphs even more of an enduring miracle. MS

▶ With readings by Adrien Brody, Ellen Burstyn, Glenn Close, Viola Davis, Paul Giamatti, Lindsay Lohan, Janet McTeer, Uma Thurman, Marisa Tomei, Evan Rachel Wood.
▶ *Dir* and *Written by* Liz Garbus, *Pro* Stanley Buchthal, Garbus and Amy Hobby, *Ph* Maryse Alberti, *Pro Des* Mike Barton, *Ed* Azin Samari, *M* Philip Sheppard.
StudioCanal/a Diamond Girl Production/a Sol's Luncheonette production-StudioCanal Limited.
107 mins. USA/France. 2012. Rel: 18 Oct. 2013. Cert. 12A.

Lovelace ★★½

Much as I admire Rob Epstein and Jeffrey Friedman I cannot feel other than disappointment with this portrayal of the famous porn actress Linda Lovelace. That's no fault of Amanda Seyfried in the title role and there's a telling cameo from a virtually unrecognisable Sharon Stone. A banal music score doesn't help, but it's the screenplay (not by Epstein and Friedman) which, in not getting to grips with the complex Lovelace, renders the unedifying story superficial. MS

▶ Amanda Seyfried, Peter Sarsgaard, Hank Azaria, Wes Bentley, Adam Brody, Bobby Cannavale, James Franco, Eric Roberts, Chloë Sevigny, Sharon Stone, Juno Temple.
▶ *Dir* Rob Epstein and Jeffrey Friedman, *Pro* Jason Weinberg, Jim Young, Heidi Jo Markel and Laura Rister, *Screenplay* Andy Bellin, *Ph* Eric Edwards, *Pro Des* William Arnold, *Ed* Robert Dalva and Matthew Landon, *M* Stephen Trask, *Cos* Karyn Wagner.

Millennium Films/an Eclectic Pictures production/
Untitled Entertainment etc.-Lionsgate UK.
93 mins. USA. 2013. Rel: 23 Aug 2013. Cert. 18.

Machete Kills ★

What began as a fake and jokey trailer fashioned
to celebrate the cheerfully cheap, exploitational
stylings of Grindhouse Cinema, and later
developed into a brazenly bloody and flat-out
bonkers B-movie, now returns as a blundering,
puerile and tedious jumble. This time around,
Machete (Danny Trejo) rumbles with a lunatic
arms dealer (Mel Gibson). The trouble with
emulating good-bad movies is that, while those
original exploitation films were entertaining for all
the wrong reasons, really more by accident than
design, if you set out to deliberately make a rubbish
film, usually you just end up with trash like this. MJ

▶ Danny Trejo, Mel Gibson, Demián Bichir, Amber
Heard, Michelle Rodriguez, Sofia Vergara, Charlie
Sheen, Lady Gaga, Antonio Banderas, Cuba
Gooding Jr, Vanessa Hudgens.
▶ Dir and Ph Robert Rodriguez, Pro Rodriguez,
Rick Schwartz, Alexander Rodnansky, Iliana Nikolic,
Sergei Bespalov and Aaron Kaufman, Screenplay Kyle
Ward, from a story by Robert and Marcel Rodriguez,
Pro Des Steve Joyner, Ed Robert and Rebecca
Rodriguez, M Robert Rodriguez and Carl Thiel,
Cos Nina Proctor.

Quick Draw Productions/AR Films/Aldamisa
Entertainment/1821 Pictures/Demarest Films/Overnight
Films-Lionsgate.
107 mins. Russia/USA. 2013. Rel: 11 Oct 2013. Cert. 15.

Mademoiselle C ★★★

In contrast to fascinating recent documentaries
set in or close to the world of fashion (I think of
films about Diana Vreeland and Bill Cunningham
in particular), this study of the stylist and
designer Carine Roitfeld seems strictly for those
fascinated by her world. It looks at her life and
work but in a superficial way as it passes from
Paris (where she was editor-in-chief for *Vogue*)
to New York where she is moving in a new
direction. MS

▶ With Carine Roitfeld, Karl Lagerfeld, Tom Ford,
Bruce Weber, Donatella Versace.
▶ Dir and Ph Fabien Constant, Pro Eric Hannezo,
Vincent Lebrun, Guillaume Lacroix and Constant,
Ed Stephanie Drean, M The Shoes.

Black Dynamite Films/Tarkovspop/Elle driver-
StudioCanal Limited.
93 mins. France. 2013. Rel: 20 Sep 2013. Cert. 12A.

A Magnificent Haunting ★★★½

It's not exactly Pirandello but this slight,
offbeat and eventually appealing work from the
Italian-based Turkish director Ferzan Ozpetek
features a would-be actor who hires a haunted
flat where he encounters theatre folk from the
past, spirits who don't realise that they died in
1943. Even a comic flight of fancy needs more
logic than we get here, yet the piece is engaging
and even touching as we follow these eight
characters in search of an audience. (Original
title: *Magnifica presenza*) MS

Ghost world:
Ambrogio Maestri,
Claudia Potenza,
Margherita Buy,
Andrea Bosca,
Beppe Fiorello,
Vittoria Puccini,
Cem Yilmaz and
Mateo Savino
in *A Magnificent
Haunting*.

▶ Elio Germano, Margherita Buy, Vittoria Puccini, Anna Proclemer, Andrea Bosca.
▶ *Dir* Ferzan Ozpetek, *Pro* Domenico Procacci, *Screenplay* Federica Pontremoli and Ozpetek, *Ph* Maurizio Calvesi, *Pro Des* Andrea Crisanti, *Ed* Walter Fasano, *M* Pasquale Catalano, *Cos* Alessandro Lai.

A Fandango and Faros production/Rai Cinema/Intesa Sanpaolo SpA-Peccadillo Pictures Ltd.
105 mins. Italy. 2012. Rel: 25 Oct 2013. Cert. 15.

Mahmut & Meryem ★★

In Turkey in 1514, the sultan of Karabag worries about his legacy and the future of his empire. His son Mahmut is nothing like him and seems more preoccupied with peaceful concerns and the love of Meryem, the daughter of a Christian monk… Not a film to be embraced by the fans of Nuri Bilge Ceylan, *Mahmut & Meryem* is terribly conventional in its telling although there is some leavening of humour. (Original title: *Mahmut ile Meryem*) CB

▶ Aras Bulut Iynemli, Eva Dedova, Fahreddin Manafov, Melahat Abbasova, Polat Bilgin.
▶ *Dir* Mehmet A. Öztekin, *Pro* Ali Kaygisiz and Sevda Kaygisiz, *Screenplay* Esref Dinçer and Yerkan Kahraman, *Ph* Serkan Güler, *Art Dir* Aziz Memedov and Baran Ugurlu, *Ed* Rusen Daghan, *M* Toygar Isikli, *Cos* Baran Ugurlu.

24 Kare Prodüksiyon/Duka Film/Salname-Cinemaster UK.
128 mins. Turkey. 2013. Rel: 5 Apr 2013. Cert. 15.

Mama ★★★

Mama is a pretty good, well-crafted Spanish version of the Japanese 'drippy water, scary videos, troubled mamas' kind of chiller. It has its tense and scary moments. Andy Muschietti's smooth and polished debut started life as a 2008 three-minute short of the same name. Executive produced by Guillermo Del Toro, and Canadian-made, it cost $15 million and scored a big hit in the States, taking over $70 million there, helped by star Jessica Chastain's Oscar nomination for *Zero Dark Thirty* [qv]. Here she's brisk and capable but none too convincing as a rich chick who becomes a concerned mama to her coma-stricken boyfriend's two feral nieces. Nikolaj Coster-Waldau has twin roles, neither very exciting nor satisfying. DW

▶ Jessica Chastain, Nikolaj Coster-Waldau, Megan Charpentier, Isabelle Nélisse, Daniel Kash, Javier Botet.
▶ *Dir* Andy Muschietti, *Pro* J Miles Dale and Barbara Muschietti, *Screenplay* Andy and Barbara Muschietti and Neil Cross, *Ph* Antonio Riestra, *Pro Des* Anastasia Masaro, *Ed* Michele Conroy, *M* Fernando Velázquez, *Cos* Luis Sequeira.

Universal Pictures/De Milo/Toma 78-Universal Pictures International.
100 mins. Canada/Spain. 2013. Rel: 22 Feb 2013. Cert. 15.

Man of Steel ★★★★½

In this dark, prodigious, incredibly violent and impossibly big reboot from producer Christopher Nolan, there is none of the cheesy charm of Christopher Reeve's Superman movies. Instead, there is an apocalyptic self-importance that draws the influences of *2001* and *Alien* into new realms. The sheer scale of it is breathtaking and at times it is almost as intellectually challenging as Nolan's

Kal-El returns (yet again): Henry Cavell is the *Man of Steel*.

own *Inception* – but with more of a (sort of) logical thrust. A PhD in physics might help to unravel some of the film's more convoluted leaps of scientific narrative, but the basic building blocks of the DC Comic original are all here. An awesome experience, both cerebrally and visually. JC-W

▶ Henry Cavill, Amy Adams, Michael Shannon, Kevin Costner, Diane Lane, Laurence Fishburne, Russell Crowe, Ayelet Zurer, Harry Lennix, Christopher Menoli, Richard Schiff.
▶ *Dir* Zack Snyder, *Pro* Christopher Nolan, Charles Roven, Emma Thomas and Deborah Snyder, *Screenplay* David S Goyer, *Ph* Amir Mokri, *Pro Des* Alex McDowell, *Ed* David Brenner, *M* Hans Zimmer, *Cos* James Acheson and Michael Wilkinson.

Warner Bros/Legendary Pictures/Syncopy-Warner Bros.
142 mins. USA/UK/Canada. 2013. Rel: 14 June 2013.
Cert. 12A.

Man to Man ★★★

Régis Wargnier's thought-provoking 2005 drama about Victorian anthropologists who hunt and capture African pygmies for study in Europe finally got a UK release in 2013. Joseph Fiennes stars as Dr Jamie Dodd who captures two pygmies and brings them to Scotland, where he's helped by Elena Van den Ende (Kristin Scott Thomas), who sells wild animals to zoos. Anthropologists Alexander and Fraser (Iain Glen, Hugh Bonneville) are certain the pygmies are the missing link between man and ape, but Dodd finds they are just as sensitive and intelligent as any other humans. Classy acting, a fascinating topic and an intelligent, literate script (partly by William Boyd) make the long wait worth it. DW

▶ Joseph Fiennes, Kristin Scott Thomas, Iain Glen, Hugh Bonneville, Lomama Boseki, Cécile Bayiha, Peter Egan.
▶ *Dir* Régis Wargnier, *Pro* Farid Lahouassa, *Screenplay* Wargnier, William Boyd, Michel Fessler and Fred Fougea, *Ph* Laurent Dailland, *Pro Des* Maria Djurkovic, *Ed* Yan Malcor, *M* Patrick Doyle, *Cos* Pierre-Yves Gayraud.

Skyline Films/Vertigo Productions/Boréales/Zen HQ Films/TPS Star etc-Vertigo Productions.
122 mins. France/South Africa/UK. 2005.
Rel: 31 May 2013. Cert. 15.

Maniac ★★★

In this remake of the low-budget 1980 slasher movie, Elijah Wood plays a serial killer with a fetish for scalps and mannequins in present day LA. But when he meets Anna (Norah Arnezeder), a French artist, he begins to have second thoughts about his appetite for murder... The action is seen from the killer's point of view – similar to *Peeping Tom* – but here his face can only be seen in either reflections or dreams.

It's stylish but brutal and extremely violent – definitely not for the faint-hearted. GS

▶ Elijah Wood, Nora Arnezeder, Genevieve Alexandra, Liane Balaban, Jan Broberg, Joshua De La Garza, Megan M Duffy, America Olivio, Sammi Rotibi.
▶ *Dir* Franck Khalfoun, *Pro* Alexandre Aja, Thomas Langmann and William Lustig, *Screenplay* Aja and Gregory Levasseur, based on Joe Spinell's 1980 screenplay, *Ph* Maxime Alexandre, *Pro Des* Stefania Cella, *Ed* Khalfoun and Baxter, *M* Robin Coudert, *Cos* Mairi Chisholm.

La Petite Reine/Studio 37/Canal+/Ciné+/Blue Underground-Wild Bunch.
89 mins. France/USA. 2012. Rel: 15 Mar 2013. Cert. 18.

Marius ★★★

Daniel Auteuil continues his homage to Marcel Pagnol with this remake of the first part of his 1930s Marseille trilogy. *Fanny* [qv] has also appeared and is easily the more successful film. That's because the opening section of this story, dealing as it does with Fanny's love for Marius being frustrated by his desire to go to sea, suffers from its restricted setting and from being rushed. But it does come from the heart and it is doubtless best to see this before viewing its superior successor in which Auteuil as César, Fanny's father, comes into his own. MS

▶ Daniel Auteuil, Raphaël Personnaz, Victoire Belezy, Jean-Pierre Darroussin.
▶ *Dir* and *Screenplay* (based on the work of Marcel Pagnol) Daniel Auteuil, *Pro* Alain Sarde and Jérôme Seydoux, *Ph* Jean-François Robin, *Pro Des* Christian Marti, *Ed* Joëlle Hache, *M* Alexandre Desplat, *Cos* Pierre-Yves Gayraud.

A.S. Films/Zack Films/ Pathé /Canal+/Ciné+ etc.-Pathé Productions.
94 mins. France. 2012. Rel: 29 Nov 2013. Cert. 12A.

Model murder: Elijah Wood and mannequin in Franck Khalfoun's brutal *Maniac*.

Sister act: Jacopo
Olmo Antinori
and Tea Falco
in Bernardo
Bertolucci's
Me and You.

May I Kill U? ★★★

This, Stuart Urban's third fiction feature, would
make an interesting double-bill with last year's *God
Bless America*. It's a defiantly small-scale offering,
turning on a London cycle cop who sustains a head
injury and turns into a serial-killing vigilante (or
"death facilitator"). More than that, he becomes
an internet hero in as scabrous a satire on modern
Britain as one could wish for. There's plenty of
gruesome wit (one of the victims, deposited in a
dumpster, is memorialised with "I just put some
white trash where it belongs forever"), though
there are lulls and longueurs too. Even so, Urban
and cinematographer Fernando Ruiz capture a
uniquely British kind of grottiness which (despite
all the technology on view) is timeless. JR

▶ Kevin Bishop, Jack Doolan, Frances Barber, Hayley-
Marie Axe, Kasia Koleczek, Rosemary Leach, Ali Craig.
▶ *Dir* and *Screenplay* Stuart Urban, *Pro* Urban and
Alan Jay, *Ph* Fernando Ruiz, *Pro Des* Sabina Sattar, *Ed*
Ruiz and Christopher Chow, *M* Haim Frank Ilfman,
Cos Cathy Lang.
**Vectis Vision/MIKU/Cyclops Vision-Miracle
Communications.**
87 mins. UK. 2012. Rel: 11 Jan 2013. Cert. 15.

McCullin ★★★★

The outstanding British photographer Don
McCullin, now a septuagenarian, is centre screen in
this compelling documentary portraying his life in
chronological order and underlining his presence
in so many war zones. If he seems addicted to this
need to produce often shocking photographs, his
sincerity and sensitivity are never in doubt as he
illustrates the madness of war. This revealing film
shows just how brilliant his imagery is. MS

▶ With Don McCullin, Sir Harold Evans.
▶ *Dir* Jacqui and David Morris, *Pro* Jacqui Morris,
Ph Richard Stewart and Michael Wood, *Ed* Andy
McGraw and David Fairhead, *M* Alex Baranowski.
**British Film Company/Rankin Film Productions/Frith
Street Films-Artificial Eye.**
95 mins. UK. 2012. Rel: 1 Jan 2013. Cert. 15.

Me and You ★★★

This film marking Bernardo Bertolucci's return to
filmmaking after being confined to a wheelchair
shows that he has lost none of his directorial
flair. However, Niccolò Ammaniti's novella,
which concerns an odd 14-year-old seeking
seclusion in a basement where he encounters his
half-sister who is in her twenties, does not seem
suited to an extended treatment. Since we know
little about these characters, we remain distant
observers. There are good moments certainly,
but as a whole it's too elusive and insubstantial.
(Original title: *Io e te*) MS

▶ Jacopo Olmo Antinori, Tea Falco, Sonia
Bergamasco, Veronica Lazar, Pippo Delbono.
▶ *Dir* Bernardo Bertolucci, *Pro* Mario Gianani,

Screenplay Niccolò Ammaniti, Umberto Contarello, Francesca Marciano and Bertolucci, from Ammaniti's novel, *Ph* Fabio Cianchetti, *Pro Des* Jean Rabasse, *Ed* Jacopo Quadri, *M* Franco Piersanti, *Cos* Metka Kosak.

A Fiction and Mario Gianani production/Wildside/ Medusa Film etc.-Artificial Eye.
96 mins. Italy/Switzerland. 2012. Rel: 19 Apr 2013. Cert. 15.

Mea Maxima Culpa: Silence in the House of God ★★★★

Alex Gibney's exposé of paedophiles within the Catholic Church is occasionally over-dramatised but much of it is compelling. The focus initially is on one priest at a church for the deaf (actors effectively give words to what victims are expressing in sign language) but, as the film goes on, it widens out becoming ever more impressive and disturbing. Ultimately it puts the responses and reactions of two popes, John Paul II and Benedict XVI, in the spotlight. MS

❱ With the voices of John Slattery, Ethan Hawke, Chris Cooper.
❱ *Dir* and *Written by* Alex Gibney, *Pro* Todd and Jedd Wider, Gibney and others, *Ph* Lisa Rinzler, *Ed* Sloane Klevin, *M* Ivor Guest and Robert Logan.

A Jigsaw production/Wider Film Projects/Below the Radar Films etc.-Element Pictures Distribution.
107 mins. USA/Ireland. 2012. Rel: 15 Feb 2013. Cert. 15.

Metallica: Through the Never ★★★★

Nimrod Antal's imaginative concert movie is actually two films for the price of one. The Metallica concert is spectacular, as can be expected, but the back story featuring the fictional adventures of Trip (Dane DeHaan) is equally impressive. Trip is a young roadie for Metallica, sent on a special mission during the band's show. The concert is terrific and so are the set-pieces focusing on Trip. GS

❱ Dane DeHaan, James Hetfield, Lars Ulrich, Kirk Hammett, Robert Trujillo, Kyle Thomson, Toby Hargrave.
❱ *Dir* Nimrod Antal, *Pro* Charlotte Huggins, Deena Sheldon and Jeff Zachary, *Screenplay* Antal, Hammett, Ulrich, Trujillo and Hetfield, *Ph* Gyula Pados, *Pro Des* Helen Jarvis, *Ed* Joe Hutshing, *M* Metallica, *Cos* Carla Hetland.

Blackened Recordings/Exclusive Media Group/Hit the Lights-Entertainment One.
93 mins. USA. 2013. Rel: 4 Oct 2013. Cert. 15.

Metro Manila ★★★

British director Sean Ellis sensibly had the initiative to make this film in the Philippines as a subtitled work. He seeks to confront social issues while also setting up a thriller about a poor man from the north working for an armoured truck company as he struggles to survive with his family in Manila. Unfortunately, on turning into a heist movie the film starts to feel decidedly fictional and an over-emphatic music score invalidates it even further. Ellis could have learnt something from Ken Loach's approach in *Bread and Roses* (2000). MS

❱ Jake Macapagal, John Arcilla, Althea Vega, Erin Panlilio, JM Rodriguez.
❱ *Dir* and *Ph* Sean Ellis, *Pro* Ellis and Mathilde Charpentier, *Screenplay* Ellis and Frank E Flowers from Ellis's story, *Pro Des* Ian Traifalgar, *Ed* Richard Metter, *M* Robin Foster, *Cos* Lumen Medrano.

Chocolate Frogs Films-Independent Distribution.
115 mins. UK. 2012. Rel: 20 Sep 2013. Cert. 15.

Michael H. Profession: Director ★★★½

Those not well versed in the films of Michael Haneke are not properly catered for in this survey of his career starting with *Amour* and working backwards. Many contributors (among whom Isabelle Huppert stands out) go unidentified and excellent film extracts carry little indication of what the films were actually about. Haneke is present but such controversial issues as his US remake of *Funny Games* are ignored. Even so, it is fascinating for his admirers. MS

❱ With Michael Haneke, Isabelle Huppert, Juliette Binoche, Jean-Louis Trintignant.
❱ *Dir* Yvers Montmayeur, *Pro* Vincent Lucassen, Ebba Sinzinger and Serge Guez, *Ph* Montmayeur and Attila Boa, *Ed* Oliver Neumann.

Wildart Film/Crescendo Films/Les Films du Losange etc.-Artificial Eye.
92 mins. Austria/France/Germany/Switzerland. 2013. Rel: 15 Mar 2013. Cert. 18.

Highly strung: James Hetfield in Nimrod Antal's *Metallica: Through the Never.*

Dreaming the dream: Eddie Redmayne as Marius Pontmercy in Tom Hooper's award-laden *Les Misérables*.

Midnight Son ★★★★

Jacob (Zak Kilberg) works as a night security guard and avoids daylight as he suffers from a rare skin disorder. But when he is later diagnosed as anaemic he resorts to drinking human blood... Kilberg is excellent as the highly sympathetic and vulnerable protagonist and Scott Leberecht's fluid direction expertly builds up suspense – perfectly accompanied by an eerie soundtrack which enhances the action. GS

▶ Zak Kilberg, Maya Parish, Jo D Jonz, Larry Cedar, Tracey Walter, Arlen Escarpeta, Kevin McCorkle, Juanita Jennings.
▶ *Dir* and *Screenplay* Scott Leberecht, *Pro* Matt Compton, *Ph* Lyn Moncrief, *Pro Des* Manuel Perez Pena, *Ed* Ian McCamey, *M* Kays Al-Atrakchi and Geoff Levin, *Cos* Mairi Chisholm.

**Free Lunch Productions-Monster Pictures.
88 mins. USA. 2011. Rel: 11 Jan 2013. Cert. 18.**

Milius ★★★½

Filmmaker John Milius came to the fore at about the same time as Spielberg, Scorsese, Lucas and Coppola, all of whom appear in this documentary portrait of him eager to praise. But if the man's right-wing opinions and his macho image invite questions, so do his films, be he writer, director or both, since they are decidedly variable in quality. Having now recovered from a stroke, Milius hopes to make a comeback. Given that situation, this film backs away from being confrontational although that is what would have brought it more fully to life. MS

▶ With John Milius, Martin Scorsese, Steven Spielberg, Oliver Stone, Walter Murch, Francis Ford Coppola, Richard Dreyfuss, Arnold Schwarzenegger, Clint Eastwood.
▶ *Dir* Joey Figueroa and Zak Knutson, *Pro* Figueroa, Knutson and Ken Plume, *Ed* Knutson, *M* Daniel Sternbaum.

**Haven Entertainment/O.G.B./a Chop Shop Entertainment production etc.-StudioCanal Limited.
103 mins. USA. 2013. Rel: 1 Nov 2013. Cert. 15.**

Les Misérables ★★★★

This is Tom Hooper's brilliantly realised film version of the musical treatment of the Victor Hugo classic; it flows so well that it readily sustains a running length of 158 minutes. For my personal taste the tale of injustice in 19th century France is at times too manipulative and sentimental, but you can blame Hugo for that. Here a fine cast, not least the stunning, award-winning Anne Hathaway, rises to the occasion. In any case the theme of the need to fight for freedom is universal and as relevant as ever. On its own terms this is a triumph. MS

▶ Hugh Jackman, Russell Crowe, Anne Hathaway, Amanda Seyfried, Eddie Redmayne, Samantha Barks, Isabelle Allen, Helena Bonham Carter, Sacha Baron Cohen.

▸ *Dir* Tom Hooper, *Pro* Tim Bevan, Eric Fellner, Debra Hayward and Cameron Mackintosh, *Screenplay* William Nicholson, Alain Boublil, Claude-Michel Schönberg and Herbert Kretzmer, from the stage musical based on the novel by Victor Hugo, *Ph* Danny Cohen, *Pro Des* Eve Stewart, *Ed* Melanie Ann Oliver and Chris Dickens, *M* Schönberg, *Cos* Paco Delgado.

A Universal Pictures presentation/a Working Title Films/ Cameron Mackintosh production etc.-Universal. 158 mins. USA/UK/Japan. 2012. Rel: 11 Jan 2013. Cert. 12A.

Mister John ★★★

There's an outstanding performance here from Aiden Gillen as a man who, with his own life in disarray, travels to Singapore when his brother, who had been married to a Thai woman, dies. Becoming caught up in the life of the widow and wearing the dead man's clothes, it is as though he is taking over his brother's identity. Ultimately this tale proves to be about mid-life crisis, but that only becomes clear at the close and meanwhile the visuals and the music score are more telling than the actual narrative, which is slow-paced and sometimes pretentious. MS

▸ Aiden Gillen, Zoe Tay, Michael Thomas, Claire Keelan.
▸ *Dir, Screenplay* and *Ed* Christine Molloy and Joe Lawlor, *Pro* David Collins, Fran Borgia and Lawlor, *Ph* Ole Birkland, *Pro Des* Daniel Lim, *M* Stephen McKeon, *Cos* Meredith Lee.

BFI/Bord Scannán na hÉireann/Irish Film Board/a Samson Films, Akanga Film Asia, Desperate Optimists production etc.-Curzon Film World. 95 mins. Republic of Ireland/Republic of Singapore/UK. 2013. Rel: 27 Sep 2013. Cert. 15.

Monsters Inc. 3D ★★★★

Another Pixar 3D conversion: this is greatly improved – probably because so much of it is about confined spaces (eg, kids' bedrooms at night) or wide open spaces. So much so, in fact, that by the time you get to the finale – lots of doors moving around whilst hanging vertically from overhead racks with a huge spatial drop below – it's hard to believe this was actually made in 2D and not 3D. Not that it wasn't hugely engaging to start with. JC

▸ Voices of John Goodman, Billy Crystal, Mary Gibbs, Steve Buscemi, James Coburn, Jennifer Tilly, Bob Peterson, John Ratzenburger, Frank Oz.
▸ *Dir* Pete Docter, David Silverman and Lee Unkrich, *Pro* Darla K Anderson, *Screenplay* Andrew Stanton, Daniel Gerson, Robert L Baird, Rhett Reese and Jonathan Roberts, based on an original story by Docter, Jill Culton, Jeff Pidgeon and Ralph Eggleston, *Pro Des* Harley Jessup and Bob Pauley, *Ed* Robert

Grahamjones and Jim Stewart, *M* Randy Newman.

Walt Disney Pictures/Pixar Animation Studios-Walt Disney Studios Motion Pictures. 92 mins. USA. 2001. Rel: 8 Feb 2002. Re-released in 3D 18 Jan 2013. Cert. U.

Monsters University ★★★½

After the success of *Monsters Inc.* (2001, but back this year in 3D: qv) there had to be a sequel. This is actually a prequel telling how little Mike and big Sulley, both monsters to their fingertips (who generate the city's power by frightening little kids out of their wits), learned how to be scary in college, as if their looks alone weren't enough to unhinge most folk. The animation is Pixar at its best, even if the script is not. The detail is splendid (Mike even wears a brace on his teeth) and the voice work by Billy Crystal as Mike, John Goodman as Sulley and Helen Mirren as the swooping Dean Hardscrabble is perfect. MHD

▸ Voices of Billy Crystal, John Goodman, Steve Buscemi, Helen Mirren, Alfred Molina, Peter Sohn, Joel Murray.
▸ *Dir* Dan Scanlon, *Pro* Kori Rae, *Screenplay* Daniel Gerson, Robert L. Baird and Dan Scanlon, *Ph* Matt Aspbury and Jean-Claude Kalach, *Pro Des* Ricky Nierva, *Ed* Greg Snyder, *M* Randy Newman.

Walt Disney Pictures/Pixar Animation Studios-Walt Disney Studios Motion Pictures. 104 mins. USA. 2013. Rel: 12 July 2013. Cert. U.

The Moo Man ★★★★½

Forget the ill-chosen title: this is a superbly made documentary from Andy Heathcote about a Sussex dairy farmer struggling to make his family business survive in difficult times. The sympathetic but unsentimental bond between the filmmaker and the farmer is ideal although one would have liked to see more of the rest of the farmer's family. Great visuals (by Heathcote

Diary of the dairy: farmer Stephen Hook in Andy Heathcote and Heike Bachelier's *The Moo Man.*

himself), great music (by Stephen Daltry) and a cinematic flow that suspends time for the viewer combine to make this an outstanding film. MS

❯ With Stephen Hook.
❯ *Dir* and *Pro* Andy Heathcote with Heike Bachelier, *Ph* Heathcote, *Ed* Bachelier, *M* Stephen Daltry.
A Trufflepig Films production-November Films/ Trufflepig Films.
98 mins. UK. 2013. Rel: 12 July 2013. Cert. U.

Moon Man ★★★★

Tomi Ungerer's 1966 story, telling how a rather bored man in the moon comes to Earth and discovers his value to children here, has now become a charming animated feature. Its ideal audience may well be very young children but it is not difficult for adults to engage too, given the film's sincerity and the fine voicing done in the version I saw by mainly Irish players. Seek it out. (Original title: *Der Mondmann*) MS

❯ With the English language voices of Katharina Thalbach, Pat Laffan, Michael McElhatton, Paul McLoone, Taylor Mooney, Helen Mooney. Narrated by Tomi Ungerer.
❯ *Dir* Stephan Schesch with Sarah Clara Weber, *Pro* and *Screenplay* (from Tomi Ungerer's book) Schesch, *Ed* Weber, *Animation Supervisors* Heidi Yilun, Chen Ceslik and Gyula Szabo.

Hip to the bone (and forever morose): Steven Patrick Morrissey in James Russell's Morrissey: 25: Live.

A Schesch Filmkreation (Germany), Le Pacte (France), Cartoon Saloon (Ireland) co-production etc.-Wildcard Distribution.
95 mins. Germany/France/Ireland. 2012. Rel: 27 Dec. 2013. Cert.U.

More Than Honey ★★★

This strange documentary was promoted as a study of 'colony collapse disorder', the worldwide phenomenon whereby bees have been vanishing and thus leaving numerous colonies decimated. Bizarrely the film is over halfway through before it gets to its true subject. Up to that point it is informative about bees in general, but that's frustrating when you are waiting for it to deal with this key issue. Furthermore, there's no real sense of shape or structure being brought to bear on material which is admittedly of interest in its own right. MS

❯ With Fred Jaggi, Fred Terry, John Miller and John Hurt (narrator).
❯ *Dir* and *Written by* Markus Imhoof, *Pro* Thomas Kufus, Helmut Grasser and Pierre-Alain Meier, *Ph* Jörg Jeshel and Attila Boa, *Ed* Anne Fabini, *M* Peter Scherer.
Zero One Film/Allegro Film/Thelma Film & Ormenis Film etc.-Eureka Entertainment.
95 mins. Germany/Austria/Switzerland. 2012. Rel: 6 Sep 2013. No Cert.

Morrissey: 25: Live ★★★★

This documentary commemorates the 25th anniversary of the former Smiths' singer's solo career. It was filmed during Morrissey's concert at the Hollywood High School in Los Angeles on 2 March 2013 and opens with fans singing the praises of their idol. Morrissey performs Smiths and solo classics to an ecstatic audience and the joy is easily transported to the screen. He is a dignified performer, but is unafraid to share his microphone with his adoring audience. A great concert film and not just for the fans. GS

❯ With Morrissey.
❯ *Dir* James Russell, *Pro* Vicki Betihavas, *Ph* Nick Wheeler, *Ed* Simon Bryant and Nicholas Meddings, *M* Morrissey.
Eagle Rock Entertainment/Nineteen Fifteen/ERP-More2Screen.
92 mins. USA. 2013. Rel: 23 Aug 2013. Cert. PG.

The Mortal Instruments: City of Bones ★½

Now that the *Harry Potter* and *Twilight* sagas have been wrapped up and put to bed, it's time for the fantastical onslaught of Cassandra Clare's literary odyssey. But whereas *Harry Potter* had wonder, charm and humour, this just accelerates with more action, more combat and

more so-called 'special' effects; in short, one damned thing after another. Top-loaded with CGI and a cast of pale and interesting anorexics (with largely English accents), the film packs in as much fantasy, romance, action, shadow hunters, demons, vampires and werewolves as its running time will allow. But it's over-long, over-scored and over-produced, full of sound and fury signifying nothing. JC-W

⟩ Lily Collins, Jamie Campbell Bower, Robert Sheehan, Kevin Zegers, Lena Headey, Kevin Durand, Aidan Turner, Jemima West, CCH Pounder, Jared Harris, Jonathan Rhys Meyers.
⟩ *Dir* Harald Zwart, *Pro* Don Carmody and Robert Kulzer, *Screenplay* Jessica Postigo Paquette, based on the novel by Cassandra Clare, *Ph* Geir Hartly Andreassen, *Pro Des* François Séguin, *Ed* Joel Negron, *M* Atli Örvarsson, *Cos* Gersha Phillips.

Constantin Film Produktion/Unique Features/Mr. Smith Productions-Entertainment One.
129 mins. USA/Germany. 2013. 21 Aug 2013.
Rel: Cert. 12A.

Moshi Monsters: The Movie
★★★½

Katsuma, Poppet, Mr Snoodle and fellow Moshi Monsters race against time to stop evil Dr Strangeglove and his Glump sidekick Fishlips from pulverising the Great Moshling Egg. That's the brilliantly daft and weirdly surreal plot and, with simple, colourful animation and a fun, boisterous script, this is ideal for three- to eight-year-old kids and tolerant adults. Bright and lively, action-packed and filled with catchy songs (including a Bollywood number!), the 80

minutes just whiz by. Any film with the character Dr Strangeglove, not to mention Buster Bumblechops and Luvli, has got to deserve at least one extra star for wit. DW

⟩ Voices of Phillipa Alexander, Steve Cleverley, Rajesh David, Boris Hiestand, Tom Clarke Hill, Ashley Slater, Emma Tate, Keith Wickham.
⟩ *Dir* Wip Vernooij, *Pro* Giles Healy and Jocelyn Stevenson, *Screenplay* Cleverley and Stevenson, *Art Dir* Cako Facioli, *Ed* Mark Edwards, *M* Sanj Sen.

Mind Candy-Universal Pictures.
81 mins. UK. 2013. Rel: 20 Dec 2013. Cert. U.

The Moth Diaries ★★★

Sarah Bolger stars as 16-year-old Rebecca who records her most intimate thoughts in a diary. She suspects that the mysterious new girl at her all-girls' boarding school, Lily Cole's Ernessa, possesses dark secrets. Rebecca is jealous of Ernessa's bond with her best friend and room mate, Lucy (Sarah Gadon), who won't listen to her warnings. The first feature in six years from Mary Harron, director of *I Shot Andy Warhol* and *American Psycho*, is another striking, compelling film with dangerously dysfunctional characters and a weird, unsettling atmosphere. Harron also scripts this satisfyingly eerie horror movie from Rachel Klein's 2002 novel. DW

⟩ Sarah Bolger, Lily Cole, Judy Parfitt, Anne Day-Jones, Sarah Gadon, Valerie Tian, Melissa Farman.
⟩ *Dir* and *Screenplay* Mary Harron, from the novel by Rachel Klein, *Pro* David Collins, Karine Martin, *Ph* Declan Quinn, *Pro Des* Sylvain Gingras, *Ed* Andrew Marcus, *M* Lesley Barber.

Cartoon madness: Wip Vernooij's *Moshi Monsters: The Movie.*

O, what men dare do!: Fran Kranz as Claudio in William Shakespeare and Joss Whedon's *Much Ado About Nothing.*

Movie 43 ★

This is a new form of deadpan comedy in which it's the viewer who remains deadpan, watching in stony-faced disbelief as a clunking series of schoolboy sketches winds its way inexorably up its own orifice. Bizarrely, Peter Farrelly's witless portmanteau boasts an all-star cast, giving you the opportunity to see Hugh Jackman with testicles where his Adam's apple should be, Anna Faris begging to be 'pooped' on, Richard Gere discussing shredded penises, Chloë Grace Moretz having her first period, and Halle Berry inserting a turkey baster up herself. Julianne Moore must have been thrilled when her sketch was dropped. (NB: The UK and US releases feature entirely different wraparound stories, meaning that British audiences didn't get to see Dennis Quaid and Greg Kinnear.) JR

❯ Richard Gere, Gerard Butler, Seth MacFarlane, Johnny Knoxville, Halle Berry, Hugh Jackman, Kate Winslet, Katie Finneran, Rocky Russo, Liev Schreiber, Naomi Watts, Anna Faris, Kieran Culkin, Kate Bosworth, Uma Thurman, Bobby Cannavale, Chloë Grace Moretz, Seann William Scott etc.
❯ *Dir* Elizabeth Banks, Steven Brill, Steve Carr, Rusty Candieff, James Duffy, Griffin Dunne, Peter Farrelly, Patrik Forsberg, Will Graham, James Gunn, Brett Ratner and Jonathan van Tullken, *Pro* Peter Farrelly, Ryan Kavanaugh, John Penoti, Charles B. Wessler etc,

Screenplay Rocky Russo, Bill O'Malley, Will Graham, Jack Kukoda, Jeremy Sosenko, James Gunn etc, *Ph* Steve Gainer, Daryn Okada, William Rexer, Tim Suhrstedt etc, *Pro Des* Toby Corbett, Jade Healy, Dina Lipton, Happy Massee, Inbal Weinberg etc, *Ed* Debra Chiate, Craig Herring, Sam Sieg, Paul Zucker etc, *M* Tyler Bates, Christophe Beck, Leo Birenberg, William Goodrum and Dave Hodge, *Cos* Anna Bingermann, Nancy Ceo, Sydney Maresca, Salvador Pérez Jr etc.

Relativity Media/Virgin Produced/GreeneStreet/Wessler Entertainment/Witness Protection Films-Momentum Pictures.
90 mins. USA. 2013. Rel: 25 Jan 2013. Cert. 15.

Much Ado About Nothing ★★★★

Setting Shakespeare's play in modern-day America makes the plot harder to follow and fans of writer-director Joss Whedon coming to the piece for the first time in this adaptation may suffer accordingly. Nevertheless Whedon's love of the play and the enthusiasm of his cast (especially Amy Acker as Beatrice) ensure that the film works. The broader comic moments are always a matter of taste, but the badinage between Beatrice and Benedick comes over beautifully and Whedon brings out well the darker side of this comedy of love. MS

❯ Amy Acker, Alexis Denisof, Clark Gregg, Nathan Fillion, Jillian Morgese.
❯ *Dir, adaptation* from Shakespeare's play and *M* Joss Whedon, *Pro* Kai Cole and Whedon, *Ph* Jay Hunter, *Pro Des* Cindy Chao and Michele Yu, *Ed*

Daniel S. Kaminsky and Whedon, *Cos* Shawna Trpcic.

A Bellwether production-Kaleidoscope Entertainment.
108 mins. USA. 2012. Rel: 14 June 2013. Cert. 12A.

Mud ★★★

This atmospheric Arkansas tale echoes both LP Hartley's *The Go-Between* and the world of Tom Sawyer and Huckleberry Finn. It centres on a boy of 14 whose youthful innocence is corrupted when he is drawn into helping out lovers, the titular Mud (Matthew McConaughey) and the abused girl he adores. Admirably acted as the film is, it is a great shame that the screenplay eventually abandons subtlety and credibility for clichés, together with a final shootout totally at odds with the persuasive account of adolescents discovering an adult world of betrayal, deceit and flawed humanity. MS

‣ Matthew McConaughey, Tye Sheridan, Sam Shepard, Michael Shannon, Reese Witherspoon, Sarah Paulson, Joe Don Baker, Bonnie Sturdivant.
‣ *Dir* and *Screenplay* Jeff Nichols, *Pro* Sarah Green, Aaron Ryder and Lisa Maria Falcone, *Ph* Adam Stone, *Pro Des* Richard A Wright, *Ed* Julie Monroe, *M* David Wingo, *Cos* Kari Perkins.

Lionsgate/Everest Entertainment/a Brace Cove/
FilmNation production-E1 Films.
130 mins. USA. 2012. Rel: 10 May 2013. Cert. 12A.

Muscle Shoals ★★★★

This sympathetic documentary ably sets out the history of the FAME recording studios in Muscle Shoals, Alabama. Inevitably the music and the singers who comment on it play a huge role, but the film is also a touching and revealing portrait of the studio's founder Rick Hall. In addition there is fascinating detail related to the way in which in its early days the studio challenged Alabama's segregationalist laws. Lasting 111 minutes, it might gain from being tauter but most viewers will be well satisfied. MS

‣ With Rick Hall, Aretha Franklin, Keith Richards, Mick Jagger, Bono.
‣ *Dir* Greg 'Freddy' Camalier, *Pro* Stephen Badger and Camalier, *Ph* Anthony Arendt, *Ed* Richard Lowe, *M Supervisor* Jill Meyer.

Ear Goggles Productions-Dogwoof.
111 mins. USA. 2013. Rel: 25 Oct 2013. Cert. PG.

Museum Hours ★★½

Filmed in Vienna, this is a minimalist work in that it devotes its 107 minutes to a situation rather than a plot. Anne (Mary Margaret O'Hara) comes from Montreal to visit a sick cousin and, alone in the city, is befriended by a gay guard (Bobby Sommer) from the Kunsthistorisches Art Museum. Almost a two-hander, the first half is an effective comment on the transience and loneliness of human life, but the second half lacks development and, despite some striking images, one longs for it to end because it has nothing to add to what has already been said. MS

‣ Bobby Sommer, Mary Margaret O'Hara, Ela Piplits.
‣ *Dir* and *Screenplay* (with contributions from the lead actors) Jem Cohen, *Pro* Paolo Calamita, Cohen and Gabriele Kranzelbinder, *Ph* Cohen and Peter Roehsler, *Ed* Cohen and Marc Vives.

Little Magnet Films/Gravity Hill/KGP Kranzelbinder
Gabriele Production-Soda Pictures.
107 mins. Austria/USA. 2012. Rel: 6 Sep 2013. Cert. 12A.

My Father and the Man in Black ★★★★

Jonathan Holiff makes his directorial debut with this excellent documentary about his father, Saul Holiff, who was Johnny Cash's personal manager from 1960 to 1973. It's a clear labour of love, exceptionally done, beautifully crafted and very moving. Cash comes over as quite a piece of work – but somehow you still can't help liking him. As it becomes a revealing story about father and son, the filmmaker bravely uses the movie as therapy. He should film a postscript scene to say if making it has healed him of his demons. It's notable that he dedicates it to his mother and not to father or both parents. There's a lot to think about here – how often can you truly say that after a film? DW

‣ With Jonathan Holiff, Harvey Glatt, Gary Holiff, David Disher, Joshua Robinson, Elli Hollands

Murky waters: Jacob Lofland, Matthew McConaughey and Tye Sheridan in Jeff Nichols' *Mud.*

Cornhusker men: Bruce Dern (in his Oscar-nominated role) and Will Forte in Alexander Payne's *Nebraska*.

▶ *Dir* and *Written by* Jonathan Holiff, *Pro* Holiff, Tanya Lyn Nazarec and Jennifer Phillips, *Pro Des* Adam Weir, *Ed* Nick Harauz and Rob Ruzic, *M* Michael Timmins, *Cos* Robyn Rosenberg.

New Chapter Productions-Ballpark Film Distributors. 87 mins. Canada. 2012. Rel: 2 Aug 2013. Cert. 15.

Nebraska ★★★★

Although not the writer this time, Alexander Payne's study of a son's relationship with his difficult near-senile father has most of the qualities that one associates with him. There's humour as the two take to the road after the old man erroneously believes that he has become a lottery winner, but at heart this is a defiantly unsentimental work evoking pity for empty and damaged lives. No praise is too high for Bruce Dern and the other leading players, for Mark Orton's music score and for Phedon Papamichael's black-and-white photography. However, I was not convinced by the upbeat ending which many may welcome but which, given its almost Capraesque tone, really belongs to another film. MS

▶ Bruce Dern, Will Forte, June Squibb, Stacy Keach, Bob Odenkirk.
▶ *Dir* Alexander Payne, *Pro* Albert Berger and Ron Yerxa, *Screenplay* Bob Nelson, *Ph* Phedon Papamichael, *Pro Des* Dennis Washington, *Ed* Kevin Tent, *M* Mark Orton, *Cos* Wendy Chuck.

Paramount Vantage/FilmNation Entertainment/a Bona Fide production etc.-Paramount Pictures UK. 115 mins. USA. 2013. Rel: 6 Dec 2013. Cert. 15.

Neighbouring Sounds ★★½

The neighbourhood is in Recife in north-eastern Brazil, where several story threads interweave although these are more akin to snapshots than fully fledged tales. The presence of a man set on revenge provides the strongest plot-line and the striking imagery means that the people are tellingly shown in their environment. But it's a long film and we come to care about the characters less and less. It's the failure to follow through which renders this genuinely individual debut by Kleber Mendonça Filho so disappointing in the long run. (Original title: *O som ao redor*) MS

▶ Irandhir Santos, Gustavo Jahn, Maeve Jinkings, WJ Solha, Irma Brown.
▶ *Dir* and *Screenplay* Kleber Mendonça Filho, *Pro* Emilie Lesclaux, *Ph* Pedro Sotero and Fabricio Tadeu, *Art Dir* Juliano Dornelles, *Ed* Mendonça and João Maria, *Soundtrack* DJ Dolores, *Cos* Ingrid Mata.

Petrobas/a CinemaScópio production etc.-Artificial Eye. 131 mins. Brazil/The Netherlands. 2012. Rel: 22 Mar 2013. Cert. 15.

Night of Silence ★★½

Far from being 'positively Hitchcockian' as the poster declares, this film from Turkey is a minimalistic exercise with a potentially touching theme about the marriage of a child bride. There's atmosphere in plenty and good acting but we know so little about either groom or bride that everything on their bridal night seems tediously slow and extended until we reach an ambiguous conclusion. (Original title: *Lal Gece*) MS

▶ Dilan Aksüt, Ilyas Salman, Sabri Tutal, Nazan Durmus, Mayseker Yücel.
▶ *Dir, Screenplay* and *Ed* Reis Çelik, *Pro* Anil Çelik, *Ph* Gökhan Tiryaki, *Art Dir* Burcu Karakas, *M* Anil Çelik.
KAZ Film Production Ltd.-Verve Pictures.
92 mins. Turkey. 2012. Rel: 28 June 2013. Cert. PG.

No ★★★½

Greatly admired by many, this is Pablo Larraín's third feature about Pinochet's Chile but quite different in tone from its predecessors *Tony Manero* and *Post Mortem*. Set in 1988 when Pinochet risked calling for a referendum on his presidency, the film uses satirical humour to make serious points. It concentrates on the opposition's use of advertising and a nightly television slot. However I found it underdramatised giving few opportunities to the distinguished cast despite a long, indeed over-long, running time. It's both interesting and honourable, but the screen shape chosen to incorporate actual video material of the time distracts. A documentary on the subject might have been more telling. MS

▶ Gael García Bernal, Alfredo Castro, Luis Gnecco, Antónia Zegers.
▶ *Dir* Pablo Larraín, *Pro* Juan de Dios Larraín and Daniel Marc Dreifuss, *Screenplay* Pedro Peirano, from the play *Referendum* by Antonio Skarmeta, *Ph* Sergio Armstrong, *Pro Des* Estefania Larrain, *Ed* Andrea Chignoli, *M* Carlos Cabezas, *Cos* Francisca Román.
Corfo Participant Media/Funny Balloons/Canana etc.-Network Releasing.
118 mins. Chile/USA/France/Mexico. 2012. Rel: 8 Feb 2013. Cert. 15.

No Fixed Abode (aka NFA) ★★

Steve Rainbow clearly has the best of intentions in this film made in Birmingham which sets out to portray a major social problem. But the movie's tag-line – 'A psychological thriller about homelessness' – underlines what is wrong with the film. If you want to engage an audience regarding a tragic social issue, why think in terms of a psychological thriller? That's even more pertinent when the story of a married man who wakes up in a hostel with no money and no memory of how he got there reveals itself as totally lacking in credibility. Well-meaning, yes, but to my mind a total misfire. MS

▶ Patrick Baladi, David Sterne, Saskia Butler, Simon Lowe, Vicky Roberts.

▶ *Dir* and *Screenplay* Steve Rainbow, *Pro* Anna Savill, Justin Edgar and Alex Usborne, *Ph* Flemming Jetmar, *Pro Des* Annabelle Bevan, *Ed* Philip Arkinstall, *M* Alex Baranowski.
104 films/WED Charitable Trust, Felix Dennis/UK Film Council-Ballpark Film Distributors.
72 mins. UK. 2012. Rel: 29 Nov 2013. Cert. 12A.

No One Lives ★½

Bad guys pick on a worse guy in this gory psycho-thriller starring Luke Evans as a nameless killer who terrorises and murders a gang of criminal toughs. Yet having monsters on both sides means there's no one to care about or root for. There's a girl in the middle, though, a traumatised hostage (Adelaide Clemens) we're supposed to want to see survive. Except it's all a bunch of immature nonsense so there's no chance of becoming engaged by any part of it. Tiresomely nasty and pretentious, it's neither scary fun nor interesting. MJ

▶ Luke Evans. Adelaide Clemens, Lee Tergesen, Derek Magyar, America Olivo, Beau Knapp, Lindsay Shaw.
▶ *Dir* Ryûhei Kitamura, *Pro* Harry Knapp and Kami Naghdi, *Screenplay* David Cohen, *Ph* Daniel Pearl, *Pro Des* Jonathan A Carlson, *Ed* Toby Yates, *M* Jerome Dillon, *Cos* Claire Breaux.
Pathé/Milk and Media/Constance Media/WWE Studios-20th Century Fox.
86 mins. USA. 2012. Rel: 6 Sep 2013. Cert. 18.

Nobody's Daughter: Haewon ★★½

Little known here outside the London Film Festival, Korea's Hong Sangsoo is unfortunate in that this off-putting film is his first to be distributed in this country. Haewon, left in Seoul

Ninguno!: a pensive Gael García Bernal in Pablo Larraín's *No*.

Habit of a lifetime: Pauline Etienne in Guillaume Nicloux's *The Nun.*

when her mother seeks a new life in Canada, is an unengaging heroine and we never come to care what happens to her relationship with a married teacher. A more vital issue for us is why Hong favours such details as a repeated emphasis on cigarette butts being stepped on! (Original title: *Nugu-ui ttal-do anin Haewon*) MS

▶ Jung Eunchae, Lee Sunkyun, Kim Eui-sung, Kim Ja-ok, Yu Jun-sang, Jane Birkin.
▶ *Dir* and *Screenplay* Hong Sangsoo, *Pro* Kim Kyounghee, *Ph* Kim Hyungkoo and Park Hongyeol, *Ed* Hahm Sungwon and Son Yeonji, *M* Jeong Yongjin.
A Jeonwonsa Film Co. production-StudioCanal Limited. 90 mins. Republic of Korea. 2013. Rel: 11 Oct 2013. Cert. 12A.

Not Another Happy Ending ★★

Doctor Who fans eager to see Karen Gillan's first significant post-Amy Pond effort will likely wander away from *Not Another Happy Ending* feeling much the same as anyone else who braves this hoary Scottish romcom: deflated, underwhelmed and certainly a little sleepy. Only Glasgow comes across well in this underwritten and feebly characterised tale of a blocked author who can only write when she's unhappy. Cue desperate publisher, deliberately depressing the poor girl while accidentally falling in love with her. Ho-ho-hopeless, I'm afraid. MJ

▶ Karen Gillan, Stanley Weber, Ian De Caestecker, Amy Manson, Kate Dickie, Freya Mavor, John Bett, Gary Lewis.

▶ *Dir* John McKay, *Pro* Claire Mundell, *Screenplay* David Solomons, *Ph* George Geddes, *Pro Des* Andy Harris, *Ed* Calum Ross, *M* Lorne Balfe, *Cos* Louise Allen.
British Film Company/Synchronicity Films-Kaleidoscope Entertainment. 102 mins. UK. 2013. Rel: 11 Oct 2013. Cert. 12A.

Now You See Me ★★★½

FBI agent Mark Ruffalo and Interpol detective Mélanie Laurent investigate a team of illusionists (Jesse Eisenberg, Woody Harrelson, Isla Fisher, Dave Franco) who, while performing in Las Vegas, declare they'll rob a bank and invite an audience member to be teleported to Paris to do it. Director Louis Leterrier's slick and handsomely produced caper thriller offers flashy sleight of hand and occasionally a touch of real movie magic. The cast is first rate and the plot's ingenious, even if the ending is frustratingly unsatisfying and full of loose ends. Still, it's mostly great fun and does the trick! It has a sequel up its sleeve. DW

▶ Jesse Eisenberg, Mark Ruffalo, Mélanie Laurent, Morgan Freeman, Michael Caine, Woody Harrelson, Isla Fisher, Dave Franco.
▶ *Dir* Louis Leterrier, *Pro* Robert Orc, Alex Kurtzman and Bobby Cohen, *Screenplay* Ed Solomon, Boaz Yakin and Edward Ricourt, from a story by Yakin and Ricourt, *Ph* Mitchell Amundsen, *Pro Des* Peter Wenham, *Ed* Robert Leighton and Vincent Tabaillon, *M* Brian Tyler, *Cos* Jenny Eagan.
Summit Entertainment/See Me Louisiana/KO Paper Products etc-Entertainment One. 115 mins. France/USA. 2013. Rel: 3 July 2013. Cert. 12A.

The Nun ★★★★

Previously filmed by Jacques Rivette as *La Religieuse* (1966), this new treatment of Diderot's classic novel has been unjustly neglected. This 18th century tale of a girl placed in a convent by her family as a matter of convenience is presented by Guillaume Nicloux (a new name to me) in a manner that would have offended neither Bresson nor Rohmer. Three mother superiors (one kind, one unfeeling, one lesbian) play roles in a work that avoids melodrama and the cast is on fine form. (Original title: *La Religieuse*) MS

▶ Pauline Etienne, Isabelle Huppert, Louise Bourgoin, Martina Gedeck, Françoise Lebrun, Agathe Bonitzer, Alice de Lencquesaing, Marc Barbé, Lou Castel.
▶ *Dir* Guillaume Nicloux, *Pro* Sylvie Pialat and Benoît Quainon, *Screenplay* Nicloux and Jérôme Beaujour, from the novel *La Religieuse* by Denis Diderot, *Ph* Yves Cape, *Pro Des* Olivier Radot, *Ed* Guy Lecorne, *M* Max Richter, *Cos* Anaïs Romand.

A Les Films du Worso/Belle Epoque Films/Versus Production co-production etc.-Metrodome Distribution Ltd.
112 mins. France/Germany/Belgium. 2013.
Rel: 1 Nov 2013. Cert. 12A.

Oblivion ★★★

Planet Earth, circa 2077, has been all but destroyed; giant generators retrieve what's left of its resources. Jack Harper (Tom Cruise), a technician living with his wife (Andrea Riseborough) on a space station, is employed to keep the machines from being savaged by gangs of alien so-called Scavengers. Basically this is a thriller about a mysterious woman (Olga Kurylenko) rescued by Harper from a crashed spaceship. In his dreams she seems familiar to him (shades of *Vertigo*?)... It could be a detective story, a gangster pic or a Western with its final shootout because, despite the seductive-looking visuals, the space setting seems like mere dressing. Cruise and company do what they can with a script based on director Joseph Kosinski's graphic novel but the whole affair is strangely uninvolving. MHD

▶ Tom Cruise, Morgan Freeman, Olga Kurylenko, Andrea Riseborough, Nikolaj Coster-Waldau, Melissa Leo.
▶ *Dir* Joseph Kosinski, *Pro* Kosinski, Peter Chernin, Dylan Clark, Duncan Henderson and Barry Levine, *Screenplay* Karl Gajdusek and Michael DeBruyn, based on Kosinski's graphic novel, *Ph* Claudio Miranda, *Pro Des* Darren Gilford, *Ed* Richard Francis-Bruce, *M* Joseph Trapanese, Anthony Gonzalez and M83, *Cos* Marlene Stewart.

Universal Pictures/Relativity Media/Monolith Pictures/ Radical Studios/Chernin Entertainment-Universal Pictures.
124 mins. USA. 2013. Rel: 10 Apr 2013. Cert. 12A.

The Odd Life of Timothy Green ★★★★

Mr and Mrs Green cannot have children; instead they put all their wishes for a child in a box and bury it in the garden. Like Jack's beanstalk, something grows and, after a stormy night, the Greens have a new son, who they name Timothy, and claim that he's adopted. Despite his one oddity – he has leaves growing out of his legs – Timothy

Alien nation: an oblivious Tom Cruise in Joseph Kosinski's *Oblivion*.

Deep purple:
Edward Hogg in
Viv Fongenie's
*Ollie Kepler's
Expanding
Purple World.*

is a force for good, bringing people together and making friends out of enemies. He even saves the local pencil factory from being sold overseas. Sentimental it may be, but taken as a fairytale fantasy this Disney film has much going for it, especially CJ Adams as the eponymous hero. MHD

▶ Jennifer Garner, Joel Edgerton, CJ Adams, M Emmett Walsh, Dianne Wiest, Odeya Rush, Shohreh Aghdashloo, Rosemarie DeWitt.
▶ *Dir* Peter Hedges, *Pro* Ahmet Zappa, Scott Sanders and James Whitaker, *Screenplay* Hedges, from a story by Zappa, *Ph* John Toll, *Pro Des* Wynn Thomas, *Ed* Andrew Mondshein, *M* Geoff Zanelli, *Cos* Susie DeSanto.

Walt Disney Pictures/Scott Sanders Productions/ Monsterfoot Productions-Walt Disney Studios Motion Pictures.
105 mins. USA. 2012. Rel: 5 Apr 2013. Cert. U.

Old Boy ★★★

Josh Brolin is great as Joe Doucett, an advertising executive abducted and locked into solitary confinement for 20 years. Inexplicably released, he embarks on an obsessive quest to find out why he was kidnapped and by whom. The trail leads to sexy young Marie Sebastian (Elizabeth Olsen), prison guard Chaney (Samuel L Jackson) and the nutter responsible, Adrian (Sharlto Copley). Director Spike Lee's bold, visceral reworking of Park Chan-wook's 2003 Korean thriller is patchy but highly effective in places. Just when you're falling under its spell, along comes a rotten scene to alienate you. Jackson is camp, Copley is terrible, but while Brolin is on screen alone it's on fire. DW

▶ Josh Brolin, Elizabeth Olsen, Sharlto Copley, Samuel L. Jackson, Michael Imperioli, Pom Klementieff.
▶ *Dir* Spike Lee, *Pro* Spike and Roy Lee and Doug Davison, *Screenplay* Mark Protosevich, based on a manga story by Garon Tsuchiya and Nobuaki Minegishi for Park Chan-wook's 2003 *Oldboy* film, *Ph* Sean Bobbitt, *Pro Des* Sharon Seymour, *Ed* Barry Alexander Brown, *M* Roque Baños, *Cos* Ruth E Carter.

Good Universe/OB Productions/40 Acres and a Mule/ Vertigo Entertainment- Universal Pictures International.
104 mins. USA. 2013. Rel: 6 Dec 2013. Cert. 18.

Ollie Kepler's Expanding Purple World ★★★

Ollie (Edward Hogg) lives a happy existence with his girlfriend Noreen (Jodie Whittaker). But when she unexpectedly dies his obsession with astronomy triggers his slow descent into hell... First shown at the Edinburgh International Film Festival in June 2010, Viv Fongenie's sensitive but bleak film is blessed with a committed performance from Hogg who manages to lift the rather one-dimensional script to another level. Whittaker is on fine form and so is Cathy Tyson as Ollie's loyal friend. GS

▶ Edward Hogg, Andrew Knott, Jodie Whittaker, Cathy Tyson, Jessica Pidsley, Mo Banerjee.
▶ *Dir, Pro* and *Screenplay* Viv Fongenie, *Ph* Mattias Nyberg, *Pro Des* Rachel Payne, *Ed* Jake Robertson, Jason de Vyea and Alexis Odiowei, *M* Isa Suarez, *Cos* Raquel Azevedo.

Fruitcake Films Limited-Nimbus Films.
90 mins. UK. 2010. Rel: 18 Feb 2013. Cert. 15.

Olympus Has Fallen ★★½

Could the White House ever be subject to attack by terrorists? Well, anything is possible – in the movies, that is. When the attack comes, all the Secret Service men are disposed of and the President (Aaron Eckhart) is taken hostage. A likely story, you may wonder, and you would be right because Antoine Fuqua's film is basically an incredible shoot-out between Korean mastermind Kang (Rick Yune) and disgraced former presidential guard Mike Banning (Gerard Butler, at his most po-faced), who wangles his way back into the White House to singlehandedly wipe out the opposition. It's noisy, it's silly and it's only moderately exciting. Morgan Freeman, Melissa Leo and Dylan McDermott are surprisingly misused. MHD

▶ Gerard Butler, Aaron Eckhart, Morgan Freeman, Angela Bassett, Rick Yune, Robert Forster, Cole Hauser, Ashley Judd, Melissa Leo, Dylan McDermott.
▶ *Dir* Antoine Fuqua, *Pro* Fuqua, Butler, Danny Lerner, Alan Siegel and Ed Cathell III. *Screenplay* Creighton Rothenberger and Katrin Benedikt, *Ph* Conrad W Hall, *Pro Des* Derek R Hill, *Ed* John Refoua, *M* Trevor Morris, *Cos* Doug Hall.

Millennium Films/Nu Image/West Coast Film Partners/ Gerard Butler Alan Siegel Entertainment-Lionsgate. 119 mins. USA. 2013. Rel: 17 Apr 2013. Cert. 15.

On Landguard Point ★★½

It is difficult to describe Robert Pacitti's debut feature, shot entirely in the east of England. It's a non-narrative film told through poetry, maps and ideas exploring the meaning of home, focusing on Landguard Point, a small peninsula in the Suffolk parish of Felixstowe. Does it sound pretentious? Well yes but, thanks to Michael Nyman's exquisite score, it is also curiously mesmerising. GS

▶ With Julia Bardsley, Dominic Johnstone, Dicky Eaton, Carla Esperanza Tommasini, Harminder Judge, Kira O'Reilly, Rajni Shah.
▶ *Dir* and *Written by* Robert Pacitti, *Pro* Nicola Gallani, *Ph* Lucy Cash and Becky Edmunds, *Ed* Hoping Chen, *M* Michael Nyman.

Pacitti Company-Green Grass Media. 83 mins. UK. 2012. Rel: 23 Aug 2013. Cert. PG.

One Chance ★★★★

Putting away the abrasive side of his personality, James Corden is surprisingly likeable in this uplifting, funny, delightfully feel-good Brit biopic. He gives an appealing, often showstopping turn as *Britain's Got Talent* winner Paul Potts, a Welsh mobile phone shop salesman, who lives the dream of becoming an opera singer. The makers want it to be *Billy Elliot*, even to casting Julie Walters again, and it very nearly is. There's plenty

of mileage in its early scenes of poor, shy, fat Paul being bullied at school and later by workmates in his generally crap life, like the pathetic if lovable loser he looks. This funny film has a huge heart, lots of good jokes and loads of good, rock-solid comedy performances. DW

▶ James Corden, Alexandra Roach, Julie Walters, Colm Meaney, Mackenzie Crook, Valeria Bilello,
▶ *Dir* David Frankel, *Pro* Simon Cowell, Brad Weston, Kris Thykier and Michael Menchel, *Screenplay* Justin Zackham, *Ph* Florian Ballhaus, *Pro Des* Martin Childs, *Ed* Wendy Greene Bricmont, *M* Theodore Shapiro, *Cos* Colleen Kelsall.

Relevant Entertainment/Syco Television-Entertainment Film Distributors. 103 mins. UK/USA. 2013. Rel: 25 Oct 2013. Cert. 12A.

One Direction: This Is Us ★★★

This 3D concert film is an intimate, all-access look at life on the road for the global phenomenon boy band. Live concert footage from London's O2 Arena mixes with unstaged footage from their lives both before and after their 2010 *X Factor* appearance. The unscripted documentary provides carefully PR-controlled insights into the preparation for their concerts, though we never really learn what it's like to be One Direction. That would be too insightful and intrusive, which isn't the point of this celebratory, fan-worshipping movie. Unrevealing though it is, it's also enjoyable, likeable and fun for fans. Morgan Spurlock directs slickly but blandly; you expect more from the maker of *Supersize Me*. DW

▶ With Niall Horan, Zayn Malik, Liam Payne, Harry Styles, Louis Tomlinson, Jon Shone, Dan Richards, Sandy Beales, Josh Devine.
▶ *Dir* Morgan Spurlock, *Pro* Spurlock, Simon Cowell, Ted Kenney, Ben Winston and Adam Milano, *Ph* Neil Harvey, *Ed* Pierre Takai, Wyatt Smith, Cori McKenna, Marrian Cho and Guy Harding, *M* Simon Franglen.

A passion above his station: James Corden (right) goofs off with Mackenzie Crook in David Frankel's *One Chance.*

Tri-Star Pictures/Warrior Poets/Fulwell 73/Syco
Entertainment-Sony Pictures Releasing.
92 mins. USA. 2013. Rel: 29 Aug 2013. Cert. PG.

One Mile Away ★★★★

Having already filmed an explosive hip hop drama
about gang warfare among the Afro-Caribbean
community in the West Midlands, director and
writer Penny Woolcock was approached by Shabba,
a real-life member of one of the Birmingham
gangs (the Johnson Crew) who was looking for a
solution to end local gang warfare activities. She
then contacted one of the stars of her 2009 film
(*1 Day*), Dylan Duffus of the Burger Bar Boys, and
got together with Shabba. The film follows the two
men as they try to talk to their own and rival gang
members, a ploy that was only partially successful.
The film, however, takes a cool look at a constant
problem that may never be solved. PL

▶ With Matthias Thompson, Shabba, Dylan Duffus,
Simeon Moore, Joel Eccleston, Daniel Davidson.
▶ *Dir* Penny Woolcock, *Pro* James Purnell,
Ph Alexander Piatti, *Ed* Alex Fry, *M* Urban Monk.

Channel 4/Creative England/Barrow Cadbury Trust/
Bertha Foundation/ Kickstarter!/Rare Day-BRITDOC
Films (Impact Distribution).
91 mins. UK. 2012. Rel: 29 Mar 2013. Cert. 15.

Only God Forgives ★★½

As a man on the outskirts of the law, Ryan
Gosling gives us another variation of his
minimalist moodiness, running both a boxing
club and a drug smuggling operation. However,
as he drifts around the neon-lit shadows of
Bangkok, his older brother (Tom Burke) takes
some rather questionable liberties with the local
female populace… As is his wont, director Nicolas
Winding Refn builds an atmosphere of menace
and unease with some finesse but, in spite of
a stand-out turn from Kristin Scott Thomas,

*Rap party:
Shabba and
Dylan Duffus in
Penny Woolcock's
One Mile Away.*

it's not enough to salvage what is essentially a
maddeningly mannered (and thin) exercise in
exotic sadism. JC-W

▶ Ryan Gosling, Kristin Scott Thomas, Vithaya
Pansringarm, Rhatha Phongam, Tom Burke.
▶ *Dir* and *Screenplay* Nicolas Winding Refn,
Pro Lene Børglum, *Ph* Larry Smith, *Pro Des* Beth
Mickle, *Ed* Matthew Newman, *M* Cliff Martinez,
Cos Wasitchaya 'Nampeung' Mochanakul.

Grand Elephant/Bold Films/Film i Väst-LionsGate.
90 mins. Denmark/France. 2013. Rel: 2 Aug 2013. Cert. 18.

Our Children ★

Inexplicably praised in some quarters, this tragic
drama defeats its very talented cast. This is partly
because its tale about an obsessive French doctor
with a hold over a Moroccan youth, one that
extends beyond the youngster's marriage, is
never clearly portrayed. But even more at fault is
the director's eccentric use of often blacked-out
screen space which is so distracting that we are
prevented from engaging with the story. This is
Brechtian with a vengeance. (Original title:
À perdre la raison) MS

▶ Niels Arestrup, Tahar Rahim, Emilie Dequenne,
Stéphane Bissot.
▶ *Dir* Joachim Lafosse, *Pro* Jacques-Henri Bronckart,
Olivier Bronckart, Sylvie Pialat and others, *Screenplay*
Lafosse, Matthieu Reynaert and Thomas Bidegain,
Ph Jean-François Hensgens, *Art Dir* Anna Falguères,
Ed Sophie Vercruysse, *Cos* Magdalena Labuz.

Versus Production/Samsa Film/Les Films du Worso/Box
Productions etc.-Peccadillo Pictures Ltd.
111 mins. Belgium/Luxembourg/France/Switzerland.
2012. Rel: 10 May 2013. Cert. 15.

Out in the Dark ★★★½

Reminiscent of last year's *Yossi* this is another gay
film from Israel but this time political elements
play a strong role. The 'Romeo and Juliet' aspect
in this gay love story arises from the fact that the
male lovers, seriously attracted, are a Palestinian
student and an Israeli lawyer. Pressure applied by
the security forces adds to the drama and the film
contrasts the inhumanity of the national conflict
with the need for love. Some plot contrivances
weaken the piece slightly but can't prevent it from
being very sympathetic. (Original title: *Alata*) MS

▶ Nicholas Jacob, Michael Aloni, Jameel Khouri,
Alon Pdut, Loai Noufi.
▶ *Dir* Michael Mayer, *Pro* Lihu Roter and Mayer,
Screenplay Yael Shafrir and Mayer, *Ph* Ran Aviad,
Pro Des Sharon Eagle, *Ed* Maria Gonzales, *M* Mark
Holden and Michael Lopez, *Cos* Hamada Atallah.

M7200 Productions/a Periscope production/Israel Film
Fund/Channel 10-Network Releasing.
96 mins. Israel/USA. 2012. Rel: 5 July 2013. Cert. 15.

Oz The Great and Powerful
★★★½

This is based on L Frank Baum's characters in his Land of Oz series, a prequel in which Oscar Diggs (James Franco), a small-time magician and conman in Kansas, gets blown over to the Land of Oz, having stolen a hot-air balloon. On arrival at the Emerald City Oscar has to fight against a couple of evil witches (Rachel Weisz and Mila Kunis) with the help of good witch Glinda (Michelle Williams). It's all a bit like the 1939 film of *The Wizard of Oz*, but with the Wizard instead of Dorothy. Horror and action specialist Sam Raimi helms the film with its ravishing special effects and Robert Stromberg's designs. The film is fine, but it just isn't *The Wizard of Oz*. MHD

▶ James Franco, Mila Kunis, Rachel Weisz, Michelle Williams, Zach Braff, Bill Cobbs, Bruce Campbell.
▶ *Dir* Sam Raimi, *Pro* Joe Roth, *Screenplay* Mitchell Kapner and David Lindsay-Abaire, from a screen story by Mitchell Kapner, based on the Oz books of L Frank Baum, *Ph* Peter Denning, *Pro Des* Robert Stromberg, *Ed* Bob Murawski, *M* Danny Elfman, *Cos* Gary Jones.
Walt Disney Pictures/Roth Films-Walt Disney Studios Motion Pictures.
130 mins. USA. 2013. Rel: 8 Mar 2013. Cert. PG.

Pacific Rim ★

Mankind's latest problem is the rise of a race of supermonsters from the depths of the Pacific, so the world's governments get together to create a line of giant, manually operated robots to combat them. Cue *Godzilla* meets *The Transformers*… To the film's credit, the extent of urban devastation probably trumps even *Avengers Assemble*, *Man of Steel* and *World War Z*, although the special effects are nowhere near as effective. It's a shame, too, that the human characters are so one-dimensional and force-fed such abominable dialogue. But then *Pacific Rim* is such a thoroughgoing mess that little could have helped it. JC-W

▶ Charlie Hunnam, Idris Elba, Rinko Kikuchi, Charlie Day, Rob Kazinsky, Ron Perlman, Burn Gorman, Clifton Collins Jr.
▶ *Dir* Guillermo del Toro, *Pro* Del Toro, Thomas Tull, Jon Jashni and Mary Parent, *Screenplay* Del Toro and Travis Beacham, *Ph* Guillermo Navarro, *Pro Des* Andrew Neskoromny and Carol Spier, *Ed* Peter Amundson and John Gilroy, *M* Ramin Djawadi, *Cos* Kate Hawley.
Warner Bros/Legendary Pictures/Disney Double Dare You (DDY)-Warner Bros.
132 mins. USA. 2013. Rel: 12 July 2013. Cert. 12A.

Pain & Gain ★

Almost entirely pain with only trace amounts of gain, Michael Bay's *Pain & Gain* is an obnoxious film about terrible people. Developing every muscle but the one between their ears, steroidal morons chase their American dreams by committing crimes so badly it would be funny if someone other than Michael Bay was at the helm. Mark Wahlberg, Dwayne Johnson and Anthony Mackie play it panto big in this muscle-headed comedy caper. MJ

Baum on troubled waters: James Franco and Mila Kunis in Sam Raimi's ingenious *Oz The Great and Powerful*.

Greek chorus:
Frank Dillane,
Georges Corraface,
Stephen Dillane,
Georgia Groome
and Thomas
Underhill in
Marcus Markou's
*Papadopoulos
and Sons.*

▶ Mark Wahlberg, Dwayne Johnson, Anthony
Mackie, Tony Shalhoub, Ed Harris, Rob Corddry,
Bar Paly, Rebel Wilson.
▶ *Dir* Michael Bay, *Pro* Bay, Donald De Line and Ian
Bryce, *Screenplay* Christopher Markus and Stephen
McFeely, based on Pete Collins' magazine articles,
Ph Ben Seresin, *Pro Des* Jeffrey Beecroft, *Ed* Thomas
A Muldoon and Joel Negron, *M* Steve Jablonsky,
Cos Colleen Kelsall and Deborah L Scott.

**Paramount Pictures/De Line Pictures-Paramount Pictures.
129 mins. USA. 2013. Rel: 30 Aug 2013. Cert. 15.**

Pandora's Promise ★★★★

Robert Stone's fascinating documentary sets out to
make a case which it knows will meet resistance
from many: its purpose is to promote nuclear
energy as the best environmental answer for our
future. Stone once had a strong anti-nuclear stance
so his change of heart is intriguing. However
fair his arguments may or may not be, this piece
surprises by offering real food for thought. MS

▶ With Robert Stone, Mark Lynas, Stewart Brand,
Gwyneth Cravens.

▶ *Dir* and *Written by* Robert Stone, *Pro* Stone,
Jim Swartz and Susan Swartz, *Ph* Stone and
Howard Shack, *Ed* Don Kleszy, *M* Gary Lionelli.

**Impact Partners/CNN Films/Vulcan Productions-
November Films.
87 mins. USA. 2013. Rel: 15 Nov 2013. Cert. 12A.**

Papadopoulos and Sons ★★★★

Debut writer-director Marcus Markou hits
the spot with this appealing tale of high-
flying, widowed catering entrepreneur Harry
Papadopoulos (Stephen Dillane) who loses his
business in the recession and is forced into
running his family's now defunct fish and chip
shop. Having not seen his estranged brother
Spiros (Georges Corraface) for many years, he
finds his new way of life is not at first an easy
ride. A subplot involving a local kebab shop
competitor with a touch of the Romeo and Juliets
adds spice to this warmly witty and affecting tale.
Good performances by Dillane and Corraface
give splendid life to Markou's script. Look out for
Film Review's very own George Savvides as the
kebab shop owner. MHD

▶ Stephen Dillane, George Corraface, Ed Stoppard, Selina Cadell, Frank Dillane, Georgia Groome, Thomas Underhill, George Savvides, Alexander Hanson.
▶ *Dir* and *Screenplay* Marcus Markou, *Pro* Sara Butler, *Ph* James Friend, *Pro Des* Julian Fullalove, *Ed* Sebastian Morrison, *M* Stephen Warbeck, *Cos* Robert Lever.

Double M Films-Miracle Communications Ltd.
109 mins. UK. 2012. Rel: 5 Apr 2013. Cert. 15.

The Paperboy ★★★

Set in 1967 but with flashbacks to the 1950s, this lurid piece of southern melodrama described as an erotic thriller was widely derided at Cannes but later reassessed by some. Nicole Kidman's central femme fatale never convinces while the tale being told rather oddly combines sex, murder and a rites of passage theme. It's all a bit of a mess and over the top in several scenes, but at 107 minutes it's fun if you're in the mood. MS

▶ Matthew McConaughey, Zac Efron, Nicole Kidman, David Oyelowo, John Cusack, Scott Glenn, Macy Gray.
▶ *Dir* Lee Daniels, *Pro* Hilary Shor, Daniels, Avi Lerner and others, *Screenplay* Pete Dexter and Daniels, from the novel by Dexter, *Ph* Roberto Schaefer, *Pro Des* Daniel T Dorrance, *Ed* Joe Klotz, *M* Mario Grigorov, *Cos* Caroline Eselin-Schaefer.

Millennium Films/a Nu Image and Lee Daniels Entertainment production-Lionsgate UK.
107 mins. USA. 2012. Rel: 15 Mar 2013. Cert. 15.

Paradise: Love ★★★★
Paradise: Faith ★★★½
Paradise: Hope ★★★½

Paradise: Love is the best part of Ulrich Seidl's connected trilogy in which each film can be seen on its own. Indeed, this one is probably the best starting point, a remarkably explicit but touching portrait of an Austrian woman visiting Kenya where her age and weight may not prevent her from being accepted as a 'Sugar Mama' by locals profiting from sex tourism. It's both shocking and compassionate and lead actress Margarethe Tiesel really does give a performance that deserves to be called brave. In contrast, *Paradise: Faith* is virtually a two-hander and almost minimalist in style. Set in Vienna throughout, it is a wholly convincing picture of a deeply Catholic woman who, seeking to convert others, is devoted to the Cult of the Wandering Madonna. After an absence her Muslim husband, who is in a wheelchair following an accident, returns but her treatment of him is far removed from any commandment to love your neighbour as yourself. This film is longer than it needs to be but is a compelling portrait of religious fanaticism viewed with pity. The remaining film, *Paradise: Hope*, turns to the younger generation

with utterly convincing portrayals of two girls at a diet camp for those who are overweight. One of them becomes sexually obsessed with the camp's doctor and all of this carries great conviction. However, it is difficult to tell if this is about potential paedophilia or a more general study of adolescent behaviour. With routines in the camp dominating the last scenes, the film never quite coheres thematically but much of it is superbly realised. (Original titles: *Paradies Liebe, Paradies Glaube* and *Paradies Hoffnung*) MS

▶ Margarethe Tiesel, Maria Hofstätter, Melanie Lenz, Peter Kazungu and Inge Maux (*Paradise: Love*), Nabil Saleh and René Rupnik *Paradise: Faith*), Verena Lehbauer and Joseph Lorenz (*Paradise: Hope*).
▶ *Dir* and *Pro* Ulrich Seidl, *Screenplay* Seidl and Veronika Franz, *Ph* Wolfgang Thaler and Ed Lachman, *Pro Des* Andreas Donhauser and Renate Martin, *Ed* Christof Schertenleib, *Cos* Tanja Hausner.

An Ulrich Seidl Film Produktion/Tatfilm/Parisienne de Production etc.-Soda Pictures.
121 mins (Love); 115 mins (Faith); 91 mins (Hope).
Austria/Germany/France. 2012.
Rel: 14 June (Love), 5 July (Faith) and 2 Aug 2013 (Hope). Cert. 18 (Love and Faith); 15 (Hope).

Paris-Manhattan ★★★

This French romantic comedy offers homage to Woody Allen who puts in a brief but rather uneasy appearance. The film's heroine has a troubled love life and turns for advice to Allen's sayings as recalled from his films while its hero is a humble technician dealing with alarm systems. The movie sounds rather better than it is, being amiable but never magical and at times heavy-handed despite being lightweight. MS

▶ Alice Taglioni, Patrick Bruel, Marine Delterme, Michel Aumont, Louis-Do de Lencquesaing, Marie-Christine Adam, Woody Allen.

Lubricious tourism: Margarethe Tiesel (and prospective partners) in Ulrich Seidl's *Paradise: Love.*

> *Dir* and *Screenplay* Sophie Lellouche, *Pro* Philippe Rouselet, *Ph* Laurent Machuel, *Art Dir* Philip L'Évèque, *Ed* Monica Coleman, *M* Jean-Michel Bernard, *Cos* Fabienne Katany.

A Vendôme Production/France 2 Cinéma/SND/Canal+ etc.-Cinefile.
78 mins. France. 2011. Rel: 5 July 2013. Cert. 12A.

Parker ★★

There is a certain novelty about seeing JLo in a Jason Statham movie, like a JSta/JLo combo. But make no mistake: this is first and foremost a Jason Statham movie. There are gunfights, some bone-crunching hand-to-hand combat and a whole lotta bad guys. This time JSta is in Palm Beach to hunt down some former colleagues after they left him for dead following an Ohio heist. We get to see him in a silver wig, a dog collar and a stetson, and he even attempts a Texan accent. And a lot of people die – dramatically. It's routine fodder, with Jennifer Lopez merely a minor distraction. JC-W

> Jason Statham, Jennifer Lopez, Michael Chiklis, Wendell Pierce, Clifton Collins Jr., Bobby Cannavale, Patti LuPone, Emma Booth, Nick Nolte.
> *Dir* Taylor Hackford, *Pro* Hackford, Les Alexander, Steven Chasman, Sidney Kimmel and Jonathan Mitchell, *Screenplay* John J McLaughlin, *Ph* J Michael Muro, *Pro Des* Missy Stewart, *Ed* Mark Warner, *M* David Buckley, *Cos* Melissa Bruning.

Incentive Filmed Entertainment/Sierra/Affinity/ Alexander/Mitchell Productions-Entertainment One. 118 mins. USA. 2013. Rel: 8 Marc 2013. Cert. 15.

Parkland ★★★½

Revisiting the assassination of President Kennedy 50 years on, this drama chooses to concentrate on individuals in Dallas on that day and on the Parkland Memorial Hospital where Kennedy died, as did his presumed killer Lee Harvey Oswald only days later. The narrow time focus adopted, just four days, excludes any hint of conspiracy theories and, whether one gives credence to them or not, that leaves us with only a partial dramatisation of events which feels odd and incomplete. MS

> Zac Efron, James Badge Dale, Marcia Gay Harden, Billy Bob Thornton, Jacki Weaver, Paul Giamatti, Mark Duplass, Jackie Earle Haley, Ron Livingston, Colin Hanks.
> *Dir* and *Screenplay* (based on the book *Four Days in November* by Vincent Bugliosi) Peter Landesman, *Pro* Tom Hanks, Gary Goetzman, Bill Paxton and others, *Ph* Barry Ackroyd, *Pro Des* Bruce Curtis, *Ed* Leo Trombetta, *M* James Newton Howard, *Cos* Kari Perkins.

The American Film Company/Millennium Entertainment/a Playtone/Exclusive Media production-Koch Media Entertainment.
94 mins. USA. 2013. Rel: 22 Nov 2013. Cert. 15.

The Patience Stone ★★★★½

This is a potent portrait of life in the Middle East from the Afghan writer-director Atiq Rahimi. Initially it appears to be an anti-war film about the suffering of civilians in an unspecified setting. But it soon builds into something else. We focus on a wife looking after her husband, wounded when a soldier and now incapable of speech. What follows becomes a stunning reflection on the position of women in this part of the world. It may be designed to deliver a message, but this is involving filmmaking of a very high standard and the film gains immensely from the brilliant performance of Golshifteh Farahani in the central role. MS

> Golshifteh Farahani, Hamidreza Javdan, Hassina Burgan, Massi Mrowat.
> *Dir* Atiq Rahimi, *Pro* Michael Gentile, *Screenplay* Jean-Claude Carrière and Rahimi, from the latter's novel *Syngué Sabour, pierre de patience*, *Ph* Thierry Arbogast, *Art Dir* Erwin Prib, *Ed* Hervé de Luze, *M* Max Richter, *Cos* Malak Djaham Khazal.

Hani Farsi/a The Film, Razor Film, Corniche Pictures, Studio 37, Arte France Cinéma, Jahan-e-Honar Productions co-production etc.-Axiom Films Limited.
102 mins. France/Germany/UK/Afghanistan. 2012. Rel: 6 Dec 2013. Cert. 15.

Percy Jackson: Sea of Monsters ★★½

Largely dismissed as a second rate *Harry Potter* clone, 2010's *Percy Jackson and the Lightning Thief* came and went without much fuss and hardly seemed successful enough to warrant a sequel. Yet here we have *Percy Jackson: Sea of Monsters*,

Finding a voice: the brilliant Golshifteh Farahani in Atiq Rahimi's *The Patience Stone*.

a contemporary teen romp following the adventurous offspring of various Greek gods. Much like the first it's an uneven affair, sporadically amusing with the odd action highlight and decent effects, but really nothing special and not a patch on Rick Riordan's lively original novels. MJ

▶ Logan Lerman, Alexandra Daddario, Douglas Smith, Anthony Head, Stanley Tucci, Leven Rabin, Brandon T Jackson, Jake Abel.
▶ *Dir* Thor Freudenthal, *Pro* Chris Columbus and Michael Barnathan, *Screenplay* Marc Guggenheim, from Rick Riordan's novel *Percy Jackson and the Olympians: The Sea of Monsters*, *Ph* Shelly Johnson, *Pro Des* Claude Paré, *Ed* Mark Goldblatt, *M* Andrew Lockington, *Cos* Monique Prudhomme.

Fox 2000 Pictures/Sunswept Entertainment/1492 Pictures/Dune Entertainment-20th Century Fox. 106 mins. USA. 2013. Rel: 7 Aug 2013. Cert. PG.

The Pervert's Guide to Ideology ★★★★

The Slovenian philosopher and film enthusiast Slavoj Žižek is his own man. Here he follows *The Pervert's Guide to Cinema* with a fresh dissertation, directed once again by Sophie Fiennes who is clearly a kindred spirit. He takes his time and uses a range of film clips to develop his idiosyncratic ideas about the power of ideologies. With much humour and striking ideas which you can't necessarily take seriously (including his views on movies and their subtexts), Žižek is someone

you either find engaging or infuriating. I take the positive view. MS

▶ With Slavoj Žižek.
▶ *Dir* Sophie Fiennes, *Pro* James Wilson, Martin Rosenbaum, Katie Holly and Fiennes, *Ph* Remko Schnorr, *Pro Des* Lucy van Lonkhuyzen, *Ed* Ethel Shepherd, *M* Magnus Fiennes, *Cos* Debbie Millington.

British Film Institute/Film4/A P Guide production/ Blinder Films etc.-Picturehouse Entertainment. 136 mins. UK/Ireland. 2012. Rel: 4 Oct 2013. Cert. 15.

Philomena ★★★★

A free treatment of a true story, this film tells of a mother's attempt late in life to trace the son who had been taken away from her when she was a young unmarried mother in Ireland in the care of Catholic nuns. In contrast to Peter Mullan's *The Magdalene Sisters* (2002) which it brings to mind, this piece for all its serious concerns sets out to entertain and is on occasion too obviously doing that. However, the title role enables Dame Judi Dench to transcend any limitations by bringing to her portrayal, quite possibly her finest ever, a sense of total truth. MS

▶ Judi Dench, Steve Coogan, Michelle Fairley, Barbara Jefford, Anna Maxwell Martin.
▶ *Dir* Stephen Frears, *Pro* Gabrielle Tana, Steve Coogan and Tracey Seaward, *Screenplay* Coogan and Jeff Pope, based on the book *The Lost Child of Philomena Lee* by Martin Sixsmith, *Ph* Robbie Ryan, *Pro Des* Alan MacDonald, *Ed* Valerio Bonelli,

The searchers: Judi Dench and Steve Coogan in Stephen Frears' *Philomena*, for which Dame Judi won the best British actress award from the London Film Critics' Circle.

Symbolically speaking: Jeong-jin Lee and Min-soo Jo in Ki-duk Kim's *Pieta*, winner of the Golden Lion.

M Alexandre Desplat, *Cos* Consolata Boyle.

Pathé/BBC Films/BFI/a Baby Cow/Magnolia Mae production/Canal+ etc.-Pathé Productions. 98 mins. UK/USA/France. 2013. Rel: 1 Nov 2013. Cert. 12A.

Pieta ★★★★

Writer-director Ki-duk Kim's twisted tragedy was South Korea's submission to the 85th Oscars as Best Foreign Language Film. Both repellent and seductive, it was a deserved winner of the Golden Lion at the Venice Film Festival in 2012. Min-soo Jo won several Best Actress awards worldwide for her astonishing role as Mi-Son, a mystery woman who turns up at the house of violent loan shark Gang-Do (Jeong-jin Lee), claiming to be his long-lost mother. This unique and extraordinary film, mixing Christian symbolism with strong and ultra-disturbing sexual content, makes a devastating impact, with its two brave and dazzling performances and brilliant, challenging screenplay. DW

❧ Min-soo Jo, Jeong-jin Lee, Ki-Hong Woo, Eunjin Kang, Jae-ryong Cho, Myeong-ja Lee, Jun-seok Heo.
❧ *Dr, Ed* and *Screenplay* Ki-duk Kim, *Pro* Kim

Soon-mo, *Ph* Jo Young-jik, *Pro Des* Hyun-joo Lee, *M* In-young Park, *Cos* Ji-yeon Ji.

Good Film/Finecut-StudioCanal. 86 mins. South Korea. 2012. Rel: 6 Sep 2013. Cert. 18.

The Place Beyond the Pines ★★★

Derek Cianfrance's follow-up to *Blue Valentine* reunites him with Ryan Gosling on outstanding form as a blond biker. On learning that he has fathered a child, he hopes to win back the girl he left behind and is prepared to turn to robbery for funds that will impress her. It's better for the audience to know no more of the plot, but this is a long three-act affair and the longer it goes on the less does it convince. The first part is the best by a substantial margin. MS

❧ Ryan Gosling, Bradley Cooper, Eva Mendes, Ray Liotta, Ben Mendelsohn, Emory Cohen, Dane DeHaan, Rose Byrne, Bruce Greenwood, Harris Yulin.
❧ *Dir* Derek Cianfrance, *Pro* Sidney Kimmel, Jamie Patricof, Lynette Howell and Alex Orlovsky, *Screenplay* Cianfrance, Ben Coccio and Darius Marder, from a story by Cianfrance and Coccio, *Ph* Sean Bobbitt, *Pro Des* Inbal Weinberg, *Ed* Jim Helton

and Ron Patane, *M* Mike Patton, *Cos* Erin Benach.

Focus Features/Sidney Kimmel Entertainment/an Electric City Entertainment production/Verisimilitude-StudioCanal Limited.
141 mins. USA. 2012. Rel: 12 Apr 2013. Cert. 15.

A Place in the Sun (reissue)
★★★★★

"Brilliantly directed, excellent, almost great adaptation of the famous Theodore Dreiser novel *An American Tragedy*." Thus F Maurice Speed's judgment in this annual's 1952 edition. Sixty years on we can delete that word 'almost' and hail George Stevens' film as the post-war masterwork it is. With social-climbing Montgomery Clift contemplating murder when caught between high-society and factory-floor sweethearts, it's exquisitely atmospheric and, bar Raymond Burr's overblown DA, exceptionally acted. The book had been filmed 20 years earlier by Josef von Sternberg, as well as being liberally borrowed from in Murnau's *Sunrise*. But Stevens' version boasts such a wealth of finely wrought detail, subliminal as well as surface, that the story takes on a grim inevitability rarely achieved in Hollywood. JR

❥ Montgomery Clift, Elizabeth Taylor, Shelley Winters, Anne Revere, Keefe Brasselle, Fred Clark, Raymond Burr, Herbert Heyes, Shepperd Strudwick, Frieda Inescort.
❥ *Dir* and *Pro* George Stevens, *Screenplay* Michael Wilson, Harry Brown, from the novel *An American Tragedy* by Theodore Dreiser, *Ph* William C Mellor, *Pro Des* Hans Dreier, Walter Tyler, *Ed* William Hornbeck, *M* Franz Waxman, *Cos* Edith Head.

Paramount Pictures-BFI Distribution.
122 mins. USA. 1951. Rel: 28 January 1952 (UK general release). Reissued: 1 February 2013. Cert. PG.

Planes ★★½

Following the success of the two *Cars* movies, Disney motors on with *Planes* but without Pixar, although John Lasseter is on the credits. *Planes*, like *Cars*, creates a non-human world but the anthropomorphism of the talking aircraft replacing mankind soon palls. The paltry script concerns a lowly little crop-dusting plane called Dusty Cropper (geddit?) who's out to win the Wings Around the Globe competition. Aided by chums Chug, a fuel truck, and Dottie, a forklift truck, he convinces the top racing planes that he is eligible to enter. Although the animation is at times spectacular, the screenplay lets it down badly. Very young kids may enjoy it, possibly looking forward to the *Planes* sequel and even *Cars 3*. MHD

❥ Voices of Dane Cook, Stacy Keach, Brad Garrett, Teri Hatcher, John Cleese, Cedric the Entertainer, Val Kilmer, Sinbad, Roger Craig Smith.

❥ *Dir* Klay Hall, *Pro* Traci Balthazor, *Screenplay* Jeffrey M Howard from a story by Hall, Howard and John Lasseter, *Pro Des* Ryan L Carlson, *Ed* Jeremy Milton, *Animation Dir* Sheryl Sardina Sackett, *M* Mark Mancina.

DisneyToon Studios/Prana Studios-Walt Disney Studios Motion Pictures.
91 mins. USA. 2013. Rel: 16 Aug 2013. Cert. U.

Play ★★★½

Based on events that took place in Gothenburg, this film by Ruben Östlund gives the impression of eavesdropping on lives. Its focus is on African youths who pick on three white boys in threatening ways and the film becomes a social portrait of hooliganism and bullying in a world in which many youngsters are left to fend for themselves. A somewhat enigmatic ending is less effective, but much of this is a persuasive exercise in minimalism. MS

❥ Anas Abdirahman, Sebastian Blyckert, Yannick Diakite, Sebastian Hegmar, John Ortiz, Abdiaziz Hilowle.
❥ *Dir* and *Screenplay* Ruben Östlund, *Pro* Erik Hemmendorff and Philippe Bober, *Ph* Marius Dybwad Brandrud, *Pro Des* and *Cos* Pia Aleborg, *Ed* Östlund and Jacob Schulsinger, *M* Saunder Jurrians and Daniel Bensi.

A Coproduction Office ApS, Parisienne de Production, Film i Väst, Sveriges Television, Sonet Film co-production etc.-Soda Pictures.
118 mins. Sweden/Denmark/France/Germany/Norway. 2011. Rel: 12 July 2013. Cert. 15.

Playing for Keeps ★

Ex-football star George (Gerard Butler) has reached rock bottom. He's out of work while his ex-wife (Jessica Biel) and son are now living with another man. George moves close to them in a desperate attempt to win back their affection... Butler delivers another smug performance while Biel

In the lap of the Gods: Montgomery Clift and Elizabeth Taylor in *A Place in the Sun*, which won six Oscars in 1952.

tries hard to keep her dignity. It's sad to see the talents of Uma Thurman, Catherine Zeta-Jones and Judy Greer being totally wasted as frustrated housewives lusting after the body of the Butler. GS

▶ Gerard Butler, Jessica Biel, Noah Lomax, Dennis Quaid, Uma Thurman, Catherine Zeta-Jones, Judy Greer.
▶ *Dir* Gabriele Muccino, *Pro* Gerard Butler, John Thompson, Alan Siegel, Jonathan Mostow, Kevin Misher and Heidi Jo Markel, *Screenplay* Robbie Fox, *Ph* Peter Menzies Jr, *Pro Des* Daniel D Dorrance, *Ed* Padraic McKinley, *M* Andrea Guerra, *Cos* Angelica Russo.

Millennium Films/Nu Image Films/Misher Films/Evil Twins/Eclectic Pictures-Lionsgate.
105 mins. USA. 2012. Rel: 1 Jan 2013. Cert. 12A.

Populaire ★★★

Set in the 1950s (it even features Leroy Anderson's *Forgotten Dreams* as a kind of theme tune) this French romcom is the story of a gauche secretary who becomes a champion typist who may win the heart of her boss. That he is an unattractive character is a weakness, but for the rest the film is faithful to every cliché of the genre – which may explain why some people love it. The stars do their best but Bérénice Bejo from *The Artist* is wasted in a subsidiary role. MS

▶ Romain Duris, Déborah François, Bérénice

Bejo, Shaun Benson, Miou-Miou.
▶ *Dir* Régis Roinsard, *Pro* Alain Attal, *Screenplay* Roinsard, Daniel Presley and Romain Compingt, *Ph* Guillaume Schiffman, *Pro Des* Sylvie Olivé, *Ed* Laure Gardette and Sophie Reine, *M* Rob Coudert and Emmanuel d'Orlando, *Cos* Charlotte David.

A Productions du Trésor, France 3 Cinéma, France 2 Cinéma, Mars Films, Wild Bunch, Panache Productions, Compagnie Cinématographique, RTBF (Télévision Belge) co-production etc.-E1/Momentum.
111 mins. France/Belgium. 2012. Rel: 31 May 2013. Cert. 12A.

Post Tenebras Lux ★★★½

The title's promise that we will move from darkness to light is not altogether realised in this drama about a well-off but troubled Mexican family living in the countryside. Stylised but not quite as difficult to follow as was claimed when it controversially won an award at Cannes, this is a very atmospheric piece which captures a sense of menace in the world today. It is not Carlos Reygadas' best work by any means but his admirers will find it suitably provocative. MS

▶ Rut Reygadas, Elezar Reygadas, Nathalia Acevedo, Adolfo Jiménez Castro, Willebaldo Torres.
▶ *Dir* and *Screenplay* Carlos Reygadas, *Pro* Jaime Romandia and Reygadas, *Ph* Alexis Zabé, *Pro Des* Gerardo Tagle, *Ed* Natalia López.

Nodream/Mantarraya/Le Pacte/ARTE France Cinéma/

The Match Factory etc.-Independent Cinema Office.
115 mins. Mexico/France/Germany/The Netherlands.
2012. Rel: 22 Mar 2013. Cert. 18.

Powder Room ★★

Based on the stage play *When Women Wee* from
2011, *Powder Room* is set in the ladies' loo of a
down-at-heel London nightclub. This frank take
on the old girls' night out saga might have worked
well on a fringe theatre stage, but the thin, gossipy
script is exposed on screen. The women all seem
like stereotypes, and not entirely appealing ones,
doing and saying such annoying things that you
think a man must have written this – but not so,
it's Rachel Hirons. The performances are at best
variable, but Sheridan Smith does well enough as
the insecure, messy Sam and Jaime Winstone is
convincingly tough and sassy as her punkish man-
eating friend Chanel. DW

❧ Sheridan Smith, Jaime Winstone, Kate Nash, Oona
Chaplin, Riann Steele, Sarah Hoare, Johnnie Fiori.
❧ *Dir* MJ Delaney, *Pro* James Cotton, Nichola Martin
and Damian Jones, *Screenplay* Rachel Hirons, based
on the play *When Women Wee* by Hirons, Jennifer
Davies, Amy Revelle, Natasha Sparkes, Amirah
Garba, Stephanie Jay, Stef O'Driscoll and Emily
Wallis*, Ph* John Lee, *Pro Des* Soraya Gilanni, *Ed* Ben
Jordan, *M* Fake Club, *Cos* PC Williams.

DJ Films-Vertigo Films.
86 mins. UK. 2013. Rel: 6 Dec 2013. Cert. 15.

Prince Avalanche ★★★

David Gordon Green here returns to the kind
of small independent movie with which he
made his name. Superbly photographed, this is a
virtual two-hander about the bond between two
men repainting lines on Texas highways where
wildfire has raged. They are contrasted types –
one being the brother of the other's girlfriend,
although that romance is now ending. The first
half is well observed, but the contrived second
half disappoints. Excellent performances. MS

❧ Paul Rudd, Emile Hirsch, Lance LeGault, Joyce
Payne, Gina Grande, Lynn Shelton.
❧ *Dir* and *Screenplay* (based on the film *Either Way*
by Hafsteinn Gunnar Sigurdsson) David Gordon
Green, *Pro* Lisa Muskat, Derrick Tseng, Green and
others, *Ph* Tim Orr, *Pro Des* Richard A Wright,
Ed Colin Patton, *M* Explosions in the Sky and David
Wingo, *Cos* Jill Newell.

A Muskat Filmed Properties & Dogfish Pictures
presentation etc.-Metrodome Distribution Ltd.
93 mins. USA. 2012. Rel: 18 Oct 2013. Cert. 15.

Prisoners ★★★

This thriller centres on the kidnapping of two
young girls and on a father's decision to take
the law into his own hands when evidence
against a prime suspect falls short. It's a sturdily
cast Hollywood movie and initially promises
much – wonderful atmospheric photography by
Roger Deakins, direction by Denis Villeneuve
who made the brilliant *Incendies* and an in-depth
approach that seeks to put this piece on the level
of *Mystic River* or *Zodiac*. What a pity, then, that
the last quarter careers downhill into improbable
melodrama. MS

❧ Hugh Jackman, Jake Gyllenhaal, Viola Davis,
Maria Bello, Terrence Howard, Melissa Leo, Paul
Dano, Len Cariou.
❧ *Dir* Denis Villeneuve, *Pro* Broderick Johnson, Kira
Davis, Andrew A Kosove and Adam Kolbrenner,
Screenplay Aaron Guzikowski, *Ph* Roger Deakins,
Pro Des Patrice Vermette, *Ed* Joel Cox and Gary
Roach, *M* Jóhan Jóhansson, *Cos* Renée April.

Alcon Entertainment/An 8.38 Productions production/
A Madhouse Entertainment production- E1 Films.
153 mins. USA. 2013. Rel: 27 Sep 2013. Cert. 15.

Project Wild Thing ★★★½

This engagingly personal documentary puts
director David Bond centre screen together
with his desire to bring back a past lifestyle for
children in which, free of Health and Safety
regulations, they can play at ease and embrace
not technology but the natural world. It's an
amiable film even if, despite its short running
time, it seems to be repeating itself in the
second half. MS

❧ With David Bond, Michael Depledge, Susan
Greenfield.
❧ *Dir* David Bond, *Pro* Ashley Jones, *Ph* Annemarie
Lean Vercoe, Amy Rose and Gavin Northover,
Ed Jesse Dixon and Alan Mackay.

The BRITDOC Foundation/a Green Lions
production-The BRITDOC Foundation/Green Lions.
83 mins. UK. 2013. Rel: 25 Oct 2013. Cert. PG.

A barrow of
laughs: Emile
Hirsch and Paul
Rudd in David
Gordon Green's
Prince Avalanche.

Home viewing:
Ethan Hawke in
James DeMonaco's
highly disturbing
The Purge.

Promised Land ★★★

Rural America is at the mercy of underhand dealing by company men out to persuade a community to approve their plan to extract gas locally by fracking. Gus Van Sant's film has a great cast but the screenplay – by two of its actors, Matt Damon and John Krasinski – fails to realise the story's potential, and that's particularly the case when the film's final stages succumb to corny sentimentality. The subject – and the cast – deserved better. MS

❧ Matt Damon, John Krasinski, Frances McDormand, Rosemarie DeWitt, Scoot McNairy. Hal Holbrook.
❧ *Dir* Gus Van Sant, *Pro* Matt Damon, John Krasinski and Chris Moore, *Screenplay* Krasinski and Damon, from a story by Dave Eggers, *Ph* Linus Sandgren, *Pro Des* David B Clancy, *Ed* Billy Rich, *M* Danny Elfman, *Cos* Juliet Polsca.

Focus Features/Participant Media/a Sunday Night, Pearl Street, Media Farm production etc.-Universal. 107 mins. USA/United Arab Emirates. 2012. Rel: 19 Apr 2013. Cert. 15.

The Punk Syndrome ★★★★

This unique music documentary tells the story of four punk musicians from Finland with learning difficulties, who call themselves Pertti Kurikka's Name Day. There is a clash of egos as they prepare for their first international tour and recording session, but there's a very funny sequence where they're all having a pedicure just before they begin their tour in Hamburg. This is an honest portrait of a group passionate for their music and also confronts attitudes towards mental disability. (Original title: *Kovasikajattu*) GS

❧ With Pertti Kurikka, Karl Aalto, Sami Helle, Toni Välitalo, Kale Pajamaa, Kyösti Välitalo.
❧ *Dir* Jukka Kärkkäinen and J-P Passi, *Pro* Sami Jahnukainen, *Written by* Kärkkäinen, Passi and Sami Jahnukainen, *Ph* J-P Passi, *Ed* Riitta Poikselkä, *M* Pertti Kurikan Nimipäivät.

Mouka Filmi Oy/Indie Film/Film I Skåne/Auto Images-November Films. 85 mins. Finland/Sweden/Norway. 2012. Rel: 1 Feb 2013. No Cert.

The Purge ★★★½

In a few years' time the US government will come up with an ingenious plan to rid the country of crime. Almost. For one night of every year, between 8.00 pm and 7.00 am, every misdemeanour, robbery and murder will go unpunished. Thus, every man, woman and child will have expunged any desire for wrongdoing for the rest of the year. So, let the killing commence... While monsters are scary, the worst excesses of human nature are something else. As a horror film, then, *The Purge* is something of a masterclass and, in its accomplished way, one of the most disturbing and frightening films of the year. JC-W

❧ Ethan Hawke, Lena Headey, Adelaide Kane, Max Burkholder, Edwin Hodge, Rhys Wakefield.
❧ *Dir* and *Screenplay* James DeMonaco, *Pro* Michael Bay, Jason Blum, Andrew Form, Bradley Fuller and Sébastien Kurt Lemercier, *Ph* Jacques Jouffret, *Pro Des* Melanie Jones, *Ed* Peter Gvozdas, *M* Nathan Whitehead, *Cos* Lisa Norcia.

Blumhouse Productions/Overlord Productions/Why Not Productions/Platinum Dunes-Universal Pictures. 85 mins. USA/France. 2013. Rel: 31 May 2013. Cert. 15.

Pussy Riot: A Punk Prayer
★★★★½

This excellent, moving documentary follows five young Russian women, members of a punk band, who dared to perform in the part of Moscow's Cathedral of Christ the Saviour where only men are admitted. They appeared in balaclava masks and with bared shoulders (also a crime) in order to make a point about the rights of the artist and the relationship between Church and State. The film shows three of the group on trial behind a glass booth and their subsequent incarceration in a penal colony. After seven months they had an appeal hearing at which one woman was freed on a technicality, while the remaining two returned to their two-year sentence. How far has Russia come since Glasnost? Not very far, it seems. (Original title: *Pokazatelnyy protsess: Istoriya Pussy Riot*) MHD

▶ With Mariya Alyokhina, Yekaterina Samutsevich, Nadezhda Tolokonnikova, Andrey Tolokonnikov, Stanislav Samutsevich, Natalia Alyokhina, Violetta Volkova, Mark Feygin, Larisa Pavlova, Gera Tolokonnikova.
▶ *Dir* and *Pro* Mike Lerner and Maxim Pozdorovkin, *Ph* Antony Butts, *Ed* Simon Barker and Esteban Uyarra, *M* Simon Russell.
Roast Beef Productions-Independent.
88 mins. UK/Russia. 2013. Rel: 5 July 2013. Cert. 18.

Quartet ★★★★

Dustin Hoffman makes his directing debut with Ronald Harwood's adaptation of his own stage play set in a retirement home for ageing musicians. To Beecham House comes a new resident, former opera singer Jean Horton (Maggie Smith), who is somewhat distressed because her ex-husband, singer Reggie Paget (Tom Courtenay), on whom she cheated years ago, is in situ. As the residents prepare for their annual concert in honour of Verdi's birthday and to raise funds for the upkeep of the house, it's touch and go whether everybody will be up for it. With Billy Connolly, Pauline Collins, Michael Gambon and real opera diva Dame Gwyneth Jones, this is English Heritage filmmaking at its most winning. MHD

▶ Maggie Smith, Tom Courtenay, Billy Connolly, Pauline Collins, Michael Gambon, Sheridan Smith, Andrew Sachs, Trevor Peacock, David Ryall, Michael Byrne, Dame Gwyneth Jones.
▶ *Dir* Dustin Hoffman, *Pro* Finola Dwyer and Stewart Mackinnon, *Screenplay* Ronald Harwood, based on his own play, *Ph* John de Borman, *Pro Des* Andrew McAlpine, *Ed* Barney Pilling, *M* Dario Marianelli, *Cos* Odile Dicks-Mireaux.
Headline Pictures/BBC Films/Finola Dwyer Productions/ DCM Productions-Momentum Pictures.
98 mins. UK. 2012. Rel: 1 Jan 2013. Cert. 12A.

Reality ★★½

Following a slow start, this Italian comedy from Matteo Garrone of *Gomorrah* (2008) focuses on a Neapolitan fishmonger who longs to become a TV celebrity by taking part in Italy's version of *Big Brother*. The atmosphere may evoke Fellini but both as comedy and as story-telling this is

We predict a riot: documenting musical dissent in Mike Lerner and Maxim Pozdorovkin's *Pussy Riot: A Punk Prayer*.

distinctly lacklustre. It may have won the Cannes Grand Prix in 2012 but at the National Press Show in London I heard not a titter – and, if it fails to garner laughs, this study of an obsessive also misses out on the opportunity for pathos. MS

▶ Aniello Arena, Loredana Simioli, Nando Paone, Giuseppina Cervizzi.
▶ *Dir* Matteo Garrone, *Pro* Domenico Procacci and Garrone, *Screenplay* Maurizio Braucci, Ugo Chiti, Garrone and Massimo Gaudioso, from a story by Garrone and Gaudioso, *Ph* Marco Onorato, *Art Dir* Paolo Bonfini, *Ed* Marco Spoletini, *M* Alexandre Desplat, *Cos* Maurizio Millenotti.

An Archimede-Fandango, Le Pacte-Garance Capital co-production/RAI Cinema etc.-Independent Distribution. 116 mins. Italy/France. 2012. Rel: 22 Mar 2013. Cert. 15.

Rebellion ★★★½

Philippe Legorjus, who wrote a book about his experiences in the French colony of New Caledonia in 1988, is the central figure in this work by Mathieu Kassovitz, who also plays him. Rebels seeking independence were treated as terrorists, with the military encouraged for political reasons to attack rather than negotiate, as Legorjus had been led to anticipate. At times confusion reigns in portraying this complex situation (the climax is a night-time attack) but if we could be drawn in more this remains a shocking story that deserves to be told and remembered. (Original title: *L'Ordre et la morale*) MS

▶ Mathieu Kassovitz, Iabe Lapacas, Malik Zidi, Alexandre Steiger, Sylvie Testud.
▶ *Dir* Mathieu Kassovitz, *Pro* Christophe Rossigon and Philip Boëffard, *Screenplay* Kassovitz, Pierre Geller, Benoît Jaubert and Serge Frydman, based on the book *La Morale et l'action* by Philippe Legorjus, *Ph* Marc Koninckx, *Art Dir* Bruno Coupé, *Ed* Kassovitz, Thomas Beard and Lionel

Devuyst, *M* Klaus Badelt, *Cos* Agnès Beziers.

Nord-Ouest Films, UGC, Studio 37 and France 2 Cinéma co-production etc.-Lionsgate UK. 135 mins. France. 2011. Rel: 19 Apr 2013. Cert. 15.

RED 2 ★½

From *Galaxy Quest* director Dean Parisot comes an old-school action offering that aims for breezy, cheeky, winky, easy fun but misses the mark entirely. It's a woeful tale of wrinkly heroes saving the world from nuclear disaster. Although there's value in the spectacle of Helen Mirren kicking ass, it's not enough to justify the existence of a film that, though rife with explosions, gun fights and chase sequences, somehow drags along slower than a biddy doing her weekly supermarket shop. MJ

▶ Bruce Willis, Helen Mirren, John Malkovich, Mary-Louise Parker, Anthony Hopkins, Catherine Zeta-Jones, Tim Pigott-Smith, Brian Cox, Steven Berkoff, Byung-hun Lee, Jong Kun Lee.
▶ *Dir* Dean Parisot, *Pro* Lorenzo di Bonaventura and Mark Vahradian, *Screenplay* Jon Hoeber and Eric Hoeber, based on characters created by Warren Ellis and Cully Hamner, *Ph* Enrique Chediac, *Pro Des* Jim Clay, *Ed* Don Zimmerman, *M* Alan Silvestri, *Cos* Beatrix Aruna Pasztor.

Di Bonaventura Pictures/Saints LA/DC Entertainment/ Etalon Film/Neoreef/Summit Entertainment-Entertainment One. 116 mins. USA/France/Canada. 2013. Rel: 2 Aug 2013. Cert. 12A.

Red Dawn ★

In this redundant remake of John Milius' 1984 right-wing actioner a group of young American teenagers are determined to fight back when North Korean paratroopers land in their town. This is another excuse for American gung-ho propaganda delivered without any irony or style. Last year Australia's *Tomorrow When the War Began* dealt with a similar premise, but that was done with craft and had fully fleshed characters – unlike this superficial and deeply annoying film. Avoid! GS

▶ Chris Hemsworth, Josh Peck, Adrianne Palicki, Isabel Lucas, Jeffrey Dean Morgan, Connor Cruise.
▶ *Dir* Dan Bradley, *Pro* Beau Flynn and Tripp Vinson, *Screenplay* Carl Elsworth and Jeremy Passmore, based on the 1984 screenplay by Kevin Reynolds and John Milius, from a story by Reynolds, *Ph* Mitchell Amundsen, *Pro Des* Dominic Watkins, *Ed* Richard Pearson, *M* Ramin Djawadi, *Cos* Catherine George.

United Artists/FilmDistrict/Contrafilm etc-Koch Media. 93 mins. USA. 2012. Rel: 15 Mar 2013. Cert. 15.

The Reef 2: High Tide ★★½

In this unexpected sequel to 2006's *The Reef* (aka *Shark Bait*), its menacing shark villain Troy

Rebel yell: Mathieu Kassovitz in his shocking, if occasionally confusing *Rebellion*.

(voice of Donal Logue) escapes from captivity. His dastardly plot is to avenge himself on the young guppy hero Pi (Drake Bell, taking over from Freddie Prinze Jr) and the other fish of the reef. Pi needs help to survive the terrible threat. The candy-coloured animation is rather flat and inexpressive, and the story is all a bit lame and clichéd, paling in comparison with the similar *Finding Nemo* and *Shark Tale*. But the film is merry and good-hearted, with enough innocent humour and simple sentiment to appeal to its young audience. DW

▶ Voices of Andy Dick, Busy Phillips, Drake Bell, Frankie Jonas, Jamie Kennedy, Donal Logue, Rob Schneider.
▶ *Dir* Mark AZ Dippé and Taedong Park, *Pro* Dippé, Ash R Shah, Daniel Chuba and Youngki Lee, *Screenplay* Chris Denk and Johnny Hartmann, *Art Dir* Junghun Kim, *Ed* Michael Rafferty and Tom Sanders, *M* Todd Haberman.
Animation Picture Company/WonderWorld Studios-Blue Sky Media.
80 mins. South Korea/USA. 2012. Rel: 28 Oct 2013. Cert. U.

Reign of Assassins ★★★

Seen in China as long ago as 2010, this visually sumptuous wuxia offering involves a classic MacGuffin – a Buddhist monk's mortal remains, hijacked by Dark Stone assassin Drizzle (Kelly Lin) and hotly pursued by others of the faction. The fights, enlivened by a lethally bendy 'Water Shedding' sword, are of course dazzling. And there are numerous outré details to divert those

for whom airborne martial arts are limited in appeal. Lin is transformed into Michelle Yeoh, for example, by means of bone-eating beetles introduced via the nostrils, while Yeoh's fearsome antagonist (Wang Xueqi) is a eunuch attracted by the MacGuffin's magical ability to regenerate body parts. "I only want to be a normal man," he says. "Am I too demanding?" (Original title: *Jianyu*) JR

▶ Michelle Yeoh, Woo-sung Jung, Kelly Lin, Wang Xueqi, Barbie Hsu, Shawn Yue, Xiangdong Guo.
▶ *Dir* and *Screenplay* Chao-Bin Su, *Pro* Terence Chang, John Woo and Shaoye Shi, *Ph* Wing-hang Wong, *Pro Des* Simon So and Baigui Yang, *Ed* Ka-Fai Cheung, *M* Peter Kam and Anthony Chue, *Cos* Emi Wada.
Lumiere Motion Picture Co/Media Asia Films/Lion Rock Productions/Stellar Entertainment/Beijing Heguchuan TV & Film Company/Beijing Galloping Horse Films Company/Zhejiang Dongyang Dragon Entertainment Venture Investment Company-Lionsgate.
117 mins. China/Taiwan/Hong Kong. 2010. Rel: 15 Feb 2013. Cert. 15.

Reincarnated ★★★½

In an effort to change his life, rap artist Snoop Dogg goes off to Jamaica with the intention of recording a reggae album. There he meets Bunny Wailer, one of the original members of Bob Marley's band, and is generally made welcome by the Jamaican community. Snoop Dogg wants to become Snoop Lion with a new outlook on life and an effort to put behind him all the negative

Remains to be seen: Michelle Yeoh in Chao-Bin Su's dazzling *Reign of Assassins.*

A thing of beauty: Michel Bouquet and Vincent Rottiers on the estate at Cagnes-sur-Mer in Gilles Bourdos' sumptuous *Renoir*.

parts of his hitherto unorthodox ways. This is the reincarnation referred to in the title of Andy Capper's entertaining documentary, which also contains some music that will be appreciated by lovers of hip hop. PL

▶ With Snoop Dogg, Bunny Wailer, Dr Dre, Daz Dillinger, Angela Hunte, Ariel Rechtshaid, Stewart Copeland, Dre Skull.
▶ *Dir* Andy Capper, *Pro* Snoop Dogg, Ted Chung and Suroosh Alvi, *Ph* William Fairman, Nick Neofitidis and Willie Toledo, *Art Dir* Matt Schoen, *Ed* Dave Gutt, Emily Wilson, Jared Perez and Bernardo Loyola, *M* Snoop Dogg.
Vice Films/Snoopadelic Films Inc-Vice Films.
96 mins. USA. 2012. Rel: 22 Mar 2013. Cert. 18.

The Reluctant Fundamentalist ★★★

Interesting but, as written, underwhelming, this treatment of Mohsin Hamid's novel is certainly a tale for our times. Its central character is a Pakistani who embraces capitalism in New York but suffers humiliation after 9/11 and is subsequently approached by terrorist extremists back in Lahore. The film, novelettish at times, is more superficial than it should be but it's well-intentioned. MS

▶ Riz Ahmed, Liev Schreiber, Kate Hudson, Kiefer Sutherland, Om Puri, Shabana Azmi, Martin Donovan.

▶ *Dir* Mira Nair, *Pro* Lydia Dean Pilcher, *Screenplay* William Wheeler, from a story by Mohsin Hamid and Ami Boghani based on the novel by Hamid, *Ph* Declan Quinn, *Pro Des* Michael Carlin, *Ed* Shimit Amin, *M* Michael Andrews, *Cos* Arjun Bhasin.
IFC Films/Doha Film Institute/a Mirabai Films and Cine Mosaic production-Mara Pictures.
130 mins. USA/India/Qatar. 2012. Rel: 10 May 2013. Cert. 15.

Renoir ★★★½

A film about the painter Auguste Renoir and his filmmaker son Jean set in 1915 and featuring the model who would become the screen actress Catherine Hessling should be fascinating, and all the more so since the talented Michel Bouquet is well cast as Renoir Senior. But in the event the narrow focus and lack of momentum limit its appeal. It compares poorly with that other rural tale from France seen recently, *The Well Digger's Daughter* (2011). MS

▶ Michel Bouquet, Christa Théret, Vincent Rottiers, Thomas Doret, Romane Bohringer.
▶ *Dir* Gilles Bourdos, *Pro* Olivier Delbosc and Marc Missonnier, *Screenplay* Jérôme Tonnerre and Bourdos with Michel Spinosa, based on *Le Tableau amoureux* by Jacques Renoir, *Ph* Mark Ping Bing Lee, *Art Dir* Benoît Barouh, *Ed* Yannick Kergoat, *M* Alexandre Desplat, *Cos* Pascaline Chavanne.

Fidélité/Wild Bunch/Mars Films/France 2 Cinéma etc.-Soda Pictures.
112 mins. France. 2012. Rel: 2013. Cert. 12A.

Riddick ★

Because no one demanded it, Vin Diesel's *Riddick* returns in a tepid tale of survival that sees the silver-eyed psycho left for dead on a hostile planet, gratingly narrating the hard-boiled hell out of his rehabilitation. Gratuitous boobs, celebrity side-boob (Katee Sackhoff) and half-hearted gore earn the movie an adult rating, even though in most other respects it's puerile stuff, from lame-brained characters poorly played by a struggling cast and a screenplay of inept exchanges to a tacked-on, alien-strewn finale that plays like out-takes from the significantly superior *Pitch Black* (2000). MJ

❯ Vin Diesel, Jordi Mollà, Matt Nable, Katee Sackhoff, Dave Bautista, Bokeem Woodbine, Raoul Trujillo.
❯ *Dir* and *Screenplay* David Twohy, based on characters created by Jim and Ken Wheat, *Pro* Diesel and Ted Field, *Ph* David Eggby, *Pro Des* Joseph C. Nemec III, *Ed* Tracy Adams, *M* Graeme Revell, *Cos* Simonetta Mariano.

One Race Productions/Riddick Canada Productions/Radar Pictures-Entertainment One.
119 mins. USA/UK. 2013. Rel: 4 Sep 2013. Cert. 15.

R.I.P.D. ★

A Frankenstein's Monster of a movie, seemingly formed of familiar bits and pieces from earlier and more successful films, it's a wonder this vapid onslaught of effects had the nerve to show its face in public. For the record, R.I.P.D. stands for Rest in Peace Department. Jeff Bridges we expected more from. Ryan Reynolds, not so much. MJ

❯ Jeff Bridges, Ryan Reynolds, Kevin Bacon, Mary-Louise Parker, Stephanie Szostak, James Hing, Marisa Miller.
❯ *Dir* Robert Schwentke, *Pro* Mike Richardson, Neal H Moritz and Michael Fottrell, *Screenplay* Phil Hay and Matt Manfredi, based on a story by Hay, Manfredi and David Dobkin, from the Dark Horse comic feature by Peter M Lenkov, *Ph* Alwin H Küchler, *Pro Des* Alec Hammond, *Ed* Mark Helfrich, *M* Christophe Beck, *Cos* Susan Lyall.

Universal Pictures/Original Film/Dark Horse Entertainment-Universal Pictures.
96 mins. USA. 2013. Rel: 20 Sep 2013. Cert. 12A.

The Road: A Story of Life and Death ★★★½

Featuring five immigrants living in London, two sharing Ireland as their homeland and two now sadly deceased, this documentary by Marc Isaacs lacks something in shaping but not in

its humane, sensitive approach. By the time we get into the film's second half we have come to respond to the people whose mode of life is well captured regardless of some weaknesses in the early stages. Ultimately, it is touching. MS

❯ With Keelta, Billy, Peggy, Birgitte, Nom Rajj, Iqbal.
❯ *Dir* and *Ph* Marc Isaacs, *Pro* Rachel Wexler and Aisling Ahmed, *Written by* Isaacs and Iqbal Ahmed, *Ed* David Charap, *M* Lance Hogan.

Bungalow Town Productions/Marc Isaacs Films/Crow Hill Films/BBC etc.-Drakes Avenue Pictures.
78 mins. UK/Republic of Ireland. 2012.
Rel: 22 Feb 2013. Cert. PG.

Robosapien: Rebooted ★★★

Robosapien, as more percipient readers may have guessed, is a robot. He's found and repaired by young Henry (Bobby Coleman), a loner and a bit of a techno-geek. But what Henry doesn't realise is that Robosapien was designed to be a weapon... If this sounds like a nightmarish scenario, *Robosapien: Rebooted* is actually a family adventure, more in keeping with *Short Circuit* than *RoboCop*. It's inoffensively old-fashioned and rather endearing, which one might expect from the director of *Soul Surfer* and *Casper: A Spirited Beginning*. CB

❯ Penelope Ann Miller, Kim Coates, David Eigenberg, Joaquim de Almeida, Jae Head, Bobby Coleman.
❯ *Dir* Sean McNamara, *Pro* Avi Arad and Steven Paul, *Screenplay* Arad and Max Botkin, *Ph* Christian Sebaldt, *Pro Des* Steve Arnold and Brad Wilson, *Ed* Jeff Canavan, *M* John Coda, *Cos* Bernadene Morgan.

Arad Productions/Crystal Sky Pictures/Brookwell-McNamara Entertainment/Arc Productions/Circle Productions/Hot Sets-Kaleidoscope Entertainment.
86 mins. USA. 2013. Rel: 3 May 2013. Cert. PG.

Robot & Frank ★★★½

Avoiding both whimsy and sentimentality, this offbeat piece set "in the very near future" shows how elderly people like Frank (a magnificent turn by Frank Langella) rely on robots to help them.

Machine fun: Robosapien and Bobby Coleman in Sean McNamara's *Robosapien: Rebooted*.

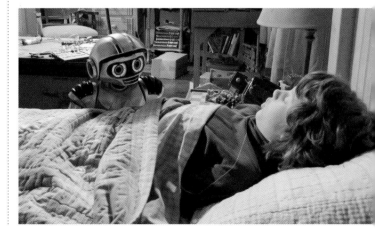

Star-crossed, *Downton Abbey* style: Lesley Manville, Hailee Steinfeld and Douglas Booth in the Julian Fellowes-scripted *Romeo and Juliet.*

It proves to be both a comic crime caper and a buddy movie with Peter Sarsgaard voicing Frank's companion. A plot contrivance and the denial of a happy ending are misjudgments, but see it because when it's good it's very, very good. MS

❧ Frank Langella, James Marsden, Liv Tyler, Jeremy Strong, Susan Sarandon and the voice of Peter Sarsgaard.
❧ *Dir* Jake Schreier, *Pro* Galt Niederhoffer and Sam Bisbee, *Screenplay* Christopher Ford, *Ph* Matthew J Lloyd, *Pro Des* Sharon Lomofsky, *Ed* Jacob Craycroft, *M* Francis and the Lights, *Cos* Erika Munro.
Samuel Goldwyn Films/Stage 6 Films/a Park Pictures feature etc.-Momentum Pictures.
89 mins. USA. 2012. Rel: 8 Mar 2013. Cert. 12A.

Romeo and Juliet ★★★★

Much reviled, this is a treatment of Shakespeare's play which, if hardly memorable and strictly traditional in its stylistic approach, could well work as intended for those youngsters who might be dubious about the Bard but love the romantic drama to be found in the *Twilight* films. In any case Paul Giamatti is a great Friar Laurence and Lesley Manville excels as the nurse. The last shot in the movie is perfectly suited to its aims. MS

❧ Hailee Steinfeld, Douglas Booth, Damian Lewis, Christian Cooke, Lesley Manville, Kodi Smit-McPhee, Stellan Skarsgård, Paul Giamatti, Natascha McElhone.
❧ *Dir* Carlo Carlei, *Pro* Ileen Maisel, Lawrence Elman,

Julian Fellowes and others, *Screenplay* Fellowes, from Shakespeare's play, *Ph* David Tattersall, *Pro Des* Tonino Zera, *Ed* Peter Honess, *M* Abel Korzeniowski, *Cos* Carlo Poggioli.
Swarovski Entertainment/Blue Lake Media Fund/an Amber Entertainment production etc.-Entertainment Film Distributors Ltd.
118 mins. UK/USA/Italy. 2013. Rel: 11 Oct 2013. Cert. PG.

Rough Cut ★★½

London-based artist turned first-time film director Jamie Shovlin explores the production of fictitious Italian director Jesus Rinzoli's 1970s exploitation flick *Hiker Meat* in his quirky, thoughtful pseudo-documentary. The film follows the troubled movie-making of an amateur crew as they head to the Lake District to re-create the slasher movie, battling bugs, botched effects and a micro-budget. Both a homage to and critique of the '70s horror genre, it's clever, enlightening and revealing up to a point, though sometimes it's frustrating as its obvious ambitions outreach its achievement. Despite its intelligence, some of it seems awfully obvious and clumsily done. DW

❧ Agnes Aspen, Ashley Houston, Bob Young, Jack Dearsley, Helen Batchelor, Aaron Cobham.
❧ *Dir* Jamie Shovlin, *Pro* Bren O'Callaghan, *Concept* and *Screenplay by* Mike Harte, *Ph* John Grey, *Ed* Shovlin and Adam Milburn, *M* Euan Rodger.
Cornerhouse Artist Film-Cornerhouse Artist Film.
90 mins. UK. 2013. Rel: 6 Dec 2013. Cert. 15.

Run for Your Wife ★

You don't have to recall, as I do, seeing Ray Cooney's classic farce on its April 1983 debut at the Shaftesbury Theatre to be left slack-jawed in amazement by this mirthless car-crash of a film version. Richard Briers and Bernard Cribbins, so brilliant in the stage production, totter through in microscopic cameos here – just two of seemingly hundreds of such appearances by Cooney's "theatre chums", as they're billed in the credits. (Several, including Briers, barely outlived the film's release date.) The complicated tale of a taxi driver who maintains one wife in Stockwell and another in Finsbury, the result raises a few smiles courtesy of Neil Morrissey (in the old Cribbins role), but is otherwise the worst kind of collectors' item. JR

▶ Danny Dyer, Denise Van Outen, Sarah Harding, Neil Morrissey, Kellie Shirley, Christopher Biggins, Lionel Blair, Nicholas Le Prevost, Cliff Richard, Barry Cryer, Rolf Harris, Vicki Michelle, Jenny Seagrove, Judi Dench, Russ Abbot, Nicky Henson, Bernard Cribbins, Richard Briers, Brian Murphy, Marcia Warren, June Whitfield, Maureen Lipman, Su Pollard, Andrew Sachs, Derek Fowlds, Anne Rogers, Simon Williams, Robin Askwith, Sylvia Syms, Donald Sinden, Wendy Craig, Geoffrey Palmer, Lynda Baron, Rona Anderson, Bill Pertwee, Tony Britton, Wanda Ventham, Derren Nesbitt, Timothy West, Prunella Scales, Jess Conrad, Tom Conti, Dennis Waterman, Ray Cooney et al.
▶ *Dir* Ray Cooney and John Luton, *Pro* James Simpson, *Screenplay* Cooney, from his own play, *Ph* Graham Fowler, *Pro Des* Fi Russell, *Ed* John Pegg, *M* Walter Christian Mair, *Cos* Tony Priestley.

Run For Your Wife Film-Ballpark Film Distributors. 94 mins. UK. 2012. Rel: 14 Feb 2013. Cert. 12A.

Runner, Runner ★

Did this ever look exciting on paper? With Leonardo DiCaprio as co-producer and Ben Affleck as the bad guy, one can only presume so. As it is, under Brad Furman's lacklustre direction this tale of the shenanigans surrounding on-line gambling shapes up as the dullest 'thriller' of the year. There are a lot of numbers, percentages and statistics – and even more shady figures in sunglasses – but the characters are plasma-screen thin and the potentially exotic locales of Puerto Rico completely squandered. They used to make films like this in the 1960s to support the main feature, but they were seldom this lifeless. JC-W

▶ Justin Timberlake, Gemma Arterton, Ben Affleck, Anthony Mackie, David Costabile, John Heard.
▶ *Dir* Brad Furman, *Pro* Arnon Milchan, Jennifer Davisson Killoran, Leonardo DiCaprio, Michael Shamberg, Stacey Sher, Brian Koppelman and David Levien, *Screenplay* Koppelman and Levien, *Ph* Mauro

Fiore, *Pro Des* Charisse Cardenas, *Ed* Jeff McEvoy, *M* Christophe Beck, *Cos* Sophie De Rakoff.

Appian Way/Double Feature Films/New Regency Pictures-20th Century Fox. 91 mins. USA. 2013. Rel: 27 Sep 2013. Cert. 15.

Rurouni Kenshin ★★★½

Keishi Ohtomo's stylish live-action adaptation of this popular manga takes place in 1868 during the last days of the Shoguns. The legendary assassin known as Battosai the Killer disappears without a trace but years later he returns as a wanderer named Kenshin Himura (Takeru Satô). He begins to save people who need his help but vows never to kill anyone again... This enjoyable adventure boasts plenty of action with cleverly choreographed martial arts sequences. (Original title: *Rurôni Kenshin: Meiji kenkaku roman tan*) GS

▶ Takeru Satô, Yû Aoi, Teruyuki Kagawa, Emi Takei, Yôsuke Eguchi, Munetaka Aoki, Kôji Kikkawa, Taketo Tanaka.
▶ *Dir* Keishi Ohtomo, *Pro* Shinzô Matsuhashi, *Screenplay* Ohtomo, Kiyomi Fujii and Nobuhiro Watsuki, *Ph* Takuro Ishizaka, *Pro Des* Hashimoto So, *Ed* Tsuyoshi Imai, *M* Naoki Sato, *Cos* Sawataishi Kazuhiro.

Warner Bros/C & I Entertainment/IMJ Entertainment/ Studio Swan/RoC Works Company-Warner Bros. 134 mins. Japan. 2012. Rel: 4 Oct 2013. Cert. 15.

Rush ★★★★

Senna (2010) may be in every sense a more authentic view of Formula One racing (it was after all a documentary) but *Rush* is a polished production and you don't have to be a motor racing enthusiast to enjoy it. Based on the rivalry between those famed contrasted drivers James Hunt and Niki Lauda (admirably played by Chris

Peace by the sword: Takeru Satô in Keishi Ohtomo's *Rurouni Kenshin*.

Brought to book: Emma Thompson as PL Travers and Tom Hanks as Walt Disney in *Saving Mr Banks*.

Hemsworth and Daniel Brühl respectively), it cleverly gives each a voice-over as the drama proceeds thus encouraging the viewers to support now one and now the other. MS

▶ Chris Hemsworth, Daniel Brühl, Olivia Wilde, Alexandra Maria Lara, Christian McKay.
▶ *Dir* Ron Howard, *Pro* Andrew Eaton, Eric Fellner, Brian Oliver, Peter Morgan, Brian Grazer and Howard, *Screenplay* Morgan, *Ph* Anthony Dod Mantle, *Pro Des* Mark Digby, *Ed* Dan Hanley and Mike Hill, *M* Hans Zimmer, *Cos* Julian Day.

Exclusive Media/Cross Creek Pictures/a Revolution Films/Working Title Films/Imagine Entertainment production etc.-StudioCanal Limited.
122 mins. UK/Germany/USA. 2013. Rel: 13 Sep 2013. Cert. 15.

Safe Haven ★★

This is the eighth film inspired by the maudlin machinery of Nicholas Sparks' bestselling novels, with two more on the way. This time around, the machinery incorporates a few thriller tactics vaguely reminiscent of *Cape Fear* and a supernatural coda lifted (to hilarious, stupefying effect) from *The Sixth Sense*. Julianne Hough is the troubled heroine on the run, Josh Duhamel the winsome widower with a couple of repugnant brats in tow, and David Lyons the glassy-eyed maniac cop who comes between them. Saccharine stuff like this is ripe for what academics call 'camp appropriation'. (Who

knows? It may already have been appropriated.) But there's no denying that, for its target audience, *Safe Haven* will be just the ticket. JR

▶ Julianne Hough, Irene Ziegler, Jon Kohler, Tim Parati, David Lyons, Josh Duhamel, Giulia Pagano.
▶ *Dir* Lasse Hallström, *Pro* Nicholas Sparks, Ryan Kavanaugh, Wyck Godfrey and Marty Bowen, *Screenplay* Dana Stevens and Gage Lansky, from the novel by Nicholas Sparks, *Ph* Terry Stacey, *Pro Des* Kara Lindstrom, *Ed* Andrew Mondshein, *M* Deborah Lurie, *Cos* Leigh Leverett.

Relativity Media/Nicholas Sparks Productions/Temple Hill Entertainment-Momentum Pictures.
115 mins. USA. 2013. Rel: 1 Mar 2013. Cert. 12A.

Sammy's Great Escape ★★

In this sequel to Belgium's CG-animated family film *A Turtle's Tale: Sammy's Adventures*, Sammy the Turtle is caught by poachers and taken with other assorted sea creatures to an aquarium in Dubai from which they plot an escape. This desperately wants to be *Finding Nemo* (re-released in 3D this same year; qv) but lacks that film's level of wit and inventiveness. The result is, consequently, unremarkable. (Original title: *Sammy's avonturen 2*) JC

▶ Voices of Pat Carroll, Carlos McCullers II, Cinda Adams, Dino Andrade, Chris Andrew Ciulla, Isabelle Fuhrman, Wesley Johnny.
▶ *Dir* Vincent Kesteloot and Ben Stassen, *Pro*

Stassen, Gina Gallo, Mimi Maynard, Domonic Paris and Caroline Van Iseghem, *Screenplay* Paris, *Art Dir* Vincent Kesteloot, *M* Ramin Djawadi.

Illuminata Pictures/Motion Investment Group/ nWave Pictures/BNP Paribas Fortis Film Fund/uFilm etc-Warner Bros.
92 mins. Belgium. 2012. Rel: 15 Feb 2013. Cert. U.

Saving Mr Banks ★★★½

PL (Pamela) Travers, author of the *Mary Poppins* books, resisted requests from Walt Disney to film her creation for over 20 years. In the early 1960s she finally caved in and went to Hollywood to discuss her terms, which included final approval and no animation or songs. Eventually Disney secured the rights and the resulting film was a huge hit. Emma Thompson as Travers and Tom Hanks as Disney are both terrific at knocking spots off each other. Mr Banks, the children's father in *Mary Poppins*, was based on Travers' own father, as we learn from flashbacks. John Lee Hancock's film is both touching and hilarious in its eye-opening look at life in Tinseltown. MHD

❧ Emma Thompson, Tom Hanks, Paul Giamatti, Jason Schwartzman, Bradley Whitford, Colin Farrell, Ruth Wilson.
❧ *Dir* John Lee Hancock, *Pro* Alison Owen, Ian Collie and Philip Steuer, *Screenplay* Kelly Marcel and Sue Smith, *Ph* John Schwartzman, *Pro Des* Michael Corenblith, *Ed* Mark Livolski, *M* Thomas Newman, *Cos* Daniel Orlandi.

Walt Disney Pictures/BBC Films/Essential Media and Entertainment/Ruby Films/Hopscotch Features-Walt Disney Studios Motion Pictures.
125 mins. USA/UK/Australia. 2013. Rel: 29 Nov 2013. Cert. PG.

Saving Santa ★★½

Considering how costly animated features are to make, it's surprising how many duff ones come along, especially at Christmas. Unless you have something original to say or have an expert eye like that of Aardman Animation, then why waste your money? *Saving Santa* is a case in point, with Bernard (Martin Freeman) as a time-travelling elf who has to keep Santa's grotto a secret from the rest of the world and especially from evil Neville Baddington (Tim Curry) who's after all of Claus's secrets. The predictable story goes nowhere fast, but then it's only for kids, so why bother? Other recognisable voices include Joan Collins as Baddington's mum. Not the best Christmas present a child might want. PL

❧ Voices of Martin Freeman, Tim Curry, Noel Clarke, Tim Conway, Pam Ferris, Ashley Tisdale, Joan Collins, Tom Baker.
❧ *Dir* Leon Joosen and Aaron Selman, *Pro* Antony Nottage, *Screenplay* Ricky Roxburgh, from a story by

Nottage, *Ed* Janie Kirkpatrick, *M* Grant Olding.

Gateway Films/Prana Animation Studios-Kaleidoscope Entertainment.
83 mins. UK/USA/Mongolia. 2013. Rel: 29 Nov 2013. Cert. U.

Scary Movie 5 ★

An all-new cast appears in this slack and shoddy fourth sequel to the 2000 hit. Ashley Tisdale and Simon Rex star as a dim suburban couple who move into a haunted house with their possessed adopted nieces and nephew. The couple experience paranormal activity and use home-surveillance cameras to find they're being stalked by a nefarious demon. It's easy to imagine what recent hits the film will parody and to predict the stale and mirthless jokes it will try to make out of them. Charlie Sheen and Lindsay Lohan only add to their career troubles by sharing the opening scene. *Fifty Shades of Grey* is spoofed even though it hadn't been made then! DW

❧ Ashley Tisdale, Simon Rex, Erica Ash, Molly Shannon, Heather Locklear, Jerry Connor, JP Manoux, Jerry O'Connell, Charlie Sheen, Lindsay Lohan.
❧ *Dir* Malcolm D Lee, *Pro* David Zucker and Phil Dornfeld, *Screenplay* Zucker and Pat Proft, *Ph* Steven Douglas Smith, *Pro Des* Clark Hunter, *Ed* Sam Seig, *M* James L Venable, *Cos* Keith G. Lewis.

Brad Grey Pictures/Dimension Films/DZE-Entertainment Film Distributors.
86 mins. USA. 2013. Rel: 12 Apr 2013. Cert. 15.

Scatter My Ashes at Bergdorf's ★★★

Compared to such documentaries as *Bill Cunningham New York* and *Diana Vreeland – The Eye Has to Travel* that also touch on fashion in America, this New York study of the Fifth Avenue store favoured by the elite is of only modest interest. A few good tales are told but the film is all bits and

Dedicated follower of fashion: Matthew Miele's *Scatter My Ashes at Bergdorf's.*

pieces, a slight work never justifying the feature length adopted. It's strictly for fashion aficionados not deterred by Bergdorf's role in catering only for those with a very extravagant lifestyle. MS

> With Linda Fargo, Karl Lagerfeld, Isaac Mizrahi and William Fichtner (narrator).
> *Dir* and *Written by* Matthew Miele, *Pro* Mallory Andrews, *Ph* and *Ed* Justin Bare.

Quixotic Endeavors/Berney Films/BG Productions-Curzon Film World.
94 mins. USA. 2013. Rel: 6 Dec 2013. Cert. PG.

The Seasoning House ★½

The action takes place in the Balkans during a terrible war and follows the story of Angel (Rosie Day), a young, mute, orphaned girl enslaved by Viktor (Kevin Howarth) in a grim place where young girls are kept for sex against their will... This is confidently directed by Paul Hyett and atmospherically photographed by Adam Etherington, but the misogynistic and misanthropic nature of the script leaves a bad taste in the mouth. GS

Horse sense: Conner Chapman in Clio Barnard's *The Selfish Giant*, winner of the Best British Film award from the London Film Critics' Circle.

> Rosie Day, David Lemberg, Amanda Wass, Sean Cronin, Kevin Howarth, Tomi May, Emily Tucker, Ema Britton.
> *Dir* Paul Hyett, *Pro* Michael Riley, *Screenplay* Hyett, Conal Palmer and Adrian Rigelsford, from an idea by Helen Solomon, *Ph* Adam Etherington, *Pro Des* Caroline Story, *Ed* Agnieszka Liggett, *M* Paul E Francis, *Cos* Raquel Azevedo.

Sterling Pictures/Filmgate Films/Templeheart Films-Kaleidoscope Film Distribution.
90 mins. UK. 2012. Rel: 21 June 2013. Cert. 18.

The Secret Life of Walter Mitty ★★

Loosely based on a James Thurber story, with little or nothing in common with Danny Kaye's delightful 1947 comedy of the same name, *The Secret Life of Walter Mitty* sees a hopeless, hapless daydreamer embark on a life-changing global journey that rivals his wildest flights of fancy. Essentially an attractive travelogue from director and star Ben Stiller, the result, though reasonably watchable, isn't much fun and certainly isn't funny. It is, however, bland and patronising, encouraging us to live our lives to the fullest. To which end we'd recommend giving it a miss. MJ

> Ben Stiller, Kristen Wiig, Shirley MacLaine, Adam Scott, Kathryn Hahn, Sean Penn.
> *Dir* Ben Stiller, *Pro* Stiller, Samuel Goldwyn Jr, John Goldwyn and Stuart Cornfeld, *Screenplay* Steve Conrad, based on the short story by James Thurber, *Ph* Stuart Dryburgh, *Pro Des* Jeff Mann, *Ed* Greg Hayden, *M* Theodore Shapiro, *Cos* Sarah Edwards.

Samuel Goldwyn Films/Red Hour Films/New Line Cinema/TSG Entertainment-20th Century Fox.
114 mins. USA. 2013. Rel: 26 Dec 2013. Cert. PG.

Seduced and Abandoned ★★★½

In making a film about the Cannes Film Festival and about his own attempt to sell a film project there to star Alec Baldwin, James Toback fails to give this documentary any sense of shape, disruptively cuts up interviews and tiresomely indulges split-screen techniques. Even so film buffs will enjoy comments from actors, directors and others about the state of cinema today, Ryan Gosling being especially astute in his observations. MS

> With Alec Baldwin, James Toback, Bernardo Bertolucci, Martin Scorsese, Ryan Gosling, Michel Ciment, Roman Polanski, Jeremy Thomas, Francis Ford Coppola.
> *Dir* and *Written by* James Toback, *Pro* Michael Mailer, Alec Baldwin and Toback, *Ph* Ruben Sluijter, *Ed* Aaron Yanes.

A Michael Mailer Films production/James Toback Films/El Dorado Pictures-Soda Pictures.
98 mins. USA. 2013. Rel: 8 Nov 2013. Cert. 15.

The Selfish Giant ★★★★

Clio Barnard's acclaimed film retains the Bradford setting of her brilliant debut *The Arbor* but this time it is a fully fledged drama with actors on screen. It centres on the friendship of two boys living bleak lives; they take metal to a scrapdealer who as it turns out will have a dramatic effect on their lives. Forget the title taken from an Oscar Wilde story, this film is akin to Shane Meadows' *A Room for Romeo Brass* (1999) but with its own local colour. Sincere, authentic but very, very downbeat. MS

❯ Conner Chapman, Shaun Thomas, Sean Gilder, Lorraine Ashbourne, Steve Evets.
❯ *Dir* and *Screenplay* (inspired by Oscar Wilde's story) Clio Barnard, *Pro* Tracy O'Riordan, *Ph* Mike Eley, *Pro Des* Helen Scott, *Ed* Nick Fenton, *M* Harry Escott, *Cos* Matthew Price.
BFI/Film4/a Moonspun Films production-Artificial Eye.
91 mins. UK. 2013. Rel: 25 Oct 2013. Cert. 15.

The Sessions ★★★★½

This American film about a polio victim visiting a therapist who offers herself as a sexual surrogate may well sound off-putting. However, with superb performances from John Hawkes and Helen Hunt, this tale based on actual events in 1988 provides one of the year's best films. A few minor details may seem contrived but at heart, in addition to capturing the man's sense of humour to lighten the tone, it sensitively expresses the sacred bond that can be found in sex. DH Lawrence would have approved. MS

❯ John Hawkes, Helen Hunt, William H Macy, Moon Bloodgood, Annika Marks.
❯ *Dir* and *Screenplay* (based on the article *On Seeing a Sex Surrogate* by Mark O'Brien) Ben Lewin, *Pro* Judi Levine, Stephen Nemeth and Lewin, *Ph* Geoffrey Simpson, *Pro Des* John Mott, *Ed* Lisa Bromwell, *M* Marco Beltrami, *Cos* Justine Seymour.
Fox Searchlight Pictures/Such Much Films/Rhino Films etc.-20th Century Fox.
95 mins. USA. 2012. Rel: 18 Jan 2013. Cert. 15.

Shell ★★★★

Rural Scotland, majestic and remote, is superbly photographed in this minimalist first feature from Scott Graham. Chloe Pirrie as a daughter aiding her father in his remote garage is outstanding. The bond with her father appears to involve incestuous feelings but Graham allows the audience to reach their own conclusions. This is a notable debut both for the filmmaker and for his lead actress, who has qualities akin to Samantha Morton and Carey Mulligan. MS

❯ Joseph Mawle, Chloe Pirrie, Michael Smiley, Iain de Caestecker, Kate Dickie.
❯ *Dir* and *Screenplay* Scott Graham, *Pro* David Smith and Margaret Matheson, *Ph* Yoliswa Gärtig, *Pro Des* James Lapsley, *Ed* Rachel Tunnard, *Cos* Rebecca Gore.
BFI/Creative Scotland/ a Brocken Spectre production/ Molinaire etc.-Verve Pictures.
91 mins. UK/Germany. 2012. Rel: 15 Mar 2013. Cert. 15.

Short Term 12 ★★★½

Destin Daniel Cretton's second film finds him creating a very effective drama as he deals in what he knows: he has himself worked in an American foster-care facility for teenagers at risk and that is the main setting here. His film portrays the lives of both staff and inmates and is wonderfully convincing until, sadly, the plot veers into dramatic contrivances towards the end. What's good is so very good that it's a film worth seeing regardless, and the casting could not be better. MS

❯ Brie Larson, John Gallagher Jr, Kaitlyn Dever, Rami Malek, Keith Stanfield.
❯ *Dir* and *Screenplay* Destin Daniel Cretton, *Pro* Maren Olson, Asher Goldstein and Astrachan Ron Najor, *Ph* Brett Pawlak, *Pro Des* Rachel Myers, *Ed* Nat Sanders, *M* Joel P West, *Cos* Mirren Gordon-Crozier and Joy Cretton.

Daddy's girl: Chloe Pirrie in Scott Graham's minimalist *Shell*.

Cinedigm/Demarest Films/a Traction Media/Animal Kingdom production-Verve Pictures.
97 mins. USA. 2013. Rel: 1 Nov 2013. Cert. 15.

Shun Li and the Poet ★★★½

Almost two works in one, this is in part an involving study of Chinese immigrants who, coming to Europe to work, suffer from the reception they get in Italy. The excellent lead actress Zhao Tao encourages us to identify with her plight but then the social comment yields to a tragic and even melodramatic love story. The mixture is less than wholly satisfying but Venice, poetically shot, provides a memorable setting. (Original title: *Io sono Li*) MS

▶ Zhao Tao, Rade Sherbedgia, Marco Paolini, Wang Yuan, Zhong Cheng.
▶ *Dir* Andrea Segre, *Pro* Francesco Bonsembiante, Francesca Feder and Nicola Rosada, *Screenplay* Marco Pettenello and Segre, from Segre's story, *Ph* Luca Bigazzi, *Art Dir* Leonardo Scarpa, *Ed* Sara Zavarise, *M* François Couturier, *Cos* Maria Rita Barbera.

A Jolefilm, Aeternam Films production/Rai Cinema etc.-Artificial Eye.
98 mins. Italy/France. 2011. Rel: 21 June 2013. Cert. 15.

Side by Side ★★★★

A documentary which complements last year's *The Last Projectionist*, this look at the digital revolution in cinema concentrates on the technical side of things. As presented by Keanu Reeves, it boasts a fine assortment of viewpoints and interviewees with the actors outnumbered by directors and others, including photographers and editors. For the technically minded, this will be absorbing. MS

▶ With Keanu Reeves, Martin Scorsese, David Lynch, David Fincher, Michael Ballhaus, Steven Soderbergh, Lars von Trier, Danny Boyle, Anne V Coates, Vittorio Storaro.
▶ *Dir* and *Written by* Chris Kenneally, *Pro* Keanu Reeves and Justin Szlasa, *Ph* Chris Cassidy, *Ed* Mike Long and Malcolm Hearn, *M* Brendan and Billy Ryan.

A Company Films, LLC production-Axiom Films Limited.
99 mins. USA. 2012. Rel: 15 Feb 2013. Cert. 15.

Side Effects ★★★½

Partly a cautionary tale about the effects of using ill-judged medication and partly a thriller (it opens with blood stains which will be explained only later), this is a pleasant but unexceptional entertainment which seems like two films in one. If anything unifies these contrasted elements it is the performance of Jude Law on his very best form as a doctor who becomes desperate to clear his name. MS

▶ Jude Law, Rooney Mara, Catherine Zeta-Jones, Channing Tatum, Vinessa Shaw.
▶ *Dir* Steven Soderbergh, *Pro* Lorenzo di Bonaventura, Gregory Jacobs and Scott Z Burns,

They'll always have Venice: Rade Sherbedgia and Zhao Tao in *Shun Li and the Poet*.

Doctor's orders: Jude Law on terrific form in Steven Soderbergh's multi-layered *Side Effects.*

Screenplay Burns, *Ph* Peter Andrews (ie, Soderbergh), *Pro Des* Howard Cummings, *Ed* Mary Ann Bernard (ie, Soderbergh), *M* Thomas Newman, *Cos* Susan Lyall.

Endgame Entertainment/Filmnation Entertainment-E1 Films.

106 mins. USA. 2013. Rel: 8 Mar 2013. Cert. 15.

Silence ★★★½

This is the real thing: an authentic artistic endeavour. Ireland's Pat Collins gives us a central character who visits areas where no man-made sound is present. In this way his film investigates the bond between people and places which can be felt when all the accretions of civilisation are removed. The viewer is invited to join in a non-religious meditation. However, the later stages have less universal relevance and the film even at 87 minutes seems too long. Nevertheless this utterly individual work has great images while, aptly enough, the soundtrack is precisely judged. MS

▶ With Eoghan Mac, Giolla Bhride, Hilary O'Shaughnessy, Andrew Bennett.
▶ *Dir* Pat Collins, *Pro* Tina Moran, *Written by* Collins, Sharon Whooley, Eoghan Mac and Giolla Bhride, *Ph* Richard Kendrick, *Ed* Tadhg O'Sullivan.

A South Wind Blows/Harvest Film production/RTÉ/Irish Film Board etc.-New Wave Films.

87 mins. Ireland. 2011. Rel: 9 Aug 2013. Cert. PG.

Simon Killer ★★★★

That talented but disquieting filmmaker Antonio Campos here tells the story of an American in Paris whose sociopathic tendencies become increasingly disturbing. The film puts us inside his head and Brady Corbet plays him uncompromisingly. There's no real sense of pathos or tragedy, but it seems compellingly real (much of it is in French with subtitles) and fans of Patricia Highsmith in particular should feel very much at home here. MS

▶ Brady Corbet, Mati Diop, Constance Rousseau, Lila Salet, Solo.
▶ *Dir* and *Screenplay* (from a story by himself, Brady Corbet and Mati Diop) Antonio Campos, *Pro* Josh Mond, Sean Durkin and Matt Palmieri, *Ph* Joe Anderson, *Pro Des* Nicolas de Boiscuillé, *Ed* Zac Stuart-Pontier, Campos and Babak Jalali, *M* Saunder Jurriaans and Danny Bensi, *Cos* Laetitia Bouix.

FilmHaven Entertainment/a Borderline Films production-Eureka Entertainment.

101 mins. USA. 2012. Rel: 12 Apr 2013. Cert. 18.

Sir Billi ★★

Sir Billi will go down in movie history as Sean Connery's comeback (his first film since *The League of Extraordinary Gentlemen* in 2003), as well as the first animated feature made entirely in Scotland. Alas, all we get is Connery's inimitable (or rather much imitated) voice as retired skateboarding veterinarian Sir Billi, who fights villainous police and powerful lairds to save Bessie Boo the beaver, who was raised by rabbits. It's short and harmless, but both the story and animation are on the weak and unimaginative side. It tries to raise laughs with smutty jokes and lame 007 references, but it all seems a bit obvious and not very funny. Shirley Bassey's singing of 'Guardian of the Highlands' is a highlight. DW

▶ Voices of Sean Connery, Alan Cumming, Patrick Doyle, Greg Hemphill, Ford Kiernan, Miriam Margolyes, Alex Norton, Ruby Wax.
▶ *Dir* Sascha Hartmann, *Pro* Sean Connery, Tessa and Sascha Hartmann and John Fortune Fraser, *Screenplay* Tessa Hartmann, *Art Dir* Sascha Hartmann, *Ed* Steven Weisberg, *Head of Animation* Kenneth Chan, *M* Patrick Doyle.

Billi Productions/Glasgow Animation-Kaleidoscope Entertainment.

76 mins. UK. 2012. Rel: 13 Sep 2013. Cert. U.

Table manners:
Aure Atika,
Bernadette Lafont,
Emmanuelle Riva,
Julie Delpy, Noémie
Lvovsky and Valérie
Bonneton in *Skylab*.

Skylab ★★★★½

A family gets together to celebrate grandmother Amandine's birthday in St Malo in 1979, the time of the Skylab crash. The parents are worried that the space station may land on their children – so no sleeping outdoors! Writer-director Julie Delpy's film is a rambling affair but none the worse for that. It depicts a family at ease, eating, drinking, talking, reminiscing, arguing, fighting, playing games, going to the beach, having a barbecue and enjoying themselves. Delpy also plays Anna, mother of ten-year-old Albertine (Lou Alvarez), who narrates this highly entertaining story. The strong cast of character actors are only too believable as members of this extended family. Good, too, to see Bernadette Lafont in one of her last films as Amandine, and Emmanuelle Riva as Anna's mother. (Original title: *Le Skylab*) MHD

❱ Julie Delpy, Bernadette Lafont, Emmanuelle Riva, Lou Alvarez, Eric Elmosnino, Aure Atika, Jean-Louis Coulloc'h, Noémie Lvovsky, Candide Sanchez.
❱ *Dir* and *Screenplay* Julie Delpy, *Pro* Michael Gentile, *Ph* Lubomir Bakchev, *Pro Des* Yves Fournier, *Ed* Isabelle Devinck, *Music Supervisor* Matthieu Siborny, *Cos* Pierre-Yves Gayraud.

The Film/France 2 Cinéma/Tempête Sous un Crâne Production/Canal+/France Télévision/CinéCinéma/ Coficup/Backup Films etc-StudioCanal. 114 mins. France. 2011. Rel: 25 Oct 2013. Cert. 15.

Sleep Tight ★★★

Jaume Balagueró of *[REC]* fame delivers a terrifying character study about a doorman in a hotel who becomes obsessed with ruining the life of a happy-go-lucky young female tenant because he wants to wipe the smile off her face. He sneaks into her room while she's asleep, initially just to be there but then, later, to do such things as infest her room with bugs. He's a thoroughly nasty type for whom it's hard to feel any sympathy; this deftly plotted thriller consequently feels somewhat soulless. (Original title: *Mientras duermes*) JC

❱ Luis Tosar, Marta Etura, Alberto San Juan, Petra Martinez, Iris Almeida, Carlos Lasarte, Roger Morilla.
❱ *Dir* Jaume Balagueró, *Pro* Julio Fernández, *Screenplay* Alberto Marini, *Ph* Pablo Rosso, *Pro Des* Javier Alvariño, *Ed* Guillermo de la Cal, *M* Lucas Vidal, *Cos* Marian Coromina.

Castelao Producciones/Coser y Cantar/Canal+ España/ Cubica/Filmax Entertainment/Ono etc-Metrodome Distribution.
102 mins. Spain. 2011. Rel: 1 Mar 2013. Cert. 15.

Smash & Grab: The Story of the Pink Panthers ★★

Havana Marking's uneven documentary attempts to shine a light on the mystery of the Pink Panthers – the world's most successful diamond thieves. The gang originates from Serbia and Montenegro and for the last ten years they have been getting away with millions from boutiques all over the world. It's intriguing but there's also a lot of redundant stuff (like the detailed history of Yugoslavia) as director Marking tries to analyse the reasons behind the gang's actions. GS

▶ With Tomislav Tom Benzon, Daniel Vivian, Jasmin Topalusic.
▶ *Dir* Havana Marking, *Pro* Mike Lerner, *Ph* Richard Gillespie and Joshua Z Weinstein, *Ed* Joby Gee, *M* Simon Russell.

Roast Beef Productions/Thought Engine Media Group-Doppelganger Releasing.
89 mins. UK/USA/Serbia & Montenegro. 2013. Rel: 27 Sep 2013. Cert. 12.

The Smurfs 2 ★★★

Curiously I enjoyed this much more than the original, which I found dull and too silly for words. But surely it's not aimed at adults but at children of a young age and other smurfs. Smurfette is kidnapped by the evil wizard Gargamel (Hank Azaria) who wants to acquire her secret spell in order to turn his creatures, called Naughties, into real Smurfs. But the Smurfs team up with their human friends in order to put a stop to his evil plans... The 3D effects are much more effective this time and, despite the silly premise, this is rather fun. GS

▶ Hank Azaria, Neil Patrick Harris, Brendan Gleeson, Jayma Mays, Jacob Tremblay, Nancy O'Dell, and the voices of Katy Perry, Christina Ricci, Jonathan Winters, JB Smoove, George Lopez, Anton Yelchin, Alan Cumming.
▶ *Dir* Raja Gosnell, *Pro* Véronique Culliford and Jordan Kerner, *Screenplay* Karey Kirkpatrick, David Ronn, Jay Scherick, David N Weiss and J David Stem, based on a story by Stem, Weiss, Scherick and Ronn, based on characters created by Peyo, *Ph* Phil Meheux, *Pro Des* Bill Boes, *Ed* Sabrina Plisco, *M* Heitor Pereira, *Cos* Véronique Marchessault and Rita Ryack.

Columbia Pictures/Sony Pictures Animation/NeoReel/Kerner Entertainment Company-Sony Pictures Releasing.
105 mins. USA. 2013. Rel: 31 July 2013. Cert. U.

Snitch ★★½

Businessman John Matthews (Dwayne Johnson) is determined to save his teenage son from an unjust prison sentence, so he goes undercover in order to infiltrate a violent gang... This is a powerful story but not entirely credible, despite the fact that it's inspired by true events. Just when you think that Johnson has changed direction for some serious acting, he suddenly turns into an action hero of epic proportions. GS

▶ Dwayne Johnson, Barry Pepper, Jon Bernthal, Susan Sarandon, Michael K Williams, Benjamin Bratt.
▶ *Dir* Ric Roman Waugh, *Pro* Dwayne Johnson,

Tobin Armbrust, Alex Brunner, Guy East, Nigel Sinclair, Jonathan King, Matt Jackson, Dany Garcia and David Fanning, *Screenplay* Waugh and Justin Hythe, *Ph* Dana Gonzales, *Pro Des* Vincent Reynaud, *Ed* Jonathan Chibnall, *M* Antonio Pinto, *Cos* Kimberley Adams-Galligan.

Exclusive Media/Participant Media/Front Street Productions/Imagenation Abu Dhabi FZ-Momentum Pictures.
112 mins. USA/United Arab Emirates. 2013. Rel: 21 June 2013. Cert. 12A.

Something in the Air ★★★½

Olivier Assayas, born in 1955, doubtless recalls his own teenage years here as he evokes the lives of French students in 1971 following the youthful upheavals of 'les événements'. Both the look and the attitudes of the time are well caught, but it is difficult to feel much for the characters unless the viewer can identify with them closely as Assayas himself obviously does. (Original title: *Après mai*) MS

▶ Clément Métayer, Lola Créton, Félix Armand, Carole Combes, Hugo Conzelmann.
▶ *Dir* and *Screenplay* Olivier Assayas, *Pro* Nathanaël Karmitz and Charles Gillibert, *Ph* Eric Gautier, *Art Dir* François-Renaud Labarthe, *Ed* Luc Barnier and Mathilde Van de Moortel, *Cos* Jurgen Doëring.

MK2/a France 3 Cinéma/Vortex Sutra co-production/Canal+/Ciné+ etc.-Artificial Eye.
122 mins. France. 2011. Rel: 24 May 2013. Cert. 15.

Song for Marion ★★★

Sincere but sentimental, this is an unexpected piece from the talented Paul Andrew Williams whose previous films have been hard-edged. A story with music much featured about an

Rue the day: Clément Métayer and Lola Créton in Olivier Assayas' *Something in the Air*.

aging long-married couple comes to turn on the consequences when one of them dies of cancer. However, it all becomes increasingly unconvincing as it reaches for an up-beat ending. Terence Stamp has been highly praised for his work here, but even more it is Vanessa Redgrave who, playing from the heart, transcends the mawkish plotting. MS

▶ Terence Stamp, Gemma Arterton, Vanessa Redgrave, Christopher Eccleston, Anne Reid, Ram John Holder.
▶ *Dir* and *Screenplay* Paul Andrew Williams, *Pro* Ken Marshall and Philip Moross, *Ph* Carlos Catalan, *Pro Des* Sophie Becher, *Ed* Daniel Farrell, *M* Laura Rossi, *Cos* Jo Thompson.

Aegis Film Fund/a Steel Mill Pictures production/ Coolmore Productions etc.-E1 Films.
93 mins. UK/Germany. 2012. Rel: 22 Feb 2013. Cert. PG.

Spike Island ★★

May 1990. A bunch of young Manchester lads play in a band and want to get their demo tape into the hands of legendary group The Stone Roses, who are playing a gig on Spike Island. But they don't have tickets so instead have to find a way of getting past security into the gig. Based around an actual, historical rock concert, this is let down by an inexperienced young cast, gratuitous multiple plot lines and a lack of directorial focus. JC

▶ Elliott Tittensor, Nico Mirallegro, Jordan Murphy, Adam Long, Oliver Heald, Emilia Clarke, Lesley Manville, Antonia Thomas, Philip Jackson.
▶ *Dir* Mat Whitecross, *Pro* Esther Douglas and Fiona Neilson, *Screenplay* Chris Coghill, *Ph* Christopher Ross, *Pro Des* Richard Bullock, *Ed* Peter Christells, *M* Ilan Eshkeri and Tim Wheeler, *Cos* Liza Bracey.

Candid camera: The Boss plays it real in Baillie Walsh's Springsteen and I.

Bankside Films/Fiesta Productions/Head Gear Films/ Revolver Entertainment/Metro Technology-Vertigo Films.
105 mins. UK. 2012. Rel: 21 June 2013. Cert. 15.

The Spirit of '45 ★★★★

As sincere as they are one-sided, Ken Loach's political views understandably shape this view of post-war Britain which eventually jumps from 1951 to the late 1970s and the Thatcher era. Containing wonderful images from the period and blending them with new interview footage, this is a masterly example of how to handle such material and how to apply an evocative music track which never becomes too assertive. The Socialist ideals of a past age are celebrated in the hope that they could be taken up again. MS

▶ With Tony Benn, Ray Davies, Julian Tudor Hart, Stan Pearce.
▶ *Dir* Ken Loach, *Pro* Rebecca O'Brien, Kate Ogborn and Lisa Marie Russo, *Ph* Stephen Standen, *Ed* Jonathan Morris, *M* George Fenton.

BFI/Film4/Sixteen Films/Fly Film etc.-Dogwoof.
98 mins. UK. 2012. Rel: 15 Mar 2013. Cert. U.

Spring Breakers ★★★

One approaches the work of the experimental filmmaker Harmony Korine with some caution (his films include *Gummo,* the unwatchable *julien donkey-boy* and *Trash Humpers*). But here Korine has taken on the beach exploitation genre and turned it into a highly cinematic experience. Far from alienating his audience, he panders to their basest instincts and fills the screen with elements a red-blooded male might like to ogle. He could have gone further (this ain't *Baise-moi*), but he goes far enough and has given James Franco plenty of room to chew the garish Florida scenery. JC-W

▶ James Franco, Selena Gomez, Vanessa Hudgens, Ashley Benson, Rachel Korine, Gucci Mane.
▶ *Dir* and *Screenplay* Harmony Korine, *Pro* Charles-Marie Anthonioz, Jordan Gertner, Chris Hanley and David Zander, *Ph* Benoît Debie, *Pro Des* Elliott Hostetter, *Ed* Douglas Crise, *M* Cliff Martinez, *Cos* Heidi Bivens.

Muse Productions/O' Salvation/Division Films-Vertigo Films.
93 mins. USA. 2012. Rel: 5 April 2013. Cert. 18.

Springsteen & I ★★★★

There are many ways to construct a documentary but this is quite a novel one. Partly inspired by the Ridley Scott-produced, crowd-sourced *Life in a Day*, Baillie Walsh's *Springsteen & I* – also produced by Scott – takes a look at the life and career of The Boss through the eyes and camera phones of his fans. Thus, we have testaments of adoration, home-movie footage of The Boss in

action and archive concert material. It's both a celebration of Springsteen and the hero worship he inspires in his admirers and you can't help but warm to him and to them. CB

▶ With Bruce Springsteen, Mitchell A. S. Hallock.
▶ *Dir* Baillie Walsh, *Pro* Svana Gisla, *Ph* Marco Tomaselli, *Ed* Ben Harrax, *M* Bruce Springsteen and the E Street Band.

Mr Wolf/Black Dog Films/Ridley Scott Associates/Scott Free Productions/RSA Films etc-NCM Fathom Events. 124 mins. UK. 2013. Rel: 22 July 2013. Cert. PG.

Stand Up Guys ★★

Oscar-winners Al Pacino, Christopher Walken and Alan Arkin rise marginally above their material in this sentimental, old folks' crime comedy from journeyman director Fisher Stevens. A trio of retired gangsters reunite for a final night of mayhem. Though one has to kill another at daybreak, they're not about to let that spoil their good time, which mainly involves eating, moaning and Viagra-assisted whore-mongering. A knockabout tale with the odd fun moment, above all else it's a squandered opportunity. MJ

▶ Al Pacino, Christopher Walken, Alan Arkin, Julianna Margulies, Mark Margolis, Lucy Punch, Vanessa Ferlito.
▶ *Dir* Fisher Stevens, *Pro* Sidney Kimmel, Jim Tauber, Gary Lucchesi and Tom Rosenberg, *Screenplay* Noah Haidle, *Ph* Michael Grady, *Pro Des* Maher Ahmad,

Ed Mark Livolsi, *M* Lyle Workman, *Cos* Lindsay McKay.

Lionsgate/Sidney Kimmel Entertainment/Lakeshore Entertainment-Entertainment Film Distributors. 95 mins. USA. 2012. Rel: 28 June 2013. Cert. 15.

Star Trek Into Darkness ★★

Like *Batman Begins* and *The Amazing Spider-Man*, JJ Abrams' 2009 reboot of *Star Trek* brought a freshness and dynamism to a tired old franchise, which makes his follow-up all the more disappointing. While there are a few nice lines of dialogue and some suitably awesome visuals, the cheese of the original Gene Roddenberry series has crawled back out of the pantry. The problem is a congestion of narrative strands pegged to a story that isn't that interesting. However, the ending is considerably more impressive than the start (the prologue is particularly mundane), but by then we have lost interest in the whole familiar shambles. JC-W

▶ John Cho, Benedict Cumberbatch, Alice Eve, Bruce Greenwood, Simon Pegg, Chris Pine, Zachary Quinto, Zoë Saldana, Karl Urban, Peter Weller, Anton Yelchin, Noel Clarke, Heather Langenkamp, Chris Hemsworth.
▶ *Dir* J.J. Abrams, *Pro* Abrams, Bryan Burk, Damon Lindelof, Alex Kurtzman and Roberto Orci, *Screenplay* Orci, Kurtzman and Lindelof, *Ph* Daniel Mindel, *Pro Des* Scott Chambliss, *Ed* Maryann Brandon and Mary Jo Markey, *M* Michael Giacchino, *Cos* Michael Kaplan.

Lost Enterprise: Zoë Saldana and Zachary Quinto in JJ Abrams' disappointing Star Trek Into Darkness.

If the shoe fits:
Mia Wasikowska
in Park Chan-
wook's *Stoker*.

Paramount Pictures/Skydance Prods/Bad Robot-
Paramount Pictures.
133 mins. USA. 2013. Rel: 9 May 2013. Cert. 12A.

Stoker ★★★★

This English-language film made in America by
South Korea's Park Chan-wook was underestimated,
perhaps because it fails to fit neatly into any single
genre. It's a superbly acted piece about sibling
rivalry, a detailed take on adolescence and a tale
in which people get murdered – but it's not really
mainstream, not quite a horror film and touches
only incidentally on the supernatural. If less than a
masterpiece, it is admirably directed, atmospheric
and certainly offbeat. Reader, I liked it. MS

▶ Mia Wasikowska, Matthew Goode, Jacki Weaver,
Nicole Kidman, Dermot Mulroney.
▶ *Dir* Park Chan-wook, *Pro* Ridley Scott, Tony Scott
and Michael Costigan, *Screenplay* Wentworth Miller,
Ph Chung-Hoon Chung, *Pro Des* Thérèse DePrez,
Ed Nicolas de Toth, *M* Clint Mansell, *Cos* Kurt
Swanson and Bart Mueller.

Fox Searchlight Pictures/Indian Paintbrush/a Scott Free
Production etc.-20th Century Fox.
99 mins. USA/UK. 2012. Rel: 1 Mar 2013. Cert. 18.

The Stoker ★★½

The Russian Aleksey Balabanov, who died in 2013,
was always something of a provocateur but, as
this story set in the north-west of his country in
the 1990s reminds us, he also created wonderfully
precise images. Released in Russia in October
2010, the film tells of criminality and corruption
eventually becoming a tale of vengeance exacted
by a father, the titular figure well played by
the late Mikhail Skryabin. With deaths on a
Shakespearean scale the piece lies somewhere
between melodrama and tragedy, but the wildly
inappropriate music score totally undermines the
work. (Original title: *Kochegar*) MS

▶ Mikhail Skryabin, Aida Tumutova, Yuri Matveev,
Anna Korotaeva.
▶ *Dir* and *Screenplay* Aleksey Balabanov, *Pro* Sergei
Selyanov, *Ph* Alexander Simonov, *Pro Des* Anastasia
Karimulina, *Ed* Tatyana Kuzmicheva, *M* Didjulja,
Cos Nadezda Vasileva.

A CTB Film Company production/Ministry of Culture of
the Russian Federation etc.-Filmhouse.
87mins. Russia. 2010. Rel: 17 May 2013. Cert. 15.

The Stone Roses: Made of Stone ★★★★

Shane Meadows' documentary about his
favourite band The Stone Roses – the legendary
group from Manchester – is told with love and
energy. He follows them with his camera as
they begin rehearsals for their much anticipated
reunion following their split 16 years earlier.
Their tour begins with various European gigs
before the grand finale at Manchester's Heaton
Park. It's a terrific film which wisely takes its time
in order to re-introduce all the band's members
before this eagerly awaited event. GS

▶ With Shane Meadows, Ian Brown, Gary
Mounfield, John Squire, Alan Wren, Eric Cantona,
Liam Gallagher.

> *Dir* Shane Meadows, *Pro* Mark Herbert, *Ph* Laurie Rose, *Ed* Chris King, Tobias Zaldua and Matthew Gray, *M* The Stone Roses.

Film 4 Productions/Warp Films-Picturehouse Entertainment.
97 mins. UK. 2013. Rel: 5 June 2013. Cert. 15.

Stories We Tell ★★★★

Sarah Polley, the actress turned director, takes another step into the unknown since this is her first documentary and also a film which explores secrets hidden within her own family. Ultimately the film seems rather long and weighed down by Polley's need to justify it to herself. Nevertheless much of it is riveting and it is a thoroughly intriguing work. The less the viewer knows in advance about what the film will uncover the better it works. MS

> With Sarah Polley, Michael Polley, Harry Gulkin, John Polley.
> *Dir* Sarah Polley, *Pro* Anita Lee, *Written by* Sarah Polley and Michael Polley, *Ph* Iris Ng, *Pro Des* Lea Carlson, *Ed* Michael Munn, *Cos* Sarah Armstrong.

The National Film Board of Canada/The CFC-NFB Documentary Program-Artificial Eye.
109 mins. Canada. 2012. Rel: 28 June 2013. Cert. 12A.

The Stroller Plan ★★★½

Marie Deville (Charlotte Lebon) and Thomas Patz (Raphaël Personnaz) fall in love at first sight. Then, three years later (to the day), she jilts him, scuppering his surprise party for her and the guests in waiting. It's an inspired and ingenious start to a love story about a man still in love with his ex. In fact, the opening scene alone would make a brilliant short film. Sure, it's formulaic and predictable (critics might dismiss it as frothy and sentimental), but its battery power – the fresh and engaging Personnaz and Lebon – makes it a date movie of a high calibre. (Original title: *La Stratégie de la poussette*) JC-W

> Raphaël Personnaz, Charlotte Lebon, Jérôme Commandeur, Camélia Jordana, Julie Ferrier, François Berléand, Clément Michel.
> *Dir* Clément Michel, *Pro* Alain Benguigui and Thomas Verhaeghe, *Screenplay* Michel and Louis-Paul Desanges, *Ph* Steeven Petitteville, *Pro Des* Maamar Ech-Cheikh, *Ed* Julie Dupré, Sylvain Ohrel, *Cos* Alexia Crisp-Jones.

Sombrero Productions/StudioCanal/TF1 Films-StudioCanal.
90 mins. France. 2012. Rel: 8 June 2013. Cert. 12A.

The Stuart Hall Project ★★★★

Jamaican-born cultural historian Stuart Hall (1932-2014) worked mostly in Britain from 1951. He was one of the founders of the British Cultural Studies movement and created *New Left Review*, the influential journal of the intellectual Left. He took over as director (from Richard Hoggart) of the Centre for Contemporary Cultural Studies at Birmingham University and was a regular writer-broadcaster. His soft, well-spoken tones became a perennial feature of BBC programmes for the Open University where he was Professor of Sociology. *The Stuart Hall Project* is a fine tribute to a cultural colossus who, through his life, his books and other media in which he appeared, demonstrated that his common-sense views on race, gender and class politics said more than the rantings of many a politician. MHD

> With Stuart Hall and Catherine Hall.
> *Dir* and *Written by* John Akomfrah, *Pro* Lina Gopaul and David Lawson, *Ph* Dewald Aukema, *Ed* Nse Asuquo, *M* Trevor Mathison and Miles Davis.

British Film Institute/BBC Archives/Arts Council England/Creation Rebel Films/Open University/Smoking Dogs Films-British Film Institute.
103 mins. UK. 2013. Rel: 6 Sep 2013. Cert. 12.

Stuck in Love ★★★★

For the Borgen family, love is a way of life. The acclaimed novelist Bill Borgen (Greg Kinnear) still loves his ex-wife Erica (Jennifer Connelly). His daughter Samantha (Lily Collins), who hates her mother, indulges in a string of one-night stands the better to enrich her literary landscape. And Rusty (Nat Wolff), a Stephen King devotee, pines for a girlfriend he believes he cannot have. Love is all around but an equally pertinent title could've been *Stuck in Literature*. Erudite, funny and moving, *Stuck in Love* heralds a promising new talent in Josh Boone and allows its cast to breathe in roles one might not always associate them with. JC-W

We are family: Sarah Polley scrutinises the Polley clan in *Stories We Tell.*

Song for Scotland:
George MacKay
and Antonia
Thomas in
Dexter Fletcher's
Sunshine on Leith.

▶ Greg Kinnear, Jennifer Connelly, Lily Collins, Logan Lerman, Nat Wolff, Kristen Bell, Liana Liberato, Spencer Breslin, Patrick Schwarzenegger.
▶ *Dir* and *Screenplay* Josh Boone, *Pro* Judy Cairo, *Ph* Tim Orr, *Pro Des* John Sanders, *Ed* Robb Sullivan, *M* Nathaniel Walcott and Mike Mogis, *Cos* Kari Perkins.
Informant Media/MICA Entertainment-Koch Media.
96 mins. USA. 2012. Rel: 14 June 2013. Cert. 15.

Summer in February ★★

Alfred Munnings was considered by many to be the greatest British painter of his generation. Whilst living in the Cornish fishing village of Lamorna, Munnings (Dominic Cooper) hobnobbed with the equally distinguished painter Harold Knight and called the latter's artistic wife, Laura, one of his closest friends. It was into this thriving artistic community in 1912 that another artist arrived, a beautiful young woman called Florence Carter-Wood (Emily Browning). Here be some meaty drama for a riveting tale of art and passion, if only any of it rang true. Sadly, stereotypes abound and much of the dialogue seems to stick in the performers' mouths. JC-W

▶ Dominic Cooper, Dan Stevens, Emily Browning, Hattie Morahan, Shaun Dingwall, Mia Austen, Michael Maloney, Nicholas Farrell, Roger Ashton Griffiths.
▶ *Dir* Christopher Menaul, *Pro* Jeremy Cowdrey, Pippa Cross and Janette Day, *Screenplay* Jonathan Smith, from his 1996 novel, *Ph* Andrew Dunn, *Pro Des* Sophie Becher, *Ed* Chris Gill and St John

O'Rorke, *M* Benjamin Wallfisch, *Cos* Nic Ede.
CrossDay Productions Ltd/Apart Films/Marwood Pictures-Metrodome Distribution.
100 mins. UK. 2013. Rel: 14 June 2013. Cert. 15.

Sunshine on Leith ★★★★★

Dexter Fletcher's second film as director is every bit as good, albeit different, as his first, *Wild Bill*. The grimness of East London is exchanged for the sunny delights of Edinburgh's Leith district as two soldiers come home from Afghanistan. You might think this is going to be a tract about the misfortunes of war, but no, for the two lads start dancing in the street, much like Gene Kelly, Frank Sinatra and Jules Munshin did in *On the Town*. Oh, so it's a musical – and throughout the film there are songs from The Proclaimers, culminating in '500 Miles'. Excellently acted, the film is reminiscent of Jacques Demy's *Les Demoiselles de Rochefort* and is just as entertaining. MHD

▶ George MacKay, Kevin Guthrie, Antonia Thomas, Freya Mavor, Peter Mullan, Jane Horrocks, Jason Flemyng, Paul Brannigan.
▶ *Dir* Dexter Fletcher, *Pro* Andrew Macdonald, Allon Reich, Kieran Parker and Arabella Page Croft, *Screenplay* Stephen Greenhorn, *Ph* George Richmond, *Pro Des* Mike Gunn, *Ed* Stuart Gazzard, *M* Paul Englishby, *Cos* Anna Robbins and Harriet Edmonds.
Black Camel Pictures/DNA Films-Entertainment Film Distributors.
100 mins. UK. 2013. Rel: 4 Oct 2013. Cert. PG.

Suspension of Disbelief ★½

Mike Figgis hasn't made a decent film since *Internal Affairs* and *Leaving Las Vegas* and this dull psychological thriller won't be the one to resurrect his career. Martin (Sebastian Koch) is a screenwriter who becomes implicated in the murder of a beautiful young Frenchwoman. Then her twin sister Therese (Lotte Verbeek) enters the scene... The plot is very confusing and is verging on the pretentious while decent actors like Koch struggle to make sense of it all. GS

❧ Sebastian Koch, Lotte Verbeek, Emilia Fox, Rebecca Night, Eoin Macken, Lachlan Nieboer, Frances de la Tour, Julian Sands, Kenneth Cranham.
❧ *Dir, Screenplay, Ph, Ed* and *M* Mike Figgis, *Pro* Figgis and Vito Di Rosa, *Pro Des* Di Rosa, *Cos* Sandy Powell and Oliver Garcia.

Sosho Production/Red Mullet/Suspension-Swipe Films.
112 mins. UK. 2012. Rel: 19 July 2013. Cert. 15.

The Swell Season ★★★½

This documentary features folk-rock singers Glen Hansard and Markéta Irglová of the band The Swell Season, who starred in the Irish film *Once*. Having won an Oscar for Best Original Song (while the soundtrack itself was Grammy-nominated), *Once* subsequently became a very successful Broadway musical, winning eight Tony awards and also repeating its success in London. During the making of the film the two leads fell in love. The documentary charts their relationship as they come to terms with a success that threatens to scupper their romance. Fans of *Once* will definitely want to see this film, although it had only a belated and limited release in the UK. PL

❧ With Glen Hansard, Markéta Irglová.
❧ *Dir* Nick August-Perna, Chris Dapkins and Carlo Mirabella-Davis, *Pro* Mirabella-Davis, *Ph* Dapkins, *Ed* Nick August-Perna, *M* Glen Hansard and Markéta Irglová.

Elkcreek Cinema-Wildcard Distribution.
91 mins. USA/Czech Republic/Ireland. 2011.
Rel: 6 Dec 2013. Cert. 15.

Tamla Rose ★★½

Adi Alfa (as Tamla Rose), Alexandra Johnston and Tisha Merry star as teenage girls in an all-girl Motown-style band who battle through their career from humble beginnings as background singers. It's easy to warm to the performances and the actresses share good screen chemistry, with Merry outstanding in the showier role as an ambitious schemer. But the story is clichéd and overfamiliar, and in the end it all depends on liking the music or not. The soundtrack will get some audiences dancing in the aisles and others

heading for the exit. Jake Abraham scores as the band's manager. DW

❧ Adi Alfa, Alexandra Johnston, Tisha Merry, Jake Abraham, Philip Olivier, Errol Smith.
❧ *Dir* and *Screenplay* Joe Scott, *Pro* Ann Scott and Lesley Wright, *Ph* David Read, *Art Dir* Brown Jan, *Ed* Andrew McKee, *M* Robbie Pollard and Laura Walton, *Cos* Rachael Prime.

Ace Film-Ace Film.
112 mins. UK. 2013. Rel: 13 Dec 2013. Cert. 12A.

The Taste of Money ★★★

This is a familiar neo-Gothic family saga of the filthy rich, destroying themselves through the standard combination of greed and aberrant lust. Our innocent Everyman guide is a youthful PA to the feckless father, unwilling stud to the monstrous mother and love interest to the guileless daughter. It's rather a slow burn until the virtually Jacobean levels of murder and betrayal kick in, though the coolly palatial production design is easy on the eye, the satire is occasionally diverting ("Money's easy, fucking's great – Korea's a fantastic country," enthuses a passing American), and director Im Sang-soo throws in arid eroticism at regular intervals. But in the end he plays it too glacial too long; we never become truly engaged. (Original title: *Do-nui mat*) JR

❧ Kim Kang-woo, Baek Yoon-sik, Youn Yuh-jung, Kim Hyo-jin, Maui Taylor, Darcy Paquet, Ju Wan-on.
❧ *Dir* and *Screenplay* Im Sang-soo, *Pro* Jill Anoba, *Ph* Woo-hyung Kim, *Pro Des* Younghee Kim and June Kim, *Ed* Eun-soo Lee, *M* Hong-jib Kim, *Cos* Yoojin Kdwon and Seunghee Rim.

Lotte Entertainment/Cinergy/Wild Side Films-Arrow Film Distributors.
115 mins. South Korea. 2013. Rel: 25 Oct 2013. Cert. 15.

Once again: Markéta Irglová and Glen Hansard in Nick August-Perna's *The Swell Season.*

Carnal knowledge: Mark Ruffalo and Gwyneth Paltrow in Stuart Blumberg's *Thanks for Sharing*.

Texas Chainsaw ★★

This is not a remake but a sequel to the original and begins where the first one left off. In an act of mob fury the people of Newt burn down the farmhouse of the Sawyer family, killing everybody including the notorious Leatherface. However, one baby is saved – Heather Miller (Alexandra Daddario), who discovers she is adopted years later when she inherits some property from her real grandmother Vera (Marilyn Burns)... The original, iconic film was shot like a documentary and was truly terrifying. This begins well but soon falls into very routine slasher-movie mode without many thrills. GS

▶ Dan Yeager, Alexandra Daddario, Tremaine 'Trey Songz' Neverson, Tania Raymonde, Shaun Sipos, Keram Malicki-Sánchez, Marilyn Burns.
▶ *Dir* John Luessenhop, *Pro* Carl Mazzocone, *Screenplay* Adam Marcus, Kirsten Elms and Debra Sullivan, from a story by Marcus, Sullivan and Stephen Susco, based on characters created by Tobe Hooper and Kim Henkel, *Ph* Anastas N. Michos, *Pro Des* William A Elliott, *Ed* Randy Bricker, *M* John Frizell, *Cos* Mary E McLeod.
Twisted Chainsaw Pictures/Lionsgate/Mainline Pictures/ Nu Image Films/Leatherface Productions/Millennium Films-Lionsgate.
92 mins. USA. 2013. Rel: 4 Jan 2013. Cert. 18.

Thanks for Sharing ★★★★½

Far from being the exclusive domain of rich, handsome and well-endowed men, sex addiction can affect anyone. Stuart Blumberg has assembled a top-notch cast for his directorial debut and has drawn up a roster of surprisingly disparate damaged characters, including a female hairdresser beautifully played by Alecia Moore (aka Pink). As the film's main outsider, Gwyneth Paltrow is a bonus as a seemingly 'perfect' woman whose own demanding sexuality is at odds with a disease she cannot understand. In short, it's reassuring to encounter an adult film in the true sense of the word, an articulate and moving drama that is neither exploitative nor sensationalist. JC-W

▶ Mark Ruffalo, Tim Robbins, Gwyneth Paltrow, Josh Gad, Joely Richardson, Alecia Moore, Patrick Fugit, Carol Kane.
▶ *Dir* Stuart Blumberg, *Pro* Miranda de Pencier, David Koplan, Bill Migliore, Leslie Urdang and Dean Vanech, *Screenplay* Blumberg and Matt Winston, *Ph* Yaron Orbach, *Pro Des* Beth Mickle, *Ed* Anne McCabe, *M* Christopher Lennertz, *Cos* Peggy Schnitzer.
Class 5 Films/Olympus Pictures-Koch Film.
112 mins. USA. 2012. Rel: 4 Oct 2013. Cert. 15.

Thérèse Desqueyroux ★★★½

This is the late Claude Miller's take on the Mauriac novel previously filmed by Georges Franju in 1962. Audrey Tautou makes a valiant stab at the title role in this period drama set in the 1920s which touches on class, a concern with outward appearances and male dominance against which the heroine (or should that be anti-heroine?) rebels. The central role is so complex that it really needs a great actress of the calibre of Dame Peggy Ashcroft but, if the film falls short, it is by no means to be dismissed and it looks ravishing. MS

▶ Audrey Tautou, Gilles Lellouche, Anaïs Demoustier, Catherine Arditi.
▶ *Dir* Claude Miller, *Pro* Yves Marmion, *Screenplay* Natalie Carter and Miller, from the novel by François Mauriac, *Ph* Gérard de Battista, *Art Dir* Laurence Brenguier, *Ed* Véronique Lange, *Cos* Jacqueline Bouchard.
UGC/a Les Films du 24 production/France 3 Cinéma/ Cool Industrie etc.-Artficial Eye.
110 mins. France. 2012. Rel: 7 June 2013. Cert. 12A.

This Ain't California ★★★★

I brought an innocent eye to this film in which friends of the late Denis Paracek (1970-2004) look back on his life and evoke those times in the 1980s when youngsters in Communist-controlled East Berlin took to skateboarding. Later I learnt that it was probably bogus, not being the documentary that it appears to be. However, this hardly matters since it summons up a past era convincingly and also catches something universal in expressing regret for lost youth. MS

▶ With David Nathan, Anneke Schwabe.
▶ *Dir* Marten Persiel, *Pro* Ronald Vietz and Michael

Schöbel, *Screenplay* Persiel and Ira Wedel, *Ph* Felix Leiberg, *Pro Des* Anne Zentgraf, *Ed* Maxine Goedicke, Bobby Good and Toni Froschhammer, *M* Lars Damm and Troy von Balthazar, *Cos* Simone Eichhorn.

Wildfremd Production and Arte/RBB/MDR-Luxin. 90 mins. Germany. 2012. Rel: 6 Dec 2013. Cert. 15.

This is 40 ★

Although some consider him a comic genius, the films of director Judd Apatow suggest otherwise: *The 40-Year-Old Virgin*, *Knocked Up*, *Funny People*… Equally disappointing is *This is 40*, a cold and cynical, charmless so-called comedy about a middle-aged couple (Paul Rudd and Leslie Mann) unhappy with their lot in life. At 134 minutes it's overlong and best left undiscovered. MJ

❭ Paul Rudd, Leslie Mann, John Lithgow, Megan Fox, Albert Brooks, Maude Apatow, Iris Apatow, Jason Segal, Chris O'Dowd, Tatum O'Neal.
❭ *Dir* and *Screenplay* Judd Apatow, *Pro* Apatow, Barry Mendel and Clayton Townsend, *Ph* Phedon Papamichael, *Pro Des* Jefferson Sage, *Ed* David L Bertman, Jay Deuby and Brent White, *M* Jon Brion, *Cos* Leesa Evans.

Apatow Productions-Universal Pictures International. 134 mins. USA. 2012. Rel: 14 Feb 2013. Cert. 15.

This is the End ★★★½

A twisted, reality-bending, reality-ending comedy that hurtles madly in many unexpected and frequently funny directions, *This is the End* unfolds in the ironically named City of Angels. After the Biblical Rapture James Franco, Seth Rogen, Jonah Hill, Jay Baruchel, Danny McBride and Craig Robinson, all playing appalling versions of themselves, are forced to face the grim reality that their pampered, artsy lives are about to get punctured by a flaming pitchfork. Strewn with demons, shameless celebrity cameos and apocalyptic bad taste, it's a true guilty pleasure. MJ

❭ James Franco, Jonah Hill, Seth Rogen, Jay Baruchel, Craig Robinson, Danny McBride, Michael Cera, Emma Watson, Rihanna, Paul Rudd, Kevin Hart.
❭ *Dir* and *Screenplay* Seth Rogen and Evan Goldberg, based on the short film *Jay and Seth vs The Apocalypse* by Rogen, Goldberg and Jason Stone, *Pro* Rogen, Goldberg and James Weaver, *Ph* Brandon Trost, *Pro Des* Chris L Spellman, *Ed* Zene Baker, *M* Henry Jackman, *Cos* Danny Glicker.

Columbia Pictures/Point Grey Pictures/Mandate Pictures-Sony Pictures Releasing. 107 mins. USA. 2013. Rel: 28 June 2013. Cert. 15.

Thor: The Dark World ★★

If the first Thor movie didn't quite live up to the original Marvel comic book, this sequel is even more lacklustre. Chris Hemsworth, who lit up the screen in *Rush*, can't seem to do the same playing the eponymous Norse God. The plot involves a wormhole through which Natalie Portman is transported to Asgard, where one of its enemies, imprisoned since ancient times, is unleashed to

Hello Berlin!: a scene from Marten Persiel's mockumentary *This Ain't California*.

In the frame: Vincent Cassel stars as the baddy (and there's a surprise) in Danny Boyle's *Trance*.

wage war. It's a lot more complicated than that, but you probably won't care. JC

▶ Chris Hemsworth, Natalie Portman, Tom Hiddleston, Anthony Hopkins, Christopher Eccleston, Jaimie Alexander, Idris Elba, Rene Russo, Stellan Skarsgård, Alice Krige, Chris O'Dowd.
▶ *Dir* Alan Taylor, *Pro* Kevin Feige, *Screenplay* Stephen McFeely, Christopher L Yost and Christopher Markus, from a story by Don Payne and Robert Rodat, based on characters created by Stan Lee, Larry Lieber and Jack Kirby, *Ph* Kramer Morgenthau, *Pro Des* Charles Wood, *Ed* Dan Lebenthal and Wyatt Smith, *M* Brian Tyler, *Cos* Wendy Partridge.

Marvel Studios-Walt Disney Studios Motion Pictures.
112 mins. USA. 2013. Rel: 30 Oct 2013. Cert. 12A.

Thursday till Sunday ★★½

This minimalist work from Chile follows a family – parents with two offspring – on a road trip from Santiago to the north of the country. Although almost too discreet and indirect, the first half is not ineffective in suggesting the impact on children of an escalating marital break-up; indeed, the ten-year-old central character is superbly played by Santi Ahumada. But as the film goes on it loses momentum and ultimately leads nowhere and that makes viewing it an increasingly frustrating experience. (Original title: *De jueves a domingo*) MS

▶ Francisco Pérez-Bannen, Paola Giannini, Santi Ahumada, Emiliano Freifeld.
▶ *Dir* and *Screenplay* Dominga Sotomayor, *Pro* Gregorio González and Benjamín Domenech, *Ph* Barbara Alvarez, *Pro Des* Estefanía Larraín, *Ed* Danielle Fillios and Catalina Marín, *Cos* Juana Diaz.

A Forastero, Cinestación production/Circe Films/Triciclo Films etc.-Day for Night.
96 mins. Chile/The Netherlands/France/Spain/Argentina. 2012. Rel: 5 Apr 2013. Cert. 15.

The To Do List ★★

This comedy takes place in 1993 and is inspired by writer-director Maggie Carey's real-life experiences. Brandy Clark (Aubrey Plaza) is a naïve young woman and still a virgin but is determined to change her nerdy image before she goes to college. She prepares a 'to do list' and starts ticking each item off after a few casual encounters... It's a fun premise, though often relying on scatological humour which sits uncomfortably with the rest of the film. GS

▶ Aubrey Plaza, Johnny Simmons, Bill Hader, Scot Porter, Alia Shawkat, Rachel Bilson, Christopher Mintz-Plaza, Andy Samberg.
▶ *Dir* and *Screenplay* Maggie Carey, *Pro* Mark Gordon, Tom Lassally, Greg Walter, Jennifer Todd and Brian Robbins, *Ph* Doug Emmett, *Pro Des* Ryan Berg, *Ed* Paul Frank, *M* Raney Shockne and Jason Boschetti, *Cos* Trayce Gigi Field.

The Mark Gordon Company/3 Arts Entertainment-Sony Pictures Releasing.
104 mins. USA. 2013. Rel: 4 Oct 2013. Cert. 15.

To the Wonder ★

If Terrence Malick's *The Tree of Life* (2010) veered between the brilliant and the ghastly, this work about an American in Oklahoma betraying his Russian wife with an old friend never engages at all. With minimal dialogue for the man who remains a cipher and reams of semi-mystical waffle elsewhere, it counts as one of the most pretentious and self-indulgent movies that I have ever seen. Not even the photography, usually a stand-out in a Malick film, can hold boredom at bay. MS

▶ Ben Affleck, Olga Kurylenko, Rachel McAdams, Javier Bardem, Tatiana Chiline.
▶ *Dir* and *Screenplay* Terrence Malick, *Pro* Sarah Green and Nicolas Gonda, *Ph* Emmanuel Lubezki, *Pro Des* Jack Fisk, *Ed* AJ Edwards, Keith Fraase, Shane Hazen, Christopher Roldan and Mark Yoshikawa, *M* Hanan Townshend, *Cos* Jacqueline West.

A FilmNation Entertainment presentation/Brothers K Productions-StudioCanal Limited.
113 mins. USA. 2012. Rel: 22 Feb 2013. Cert. 12A.

Trance ★★★½

Danny Boyle's film sounds rather like a Hollywood thriller of the 1960s since it involves a stolen painting and an auctioneer (James McAvoy) who, although in liaison with a thief (Vincent Cassel), claims that due to amnesia he cannot remember where he has hidden it. However, Boyle's take on this material turns it into a game-playing movie shot in a stylised way to echo other films and to tease us as to what is real and what is hallucinatory. *Trance* doesn't entirely sustain this, but on the whole it's fun. MS

James McAvoy, Vincent Cassel, Rosario Dawson, Tuppence Middleton.

Dir Danny Boyle, *Pro* Christian Colson, *Screenplay* Joe Ahearne and John Hodge from the former's story, *Ph* Anthony Dod Mantle, *Pro Des* Mark Tildesley, *Ed* Jon Harris, *M* Rick Smith, *Cos* Suttirat Larlarb.

Pathé/Fox Searchlight Pictures/Film4/a Cloud Eight/ Decibel Films production etc.-Pathé.
101 mins. USA/UK/Australia. 2013. Rel: 27 Mar 2013. Cert. 15.

Trap for Cinderella ★★½

A thriller in which issues of identity prove crucial, this is a second screen treatment of Sébastien Japrisot's novel but strikingly different in key plot points from André Cayatte's rather better 1965 version. Set in France but played in English, it comes across as an increasingly improbable tale with a tiresomely enigmatic ending. The cast are talented but can't bring conviction to such ridiculous material. MS

Tuppence Middleton, Alexandra Roach, Kerry Fox, Aneurin Barnard, Stanley Weber, Emilia Fox, Alex Jennings, Frances de la Tour.

Dir and *Screenplay* (from the novel *Piège pour Cendrillon* by Sébastien Japrisot) Ian Softley, *Pro* Robert Jones, Dixie Linder and Softley, *Ph* Alex Barber, *Pro Des* Gary Williamson, *Ed* Stuart Gazzard, *M* Christian Henson, *Cos* Verity Hawkes.

UK Film Council/Lipsync Productions/a Forthcoming Films and Jonescompany Production etc.-Lionsgate UK.
100 mins. UK/USA. 2011. Rel: 12 July 2013. Cert. 15.

Trashed ★★★

Narrator, star and executive producer Jeremy Irons travels the world to discover the extent and effects of the global waste problem. He visits places tainted by pollution and turned into landfills,

scandalised by the trash we produce unnecessarily and dump irresponsibly. Irons looks bewildered by the scale and stupidity of it all but goes on to show how we can change. San Francisco offers hope by recycling three quarters of its waste, generating thousands of jobs and recuperating valuable resources. Deviser-director Candida Brady won an award at the Tokyo International Film Festival for her meticulous investigative documentary. The Vangelis score is an asset. DW

Narrated by Jeremy Irons.

Dir and *Written by* Candida Brady, *Pro* Brady and Titus Ogilvy, *Ph* Sean Bobbitt, *Art Dir* Garry Waller, *Ed* Kate Coggins, Jamie Trevill and James Coward, *M* Vangelis.

Blenheim Films-Blenheim Films.
98 mins. USA. 2012. Rel: 1 Mar 2013. Cert. 12A.

Tropicália ★★

Anyone unfamiliar with the Brazilian artistic movement known as Tropicalismo, prominent in the late 1960s and early 1970s, will find that this documentary fails to present its history effectively. There's too much emphasis on the pop music aspect of it (but no subtitles for the song lyrics) and the quality of the old footage used is often poor. The film should have been informative and entertaining, but it isn't: a wasted opportunity in fact. MS

With Gilberto Gil, Caetano Veloso.

Dir Marcelo Machado, *Pro* Denise Gomes and Paula Cosenza, *Screenplay* Machado and Di Moretti, from an idea by Vaughn Glover and Maurice James, *Ph* Eduardo Piagge, *Art Dir* Ricardo Fernandes, *Ed* Oswaldo Santana, *M* Alexandre Kassin.

Mojo Pictures/Record Entretenimento, Vh1, DLA etc.-Mr Bongo Worldwide Ltd.
87 mins. Brazil/USA/UK. 2012. Rel: 5 July 2013. Cert. 12A.

All that he surveys: Jeremy Irons in Candida Brady's *Trashed.*

Turbo ★★★

In this CG-animated children's film from
DreamWorks Turbo dreams of being a racing
driver. Sadly he's a snail. But then he becomes
super-fast thanks to a freak accident, so resolves
to enter the Indianapolis 500. There are some nice
characterisations – racing rivals both snail and
human, plus two Mexican human brothers who
run a taco stand and become Turbo's backers. And
the whole moves along at a decent pace. But it's
nothing exceptional: just passable family fare. JC

❱ Voices of Ryan Reynolds, Paul Giamatti, Michael
Peña, Samuel L Jackson, Lis Guzmán, Bill Hader,
Snoop Dogg, Maya Rudolph.
❱ *Dir* David Soren, *Pro* Lisa Stewart, *Screenplay*
Soren, Darren Lemke and Robert D Siegel, from
a story by Soren, *Ph* Chris Stover, *Pro Des* Michael
Isaak, *Ed* James Ryan, *M* Henry Jackman.
DreamWorks Animation-20th Century Fox.
96 mins. USA. 2013. Rel: 17 Oct 2013. Cert. U.

Upstream Colour ★★★★★

You have to work hard to follow the plot of
Upstream Colour. For those who can it's worth
the effort, but others may simply be alienated.
Constituent elements include abduction,
impregnation of people with insects, and pig
farming. It's also a love story about two people
who've been through a similar, traumatic
experience. Visually beautiful and aurally ravishing,
it's recommended for anyone who can get on its
wavelength. (Original title: *Upstream Color*) JC

Waiting for Babe:
Andrew Sensenig
in Shane Carruth's
Upstream Colour.

❱ Amy Seimetz, Shane Carruth, Andrew Sensenig,
Thiago Martins, Kathy Carruth, Meredith Burke.
❱ *Dir, Screenplay, Ph* and *M* Shane Carruth, *Pro*
Carruth, Casey Gooden and Ben LeClair, *Pro Des*
Thomas Walker, *Ed* Carruth and David Lowery.
ERBP-Metrodome Distribution.
96 mins. USA. 2013. Rel: 30 Aug 2013. Cert. 12.

Utopia ★★★★

If some see John Pilger less as an objective
reporter and more as a crusader, it is certainly the
case that he picks the right crusades. In evidence
of that we have this absorbing study of how
Australia has treated, and still treats, its original
native population, the Aborigines. It's powerful
stuff ranging from the 19th to the 21st century,
from mass extermination to recent deceits
falsely linking Aborigines with paedophilia.
Recommended. MS

❱ With John Pilger, Bob Randall, Arthur Murray,
Amy McQuire, Kevin Rudd.
❱ *Dir* John Pilger and Alan Lowery, *Pro* and *Written
by* Pilger, *Ph* Preston Clothier, *Ed* Joe Frost.
**A Dartmouth Films production/SBS-TV Australia-
Dartmouth Films.**
110 mins. UK/Australia. 2013. Rel: 15 Nov 2013. Cert. 12A.

uwantme2killhim? ★★★

Sixteen-year-old Mark stabbed his geeky friend
John "for the greater good," he says, adding
deludedly "I'm a hero." Rewinding from this
tantalising start, director Andrew Douglas renders

a genuinely bizarre true story in coldly social-realist hues, shooting in the 'new town' aridness of Harlow rather than the Mancunian locations in which it actually took place. Jamie Blackley and Toby Regbo are excellent as the teen protagonists, hypnotised by their computer screens like an internet-savvy Leopold and Loeb and surrounded by weird satellite characters who make sense only at the end. This cautionary tale – from a time (2003) described by co-producer Bryan Singer as "the Wild West of social networking" – is determinedly low-key but still stokes up a doom-laden atmosphere of paranoia. JR

‣ Jamie Blackley, Toby Regbo, Joanne Froggatt, Liz White, Jaime Winstone, Mark Womack, Amy Wren.
‣ *Dir* Andrew Douglas, *Pro* Bryan Singer, Simon Crocker, Steve Golin, Peter Heslop and Jason Taylor, *Screenplay* Mike Walden, *Ph* Tim Wooster, *Pro Des* Paul Cripps, *Ed* Michael Elliot, *M* Jon Hopkins, *Cos* Caroline Harris.

The Weinstein Company/Tribeca Film/Bad Hat Harry Productions/Anonymous Content/eOne Entertainment etc-Jumping Jack Films.
92 mins. UK. 2013. Rel: 6 Sep 2013. Cert. 15.

V/H/S ★★★

This anthology of VHS 'nasties' begins when a group of petty criminals are hired to retrieve some mysterious videotapes from a rundown house in the middle of nowhere. But the temptation to watch them is irresistible... Each segment is filmed by a different director and, although there is no connection between these horrible and truly scary stories, they're all shot in a rough and raw style that takes a while to get used to. There are some genuinely frightening moments, especially the tape where one couple attempts to build up a relationship on Skype. GS

‣ Calvin Reeder, Lane Hughes, Kentucker Audley, Hannah Fiermanm, Mike Donlan, Joe Swanberg, Sophia Takai, Drew Moerlein, Jason Yachanin, Helen Rogers, Daniel Kaufman, Chad Villella, Paul Natonek, Tyler Gillett etc.
‣ *Dir* Matt Bettineli-Olpin, Adam Wingard, Ti West, David Bruckner, Tyler Gillett, Chad Villella, Joe Swanberg, Glenn McQuaid, Radio Silence and Justin Martinez, *Pro* Roxanne Benjamin, Gary Binkow and Brad Miska, *Screenplay* Bettinelli-Olpin, West, Bruckner, McQuaid, Gillett, Martinez, Villella, Radio Silence, Simon Barrett and Nicolas Tecosky, from a concept by Brad Miska, *Ph* Gillett, Martinez, Wingard, Eric Branco, Andrew Droz Palermo, Victoria K Warren and Michael J Wilson, *Art Dir* Raymond Carr, Roger Vianna and Lanie Faith Marie Overton, *Ed* Bettineli-Olpin, Gillett, McQuaid, Swanberg, West, Wingard and Joe Gressis, *M* Lucas Clyde, *Cos* Elisabeth Vastola.

The Collective/Bloody Disgusting-Momentum Pictures.
116 mins. USA. 2012. Rel: 18 Jan 2013. Cert. 18.

Video nasty: a scene from the 'A Ride in the Park' segment of *V/H/S/2*.

V/H/S/2 ★★★½

In the gory and ingenious sequel to the 2012 horror hit (reviewed left), two private investigators searching for a missing student break into his house and find a collection of VHS tapes from the first film. There follows a series of found-footage shorts directed by several hands, including Adam Wingard from the original film. There's a lot to pack in, in just 96 minutes, but they do it imaginatively and well. It's a shame that the first two stories (in which a man's mechanical eye transplant allows him to see dead people and a biker turns into a zombie) are the best, but the others are acceptable too. A third film *V/H/S Viral* is on its way. DW

‣ Lawrence Michael Levine, Kelsy Abbott, LC Holt, Adam Wingard, Hannah Hughes, John T Woods, Jay Saunders, Bette Cassatt, Dave Coyne, Fachry Albar, Hannah Al Rashid, Oka Antara, Becca Babcock, Zachary Ford etc.
‣ *Dir* Simon Barrett, Adam Wingard, Timo Tjahjanto, Jason Eisener, Gareth Huw Evans, Eduardo Sánchez and Gregg Hale, *Pro* Gary Binkow and Brad Miska, *Screenplay* Barrett, Evans, Tjahjanto, Eisener, Sánchez, Jamie Nash and John Davies, based on a concept by Brad Miska, *Ph* Jeff Wheaton, Tarin Anderson, Abdul Dermawan Habir, Stephen Scott and Seamus Tierney, *Pro Des* Thomas S Hammock, *Ed* Eisener, Evans, Sánchez, Wingard, David Geis and Bob Rose, *M* Fajar Yuskemal, Aria Prayogi, Steve Moore and James Guymon, *Cos* Avon Dorsey and Autumn Steed.

The Collective/Bloody Disgusting/Haxan Films/Snoot Entertainment/8383 Productions/Yer Dead Productions-Jade Films.
96 mins. USA/Canada/Indonesia. 2013. Rel: 14 Oct 2013. Cert. 18.

Vehicle 19 ★★

'Vehicle 19' is the wrong vehicle. When Michael Woods (the late Paul Walker) picks up his Hertz

rental from the airport car park in Johannesburg there is a mix-up. Not good news for Hertz – nor Michael Woods. In the event, it's the set-up for a chase movie in which the only visual nourishment is Walker's baby blues and the colourful streets of Jo'burg. In its sleek simplicity, Mukunda Michael Dewil's film is like a low-rent *Speed*, except without the concept, a hissable villain or a beautiful babe. High-speed chase movies shouldn't be this soporific. JC-W

❯ Paul Walker, Naima McLean, Gys de Villiers, Laila Haidarian, Andrian Mazive.
❯ *Dir* and *Screenplay* Mukunda Michael Dewil, *Pro* Paul Walker, Gary King, Peter Safran and Ryan Haidarian, *Ph* Miles Goodall, *Ed* Megan Gill, *M* Daniel Matthee and James Matthes.
Forefront Media Group/The Safran Company/The Industrial Development Corporation of South Africa-StudioCanal.
85 mins. USA. 2013. Rel: 10 May 2013. Cert. 12A.

Vendetta ★★★

Vendetta proves to be a gripping, pretty good, all-action London revenge thriller. Rarely pausing for breath or subtlety, it's plenty tough and busy throughout. Danny Dyer is on good form as SAS Special Ops interrogation officer Jimmy Vickers, who goes on the Charlie Bronson vengeance trail after his parents are gruesomely burnt alive. With the cops closing in and his old unit on his trail, he has to evade capture long enough to remove all the killers. Stephen Reynolds writes

and directs briskly and capably. Job done. The film has the right doomy mood and noir-ish photography. The action and violence are pretty nasty and scary, so there's a realistic, credible spin to the movie. DW

❯ Roxanne McKee, Danny Dyer, Vincent Regan, Josef Altin, Emma Samms, Simona Brhlikova, Bruce Payne.
❯ *Dir, Screenplay* and *Ed* Stephen Reynolds, *Pro* Jonathan Sothcott, *Ph* Haider Zafar, *Pro Des* Anthony Neale, *M* Phil Mountford, *Cos* Lenka Padysakova.
Richwater Films-Anchor Bay Entertainment.
106 mins. UK. 2013. Rel: 23 Dec 2013. Cert. 18.

Venus and Serena ★★★★

This illuminating documentary tells the story of the Williams sisters – the tennis champions Venus and Serena. From a young age these amazing athletes were determined to reach perfection and become number one, and it wasn't too long before they reached their goal under the strict guidance of their father. It's an honest portrait not only of solidarity, dedication and commitment but also of their inevitable rivalry. GS

❯ With Venus Williams, Serena Williams, Richard Williams, Oracene Price, Billie Jean King, John McEnroe, Anna Wintour.
❯ *Dir and Pro* Maiken Baird and Michelle Major, *Ph* Cliff Charles, Stephanie Johnes and Rashidi Harper, *Ed* Samuel D Pollard, *M* Wyclef Jean.
Magnolia Pictures-Kaleidoscope Entertainment.
99 mins. USA. 2012. Rel: 28 June 2013. Cert. 12A.

Verity's Summer ★

When Verity (Indea Barbe-Wilson) finishes boarding school she returns to her parents' house off the Northumberland coast. Ex-soldier Castle (Martin McGlade) also arrives in this remote village following tours of Iraq and he soon begins to haunt Verity's policeman father (James Doherty)... The plot of Ben Crowe's muddled film debut is often confusing and lacks pace as well as clarity. The performances are not bad, but the tempo is so slow that it makes the whole experience very dull. GS

▶ Indea Barbe-Wilson, James Doherty, Martin McGlade, Nicola Wright, Cristi Hogas.
▶ *Dir, Screenplay* and *Ed* Ben Crowe, *Pro* Crowe and Emma Biggins, *Ph* Sara Deane, *Art Dir* Zsuzsanna Mehrli, *M* Alexandros Miaris.

Verity Pictures-Multistory Films.
102 mins. UK. 2013. Rel: 5 Mar 2013. Cert. 15.

Very Extremely Dangerous ★★★½

Jerry McGill is not only very, extremely dangerous, but his cinematic biographer is also obviously terrified of him. Indeed, Paul Duane's documentary opens with his subject attacking his girlfriend, Joyce, as she's driving the car in which the three of them are riding. McGill is a loose cannon but, aged 70 and diagnosed with cancer, he has decided to revive his musical career (he once knew Elvis). However, his criminal ways have become so entrenched that Duane can but record a journey of discord and mayhem. Grimly fascinating stuff. CB

▶ With Jerry McGill, Joyce Rosic, Jim & Jill Lancaster, Paul Clements.
▶ *Dir* Paul Duane, *Pro* Duane and Robert Gordon, *Ph* Duane, Gordon, John T. Davis and David Leonard, *Ed* Colm O'Brien and Fiona Starogardzki, *M* Jim Lancaster.

Screenworks-Screenworks.
85 mins. USA/Ireland. 2013. Rel: 18 Oct 2013. Cert. 15.

Village at the End of the World ★★★½

The village in question is Niaqornat in north-western Greenland and Sarah Gavron's documentary shows footage taken over a period of 12 months or more starting in the summer of 2009. So isolated that less than 60 inhabitants have chosen to remain, this is a sympathetic portrait of a potentially dying homestead but one that, perhaps unintentionally, fails to make a strong case for preserving so bleak a community. MS

▶ With Lars, Karl, Annie, Ilannguaq.
▶ *Dir* Sarah Gavron with David Katznelson, *Pro* Al Morrow, *Ph* Katznelson, *Ed* Hugh Williams, Russell Crockett and Jerry Rothwell, *M* Jonas Colstrup and Max de Wardener.

Met Films/Made in Copenhagen/Film4/Danish Film Institute etc.-Dogwoof.
81 mins. UK/Denmark. 2012. Rel: 10 May 2013. Cert. 12A.

Vinyl ★★½

Phil Daniels and Keith Allen play clapped-out rockers who use a teenage punk band to front their new tunes. A gentle comedy drama for folks of a certain age, it shows old dogs teaching young whippersnappers a thing or two, and provides the kind of in-one-eye-and-out-the-other sort of entertainment that might just about pass muster on a tipsy Sunday afternoon. Apparently based on a true story, it's a cheerful, tuneful, modest little movie with a chirpy central performance from

Bleak momentum: the outpost of Niaqornat in Sarah Gavron and David Katznelson's *Village at the End of the World.*

Daniels and a lively young supporting cast who keep things from becoming intolerably cosy. MJ

▶ Phil Daniels, Jamie Blackley, Perry Benson, Keith Allen, Julia Ford, Christopher Roy Turner, James Cartwright, Alexa Davies.
▶ *Dir* Sara Sugarman, *Pro* Sugarman, John H Williams and Clay Reed, *Screenplay* Sugarman and Jim Cooper, *Ph* Benji Bakshi, *Pro Des* Anna Lavelle, *Ed* Hazel Baillie, *M* Steve Allan Jones and Mike Peters, *Cos* Claire Lester.

Vanguard Films/Traction Media/Preston Clay Reed Films/ Mrs Jones Presents/H20 Motion Pictures-Pearl and Dean. 85 mins. USA/UK. 2012. Rel: 15 Mar 2013. Cert. 15.

Viramundo ★★★★

Following the recent *Tropicália* [qv] this is another documentary which celebrates Brazilian music. Acclaimed musician Gilberto Gil embarks on a long journey to Australia and South Africa in order to share his music and sounds with the natives. Gil, Brazil's first black Minister of Culture, exchanges his love and enthusiasm for his work and shares his vision for the future. A work of great dignity and grace accompanied by superb sounds. GS

▶ With Peter Garrett, Gilberto Gil, Paul Hanmer, Vusi Mahlasela.
▶ *Dir* Pierre-Yves Borgeaud, *Pro* Emmanuel Gétaz, Clément Duboin and Frédéric Corvez, *Ph* Camille Cottagnoud and Leandro Monti, *Ed* Daniel Gibel.

Dreampixies/Urban Factory-Soda Pictures. 95 mins. France/Switzerland. 2013. Rel: 2 Aug 2013. Cert. PG.

Wheel of misfortune: Waad Mohammed in Haifaa al Mansour's *Wadjda*, the first Saudi film to be officially submitted for an Oscar.

Vivan las Antipodas! ★★★★

Russian documentary filmmaker Victor Kossakovsky has produced a beautiful study of four sets of Antipodean places, comparing these diametrically opposite locations that are literally half a world away on the other side of the globe.

He contrasts Madrid in Spain with Wellington New Zealand, Hawaii with Kubu Island in Botswana, Entre Rios in Argentina with Shanghai in China, and Patagonia in Chile with Lake Baikai in Russia. Without any narration or dialogue he conveys solely through his stunning visuals how different these locations are. He takes his time, composing his film at a very measured pace which only makes the finished work even more seductive. PL

▶ *Dir, Ph* and *Ed* Victor Kossakovsky.

Arte/Gema Films/NHK/Lemming Film/Westdeutscher Rundfunk/ZDF/Ma.Ja.De Filmproduktion etc-Filmhouse. 108 mins. Germany/Argentina/Netherlands/Chile. 2011. Rel: 22 Nov 2013. Cert. U.

Wadjda ★★★★★

This superb ground-breaking film shot on location in Riyadh has a woman writer-director, Haifaa al Mansour, finding a wonderfully engaging storyline to express the position of women and girls in Saudi Arabia today. Wadjda, magnificently incarnated by Waad Mohammed, is a schoolgirl with an ambition to own a bicycle despite that being a male province. This is central but the situation of her mother widens the focus. Not since *Bicycle Thieves* (1948) has a bicycle played such a key role in a deeply humane work of social comment. MS

▶ Waad Mohammed, Reem Abdullah, Abdullrahman Algohani, Ahd, Sultan Al Assaf.
▶ *Dir* and *Screenplay* Haifaa al Mansour, *Pro* Roman Paul and Gerhard Meixner, *Ph* Lutz Reitemeier, *Pro Des* Thomas Molt, *Ed* Andreas Wodraschke, *M* Max Richter, *Cos* Peter Pohl.

Razor Film/High Look Group/Rotana Studios/ Norddeutscher Rundfunk etc.-Soda Pictures. 97 mins. Germany/Saudi Arabia/USA/United Arab Emirates. 2012. Rel: 19 July 2013. Cert. PG.

Walesa: Man of Hope ★★★★

The amazing story of Lech Walesa, the electrician at the Gdansk shipyards who became the first president of the new Polish democracy and won a Nobel Peace Prize, is brought vividly to life in Andrzej Wajda's excellent biopic. The story focuses on Walesa's Solidarity movement during the 1970s and '80s which helped bring about the revolution in Poland. Wajda extracts a phenomenal performance from Robert Wieckiewicz, who brilliantly conveys Walesa's immense commitment and personal sacrifice. (Original title: *Walesa, Czlowiek z nadziei*) GS

▶ Robert Wieckiewicz, Agnieszka Grochowska, Iwona Bielska, Zbigniew Zamachowski, Maria Rosaria Omaggio.
▶ *Dir* Andrzej Wajda, *Pro* Michal Kwieciński, *Screenplay* Janusz Glowacki, based on his own story, *Ph* Pawel Edelman, *Pro Des* Magdalena Dipont,

Ed Milenia Fiedler and Grazyna Gradon, *M* Pawel Mykietyn, *Cos* Magdalena Biedrzycka.

Akson Studio/Canal+ Polska/Telewizja Polska-Project London Films.
127 mins. Poland. 2013. Rel: 18 Oct 2013. Cert. 12A.

Walking with Dinosaurs: The 3D Movie ★

This is an animated feature made by the people behind the eponymous BBC series which brought prehistoric beasts to the small screen with CGI. On the big screen, their work looks just as impressive. But someone, or some committee, at the studio decided that dinosaurs alone wouldn't hold the attention; they needed to talk. Worse, the redundant dubbing has infant dinosaurs talking non-stop like hyperactive contemporary American kids, turning a potential masterpiece into the Turkey of the Year. A travesty. JC

▶ Voices of Charlie Rowe, Karl Urban, Angourie Rice, plus the voices of John Leguizamo, Justin Long, Skyler Stone, Tiya Sircar.
▶ *Dir* Barry Cook and Neil Nightingale, *Pro* Mike Devlin, Deepak Nayar, Amanda Hill and Luke Hetherington, *Screenplay* John Collee, *Ph* John Brooks, *Art Dir* Ken Turner, *Ed* John Carnochan, *M* Paul Leonard-Morgan.

BBC Earth/BBC Worldwide/Animal Logic/Evergreen Films/Reliance Big Entertainment-20th Century Fox.
87 mins. USA/UK/India. 2013. Rel: 19 Dec 2013. Cert. U.

The Wall ★★★★

This astonishing first feature from Austria's Julian Roman Pölsler includes a great performance from Martina Gedeck who for much of the time is alone on the screen save for some animals. Arguably more Kafkaesque than sci-fi, the film posits a situation in which an invisible wall prevents the woman from leaving the mountains where she inhabits a weekend hunting lodge. Her need to find ways to survive in isolation seems to take us back to the Garden of Eden but the outside world threatens and innocence may be lost. The sound design is brilliant and this haunting, imaginative work encourages speculation. (Original title: *Die Wand*) MS

▶ Martina Gedeck, Lynx, Karl Heinz Hackl, Ulrike Beimpold, Wolfgang Maria Bauer.
▶ *Dir* and *Screenplay* (from the novel by Marlen Haushofer) Julian Roman Pölsler, *Pro* Bruno Wagner, Rainer Kölmel, Antonin Svoboda and others, *Ph* JRP Altmann, Christian Berger, Martin Gschlacht and others, *Pro Des* Renate Schmaderer, Enid Löser, Petra Heim and Hajo Schwarz, *Ed* Bettina Mazakarini, Natalie Schwager and Thomas Kohler, *Sound* Uve Haussig, Gregor Kienel and Markus Kathriner, *Cos* Ingrid Leibezeder.

A coop99 filmproduktion/Starhaus Filmproduktion/BR and Arte etc.-New Wave Films.
108 mins. Austria/Germany. 2011. Rel: 5 July 2013. Cert. 12A.

The War of the Worlds: Alive on Stage! The New Generation ★★★½

Watching this film of the stage version of Jeff Wayne's 1978 concept album is an odd, eerie experience. But it fits the material neatly as HG Wells' iconic alien invasion story imaginatively unfolds. The show mixes stage performance and cinema, with its star Liam Neeson ironically emerging as 'real' despite appearing in hologram form as the narrator. Equally impressive actual performers include Jason Donovan as a deranged preacher, Marti Pellow as The Sung Thoughts of The Journalist and Kaiser Chiefs frontman Ricky Wilson as The Artilleryman. While an amazing-looking Martian attack CGI film plays in the background, Wayne conducts the orchestra on stage and singers come on and perform. *The War of the Worlds* rocks! DW

Dead romantic: Nicholas Hoult in Jonathan Levine's *Warm Bodies.*

❯ Jason Donovan, Kerry Ellis, Michael Falzon, Liam Neeson, Gary Osborne, Daniel Osgerby, Marti Pellow, Anna-Marie Wayne, Jerry Wayne, Ricky Wilson.
❯ *Dir* Nick Morris, *Pro* Dionne Orrom, *Screenplay* Jeff Wayne, based on the novel by HG Wells, *Ed* Nick Morris, *M* Jeff Wayne.

Sony Music Entertainment-More2Screen.
118 mins. UK. 2013. Rel: 11 Apr 2013. Cert. PG.

Warm Bodies ★★★★

A surprisingly sweet romantic comedy with an undead Romeo and kick-ass Juliet, *Warm Bodies* is a film with a bit of everything that works like some delicious movie salad full of brains and hearts and guts. British up-and-comer Nicholas Hoult takes the lead as slacker zombie R. Australian starlet Teresa Palmer holds her own as Julie, a girl so all-round awesome that she shocks R's heart into gear and heralds a positive upswing in living-dead relations. Funny and charming and creepy and strange. MJ

❯ Nicholas Hoult, Teresa Palmer, Analeigh Tipton, Rob Corddry, Dave Franco, John Malkovich, Cory Hardrict, Daniel Rindress-Kay.
❯ *Dir* and *Screenplay* Jonathan Levine, from the novel by Isaac Marion, *Pro* Bruce Papandrea, Todd Lieberman and David Hoberman, *Ph* Javier Aguirresarobe, *Pro Des* Martin Whist, *Ed* Nancy Richardson, *M* Marco Beltrami and Buck Sanders, *Cos* George L Little.

Mandeville Pictures/Summit Entertainment/Make Movies-Entertainment One.
98 mins. USA. 2013. Rel: 8 Feb 2013. Cert. 12A.

The Way Way Back ★★½

Intended as a film blending comedy and drama, this is an ill-judged piece which centres on a 14-year-old boy whose mother is inexplicably drawn to an insensitive man likely to become the boy's stepfather. It has a distinguished cast but the writing (which arguably fails to recognise how unappealing many of the characters are) lets them down. One is reminded of the admirable *Adventureland* (2008) which really involved one and is everything that this film is not. MS

❯ Steve Carell, Toni Collette, Allison Janney, Liam James, AnnaSophia Robb, Sam Rockwell, Maya Rudolph, Amanda Peet, Nat Faxon, Jim Rash.
❯ *Dir* and *Screenplay* Nat Faxon and Jim Rash, *Pro* Kevin J Walsh and Tom Rice, *Ph* John Bailey, *Pro Des* Mark Ricker, *Ed* Tatiana S Riegel, *M* Rob Simonson, *Cos* Ann Roth and Michelle Matland.

Fox Searchlight Pictures/a Sycamore Pictures, Walsh Company, OddLot Entertainment production/What Just Happened Productions etc.-20th Century Fox.
103 mins. USA. 2013. Rel: 28 Aug 2013. Cert. 12A.

We Steal Secrets: The Story of WikiLeaks ★★★★

Alex Gibney's engrossing coverage of the now-exiled Julian Assange's Wiki-Leaks website uses archive footage to build up a picture of the man

and his courageous attempt to reveal secrets about the US. This is shown in parallel with the story of the disturbed American soldier, Bradley Manning, who downloaded thousands of documents from US military and diplomatic servers and was jailed for his trouble. In the current climate of openness both men are revealed as fervent supporters of public access to government information, although when it came to the crunch they faced a wall of silence from authorities embarrassed by such a vast security leak. It is difficult not to feel support for these martyrs of the mass medium we call the internet. MHD

▶ With Julian Assange, Bradley Manning, John McMahon, Professor Robert Manne, Heather Brooke, General Michael Hayden, J William Leonard etc.
▶ *Dir* and *Written by* Alex Gibney, *Pro* Gibney, Marc Shmuger and Alexis Bloom, *Ph* Maryse Alberti, *Ed* Andy Grieve.
Universal Pictures/Jigsaw/Global Produce-Universal Pictures.
130 mins. USA. 2013. Rel: 12 July 2013. Cert. 15.

We Went to War ★★★★

In 1970 Michael Grigsby made a film called *I Was a Soldier* about Vietnam veterans returning home to Texas. Here Grigsby (who died shortly before the film's release) and his producer Rebekah Tolley revisit the people he previously encountered and they examine how the veterans' war experiences have affected their lives as well as those of their families. It is a powerful document about their ghastly war experiences and it wisely draws comparisons with those of Iraq veterans. A sad but compelling piece of filmmaking. GS

▶ With David Johnson, Dennis Bolinger.
▶ *Dir* Michael Grigsby, *Pro* Rebekah Tolley, *Written by* Grigsby and Tolley, *Ph* Jonas Mortensen, *Ed* Emer Reynolds, *M* Gallagher & Lyle.
Soho Moon Pictures-Tarian Films.
77 mins. UK. 2012. Rel: 29 Mar 2013. No Cert.

The Wee Man ★★★

Set in Glasgow in the 1970s and '80s, writer-director Ray Burdis' gritty, hard-hitting film follows the true story of Paul Ferris and his rise through Scotland's underworld. It portrays Ferris as a family man forced by local bullies and nasty cops into a life of crime, which may not be the whole truth but does make for an exciting Brit gangster film. Martin Compston gives a compelling star performance as Ferris and there's strong support, especially by Patrick Bergin as the local Godfather. Strathclyde Police refused to co-operate, so the film was shot in London. DW

▶ Martin Compston, Patrick Bergin, Simon DeSilva, Hannah Blamires, Denis Lawson, Rita Tushingham, Steve Daly, Alastair Thomson-Mills.
▶ *Dir* and *Screenplay* Ray Burdis, *Pro* Mike Loveday, *Ph* Ali Asad, *Pro Des* Belinda Cusmano and Alice Norris, *Ed* Will Gilbey, *M* John Beckett, *Cos* Hayley Nebauer.
Carnaby International Productions/Wee Man Productions/VTR Media-Carnaby Films.
106 mins. UK. 2013. Rel: 18 Jan 2013. Cert. 18.

Crime laird: Martin Compston in Ray Burdis' *The Wee Man.*

French leave: Jim Broadbent and Lindsay Duncan in Stephen Frears' *Le Week-End.*

Le Week-End ★★★½

To mark their 30th wedding anniversary, academics Nick and Meg (Jim Broadbent and Lindsay Duncan) go to Paris to see if they can rekindle their marriage flame. They have some fun by swapping their modest accommodation for a posh hotel, muck about like kids, run off without paying a bill, and meet an old American friend, Morgan (Jeff Goldblum). Both Nick and Meg are probably jealous of him when he introduces them to his new young wife. Hanif Kureishi, following his previous screenplays about age and sex (*The Mother* and *Venus*), paints a sorry picture of a marriage on the rocks, but one not without humour, in which the protagonists refuse to give up completely. MHD

▸ Lindsay Duncan, Jim Broadbent, Jeff Goldblum, Olly Alexander, Brice Beaugier, Charlotte Léo, Lee Michelsen.
▸ *Dir* Roger Michell, *Pro* Kevin Loader, *Screenplay* Hanif Kureishi, *Ph* Nathalie Durand, *Pro Des* Emmanuelle Duplay, *Ed* Kristina Hetherington, *M* Jeremy Sams, *Cos* Natalie Ward.

Film 4/Free Range Films/Le Bureau-Curzon Film World. 93 mins. UK/France. 2013. Rel: 11 Oct 2013. Cert. 15.

Welcome to the Punch ★½

'The Punch' is the name of a self-storage unit in the City of London. But that's not important. Nor, apparently, is the plot, the characters or the plausibility of it all. This is one of those crime thrillers – executive-produced by Ridley Scott, no less – in which shoot-outs, sweeping cityscapes and constant motion hope to be enough. James McAvoy plays an East End cop with a grudge and a girlfriend, two elements that come into play when an old crook (Mark Strong) pops out of hiding. The rest is just filler. JC-W

▸ James McAvoy, Mark Strong, Andrea Riseborough, Johnny Harris, David Morrissey, Daniel Kaluuya, Peter Mullan, Daniel Mays, Jason Maza, Jason Flemyng, Ruth Sheen.
▸ *Dir* and *Screenplay* Eran Creevy, *Pro* Rory Aitken, Brian Kavanaugh-Jones and Ben Pugh, *Ph* Ed Wild, *Pro Des* Crispian Sallis, *Ed* Chris Gill, *M* Harry Escott, *Cos* Natalie Ward.

Worldview Entertainment/Between The Eyes/Automatik Entertainment-Momentum Pictures.
99 mins. UK/USA. 2013. Rel: 15 Mar 2013. Cert. 15.

We're the Millers ★★★½

Like the Griswolds in *National Lampoon's Vacation*, the Millers – Mr and Mrs, plus one son and one daughter – are on the road to misadventure. But this being 2013, the Millers are a little more 'street.' They're actually conveying $43,000 worth of weed, while the family 'look' is merely a cover for their criminal operation… Unlike the recent sludge of American gross-out comedies, *We're the Millers* is actually crude and funny at the same time. There's also a plot, lashings of incidental humour and some wonderful comic timing, along with a fistful of very funny lines. ("Hey, you kiss a lot better than my sister.") JC-W

▶ Jennifer Aniston, Jason Sudeikis, Emma Roberts, Will Poulter, Ed Helms, Nick Offerman, Kathryn Hahn, Molly Quinn, Tomer Sisley, Luis Guzmán.
▶ *Dir* Rawson Marshall Thurber, *Pro* Chris Bender, Vincent Newman, Tucker Tooley and Happy Walters, *Screenplay* Bob Fisher, Steve Faber, Sean Anders and John Morris, *Ph* Barry Peterson, *Pro Des* Clayton Hartley, *Ed* Michael L Sale, *M* Ludwig Göransson and Theodore Shapiro, *Cos* Shay Cunliffe.

New Line Cinema/Newman/Tooley Films/Slap Happy Prods-Warner Bros.
109 mins. USA. 2013. Rel: 23 Aug 2013. Cert. 15.

What Maisie Knew ★★★½

The talented team of Scott McGehee and David Siegel returns to direct this modernised treatment of the Henry James novel about an instinctively wise young child, Maisie, who has to rally when the marriage of her parents breaks up. Child actress Onata Aprile is splendid and is backed up by quality work from Julianne Moore and Joanna Vanderham in particular. Unexpectedly the adaptation, which until then has seemed subtle and intelligent as befits the original, chooses to offer an appalling Hollywood-style final scene. MS

▶ Julianne Moore, Onata Aprile, Alexander Skarsgard, Joanna Vanderham, Steve Coogan.
▶ *Dir* Scott McGehee and David Siegel, *Pro* Daniela Taplin Lundberg, Daniel Crown, William Teitler and Charles Weinstock, *Screenplay* Nancy Dayne and Carroll Cartwright, from the novel by Henry James, *Ph* Giles Nuttgens, *Pro Des* Kelly McGehee, *Ed* Madeline Gavin, *M* Nick Urata, *Cos* Stacey Battat.

A Red Crown production/Koda Entertainment/ Dreambridge Films etc.-Curzon Film World.
99 mins. USA. 2013. Rel: 23 Aug 2013. Cert. 15.

What Richard Did ★★★★

Richard, superbly played by Jack Reynor, is a teenager who lives in South Dublin and is about to start his first year at university. The film, which also introduces us to his Danish father and Irish mother, shows him amongst friends of his own age and persuasively conveys what it means to be 18 in today's world. The drama tightens when an unpremeditated act threatens Richard's future. The ending may be inconclusive but there's a pitch-perfect scene at the climax between father (Lars Mikkelsen) and son. MS

▶ Jack Reynor, Lars Mikkelsen, Róisín Murphy, Sam Keeley, Fionn Walton.
▶ *Dir* Lenny Abrahamson, *Pro* Ed Guiney, *Screenplay* Malcolm Campbell based on Kevin Power's book *Bad Day in Blackrock*, *Ph* David Grennan, *Pro Des*

Stephanie Clerkin, *Ed* Nathan Nugent, *M* Stephen Rennicks, *Cos* Leonie Prendergast.

Element Pictures/Bord Scannán na hÉireann/the Irish Film Board etc.-Artificial Eye.
88 mins. Ireland. 2012. Rel: 11 Jan 2013. Cert. 15.

When the Dragon Swallowed the Sun ★★★

Seven years in the making, this seriously over-extended documentary was set up to mark the 50th anniversary of the takeover of Tibet by the Chinese in 1949. It is the tragic history of Tibet and its people which is treated here. The Dalai Lama is an honourable screen presence, but the subject has been treated before and revisiting it for the anniversary means that the film records what seems to be an impasse. Consequently the film itself seems to be going nowhere slowly and its tone, including its use of music, tends to be over-emphatic. MS

▶ With Kungpo-Dawa Tsetan, Yangchen Dolkar and Dennis Haysbert (Narrator).
▶ *Dir* and *Written by* Dirk Simon, *Pro* Simon and Vanessa Phillipe, *Ph* Robert Muratore and Jeff Pointer, *Set Des* Sidharth Mathawan and Meghna Singh, *Ed* Dave Krahling, *M* Philip Glass, Damien Rice and Thom Yorke.

Free Motion Films-Arrow Films.
114 mins. USA. 2011. Rel: 16 Aug 2013. Cert. 15.

Which Way is the Front Line from Here? ★★★★

In 2010 Sebastian Junger co-directed the memorable documentary *Restrepo* with the photojournalist Tim Hetherington. Now, following Hetherington's death in Libya aged 40, Junger offers this heartfelt tribute to his dead friend. In telling his life story, it also captures the spirit of the man. In passing it makes an intriguing comparison with another fine documentary, *McCullin* [qv].

Affront to humanity: Sebastion Junger and Tim Hetherington in Junger's *Which Way is the Front Line from Here?*

This film is not only deeply committed but well-judged and ultimately very moving. MS

➤ With Tim Hetherington, Sebastian Junger, Alistair Hetherington, Idil Ibraham.
➤ *Dir* Sebastian Junger, *Pro* Nick Quested and James Brabazon, *Ph* Brabazon, Tim Hetherington and Junger, *Ed* Geeta Gandhbir and Maya Mumma, *M* Joel Goodman.

HBO Documentary Films/a Tripoli Street, Goldcrest Films production-Kaleidoscope Entertainment. 78 mins. USA/UK. 2013. Rel: 11 Oct 2013. Cert. 15.

White Elephant ★★★½

Set in the slums of Buenos Aires, this social drama shows the Catholic Church engaged in seeking to help the homeless, people caught between criminal bands and politicians with their own agendas. Similar in tone and concern to its predecessor, *Carancho* (2010), Pablo Trapero's film is sincere, tough and involved but there's less depth of characterisation this time around to involve us in the personal storylines linked to the real-life situation depicted. (Original title: *Elefante blanco*) MS

➤ Ricardo Darín, Jérémie Renier, Martina Gusman, Federico Benjamin Barga.
➤ *Dir* Pablo Trapero, *Pro* Juan Gordon, Trapero, Juan

Vera and others, *Screenplay* Alejandro Fadel, Martín Mauregui, Santiago Mitre and Trapero, *Ph* Guillermo Nieto, *Pro Des* Juan Pedro de Gaspar, *Ed* Trapero and Nacho Ruiz Capillas, *M* Michael Nyman, *Cos* Marisa Urruti.

A Morena Films, Matanza Cine, Patagonik production/ Full House/Arte France Cinéma etc.-Axiom Films Limited. 110 mins. Spain/Argentina/France. 2012. Rel: 26 Apr 2013. Cert. 15.

White House Down ★★★★

If Roland Emmerich's *White House Down* was the popcorn blockbuster of the summer, it was chilli-flavoured popcorn. A thrilling and even frightening rollercoaster ride from the man who routinely places our planet under deadly threat (cf, *Independence Day*, *The Day After Tomorrow*, *2012*), *White House Down* starts off as a photocopy of *Olympus Has Fallen* [qv] and then gets even more ridiculous. But in its gung-ho, brutal, over-the-top, even sentimental way, it's an insanely entertaining ride. JC-W

➤ Channing Tatum, Jamie Foxx, Maggie Gyllenhaal, Jason Clarke, Richard Jenkins, James Woods, Joey King, Michael Murphy, Rachelle Lefevre.
➤ *Dir* Roland Emmerich, *Pro* Emmerich, Bradley J Fischer, Harald Kloser, James Vanderbilt, Larry Franco and Laeta Kalogridis, *Screenplay* James

Capital punishment: Channing Tatum to the rescue in Roland Emmerich's *White House Down*.

Vanderbilt, *Ph* Anna J Foerster, *Pro Des* Kirk
M Petruccelli, *Ed* Adam Wolfe, *M* Harald Kloser and
Thomas Wander, *Cos* Lisy Christl.

**Columbia Pictures/Mythology Entertainment/
Centropolis Entertainment-Sony Pictures Releasing.
131 mins. USA. 2013. Rel: 13 Sep 2013. Cert. 12A.**

Who Needs Enemies ★★★½

Ex-boxer Tom Sheridan (Ian Pirie) begins to
regret deeply his decision to rent his club to
his old friend and fellow gangster Ian Levine
(Michael McKell). Meanwhile, three other thugs
are at each other's throats when their loyalty is
tested... Peter Stylianou makes an assured feature
film debut with this low-budget but stylish crime
thriller, the strength of which lies in a clever and
unpredictable script that manages to bring a fresh
perspective to an overfamiliar setting. GS

▶ Michael McKell, Ian Pirie, Emma Barton, Kris
Johnson, Glen Fox, Tom Carey, Victoria Donovan,
Nick Lavelle, Dona Preston.
▶ *Dir, Screenplay, Ed, Special Effects* and *Art Dir* Peter
Stylianou, *Pro* Tony Currier, *Ph* Andre Govia,
M Christopher Blake, *Cos* Catherine Stylianou.

**Red Guerilla Films-Ballpark Film Distributors.
91 mins. UK. 2013. Rel: 29 Nov 2013. Cert. 18.**

Winter of Discontent ★★★½

This fine drama was inspired by the protests
in Cairo's Tahrir Square on 25 January 2011
and, reflecting what it meant to be a citizen
living there at that time, it convincingly finds
representative figures to cover contrasted
viewpoints. That the film arrived here just when
the hopes consequent on President Mubarak
stepping down were overturned only made for
an even greater impact. Any weaknesses are
minor and, even more tellingly than the later
documentary *The Square*, this film stands as a
work of historical importance both for Egypt and
for the world. (Original title: *El sheita elli fat*) MS

▶ Amr Waked, Frah Youssef, Tamer Diaey, Salah
Al Hanafy, Ali Mohy El Din.
▶ *Dir* Ibrahim El Batout, *Pro* Amr Waked, Salah Al
Hanafy and Batout, *Screenplay* Batout, Ahmed Amer,
Yasser Naeim and Habbi Seoud, *Ph* Victor Credi,
Art Dir Mustafa Emam, *Ed* Hisham Saqr, *M* Ahmed
Mostafa Saleh, *Cos* Dalia Haikal.

**A Zad Communication & Production LLC film/Material
House Film Production etc.-New Wave Films.
96 mins. Egypt. 2012. Rel: 23 Aug 2013. Cert. 15.**

Wolf Children ★★★★

This is a charming Japanese anime film and not
the horror story its title might suggest. Young
Hana meets a werewolf and falls in love with
him. Apparently he's the last of a long line and

leads a quiet life as a removal man, although
he still ventures out at night to stalk pheasants.
One evening a hunting trip ends in his death
and Hana is left with their two baby werewolves.
The film shows how she copes as they grow up
and get into every kind of mischief. Will she lose
them if they decide to live as werewolves rather
than humans? As an antidote to the current
Disney/Pixar output, this delightfully animated
piece deserves a wider audience. (Original title:
Ookami kodomo no Ame to Yuki) PL

▶ Voices of Aoi Miyazaki, Takao Osawa, Haru Kuroki,
Yukito Nishii, Momoka Ohno, Amon Kabe.
▶ *Dir* Mamoru Hosoda, *Pro* Takuya Itô, Yuichiro
Sato, Takafumi Watanabe, Justin Cook and Carly
Hunter, *Screenplay* Hosoda and Satoko Okudera,
Art Dir Hiroshi Ohno, *Ed* Shigeru Nishiyama,
M Masakatsu Takagi, *Cos* Daisuke Iga.

**Studio Chizu/Dentsu/Hiroshima Telecasting/Toho/
Yomiuri TV Enterprise/Nippon Television Network etc-
Manga Entertainment.
117 mins. Japan. 2012. Rel: 25 Oct 2013. Cert. PG.**

The Wolverine ★★★

This solo outing for Hugh Jackman's popular,
blade-knuckled character from Marvel's *X-Men*
franchise is a peculiar hybrid of expected
superhero movie and present-day samurai epic
set mostly in Japan. It boasts some impressive
character development and terrific action set-
pieces but, as these eventually give way to
formulaic superhero plotting, it becomes harder
to care about anyone involved. JC

▶ Hugh Jackman, Tao Okamoto, Rila Fukushima,
Hiroyuki Sanada, Svetlana Khodcenkova, Brian Tee,
Haruhiko Yamanouchi, Famke Janssen.
▶ *Dir* James Mangold, *Pro* Jackman, Hutch Parker
and Lauren Shuler Donner, *Screenplay* Mark
Bromback and Scott Frank, *Ph* Ross Emery, *Pro Des*

Baulk like an
Egyptian: Amr
Waked in Ibrahim
El Batout's *Winter
of Discontent*.

Avoiding clichés like the plague: Brad Pitt, Abigail Hargrove, Mireille Enos and Sterling Jerins in *World War Z*.

François Audouy, *Ed* Michael McCusker, *M* Marco Beltrami, *Cos* Isis Mussenden.

20th Century Fox/Marvel Entertainment/Big Screen Productions/ Ingenious Media/Donners' Company/TSG Entertainment-20th Century Fox.
126 mins. USA/UK. 2013. Rel: 25 July 2013. Cert. 12A.

Won't Back Down ★★★

Maggie Gyllenhaal plays Jamie Fitzpatrick, a single mother juggling her commitments as parent and breadwinner. However, she's not impressed by the amount of time her daughter's crippling dyslexia is allocated in class. The wonderful Viola Davis is Nona Alberts, a teacher at the same Pittsburgh school who has lost her will to inspire. But, together, they might just be able to change things… Not a critics' film, *Won't Back Down* does push some of its emotional buttons a little obviously, but it has intelligence to spare. And some provocative food for thought. JC-W

▶ Maggie Gyllenhaal, Viola Davis, Holly Hunter, Oscar Isaac, Rosie Perez, Lance Reddick, Ving Rhames, Marianne Jean-Baptiste, Bill Nunn.
▶ *Dir* Daniel Barnz, *Pro* Mark Johnson, *Screenplay* Barnz and Brun Hill, *Ph* Roman Osin, *Pro Des* Rusty Smith, *Ed* Kristina Boden, *M* Marcelo Zarvos, *Cos* Luca Mosca.

Walden Media/Gran Via Prods/Lemodeln Model & Talent Agency-Walt Disney Pictures.
121 mins. USA. 2012. Rel: 25 Jan 2013. Cert. PG.

World War Z ★★★★½

The zombie genre has gone through a series of mutations, from the low-budget horror of *Night of the Living Dead* to the comic irony of *Shaun of the Dead* through to the feel-good romanticism of this year's *Warm Bodies*. But now the zombie film comes of age. It's not a sequel, it's not a remake and it's not a brainless rip-off of a video game. It's a mainstream epic in which the undead are scarier, faster and yet more credible than we've ever previously seen them. Although another apocalyptic scenario to add to this year's haemorrhaging list, in the capable hands of Marc Forster it is intelligently put together and frighteningly plausible. JC-W

▶ Brad Pitt, Mireille Enos, Daniella Kertesz, James Badge Dale, Matthew Fox, David Morse, Peter Capaldi, Ruth Negga, Moritz Bleibtreu, David Andrews, John Gordon Sinclair, Lucy Russell.
▶ *Dir* Marc Forster, *Pro* Brad Pitt, Dede Gardner, Jeremy Kleiner and Ian Bryce, *Screenplay* Matthew Michael Carnahan, Drew Goddard and Damon Lindelof, *Ph* Ben Seresin, *Pro Des* Nigel Phelps, *Ed* Roger Barton and Matt Chesse, *M* Marco Beltrami, *Cos* Mayes C Rubeo.

Paramount Pictures/Skydance Productions/Hemisphere Media Capital/Plan B-Paramount Pictures.
115 mins. USA/UK/Malta. 2013. Rel: 21 June 2013. Cert. 15.

The World's End ★★

You wait ages for a comedy about the end of the world… Actually, this is not so much an apocalyptic laugh-fest as the final nail in the coffin of the so-called 'Cornetto trilogy,' three spoofs starring Simon Pegg and Nick Frost and directed by Edgar Wright. Tapping into the same comedic vein of *The Hangover* – where grown men behave like moronic teenagers – *The World's End* is essentially a farce about the 20-year anniversary of an epic pub crawl. While the effects are pretty good and the energy level well maintained, the film falls down on the essential element of comedy: it isn't that funny. JC-W

‣ Simon Pegg, Nick Frost, Paddy Considine, Martin Freeman, Eddie Marsan, Rosamund Pike, Pierce Brosnan, Reece Shearsmith, Darren Boyd, Steve Oram, Rafe Spall, Alice Lowe, David Bradley, Michael Smiley.
‣ *Dir* Edgar Wright, *Pro* Nira Park, Tim Bevan and Eric Fellner, *Screenplay* Simon Pegg and Edgar Wright, *Ph* Bill Pope, *Pro Des* Marcus Rowland, *Ed* Paul Machliss, *M* Steven Price, *Cos* Guy Speranza.

Universal Pictures/Focus Features/Relativity Media/ Working Title/Big Talk Productions/ Dentsu/Fuji Television Network-Universal Pictures.
108 mins. UK. 2013. Rel: 19 July 2013. Cert. 15.

Wreck-It Ralph ★★★★★

Just like Woody, Buzz Lightyear and comrades in *Toy Story*, the playful entities in *Wreck-It Ralph* take on a life of their own once the humans are gone… To have an adventure incorporating everything from computer viruses to virtual reality packaged into a kid's cartoon – Walt Disney's 52nd 'official' animated feature – is a stroke of genius. Every single minute is stuffed with allusions, running the gamut from Lewis Carroll to *Alien*; but the film is also rich in real ideas, imagery, wit and priceless dialogue. The fact that it's also very funny – and even touching – is just icing on the cake. JC-W

‣ Voices of John C Reilly, Sarah Silverman, Jack McBrayer, Jane Lynch, Alan Tudyk, Ed O'Neill, Dennis Haysbert.
‣ *Dir* Rich Moore, *Pro* Clark Spencer, *Screenplay* Phil Johnston and Jennifer Lee, *Art Dir* Ian Gooding, *Ed* Tim Mertens, *M* Henry Jackman.

Walt Disney Animation Studios-Walt Disney Studios Motion Pictures.
107 mins. USA. 2012. Rel: 8 Feb 2013. Cert. PG.

You're Next ★★★

A family gathering in a house in the middle of nowhere turns nasty as a small number of assailants start violently killing off family members one by one. But they've reckoned without the survivalist-schooled member (Sharni Vinson) who will prove more than their match… This clever reworking of the 'final girl' stereotype should more than satisfy most horror fans, although otherwise there's nothing particularly remarkable here. JC

‣ Sharni Vinson, Nicholas Tucci, Wendy Glenn, Joe Swanberg, AJ Bowen, Sarah Myers, Ti West, Amy Seimetz.
‣ *Dir* Adam Wingard, *Pro* Jessica Wu, Kim Sherman, Keith Calder and Simon Barrett, *Screenplay* Barrett, *Ph* Andrew Droz Palermo, *Pro Des* Thomas S Hammock, *Ed* Adam Wingard, *M* Mads Heldtberg, Kyle McKinnon and Jasper Justice Lee, *Cos* Emma Potter.

HanWay Films/Snoot Entertainment-Icon Film Distribution.
95 mins. USA. 2013. Rel: 28 Aug 2013. Cert. 18.

Zero Dark Thirty ★★★½

Jessica Chastain and Jennifer Ehle give memorable performances in this account of how the CIA tracked down Osama bin Laden, resulting in his death. Although found controversial by some, this long work largely leaves it to the audience to draw their own conclusions. Chastain's character is so crucial to the mission that one wonders just how much the truth has been embroidered. Reality is fully observed in the night-time attack at the climax but it does render it difficult to identify exactly what is happening. MS

‣ Jessica Chastain, Jason Clarke, Joel Edgerton, Jennifer Ehle, Mark Strong, Kyle Chandler, James Gandolfini, Mark Duplass.
‣ *Dir* Kathryn Bigelow, *Pro* Mark Boal, Bigelow and Megan Ellison, *Screenplay* Boal, *Ph* Greig Fraser, *Pro Des* Jeremy Hindle, *Ed* Dylan Tichenor and William Goldenberg, *M* Alexandre Desplat, *Cos* George L Little.

An Annapurna production/a First Light production/a Mark Boal production-Universal.
157 mins. USA. 2012. Rel: 25 Jan 2013. Cert. 15.

Game for a laugh: Vanellope von Schweetz and Ralph in Rich Moore's *Wreck-It Ralph*.

Awards and Festivals

86th American Academy of Motion Picture Arts and Sciences Awards ('The Oscars') and Nominations for 2013
2 March 2014

➤ **Best Film**: *12 Years a Slave*. Nominations: *American Hustle*; *Captain Phillips*; *Dallas Buyers Club*; *Gravity*; *Her*; *Nebraska*; *Philomena*; *The Wolf of Wall Street*.

➤ **Best Director**: Alfonso Cuarón, for *Gravity*. Nominations: Steve McQueen, for *12 Years a Slave*; Alexander Payne, for *Nebraska*; David O Russell, for *American Hustle*; Martin Scorsese, for *The Wolf of Wall Street*.

➤ **Best Actor**: Matthew McConaughey, for *Dallas Buyers Club*. Nominations: Christian Bale, for *American Hustle*; Bruce Dern, for *Nebraska*; Leonardo DiCaprio, *The Wolf of Wall Street*; Chiwetel Ejiofor, for *12 Years a Slave*.

➤ **Best Actress**: Cate Blanchett, for *Blue Jasmine*. Nominations: Amy Adams, for *American Hustle*; Sandra Bullock, for *Gravity*; Judi Dench, for *Philomena*; Meryl Streep, for *August: Osage County*.

➤ **Best Supporting Actor**: Jared Leto, for *Dallas Buyers Club*. Nominations: Barkhad Abdi, for *Captain Phillips*; Bradley Cooper, for *American Hustle*; Michael Fassbender, for *12 Years a Slave*; Jonah Hill, for *The Wolf of Wall Street*.

➤ **Best Supporting Actress**: Lupita Nyong'o, for *12 Years a Slave*. Nominations: Sally Hawkins, for *Blue Jasmine*; Jennifer Lawrence, for *American Hustle*; Julia Roberts, for *August: Osage County*; June Squibb, for *Nebraska*.

➤ **Best Original Screenplay**: Spike Jonze, for *Her*. Nominations: Eric Warren Singer and David O Russell, for *American Hustle*; Woody Allen, for *Blue Jasmine*; Craig Borten and Melisa Wallack, for *Dallas Buyers Club*; Bob Nelson, for *Nebraska*.

➤ **Best Screenplay Adaptation**: John Ridley, for *12 Years a Slave*. Nominations: Richard Linklater, Julie Delpy and Ethan Hawke, for *Before Midnight*; Billy Ray, for *Captain Phillips*; Steve Coogan and Jeff Pope, for *Philomena*; Terence Winter, for *The Wolf of Wall Street*.

➤ **Best Cinematography**: Emmanuel Lubezki, for *Gravity*. Nominations: Philippe Le Sourd, for *The Grandmaster*; Bruno Delbonnel, for *Inside Llewyn Davis*; Phedon Papamichael, for *Nebraska*; Roger Deakins, for *Prisoners*.

➤ **Best Editing**: Alfonso Cuarón and Mark Sanger, for *Gravity*. Nominations: Jay Cassidy, Crispin Struthers and Alan Baumgarten, for *American Hustle*; Christopher Rouse, for *Captain Phillips*; John Mac McMurphy and Martin Pensa, for *Dallas Buyers Club*; Joe Walker, for *12 Years a Slave*.

➤ **Best Original Score**: Steven Price, for *Gravity*. Nominations: John Williams, for *The Book Thief*; William Butler and Owen Pallett, for *Her*; Alexandre Desplat, for *Philomena*; Thomas Newman, for *Saving Mr Banks*.

▶▶ Best Original Song: 'Let It Go' from *Frozen*, by Kristen Anderson-Lopez and Robert Lopez. Nominations: 'Happy' from *Despicable Me 2*, by Pharrell Williams; 'The Moon Song' from *Her*, by Karen O (music) and Karen O and Spike Jonze (lyrics); 'Ordinary Love' from *Mandela: Long Walk to Freedom*, by Paul Hewson, Dave Evans, Adam Clayton and Larry Mullen (music) and Paul Hewson (lyrics).

▶▶ Best Production Design: Catherine Martin (production design) and Beverley Dunn (set decoration), for *The Great Gatsby*. Nominations: Judy Becker (production design) and Heather Loeffler (set decoration), for *American Hustle*; Andy Nicholson (production design) and Rosie Goodwin and Joanne Woollard (set decoration), for *Gravity*; KK Barrett (production design) and Gene Serdena (set decoration), for *Her*; Adam Stockhausen (production design) and Alice Baker (set decoration), for *12 Years a Slave*.

▶▶ Best Costume Design: Catherine Martin, for *The Great Gatsby*. Nominations: Michael Wilkinson, for *American Hustle*; William Chang Suk Ping, for *The Grandmaster*; Michael O'Connor, for *The Invisible Woman*; Patricia Norris, for *12 Years a Slave*.

▶▶ Best Sound Editing: Glenn Freemantle, for *Gravity*. Nominations: Steve Boeddeker and Richard Hymns, for *All is Lost*; Oliver Tarney, for *Captain Phillips*; Brent Burge and Chris Ward, for *The Hobbit: The Desolation of Smaug*; Wylie Stateman, for *Lone Survivor*.

▶▶ Best Sound Mixing: Skip Lievsay, Niv Adiri, Christopher Benstead and Chris Munro, for *Gravity*. Nominations: Chris Burdon, Mark Taylor, Mike Prestwood Smith and Chris Munro, for *Captain Phillips*; Christopher Boyes, Michael Hedges, Michael Semanick and Tony Johnson, for *The Hobbit: The Desolation of Smaug*; Skip Lievsay, Greg Orloff and Peter F Kurland, for *Inside Llewyn Davis*; Andy Koyama, Beau Borders and David Brownlow, for *Lone Survivor*.

▶▶ Best Makeup and Hairstyling: Adruitha Lee and Robin Mathews, for *Dallas Buyers Club*. Nominations: Stephen Prouty, for *Jackass Presents: Bad Grandpa*; Joel Harlow and Gloria Pasqua-Casny, for *The Lone Ranger*.

▶▶ Best Visual Effects: Tim Webber, Chris Lawrence, David Shirk and Neil Corbould, for *Gravity*. Nominations: Joe Letteri, Eric Saindon, David Clayton and Eric Reynolds, for *The Hobbit: The Desolation of Smaug*; Christopher Townsend, Guy Williams, Erik Nash and Dan Sudick, for *Iron Man 3*; Tim Alexander, Gary Brozenich, Edson Williams and John Frazier, for *The Lone Ranger*; Roger Guyett, Patrick Tubach, Ben Grossmann and Burt Dalton, for *Star Trek Into Darkness*.

▶▶ Best Animated Short Film: *Mr. Hublot*. Nominations: *Feral*; *Get a Horse!*; *Possessions*; *Room On the Broom*.

▶▶ Best Live Action Short Film: *Helium*. Nominations: *Aquel no era yo (That Wasn't Me)*; *Avant que de tout perdre (Just Before Losing Everything)*; *Pitääkö Mun Kaikki Hoitaa? (Do I Have to Take Care of Everything?)*; *The Voorman Problem*.

▶▶ Best Animated Feature: *Frozen*. Nominations: *The Croods*; *Despicable Me 2*; *Ernest & Celestine*; *The Wind Rises*.

▶▶ Best Documentary Feature: *20 Feet from Stardom*. Nominations: *The Act of Killing*; *Cutie and the Boxer*; *Dirty Wars*; *The Square*.

▶▶ Best Documentary Short: *The Lady in Number 6: Music Saved My Life*. Nominations: *CaveDigger*; *Facing Fear*; *Karama Has No Walls*; *Prison Terminal: The Last Days of Private Jack Hall*.

▶▶ Best Foreign-Language Film: *The Great Beauty* (Italy). Nominations: *The Broken Circle Breakdown* (Belgium); *The Hunt* (Denmark); *The Missing Picture* (Cambodia); *Omar* (Palestine).

The 64th Berlin International Film Festival
6-16 February 2014

▶▶ Golden Bear for Best Film: *Black Coal, Thin Ice* (China), by Diao Yinan.

▶▶ Silver Bear, Jury Grand Prix: *The Grand Budapest Hotel* (USA), by Wes Anderson.

▶▶ Silver Bear, Best Director: Richard Linklater, for *Boyhood* (USA).

▶▶ Silver Bear, Best Actress: Haru Kuroki for *The Little House* (Japan).

▶▶ Silver Bear, Best Actor: Liao Fan, for *Black Coal, Thin Ice*.

▶▶ Silver Bear for Outstanding Artistic Achievement for Cinematography: Lou Ye, for *Blind Massage* (China/France).

▶▶ Best Screenplay: Dietrich Brüggemann, for *Stations of the Cross* (Germany).

▶▶ Alfred Bauer Prize for a work of particular innovation: *Aimer, boire et chanter (Life of Riley)* (France), by Alain Resnais.

▶▶ Special Mention: *Hitono Nozomino Yorokobiyo (Joy of Man's Desiring)* (Japan), by Masakazu Sugita.

▶▶ Golden Bear for Best Short Film: *Tant qu'il nous reste des fusils à pompe (As Long As Shotguns Remain)* by Caroline Poggi and Jonathan Vinel.

▶▶ Teddy Award: *The Way He Looks* (Brazil), by Daniel Ribeiro.

❯ Jury: *James Schamus* (president), and *Barbara Broccoli, Trine Dyrholm, Mitra Farahani, Greta Gerwig, Michel Gondry, Tony Leung, Christoph Waltz.*

Above: Liao Fan in *Black Coal, Thin Ice*.

Opposite: Barkhad Abdi, Tom Hanks and Faysal Ahmed in *Captain Phillips*.

The 2013 British Academy of Film and Television Arts Awards ('Baftas'), Royal Opera House, Covent Garden, London
16 February 2014

▶▶ **Best Film**: *12 Years a Slave*.
▶▶ **Outstanding British Film**: *Gravity*.
▶▶ **Best Director**: Alfonso Cuarón, for *Gravity*.
▶▶ **Best Actor**: Chiwetel Ejiofor, for *12 Years a Slave*.
▶▶ **Best Actress**: Cate Blanchett, for *Blue Jasmine*.
▶▶ **Best Supporting Actor**: Barkhad Abdi, for *Captain Phillips*.
▶▶ **Best Supporting Actress**: Jennifer Lawrence, for *American Hustle*.
▶▶ **Best Original Screenplay**: Eric Warren Singer and David O Russell, for *American Hustle*.
▶▶ **Best Adapted Screenplay**: Steve Coogan and Jeff Pope, for *Philomena*.
▶▶ **Best Cinematography**: Emmanuel Lubezki, for *Gravity*.
▶▶ **Best Production Design**: Catherine Martin and Beverley Dunn, for *The Great Gatsby*.
▶▶ **Best Editing**: Dan Hanley and Mike Hill, for *Rush*.
▶▶ **Best Music**: Steven Price, for *Gravity*.
▶▶ **Best Costumes**: Catherine Martin, for *The Great Gatsby*.
▶▶ **Best Sound**: Glenn Freemantle, Skip Lievsay, Christopher Benstead, Niv Adiri and Chris Munro, for *Gravity*.
▶▶ **Best Special Visual Effects**: Tim Webber, Chris Lawrence, David Shirk, Neil Corbould and Nikki Penny, for *Gravity*.
▶▶ **Best Make-Up/Hair**: Evelyne Noraz, Lori McCoy-Bell and Kathrine Gordon, for *American Hustle*.
▶▶ **Best Non-English Language Film**: *The Great Beauty* (Italy).
▶▶ **Best Documentary**: *The Act of Killing*.
▶▶ **Best Short Film**: *Room 8*.
▶▶ **Best Animated Film**: *Frozen*.
▶▶ **Best Short Animated Film**: *Sleeping With the Fishes*.
▶▶ **Best Outstanding Debut by a British Writer, Director or**

Producer: Kieran Evans (writer-director), for *Kelly + Victor*.
▶▶ **The Orange Rising Star Award**: Will Poulter.
▶▶ **BAFTA Fellowship**: Dame Helen Mirren.
▶▶ **Outstanding British Contribution to Cinema**: Peter Greenaway.

The 66th Cannes Film Festival Awards
15-26 May 2013

▶▶ **Palme d'Or (Golden Palm)**: *Blue is the Warmest Colour* (France/Belgium/Spain), by Abdellatif Kechiche.
▶▶ **Grand Prix du Jury**: *Inside Llewyn Davis* (USA), by Joel and Ethan Coen.
▶▶ **Jury Prize**: *Like Father, Like Son* (Japan), by Hirokazu Koreeda.
▶▶ **Camera d'Or** (first-time filmmaker): Anthony Chen, for *Ilo Ilo* (Singapore).
▶▶ **Best Actor**: Bruce Dern, for *Nebraska* (USA).
▶▶ **Best Actress**: Bérénice Bejo, for *The Past* (France/Italy).
▶▶ **Best Director**: Amat Escalante, for *Heli* (Mexico).
▶▶ **Best Screenplay**: Jia Zhangke, for *A Touch of Sin* (China).
▶▶ **Un Certain Regard Prize**: *The Missing Picture* (Cambodia/France), by Rithy Panh.
▶▶ **Special Jury Prize**: *Omar* (Palestine), by Hany Abu-Assad.
▶▶ **Best Director**: Alain Guiraudie, for *Stranger by the Lake* (France).
▶▶ **Best First Film**: *Fruitvale Station* (USA), by Ryan Coogler.
▶▶ **A Certain Talent**: Diego Quemada-Diez, writer-director of *The Golden Cage* (Mexico).
▶▶ **Palme d'Or – Short Film**: *Safe* (South Korea), by Moon Byoung-gon.

❯ **Jury**: *Steven Spielberg* (president), and *Daniel Auteuil, Vidya Balan, Naomi Kawase, Nicole Kidman, Ang Lee, Cristian Mungiu, Lynne Ramsay, Christoph Waltz.*

The 34th Golden Raspberries ('The Razzies')
1 March 2014

▶▶ **Worst Picture**: *Movie 43*.
▶▶ **Worst Actor**: Jaden Smith, for *After Earth*.
▶▶ **Worst Actress**: Tyler Perry, for *A Madea Christmas*.
▶▶ **Worst Supporting Actor**: Will Smith, for *After Earth*.
▶▶ **Worst Supporting Actress**: Kim Kardashian, for *Temptation: Confessions of a Marriage Counselor*.
▶▶ **Worst Director**: The 13 directors of *Movie 43*.
▶▶ **Worst Screenplay**: *Movie 43*.
▶▶ **Worst Prequel, Remake, Rip-off or Sequel**: *The Lone Ranger*.
▶▶ **Worst Screen Combo**: Jaden Smith and Will Smith 'on planet nepotism', for *After Earth*.

The 71st Hollywood Foreign Press Association ('Golden Globes') Awards
12 January 2014

▶▶ **Best Motion Picture – Drama**: *12 Years a Slave*.
▶▶ **Best Motion Picture – Musical or Comedy**: *American Hustle*.

Chiwetel Ejiofor and Michael Fassbender in *12 Years a Slave*.

➤ **Best Director**: Alfonso Cuarón, for *Gravity*.
➤ **Best Actor – Drama**: Matthew McConaughey, for *Dallas Buyers Club*.
➤ **Best Actress – Drama**: Cate Blanchett, for *Blue Jasmine*.
➤ **Best Actor – Musical or Comedy**: Leonardo DiCaprio, for *The Wolf of Wall Street*.
➤ **Best Actress – Musical or Comedy**: Amy Adams, for *American Hustle*.
➤ **Best Supporting Actor**: Jared Leto, for *Dallas Buyers Club*.
➤ **Best Supporting Actress**: Jennifer Lawrence, for *American Hustle*.
➤ **Best Foreign Language Film**: *The Great Beauty* (Italy).
➤ **Best Animated Feature Film**: *Frozen*.
➤ **Best Screenplay**: Spike Jonze, for *Her*.
➤ **Best Original Score**: Alex Ebert, for *All is Lost*.
➤ **Best Original Song**: 'Ordinary Love', music and lyrics by U2 and Danger Mouse, from *Mandela: Long Walk to Freedom*.

The 34th London Film Critics' Circle Awards 2013, The Mayfair Hotel, London
2 February 2014

➤ **Film of the Year**: *12 Years a Slave*.
➤ **British Film of the Year**: *The Selfish Giant*.
➤ **Foreign Language Film of the Year**: *Blue is the Warmest Colour* (France/Belgium/Spain).
➤ **Documentary of the Year**: *The Act of Killing*.
➤ **Director of the Year**: Alfonso Cuarón, for *Gravity*.
➤ **Breakthrough British Film-Maker**: Jon S Baird, for *Filth*.
➤ **Technical Achievement**: Tim Webber, visual effects, for *Gravity*.
➤ **Actor of the Year**: Chiwetel Ejiofor, for *12 Years a Slave*.
➤ **Actress of the Year**: Cate Blanchett, for *Blue Jasmine*.
➤ **British Actor of the Year**: James McAvoy, for *Filth*.
➤ **British Actress of the Year**: Judi Dench, for *Philomena*.
➤ **Supporting Actor of the Year**: Barkhad Abdi, for *Captain Phillips*.
➤ **Supporting Actress of the Year**: Lupita Nyong'o, for *12 Years a Slave*.
➤ **Screenwriters of the Year**: Ethan Coen and Joel Coen, for *Inside Llewyn Davis*.
➤ **Young British Performer of the Year**: Conner Chapman, for *The Selfish Giant*.
➤ **Dilys Powell Award for Excellence in Film**: Gary Oldman.

70th Venice International Film Festival
28 August-7 September 2013

➤ **Golden Lion for Best Film**: *Sacro Gra*, by Gianfranco Rosi (Italy/France).
➤ **Silver Lion for Best Director**: Alexandros Avranas, for *Miss Violence* (Greece).
➤ **Special Jury Prize**: *Die Frau des Polizisten*, by Philip Gröning (Germany).
➤ **Grand Jury Prize**: *Jiaoyou*, by Tsai Ming-liang (Chinese Taipei/France).
➤ **Coppa Volpi for Best Actor**: Themis Panou, for *Miss Violence*.

Cate Blanchett in *Blue Jasmine*.

➤ **Coppa Volpi for Best Actress**: Elena Cotta, for *Via Castellana Bandiera* (Italy/Switzerland/France).
➤ **Marcello Mastroianni Award for Best New Young Actor or Actress**: Tye Sheridan, for *Joe* (USA).
➤ **Best Screenplay**: Steve Coogan and Jeff Pope, for *Philomena* (UK).
➤ **Lion of the Future – 'Luigi De Laurentiis' Venice Award for a Debut Film**: *White Shadow,* by Noaz Deshe (Italy/Germany/Tanzania).
➤ **Golden Lion for Lifetime Achievement**: William Friedkin.
➤ **Jaeger-LeCoultre Glory to the Filmmaker Award**: Ettore Scola.
➤ **Persol Award**: Andrzej Wajda.
➤ **L'Oréal Paris Award for Cinema**: Eugenia Costantini.

❱ The Orizzonti section of the festival highlights the newest trends in world cinema (chaired by Paul Schrader):
➤ **Orizzonti Award** (full-length film): *Eastern Boys*, by Robin Campillo (France).
➤ **Special Orizzonti Jury Prize** (full-length film): *Ruin*, by Michael Cody and Amiel Courtin-Wilson (Australia).
➤ **Orizzonti Award for Best Director**: Uberto Pasolini, for *Still Life* (United Kingdom/Italy).
➤ **Orizzonti Award for Best Short Film**: *Kush*, by Shubhashish Bhutiani (India).
➤ **Special Orizzonti Award for Innovative Content**: *Mahi Va Gorbeh*, by Shahram Mokri (Iran).
➤ **European Short Film Award** (2013-EFA): *Houses With Small Windows*, by Bülent Öztürk (Belgium).

❱ **Jury**: *Bernardo Bertolucci* (chair), and *Andrea Arnold, Renato Berta, Carrie Fisher, Martina Gedeck, Jiang Wen, Pablo Larraín, Virginie Ledoyen and Ryuichi Sakamoto.*

Wall to Wall Women

With men pretty much excluded from the cast of Powder Room, ***Jonathan Rigby** recalls some of its all-female predecessors and looks forward to more.*

Sheridan Smith and Jaime Winstone in MJ Delaney's 2013 release *Powder Room* (reviewed on page 129).

"Quite good, straightforward adaptation of the stage play about a lodging house for unmarried mothers and their babies, and the terrible harridan who runs it."

Way back in 1953, in the tenth edition of this annual, F Maurice Speed didn't devote much space to the film version of Sylvia Rayman's controversial West End hit *Women of Twilight*. With a word count of just 25, he had no room to touch upon the film's treatment of several combustible social issues, nor could he reflect on a curious casting detail. For Rayman's all-women play had reached the screen graced by such top-flight female talent as Freda Jackson, Rène Ray and Lois Maxwell – but also the conspicuously male Laurence Harvey.

Having recently directed a London revival of Rayman's original (the first revival, as far as I know, for over half a century), I can testify to the fact that it plays a great deal better without Laurence Harvey. But British film producers getting cold feet about all-female subjects had a precedent in the form of *Nine Till Six*. This 1930 play by Aimée and Philip Stuart – set, rather racily, in a Regent Street dress shop – retains a certain historical significance in that it became the first film ever made at the newly opened Ealing Studios. (Fact fans may like to know that it started shooting on 2 December 1931.) But producer-director Basil Dean clearly felt such actresses as Elizabeth Allan, Kay Hammond and Jeanne de Casalis needed a bit of bolstering – by Richard Bird and various male supernumeraries.

Flash forward to 2012 and Rachel Hirons' play *When Women Wee* – set in the ladies' loo of a nightclub and originally a showcase for five actresses playing multiple roles – was fast-tracked onto film almost as rapidly as *Women of Twilight* 60 years before. Again, some negligible males were added to the cast, but this didn't worry Deborah Orr, writing in the *Guardian* a few weeks before the film's December 2013 release. For Orr, *Powder Room*, as it was now called, was "surprising, if not unique. If a feature film with a higher female-to-male on-camera ratio has ever been made," she asked, "then I'd like to know what it is."

Well, *Women of Twilight* and *Nine Till Six* are good examples for starters, but we can also mention a few films where men were banished from the screen altogether. The two classic

instances come from the 1930s, both derived from (as per the three films already cited) plays by women.

Based on an original by Christa Winsloe, Leontine Sagan's *Mädchen in Uniform* (1931) remains a genuinely moving portrait of life in a Prussian girls' boarding school, with a surprisingly frank emphasis on the same-sex passions blooming in its hothouse atmosphere. (The sole male presence is film star Hans Albers, but only as a series of fan photos pasted inside one of the girls' lockers.) Similarly, George Cukor's 1939 film of the Clare Boothe Luce play *The Women* made much of its all-female cast of 130, headed by such legendary names as Norma Shearer, Joan Crawford and Rosalind Russell – all playing what Luce called "Park Avenue pushovers" and feminist critic Molly Haskell dubbed "Park Avenue parasites".

In 2008, Diane English's misconceived remake (reportedly inspired by the success of the TV series *Sex and the City*) squandered such contemporary names as Meg Ryan, Eva Mendes and Annette Bening. (An earlier makeover, the 1956 musical *The Opposite Sex*, added men.) *Mädchen in Uniform*, too, was accorded a remake – a lusciously Eastmancolored 1958 version starring Lilli Palmer and Romy Schneider.

Going back to the UK, Nell Dunn's all-female play *Steaming*, set in a women's bath house, was the basis of Joseph Losey's final picture in 1984, and ten years later Wendy Kesselman's *My Sister in This House* (founded on the Papin murder case of 1933) became the Nancy Meckler film *Sister My Sister*. If it seems that plays written by women are the only means of getting producers to back all-female films, we can cite a few exceptions, notably the 1990 release *Eating*, a screen original by writer-director Henry Jaglom. Rainer Werner Fassbinder based his classic 1972 chamber piece *The Bitter Tears of Petra von Kant* on his own play. Two years later came a film (with men fleetingly added) of Genet's *The Maids*, based on the same case as *Sister My Sister*. In the 1980s there were Mexican and Spanish film versions of Lorca's classic drama *The House of Bernarda Alba*. And in 2001 François Ozon derived *8 Femmes* – in which the only male, a murder victim, is barely

visible – from a play by Robert Thomas. Tellingly, Ozon's original intention (until confounded by copyright problems) had been to mount a French remake of *The Women*.

Sidney Lumet's *The Group*, based on Mary McCarthy's candid satire of her Vassar College friends, made men into subordinate figures but struggled to reproduce the 1930s from the big-haired vantage point of 1965. For Lumet it was a change of pace after the relentlessly male *12 Angry Men*, while Candace Bushnell would use McCarthy's original novel as an imaginative springboard when creating *Sex and the City*. Coincidentally or otherwise, Candice Bergen, one of the eight 'group' members in Lumet's film, later appeared in *Sex and the City* (TV and film) and the 2008 retread of *The Women*.

Other films conform to the school-bound *Mädchen in Uniform* template, among them Jacqueline Audry's *Olivia* (1950), the Mexican ghost story *Even the Wind is Afraid* (1967, remade 2007), South Korea's supernatural 'Whispering Corridors' series (particularly the 1999 entry *Memento Mori*) and Jordan Scott's 2008 film *Cracks*. That female-focused films, in order to exclude men, often need to be set in institutions of one sort or another is confirmed by Mai Zetterling's borstal drama *Scrubbers* (1982), not forgetting a long procession of 'women in prison' and 'nunsploitation' potboilers. Finally, in 2005 claustrophobic confinement became literal in Neil Marshall's *The Descent*, in which a half-dozen female pot-holers encounter inhuman 'crawlers' (played largely by men) in the bowels of the earth.

So Deborah Orr's suggestion that *Powder Room* might be unique was somewhat wide of the mark. She was spot on, however, in noting that "One of the problems that arises out of the paucity of material focused on women and their lives is that when something like *Powder Room* does come along, the temptation is to see it

Above left:
Sobbing boarder Joan Dowling and 'terrible harridan' Freda Jackson in *Women of Twilight* (1952).

Above:
Annemarie von Rochhausen consoles motherless new girl Hertha Thiele in *Mädchen in Uniform* (1931).

Below:
Elizabeth Allan and Hilda Sims in Basil Dean's almost all-female *Nine Till Six* (1932).

as universal, a comment on what all women's lives are like, not just a narrative about one bunch of people in a certain place at a certain time." Here, of course, we have a double standard, for the fact that titles like *Lawrence of Arabia* (with its single, uncredited nurse) and *Reservoir Dogs* (with its 'shocked woman' and 'shot woman') are otherwise all-male is never remarked upon by anyone; apparently it's just part of the natural (male-dominated) order of things. All-female subjects, by contrast, are so scarce they become burdened with the unwonted significance referred to by Orr.

As it happens, *Powder Room* came along at a time when representations of women had once again become a hot topic. The Bechdel Test, conceived back in 1985, finally became common currency, evaluating films on the basis of whether they feature two women talking to each other about something other than a man; the results have been predictably dispiriting. In the same vein, Cate Blanchett, picking up her Oscar for *Blue Jasmine* in March 2014, used the occasion to explode the industry misconception that "female films with women at the centre are niche experiences." "They are not," she affirmed. "Audiences want to see them. In fact, they earn money." Her words echoed those of Meryl Streep, reported in *Vanity Fair* two years previously. Citing several massively successful films of recent times – including two of her own, *The Iron Lady* and *The Devil Wears Prada* – she was at a loss to understand why producers didn't make such female-targeted pictures on a routine basis: "Don't they want the money?"

As far back as 1974, Molly Haskell, in her groundbreaking book *From Reverence to Rape: The Treatment of Women in the Movies*, identified a catastrophic collapse in the value of women's roles since the female-centric heyday of the 1930s. The book's tag-line – "You've Come a Long Way, Baby … And It's All Been Downhill" – was echoed inside by the urgent question, "How will women break through the barriers of a commercial cinema more truly monolithic in its sexism than it ever was in the old days of Hollywood?"

Forty years on, with the old-fashioned phrase 'woman's picture' long since supplanted by the contemptuous 'chick flick', that monolithic sexism seems to be alive and well, with women reportedly accounting for only 28.4 per cent of the speaking roles in 2012's top 100 films. "We are in effect enculturating kids from the very beginning to see women and girls as not taking up half of the space," noted Geena Davis in *The Hollywood Reporter*.

Sexism is depressingly evident, too, in the semi-literate, hair-raisingly horrible and absolutely genuine casting briefs faithfully preserved by the pseudonymous Miss L on her website Casting Call Woe. In February 2014, for example, one employer called for "A woman who can more than hold her own in a male-dominated profession. Her cleavage is her best feature." In the same week: "Male lead – a strong, confident performer. Female lead – she doesn't have any lines." And among calls put out in late May/early June: "If you fill out a bikini nicely, this might be for you." "Male: must be comfortable speaking German. Female: must be comfortable wearing lingerie." "She doesn't require speaking experience as [she has] no dialogue and is very much supporting the male lead." Not forgetting the exploitative high-water mark: "This production will require no nudity on camera however nudity will be required on set."

For the most part, of course, these ads were placed by the UK industry's opportunistic bottom-feeders. But in higher echelons more encouraging signs can occasionally be spotted. In 2013, for example, Denmark's Nicolas Winding Refn – responding to accusations of violent misogyny in his films – told *IndieWire* that "I always set out wanting to make films about women, but it always ends up being about men. Maybe it was because I was afraid of women when I was younger … [or] maybe it's because I don't know how to write them." To combat this problem, he set up a new film for production in 2014 and gave it two distinctive features.

First, *I Walk with the Dead* is co-scripted by British playwright Polly Stenham. And second, it's all-female.

The Year in Subtitles

Mansel Stimpson reports on the year's most significant foreign language films.

The number of cinemas screening subtitled product may be limited but during 2013 such films reached us at a rate of not less than one per week. Consequently this brief overall view cannot possibly mention every title. But I hope that it will point the reader to many films noted in more detail in our review pages.

The most encouraging aspect that emerges from this deluge of films is that, while established directors continue to feature, a number of the very best films have come from filmmakers either making their feature debut or not previously known to us in Britain.

But first I will turn to the more familiar names despite the fact that their standing was not always a guarantee of a good film. Take Pedro Almodóvar, for instance: although his lightweight comedy *I'm So Excited!* may have appealed to some audiences usually not drawn to subtitled films, nobody would claim that it found him on his best form. In contrast Italy's Taviani Brothers, now octogenarians, came back into the spotlight with a totally original work, *Caesar Must Die*, centred on staging Shakespeare's *Julius Caesar* in a prison in Rome: it counts as one of the year's finest films. Also making a comeback was Bernardo Bertolucci with *Me and You*, but that was less successful. It was a pleasure, however, to

discover a new work by Margarethe von Trotta who, aided by the superb actress Barbara Sukowa (who played the title role in von Trotta's 1986 film *Rosa Luxemburg*), gave us another memorable piece about one of her real-life heroines in *Hannah Arendt*.

Not so long established but already making a name for himself in Hollywood as well as Iceland, Baltasar Kormákur impressed with *The Deep*, the true story of an Icelandic fisherman who survived a shipwreck in 1984. Furthermore, two directors came up with a couple of films each. France's prolific François Ozon gave us *In the House*, a kind of postmodern comedy which was popular, and followed it with the controversial but to my mind superior *Jeune et Jolie*, a properly disturbing view of today's arguably over-sexualised society. From Japan Kore-eda Hirokazu gave us both *I Wish*, a study of childhood overshadowed by the work of his great predecessor Ozu, and *Like Father, Like Son* which looked to be shaping up as a masterpiece until (in my eyes at least) it went on too long. Also from Japan was the film that the Iranian Abbas Kiarostami made there, *Like Someone in Love*. Here I was worried not by it going on when it should have ended but by its abrupt and indecisive close. Save for that, it is memorable as being both true to Japan and to the filmmaker.

Octogenarian brilliance: Paolo and Vittorio Taviani on the set of *Caesar Must Die*.

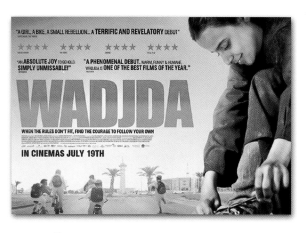

Above:
Haifa al Mansour's wonderfully sensitive *Wadjda*.

Above right:
Audrey Tautou and Gilles Lellouche in Claude Miller's final film, *Thérèse Desqueyroux*.

Below: The second instalment of Ulrich Seidl's ambitious trilogy, *Paradise: Faith*.

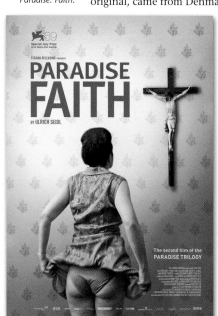

With some of the known names I have space only to list their films. Here we have Olivier Assayas (*Something in the Air*), Bruno Dumont (*Hors Satan*), Mathieu Kassovitz (*Rebellion*), Pablo Larraín (*No*), Cristian Mungiu (*Beyond the Hills*), Ferzan Ozpetek (*A Magnificent Haunting*), Carlos Reygadas (*Post Tenebras Lux*) and Pablo Trapero (*White Elephant*). Sadly I missed Andrzej Wajda's *Walesa, Man of Hope* which came and went in a twinkling.

I must also note two films from directors no longer with us. Russia's controversial Aleksey Balabanov was represented by *The Stoker* (visually striking but with the weirdest of music tracks), while France's Claude Miller bowed out with his ambitious and beautifully mounted adaptation of Mauriac's *Thérèse Desqueyroux*. An established name happily still with us is Daniel Auteuil who, having turned director with the admirable Pagnol remake *The Well-Digger's Daughter* in 2011, has now set out to do the same for Pagnol's famous Marseille trilogy. *César* has yet to appear but both *Marius* and *Fanny*, the latter by far the more successful, reached us towards the end of 2013. Another example of popular cinema, a screen original, came from Denmark in the shape of Susanne Bier's *Love is All You Need*, which partnered Pierce Brosnan with the splendid Danish actress Trine Dyrholm. Also in the popular mould, as its very title hinted, was *Populaire* from Régis Roinsard.

Before moving on to the most memorable new talents I must mention in slightly greater detail a handful of titles of particular interest. The first of these is the work which for many was the outstanding film of the year, Paolo Sorrentino's *The Great Beauty* from Italy. Here, if not quite a lone voice, I appear to be in the minority in that I found it a vacuous film about vacuous people. (Our review section reveals Michael Darvell's take on it.) I should stress that I was deeply impressed by *Il Divo* on which Sorrentino and Toni Servillo also collaborated and my possibly minority attitude swings the other way in my strong support for its predecessor, Sorrentino's much criticised *This Must Be the Place*. It is also the case that I cannot share the extreme admiration of many for the other most discussed foreign film of 2013, *Blue is the Warmest Colour*. Set in France and made by Abdellatif Kechiche, who became an international name with *Couscous*, this lesbian drama contains much that is brilliantly persuasive and the lead actresses, Léa Seydoux and Adèle Exarchopoulos, are superb. My reservations concern the extensive running time (179 minutes) and the fact that, even then, there is no sense of reaching a conclusion. The French title referred to it as being Chapters 1 and 2 so just possibly it is a case of 'to be continued'.

The other three films calling for special mention are linked, being the Paradise trilogy by the Austrian filmmaker Ulrich Seidl. This hugely ambitious work, conceived as a single project but converted into three connected films, *Paradise: Love*, *Paradise: Faith* and *Paradise: Hope*, is certainly less than perfect. But the first of the trio is stunning, albeit unsuitable for those who dislike sexually explicit material. In any case, despite some miscalculations, the trilogy is such a remarkable endeavour that it elevates Seidl's standing. I would also mention at this stage two very sympathetic gay films from lesser-known directors: from Poland Malgoska Szumowska's *In the Name of...* and from Israel Michael Mayer's *Out in the Dark*.

When it comes to new names, selling their work to the public can be a problem, especially with the number of weekly releases leading to the quick disappearance of so many titles from cinemas. Happily that was not the case with my favourite film of the year *Wadjda*, that wonderfully sensitive view of life in Saudi Arabia today from a

female perspective, with Waad Mohammed in the title role proving herself an unforgettable child actor (although truth to tell she never appears to be acting) and writer-director Haifaa al Mansour establishing her viewpoint superbly.

But many of the following films deserve to be better known. Three titles stood out not just for their quality but because they contained performances of the very highest calibre from their leading actresses. In *Child's Pose*, a Romanian film by Călin Peter Netzer, Luminita Gheorghiu had a great role: that of a mother strong enough to make us admire her initially but then revealing a domination and control that could suggest either ruthlessness or self-deception. This was truly an in-depth portrayal. Turn to *The Wall* from Austria's Julian Roman Pölsler and we have Martina Gedeck sustaining this Kafkaesque allegory while most of the time being alone on screen: it's a tour de force. No less distinguished is Golshifteh Farahani in Atiq Rahimi's *The Patience Stone* playing a woman looking after her comatose husband, a soldier wounded in a Middle East conflict. What initially seems to be a powerful anti-war film soon becomes even more tellingly a compelling view of women's position in a patriarchal society. Dealing more specifically with the situation of one young woman in a Hassidic community, Rama Burshtein's *Fill the Void*, set in Tel Aviv, contains a splendid turn from Hadas Yaron as a daughter expected to follow tradition and marry the man who, until her elder sister's death, had been her brother-in-law.

I end with a group of titles that ought not to be overlooked. Tobias Lindholm's *A Hijacking* is an impressive work from Denmark. Its subject matter links it to the Tom Hanks film *Captain Phillips*, but it offers a quite different take on the drama that ensues when a vessel in the Indian Ocean is seized by Somali pirates. The emphasis here is on the negotiations that follow and the result is a compelling and totally persuasive piece. Also powerful but decidedly downbeat is Sergei Loznitsa's Second World War tale *In the Fog*, a tragic account of the fate of Belarussians trying to survive: it's a film enhanced by the exceptional colour photography of Oleg Mutu. A period piece

of a quite different kind (the period being the 18th century) is to be found in *The Nun*, a French adaptation of Diderot's classic novel handled with absolute assurance by a filmmaker unknown to me, Guillaume Nicloux. *Winter of Discontent* is the opposite of a period piece: a view of recent events in Egypt shot when hopes were high but totally relevant to the continuing suffering of the Egyptian people. Made by Ibrahim El Batout, it uses actors but speaks with absolute authenticity and is handled with true artistry.

Art is no less apparent in Pablo Berger's *Blancanieves*, a variation on the Snow White story involving a matador in 1920s Spain. It's presented as a silent film in the manner of *The Artist* and, actually conceived first, has been unjustly overshadowed by that film. Also unlucky – but this time with the critics largely to blame – has been the woefully underestimated *Home (Yurt)*, a film from Turkey by Muzaffer Özdemir. It's less a piece of story-telling than a poetic meditation linked to environmental issues and to the state of life today. Splendidly atmospheric, there is not a shot that isn't beautifully composed.

But for the most haunting film of the year I turn to a documentary. Marc Wiese's *Camp 14 Total Control Zone* concerns Shin Donghyuk who was born in captivity in North Korea in 1983 and grew up knowing no other conditions and therefore accepting that lifestyle as normal. It is a remarkable story presented most movingly by Wiese who introduces no gimmicks into this true tale but handles it with a sensitivity that makes his film a work of art. It is certainly the best documentary of the year but also one of the best 2013 releases of any kind.

Above left:
A tour de force from Martina Gedeck in *The Wall*.

Above:
The splendidly atmospheric *Home (Yurt)* came from Turkey.

Below:
Most haunting film of the year – *Camp 14 Total Control Zone*.

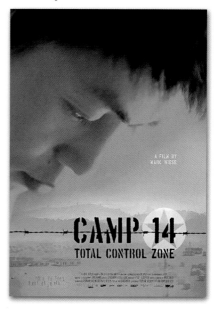

Joan Fontaine (see page 186)

In Memoriam

2013

by **Jonathan Rigby**

Given the hundreds of film personalities who died during 2013, the following selection of just 70 is, inevitably, a purely personal one. Pressure of space has excluded numerous important people, over 250 of whom are noted in supplements to the main entries.

RONA ANDERSON
Born: *3 August 1926, Edinburgh, Scotland.*
Died: *23 July 2013, London, England.*
This engaging Scottish actress moved, post-war, from the Glasgow Citizens Theatre into a long string of British second features. She began and ended with 'A' films – *Sleeping Car to Trieste* in 1948 and *The Prime of Miss Jean Brodie* some 20 years later. But more typical were such titles as *The 20 Questions Murder Mystery*, *Whispering Smith Hits London*, *The Black Rider*, *Soho Incident* and *Devils of Darkness*. In 2009 she was an apt choice as cover star of the BFI book *The British 'B' Film*. "I wish we could see more of these films today," she wrote inside, "as those we do see on television so often look better than we thought at the time. Looking back, I think what a great lark it all was – and what a great life."

VIVI BACH
Born: *3 September 1939, Copenhagen, Denmark.*
Died: *22 April 2013, Ibiza, Spain.*
Vivi Bach made her debut in *Krudt og klunker* in 1957 and within a couple of years had made the transition to German and Austrian films, gaining fame as 'die dänische Bardot'. Many of her showcases, notably *Kriminaltango* and *Schlager-Raketen* (both 1960), were anodyne musical comedies, though she journeyed further afield to star in Italian spy spoofs (*The Spy with Ten Faces*), sex comedies (*Love Italian Style*) and Westerns (*Bullets Don't Argue*). Her German celebrity prompted the British entrepreneur Harry Alan Towers to feature her in two of his mid-1960s multi-national potboilers, *Death Drums Along the River* and *Mozambique*. In similar vein, she also appeared in Curt Siodmak's *Ski Fever* and Val Guest's *Assignment K*, later becoming a game-show host.

❧ Comic actor **Eddi Arent** appeared with Bach in two *Schlagerparade* films but was better known for Euro-Westerns and Edgar Wallace thrillers; he died in May, aged 88. British DJ **Chris Howland**, who acted with Bach and Arent in *Schlagerparade 1961*, died in November at 85; another regular in krimis and Westerns, he also starred in a couple of films for Jesús

Vivi Bach

Franco [qv]. Other German actors who died in 2013 included **Jack Recknitz** and **Peter Fitz** (both in January, both 81), **Otto Sander** (September, 72) and **Hans von Borsody** (November, 84).

ALEKSEY BALABANOV
Born: *25 February 1959, Sverdlovsk, USSR.*
Died: *18 May 2013, Saint Petersburg, Russia.*
Undoubtedly the most confrontational of Russia's post-Soviet writer-directors, Aleksey Balabanov began his feature career with adaptations of Samuel Beckett (*Happy Days*) and Franz Kafka (*The Castle*), after which his world-view only became darker and more scabrous. His explosively populist late-1990s breakthrough movies – superficially likened to Quentin Tarantino – were the gangster melodramas *Brat* and *Brat-2*, between which he wrong-footed audiences with a subversive, sepia-tinted study of pioneer pornographers, *Of Freaks and Men*. Routinely attracting equal parts adoration and outrage with films like *War* and *Morphia*, he reached a divisive peak with the ersatz horror picture *Cargo 200*, a uniquely disturbing anatomisation of Soviet corruption

Karen Black

Antonia Bird

derived from William Faulkner. Balabanov – who, though not short of awards, was strangely ignored by the major festivals – signed off with *The Stoker* (reviewed on page 148) and, in 2012, *Not Me*.

❧ A taboo-breaking Russian director of an earlier generation, **Pyotr Todorovsky** (whose 1983 film *Wartime Romance* was nominated for an Oscar), died aged 87 the week after Balabanov. Other international directors who died in 2013 included Mexico's **Marcel Sisniega** (53) in January, South Korea's **Park Cheul-soo** (66) and Croatia's **Krsto Papić** (79), both in February, Germany's **Peter Sehr** (61) in May and Poland's **Ewa Petelska** (92) in August. Cuban **Daniel Díaz Torres** (64) and Bulgarian **Rangel Vulchanov** (84) both died in September, followed by Norway's **Haakon Sandberg** (89) and Hungary's **Gyula Maár** (79) in December. Czechoslovakia lost **Jiří Krejĉík** (August, 95) and **Peter Solan** (September, 84) and Romania **Sergiu Nicolaescu** (January, 82), **Geo Saizescu** (September, 80) and **Dinu Cocea** (December, 84).

NORMA BENGELL

Born: *21 September 1935, Rio de Janeiro, Brazil.*
Died: *9 October 2013, Rio de Janeiro, Brazil.*
Norma Bengell first appeared in the 1959 comedy *O homem do Sputnik* and three years later starred in one of the key titles in Brazil's Cinema Novo movement. Ruy Guerra's *Os Cafajestes* was also significant in that it included an extraordinarily protracted beach scene showing Bengell frontally nude – reputedly a world 'first' for a name actor. Another of her 1962 releases, *Keeper of Promises*, was an Oscar-nominated Palme d'Or winner. Marrying actor Gabriele Tinti, she moved to Italy and made such films as Alberto Lattuada's

Mafioso, Mario Bava's *Planet of the Vampires* and Sergio Corbucci's *Hellbenders*. Returning to Brazil, she received an APCA Trophy for the 1970 film *A casa assassinada*, winning three further awards prior to her retirement from features in 1993. She also directed two films, *Eternamente Pagu* (1987) and *O Guarani* (1996).

❧ Other Brazilian performers who died in 2013 included **Walmor Chagas** (82), **Lídia Mattos** (88) and **Zózimo Bulbul** (75), all in January. Chile's **Pablo Krögh** died at 50 in September, while Argentina lost **Patricia Castell** (September, 87), **Aldo Barbero** (October, 80) and, in December, **Nya Quesada** (94) and **Duilio Marzio** (89).

ANTONIA BIRD

Born: *27 May 1951, London, England.*
Died: *24 October 2013, London, England.*
In the mid-1980s, director Antonia Bird moved from the Royal Court Theatre to the BBC, where her work on *EastEnders* and *Casualty* prefigured her hard-hitting approach to such socially conscious TV dramas as *Safe* (1993), *Care* (2000) and *Rehab* (2003). Between the two BAFTA awards she received for *Safe* and *Care* she made her feature debut in 1994 with *Priest* (which, though made for Screen Two, was released theatrically). From this powerful anatomisation of the Catholic church she proved her versatility with the Hollywood teen runaway drama *Mad Love* (1995), the British mockney gangster thriller *Face* (1997) and her final film, the demented cannibal shocker *Ravenous* (1999). Returning to TV, her later work included the feature-length 9/11 drama *The Hamburg Cell* (2004).

KAREN BLACK

Born: *1 July 1939, Park Ridge, Illinois, USA.*
Died: *8 August 2013, Los Angeles, California, USA.*
Ranking high among the most compelling actors brought to prominence in the New Hollywood of the early 1970s, Karen Black first made an impact in Francis Coppola's 1966 film *You're a Big Boy Now.*

Les Blank

Eileen Brennan

Thereafter, from 1969 to 1977 the iconic titles, and performances, just kept coming – *Easy Rider*, an Oscar nomination and Golden Globe for *Five Easy Pieces*, *Drive He Said*, *Cisco Pike*, *Portnoy's Complaint*, *The Outfit*, *The Great Gatsby* (another Golden Globe), *The Day of the Locust*, *Nashville*, the TV movie *Trilogy of Terror*, *Family Plot*, *Burnt Offerings*, *Capricorn One*, even the fondly remembered *Airport 1975*. There were also early '80s high spots like *Come Back to the 5 and Dime, Jimmy Dean, Jimmy Dean* and *Can She Bake a Cherry Pie?* Exploitation films predominated in Black's latter years, notably the 2003 release *House of 1000 Corpses*.

LES BLANK
Born: *27 November 1935, Tampa, Florida, USA.*
Died: *7 April 2013, Berkeley, California, USA.*
Having made the 20-minute documentary *Werner Herzog Eats His Shoe* in 1979, Les Blank won a BAFTA four years later for the feature-length *Burden of Dreams*, in which he chronicled the freakishly embattled production of Herzog's *Fitzcarraldo* in the Peruvian jungle. Yet Blank's ethnographic style – humane, often whimsical, always intimately observed – was generally focused on far less high-profile subjects, pockets of fringe Americana exemplified by the marginalised musicians of *A Well Spent Life* and *Chulas Fronteras*, the food and drink fixations of *Garlic is as Good as Ten Mothers* and *All in This Tea*, and the outsider communities of *Dry Wood*, *Hot Pepper* and *God Respects Us When We Work But He Loves Us When We Dance*. He was the recipient of Lifetime Achievement awards in 1990 and 2011.

❧ Blank's British contemporary **Michael Grigsby** died, aged 76, in March, just a few weeks before the release of his final film, *We Went to War*. (See page 163.) Austrian underwater explorer **Hans Hass**, famous for the prize-winning 1951 film *Under the Red Sea* and numerous collaborations with his wife Lotte, died at 94 in June. Among American documentarists, **Peter**

Thompson (68), **Jean Bach** (94) and **William Miles** (82) all died in May, **Bert Stern** (83) in June, **Saul Landau** (77) in September and **Ed Pincus** (75) in November. Australian **Dennis O'Rourke**, winner of three AFI awards, died at 67 in June.

EILEEN BRENNAN
Born: *3 September 1932, Los Angeles, California, USA.*
Died: *28 July 2013, Burbank, California, USA.*
Having appeared in the original Broadway production of *Hello, Dolly!* in 1964, Eileen Brennan made her first film, *Divorce American Style*, three years later. After a BAFTA nomination for her jaded waitress, Genevieve, in Peter Bogdanovich's *The Last Picture Show* (1971), she followed up with *Scarecrow*, *The Sting*, *Daisy Miller*, *At Long Last Love*, *Hustle*, *Murder by Death*, *The Cheap Detective* and *FM*. Her corncrake voice and deliciously pugnacious style were best showcased as the comic tyrant Captain Doreen Lewis in *Private Benjamin* (1980); the film brought her an Oscar nomination, with an Emmy and a Golden Globe reserved for the subsequent TV spin-off. After a severe car accident in 1982, her later roles included *Clue*, *Stella*, *Texasville* (as Genevieve again), *White Palace* and *Jeepers Creepers*.

❧ Other US actresses who died in 2013 included **Barbara Werle** (in January, aged 84), **Donna Anderson** (March, 74), **Christine White** (86), **Virginia Gibson** (85) and **Jacqueline Brookes** (82), all in April, **Jeanne Cooper** (84) and **Helen Hanft** (79), both in May, **Barbara Trentham** (August, 68), **Patricia Blair** (originally Patricia Blake, 82), **Kim Hamilton**

Patrice Chéreau

Louise Currie

(81), **Marta Heflin** (68) and **Jane Connell** (87), all in September, **Mary Carver** (October, 89), **Barbara Lawrence** (83, November) and **Sheila Guyse** (88, December). **Susan Douglas**, Austrian-born actress in the US and Canada, died at 87 in January and French-Canadian actress **Hélène Loiselle** at 85 in August.

ALAN BRIDGES
Born: *28 September 1927, Liverpool, England.*
Died: *7 December 2013, [location unknown], England.*
Beginning as an actor, Alan Bridges switched rapidly to directing and in the 1960s became a major figure in the BBC's *Wednesday Play* and *Play for Today* strands. He also squeezed in eight feature films, starting at Merton Park in 1964-65 with the Edgar Wallace 'B' feature *Act of Murder* and the SF curio *Invasion*. More momentously, his 1973 film *The Hireling* won him the Palme d'Or at Cannes; its waspish elegance was echoed in the 1980s by two further period pieces, *The Return of the Soldier* and *The Shooting Party*. In between he went to Dorset for *Out of Season* (1974), Ontario for *Age of Innocence* (1976) and France for *La petite fille en velours bleu* (1978). His last film, *Apt Pupil* (1987), was abandoned mid-shooting for lack of funds.

❖ British TV director **Jim Goddard**, whose three features included *Shanghai Surprise* (1986), died in June, aged 77. Theatre director **Patrick Garland**, whose sole feature credit was *A Doll's House* in 1973, died at 78 in April. **Peter Maxwell**, director of several British second features and a number of Australian films, also died in April, aged 92. Other British filmmakers who died in 2013 included three-time

BAFTA-winning editor **Gerry Hambling** (February, 86), Oscar- and BAFTA-winning production designer **Brian Ackland-Snow** (March, 72), film and sound editor **David Campling** (May, 74) and Oscar-winning set decorator **Stephenie McMillan** (71, August).

PATRICE CHÉREAU
Born: *2 November 1944, Lézigné, France.*
Died: *7 October 2013, Paris, France.*
As well as his directorship of several distinguished French theatre companies, Patrice Chéreau revolutionised opera production with his 1976 *Ring* cycle at Bayreuth. On top of all this, he directed ten feature films, starting with the lurid James Hadley Chase adaptation *The Flesh of the Orchid* in 1974. Discussions of his work inevitably centre around his grandiloquent international hit *La Reine Margot*, which in 1994 sparked off a French vogue for lavish historical epics, and the 'unsimulated sex' controversy surrounding his single English-language film, *Intimacy* (2001). But there were several other striking titles too, among them *Judith Therpauve, L'Homme blessé, Those Who Love Me Can Take the Train, Son frère, Gabrielle* and *Persécution*. A two-time César winner, he also acted in such films as *Adieu Bonaparte* and *The Last of the Mohicans*.

LOUISE CURRIE
Born: *7 April 1913, Oklahoma City, Oklahoma, USA.*
Died: *8 September 2013, Santa Monica, California, USA.*
In 1940, regal-looking Louise Currie had an uncredited but eye-catching role in the Karloff-Lugosi-Lorre comedy *You'll Find Out* and took a moment to pop over to another RKO soundstage to play a Rosebud-querying reporter in *Citizen Kane*. But small – indeed, Poverty Row – films were to be her bread and butter. Her numerous 'B' Westerns included *The Pinto Kid, Dude Cowboy* and *Gun Town*, and she got to act opposite Bela Lugosi again in the imperishable Monogram chillers

The Ape Man and *Voodoo Man*. ("Monogram called me their Katharine Hepburn," she claimed in 1988.) For Republic, meanwhile, she was the female lead in the highly regarded serials *Adventures of Captain Marvel* and *The Masked Marvel*. Retiring in the mid-1950s, she became a successful interior decorator.

❧ Other centenarians who died in 2013 included Márta Eggerth [qv], Oscar-winning French costume designer **Rosine Delamare** (in March, aged 101), Puerto Rico's 'Latin Bombshell' **Diosa Costello** (June, 100), Chinese writer-director **Chen Liting** (August, 102), actor-magician **John Calvert** (September, also 102) and, in December, Argentina's actress-singer **Nelly Omar** (102) and 103-year-old US producer **Ted Richmond**. Spanish writer-director **Miguel Morayta**, a key figure in the Golden Age of Mexican cinema, died at 105 in June.

DAMIANO DAMIANI

Born: *23 July 1922, Pasiano di Pordenone, Italy.*
Died: *7 March 2013, Rome, Italy.*
This eclectic writer-director bookended the 1960s with tough crime dramas (*Lipstick* and *The Hit Man* at one end, *Mafia* and *The Most Beautiful Wife* at the other), filling in with adaptations from Elsa Morante and Alberto Moravia (*Arturo's Island*, *The Empty Canvas*) together with a cerebral Gothic (*The Witch in Love*) and a seminal Euro-Western (*A Bullet for the General*). Successful 1970s thrillers like *Confessions of a Police Commissioner* and *A Man on His Knees* (starring Giuliano Gemma, qv) led to his smash 1984 Mafia mini-series *The Octopus*, and in the meantime Dino De Laurentiis sponsored his sole Hollywood film, the gaudily exploitative *Amityville II: The Possession* (1982). His last of eight international awards, a 1987 David, went to the Messianic mystery *The Inquiry*, and 15 years later he bowed out, aged 79, with *Killers on Holiday*.

❧ Other Italian writer-directors who died in 2013 included **Giancarlo Zagni** (in March, aged 86), **Luciano Martino** (also a prolific producer; in August, 79) and two-time David winner **Luigi Magni** (October, 85). Another two-time David winner, **Carlo Lizzani** (who was also Oscar-nominated in 1951 for *Bitter Rice*) died in October at 91. Cinematographer **Marcello Gatti** – who worked once with Damiano but was best known for his three collaborations with Gillo Pontecorvo – died aged 89 in November.

NIGEL DAVENPORT

Born: *23 May 1928, Great Shelford, Cambridgeshire, England.*
Died: *25 October 2013, [location unknown], Gloucestershire, England.*
Too preoccupied with the Stratford Memorial Theatre and English Stage Company to bother much with films, the formidable figure of Nigel Davenport nevertheless popped up in such early pictures as *Peeping Tom*, *The Entertainer* and *Ladies Who Do*. Then, starting with *A High Wind in Jamaica* in 1965, he had a pretty remarkable 20-year run as an in-demand

character star, racking up such credits as *A Man for All Seasons*, *Play Dirty*, *Sinful Davey*, *The Last Valley*, *Villain*, *Mary Queen of Scots*, *Charley-One-Eye*, *Stand Up Virgin Soldiers*, *The Island of Dr Moreau*, *Zulu Dawn*, *Chariots of Fire*, *Nighthawks*, *Greystoke* and *Caravaggio*. In addition he gained top billing in three early 1970s titles, *No Blade of Grass*, *Living Free* and *Phase IV*.

❧ Other British actors who died in 2013 included **Bernard Horsfall** (in January, aged 82), **Robin Sachs** (61), **Peter Gilmore** (81) and **Richard Briers** (79), all in February, **Frank Thornton** (March, 92), **Nosher Powell** (84) and **Norman Jones** (78), both in April, **Aubrey Woods** (85) and **Bill Pertwee** (86), both in May, **Paul Bhattacharjee** (July, 53), **Bill Wallis** (September, 76), **Paul Rogers** (96) and **Graham Stark** (91), both in October, **Lewis Collins** (November, 67) and, in December, **Barry Jackson** (75) and **John Fortune** (74). **Arthur Malet** (85: British actor working in the US) and **Richard LeParmentier** (66: American actor working in the UK) died in April and May.

DEANNA DURBIN

Born: *4 December 1921, Winnipeg, Manitoba, Canada.*
Died: *20 April 2013, Neauphle-le-Château, Yvelines, France.*
Deanna Durbin's special 1939 Oscar was for "bringing to the screen the spirit and personification of youth." It was this spirit – rejected by MGM – that saved an 'under new management' Universal from financial disaster. Durbin's fresh-faced vivacity and marvellous singing voice were first showcased in *Three Smart Girls* (1936), after which she scored hit after hit – *One Hundred Men and a Girl*, *Mad About Music*, *That Certain Age*, *First Love*, *It's a Date*, *Spring Parade*, *Nice Girl?*, *It Started with Eve* and more. There was just one

Nigel Davenport

Deanna Durbin

colour film, _Can't Help Singing_ (1945), flanked by two surprising ventures into film noir, _Christmas Holiday_ and _Lady on a Train_. But the star of the 1939 sequel _Three Smart Girls Grow Up_ was acutely conscious of not being allowed to, so after _For the Love of Mary_ (1948) she retired to France.

❧ **Patty Andrews**, one-third of the Universal-contracted wartime singing stars the Andrews Sisters, died at 94 in January. The 1950s recording star **Patti Page**, who had a few film roles in the following decade, also died in January, aged 85.

MÁRTA EGGERTH

Born: _17 April 1912, Budapest, Hungary._
Died: _26 December 2013, Rye, New York, USA._
The queen of Viennese operetta, Márta Eggerth's dazzling coloratura soprano was first heard in cinemas just after her 18th birthday. In those days of films being made in alternate versions for different markets, she soon became a truly international star, defying language barriers by effectively starring in the same film several times over. Britain's _Where is This Lady?_ was the same as Germany's _Es war einmal ein Walzer_, for example, just as Italy's _Casta diva_ was replicated with a British cast as _The Divine Spark_. Fleeing the Nazis, she fetched up at MGM in Hollywood, where playing second fiddle to Judy Garland in _For Me and My Gal_ and _Presenting Lily Mars_ was not to her taste. Post-war she starred with her husband, Jan Kiepura, in a few French, Italian and German pictures, finally retiring from films in 1957.

❧ Opera singer **Risë Stevens**, who in the 1940s starred with Nelson Eddy in _The Chocolate Soldier_ and Bing Crosby in _Going My Way_, died at 99 in March.

ROSSELLA FALK

Born: _10 November 1926, Rome, Italy._
Died: _5 May 2013, Rome, Italy._
Rossella Falk's 2006 autobiography was entitled _L'ultima diva_, a suitably grandiose choice for the regal actress known to Italian theatregoers as 'la Greta Garbo italiana'. Sadly, her stage celebrity precluded much in the way of a film career, though her first credit was in 1948 and her CV included a substantial role in Fellini's _8½_. She was accordingly cast in two English-language films, Joseph Losey's _Modesty Blaise_ (as scintillating villainess Mrs Fothergill) and as Peter Finch's heroin-addicted companion in Robert Aldrich's _The Legend of Lylah Clare_. She also played Jane Birkin's mother in _May Morning_ and in the early 1970s was well suited to several giallo thrillers (_Black Belly of the Tarantula_, _The Fifth Cord_, _Seven Blood-Stained Orchids_, _The Killer is on the Phone_), a mode she returned to for her last feature, _Sleepless_ (2000).

❧ Another Italian stage star, **Regina Bianchi**, who won Silver Ribbon awards for _The Four Days of Naples_ (1962) and _Camerieri_ (1994), died in April, aged 92. Yet another, **Anna Proclemer** (winner of an honorary Ribbon in 2012), died at 89 the same month.

JOAN FONTAINE

Born: _22 October 1917, Tokyo, Japan._
Died: _15 December 2013, Carmel, California, USA._
This fine-boned British beauty, younger sister of Olivia de Havilland, got her start in Hollywood in such late-1930s films as _Quality Street_, _A Damsel in Distress_,

Márta Eggerth

Gunga Din and *The Women*, though all these were really just a prelude to her career-making performance in Alfred Hitchcock's *Rebecca*. Oscar-nominated for her performance, in 1941 she brought the same appealing fragility to another Hitchcock film, *Suspicion*, and this time the Oscar was hers. She was also a natural for *The Constant Nymph* (another Oscar nomination) and *Jane Eyre* in 1943, subsequently sustaining her star career through such disparate titles as *Ivy*, *Born to be Bad*, *Ivanhoe*, *The Bigamist*, *Serenade*, *A Certain Smile*, *Tender is the Night* and finally, in 1966, *The Witches*. Her best film, however – produced by her own company – was Max Ophüls' sublime 1948 masterwork *Letter from an Unknown Woman*.

BRYAN FORBES

Born: *22 July 1926, London, England.*
Died: *8 May 2013, Virginia Water, Surrey, England.*
A major force in British cinema, Bryan Forbes started as an actor in such films as *An Inspector Calls*, *The Colditz Story* and *Quatermass 2*. His Oscar-nominated, BAFTA-winning script for *The Angry Silence* (1960) was followed by *The League of Gentlemen* and *Only Two Can Play*, then he turned director with *Whistle Down the Wind*. Further monochrome gems – *The L-Shaped Room*, *Seance on a Wet Afternoon*, *King Rat*, *The Whisperers* – alternated with colourful divertissements like *The Wrong Box* and *Deadfall*, then in 1969 he became head of production at EMI-MGM Elstree Studios. An unhappy two years in this role, yielding his own project *The Raging Moon*, was followed by freelance assignments like *The Stepford Wives*, *International Velvet* and, in 1984, *The Naked Face*. His final work, co-writing the 1992 film *Chaplin*, was followed in 2007 by a BAFTA Lifetime Achievement award.

JESÚS FRANCO

Born: *12 May 1930, Madrid, Spain.*
Died: *2 April 2013, Málaga, Andalucía, Spain.*
US critic Tim Lucas once said, "You can't see one

Bryan Forbes

Jess Franco film until you've seen them all." This is a daunting prospect, not merely because the Franco filmography tops the 200 mark but because there are many who'll tell you his films are unwatchable. With such a prolific writer-director there are, inevitably, areas where you have to tread carefully, notably the 1980s period dubbed by Lucas the 'Porno Holocaust' years. But the man was a true original, creating in his better films a bizarrely atmospheric fusion of sex and horror that is absolutely unique. Among these is Spain's first horror film, *The Awful Dr Orlof*, in 1961, together with *Succubus*, *Venus in Furs*, *De Sade 70*, *El Conde Drácula*, *Vampyros Lesbos*, *She Killed in Ecstasy*, *La Comtesse perverse*, *Lorna the Exorcist* and the outrageous 1987 *Orlof* retread *Faceless*.

❧ French actress **Françoise Blanchard**, who worked not only for Franco but also his French and Italian counterparts Jean Rollin and Bruno Mattei, died in May, aged 58.

STUART FREEBORN

Born: *5 September 1914, London, England.*
Died: *5 February 2013, London, England.*
The young Stuart Freeborn arrived at Denham Studios as a trainee make-up artist in 1935. From finessing such beauties as Annabella, Marlene Dietrich and Vivien Leigh he achieved notoriety in 1948 with his uniquely grotesque Fagin make-up for *Oliver Twist*. Though nearly killed in a Sri Lankan car accident while making another David Lean film, *The Bridge on the River Kwai*, he bounced back with several versions of Peter Sellers in Stanley Kubrick's *Dr Strangelove* and perfected the revolutionary ape suits for Kubrick's *2001*. His supreme mastery of creature effects was then confirmed by iconic characters like Chewbacca and Yoda (something of a self-portrait) in the initial *Star Wars* films. Other credits included *Oh! What a Lovely War*, *Murder on the Orient Express*, *The Omen*, *Superman* and *Top Secret!*

Jesús Franco

David Frost

Annette Funicello

> Three weeks Funicello's junior, **Mikki Jamison** – who also featured in *Ski Party*, plus a handful of other films – died in June, aged 70.

JAMES GANDOLFINI

Born: *18 September 1961, Westwood, New Jersey, USA.*
Died: *19 June 2013, Rome, Italy.*
Having appeared uncredited in Tony Scott's *The Last Boy Scout* in 1991, James Gandolfini first made an impact on audiences two years later, playing hit man Virgil in Scott's *True Romance*. He remained faithful to Scott in later years, appearing for him in *Crimson Tide* (1995) and *The Taking of Pelham 123* (2009). In the meantime his brilliant performance as gang leader Tony Soprano in the smash HBO series *The Sopranos* (1999-2007) had brought him international superstar status and three Emmy awards. Claiming to be "just like a 260lb Woody Allen" rather than the brooding heavies he was normally called upon to play, his other film appearances included *Terminal Velocity*, *Get Shorty*, *Fallen*, *8MM*, *All the King's Men*, *Killing Them Softly*, *Zero Dark Thirty* and *Enough Said* (reviewed on page 58).

> Also seen in *Get Shorty* was character star **Dennis Farina**, who died at 69 in July. Other US actors who died in 2013 included **Lou Myers** (February, 77), **Robert Nichols** (March, 88), **Linden Chiles** (May, 80), **Dennis Burkley** (July, 67), **Ed Lauter** (74) and **Jon Locke** (86), both in October, **Al Ruscio** (November, 89) and, all in December, **Christopher Evan Welch** (48), **Joseph Ruskin** (89) and **James Avery** (65). Canadian-born actors **Conrad Bain** (89) and **August Schellenberg** (77) died in January and August respectively.

GIULIANO GEMMA

Born: *2 September 1938, Rome, Italy.*
Died: *1 October 2013, Civitavecchia, Italy.*
A keen athlete, Giuliano Gemma initially intended to be a stunt man, though his heartthrob good looks soon diverted him towards acting. Brief appearances in *Ben-Hur* and *The Leopard* alternated with numerous

DAVID FROST

Born: *7 April 1939, Tenterden, Kent, England.*
Died: *31 August 2013, MS Queen Elizabeth (at sea)*
Knighted in 1993, this inquisitorial titan of British broadcasting first came to prominence some 30 years earlier as the youthful satirist of BBC TV's *That Was the Week That Was*. Around the same time, he appeared – as, appropriately, 'Reporter' – in Anthony Asquith's *The V.I.P.s*. Taking his own middle name for his various Paradine companies, Frost turned film producer in the 1970s with such titles as *Futtocks End*, *The Rise and Rise of Michael Rimmer*, *Rentadick*, *Charley-One-Eye*, *Leadbelly* and *The Slipper and the Rose* (directed by Bryan Forbes, qv), resurrecting this sideline for the millennial titles *Rogue Trader*, *In Your Dreams* and *Retreat*. *Frost/Nixon*, a fanciful riff on his 1977 interview with the former US President, was a 2006 play and 2008 film in which Frost was portrayed by Michael Sheen.

ANNETTE FUNICELLO

Born: *22 October 1942, Utica, New York, USA.*
Died: *8 April 2013, Bakersfield, California, USA.*
Annette Funicello was a bracingly wholesome idol to US baby-boomers twice over, first as a teen 'Mouseketeer' in Disney's 1955-58 TV series *The Mickey Mouse Club*, then as the pretty protagonist of a handful of 1960s beach movies. Her earliest films, *The Shaggy Dog* and *Babes in Toyland*, were under the Disney wing, after which she was farmed out to AIP for *Beach Party*, *Muscle Beach Party*, *Bikini Beach*, *Pajama Party*, *Beach Blanket Bingo*, *Ski Party*, *How to Stuff a Wild Bikini* and *Fireball 500*, starring with Frankie Avalon throughout. She recorded several hit singles too. Other films included *Thunder Alley* and the Monkees vehicle *Head*, with a fondly satirical Avalon reunion, *Back to the Beach*, cropping up as late as 1987.

Giuliano Gemma

Richard Griffiths

peplum (sword-and-sandal) pictures, among them
Messalina, *Two Gladiators* and *Revolt of the Praetorians*.
With the 1965 release *A Pistol for Ringo*, however, he
became a key figure in the Western all'italiana genre,
providing a homegrown riposte to Clint Eastwood
in such titles as *The Return of Ringo*, *Arizona Colt*, *Day
of Anger* and *Alive or Preferably Dead*. Diversifying in
the late 1970s into more complex roles, he appeared
in *Desert of the Tartars*, *Il prefetto di ferro* and *Corleone*,
winning a David award for the first. Working
consistently in later years, he bowed out in 2011
with Woody Allen's *To Rome with Love*.

❧ Other Italian actors who died in 2013 included
Ennio Girolami (February, 78), **Carlo Monni** (May,
69), **Aldo Massasso** (October, 80) and **Antonio Allocca**
(December, 76).

BOB GODFREY
Born: *27 January 1921, West Maitland, New South Wales,
Australia.*
Died: *21 February 2013, [location unknown], England.*
Britain's master cartoonist and animator may have been
best known for the evergreen BBC series *Roobarb* (1974)
and *Henry's Cat* (1983), but his career stretched right
back to the Gaumont-British Animation unit in the
1940s. Delightfully whimsical early works like *Polygamous
Polonius* and *The Rise and Fall of Emily Sprod* were followed
in the 1970s by a quartet of satirical sex cartoons – the
BAFTA-winning *Henry 9 'til 5*, the Oscar-nominated *Kama
Sutra Rides Again* (part-financed by the Boulting Brothers),
Dear Margery Boobs (lampooning agony aunt Marjorie
Proops) and the Oscar-nominated *Dream Doll*. In the
midst of all this his 1975 masterpiece *GREAT (Isambard
Kingdom Brunel)* won both an Oscar and a BAFTA. In
1994 *Small Talk* brought yet another Oscar nomination,
and five years later his last film, *Millennium the Musical*,
sprinted through 1000 years in 22 minutes.

❧ Three other key British animators died in 2013 –
Jack Stokes (*Yellow Submarine*) in March at 92, **John**

David Wilson (*Shinbone Alley*) at 93 in June, and **Harold
Whitaker** (*Animal Farm*) in December, also at 93. Canada's
two-time Oscar winning animator **Frédéric Back** (*The
Man Who Planted Trees*) died aged 89 in December, and
America's **Ed Levitt** (*Gay Purr-ee*) at 96 in April.

RICHARD GRIFFITHS
Born: *31 July 1947, Thornaby-on-Tees, Yorkshire, England.*
Died: *28 March 2013, Coventry, West Midlands, England.*
Richard Griffiths made his first film, *It Shouldn't Happen
to a Vet*, in 1975, a year before joining the Royal
Shakespeare Company. As his stage celebrity took
flight, there was room in the 1980s for further films
– *The French Lieutenant's Woman*, *Gandhi*, *Gorky Park*,
Greystoke, *A Private Function*, *Shanghai Surprise*
and his cult performance as Uncle Monty in *Withnail
and I*. After a Hollywood flirtation in the early 1990s
(*The Naked Gun 2½*, *Blame It on the Bellboy*, *Guarding
Tess*), he bounced back in the 21st century as Uncle
Vernon Dursley in five of the eight *Harry Potter* films.
His most famous latterday role, however, was Hector
in Alan Bennett's *The History Boys*, which brought him
Olivier and Tony awards on stage (2004-06) and
a BAFTA nomination on film (2007).

HAJI
Born: *24 January 1946, Quebec, Canada.*
Died: *9 August 2013, Oxnard, California, USA.*
Born Barbarella Catton, Haji had just the right exotic
looks and eye-popping figure to interest 'nudie-cutie'
maestro Russ Meyer. Accordingly, aged just 19, she
starred in his 1965 cult classics *Motorpsycho!* and *Faster,
Pussycat! Kill! Kill!* Becoming an indispensable part of
the Meyer team behind the camera as well as in front
of it, she went on to appear in *Good Morning … and
Goodbye!*, *Beyond the Valley of the Dolls* and finally, in

1974, *Supervixens*. Apart from John Cassavetes' 1975 film *The Killing of a Chinese Bookie*, her remaining credits were all in sexploitation vein, including *Wham! Bam! Thank You Spaceman*, *Ilsa Harem Keeper of the Oil Sheiks* and, in the 21st century, *The Double-D Avenger*.

◆ **Roger Ebert**, celebrated American film critic and screenwriter of Meyer's *Beyond the Valley of the Dolls*, died in April, aged 70.

JULIE HARRIS

Born: *2 December 1925, Grosse Pointe Park, Michigan, USA.*
Died: *24 August 2013, West Chatham, Massachusetts, USA.*
A six-time Tony winner, Julie Harris made her Broadway debut aged 19 and only bowed out at 71. Her first major successes, *The Member of the Wedding* and *I Am a Camera*, were duly adapted for the screen, the former bringing her a 1952 Oscar nomination. After co-starring mid-decade with James Dean in *East of Eden*, she waited till the 1960s for her next worthwhile film roles, in *The Haunting*, *Harper*, *You're a Big Boy Now* and *Reflections in a Golden Eye*. Typifying her apparently contradictory blend of nerviness and serenity, the first and last of these mysteriously failed to attract any award nominations. From 1970, films were few – among them, *The People Next Door*, *The Hiding Place*, *Voyage of the Damned*, *Gorillas in the Mist*, *HouseSitter* and *The Dark Half*. She made her last, *The Lightkeepers*, in 2009.

Julie Harris

Ray Harryhausen

RAY HARRYHAUSEN

Born: *29 June 1920, Los Angeles, California, USA.*
Died: *7 May 2013, London, England.*
Without question the premier mythmaker of post-war fantasy cinema, Ray Harryhausen became fixated on *King Kong* aged 13 and by the late 1940s was collaborating with *Kong* animator Willis O'Brien on *Mighty Joe Young*. Going it alone, his stop-motion brilliance created the revived Rhedosaur of *The Beast from 20,000 Fathoms* (1953). Thereafter, with the exception of Irwin Allen's *The Animal World* and Hammer's *One Million Years BC*, he worked exclusively with producer Charles H Schneer, perfecting the monstrous wonders of, among others, *It Came from Beneath the Sea*, *20 Million Miles to Earth*, *The 7th Voyage of Sinbad*, *Mysterious Island*, *Jason and the Argonauts*, *First Men in the Moon*, *The Valley of Gwangi*, *The Golden Voyage of Sinbad*, *Sinbad and the Eye of the Tiger* and finally, in 1981, *Clash of the Titans*. He received an honorary Oscar in 1992.

ANTHONY HINDS

Born: *19 September 1922, Ruislip, Middlesex, England.*
Died: *30 September 2013, Oxford, Oxfordshire, England.*
The driving force, creatively speaking, behind the phenomenal success of Hammer Film Productions, writer-producer Anthony Hinds joined the company straight after the war and inaugurated a policy of filming economically in country houses rather than conventional studios. In 1955, another canny policy – that of choosing pre-sold subjects – gave Hammer a huge hit with *The Quatermass Xperiment*, after which Hinds steered Terence Fisher's *The Curse of Frankenstein* and *Dracula* to international notoriety. In 1960, adopting the pen name John Elder, he wrote his first script, *The Curse of the Werewolf*, keeping his hand in thereafter with such intriguingly outré

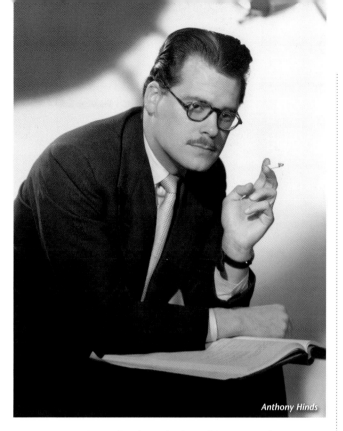

Anthony Hinds

Fay Kanin

scenarios as *Frankenstein Created Woman* and *Taste the Blood of Dracula*. Resigning from the company in 1970, he continued to provide scripts both for them (*Frankenstein and the Monster from Hell*) and other producers (*The Ghoul*), afterwards enjoying a long, publicity-shy retirement.

FAY KANIN

Born: *9 May 1917, New York City, New York, USA.*
Died: *27 March 2013, Santa Monica, California, USA.*
Having started out as a humble RKO script reader, Fay Kanin received her first screenplay credit, alongside her husband Michael, for the MGM programmer *Sunday Punch* in 1942. Her hit play *Goodbye, My Fancy* became a Joan Crawford vehicle in 1951, while the Kanins' jointly written drama *Rashomon* became *The Outrage* 13 years later. In the meantime, the couple's original screenplays in the 1950s – briefly impeded when they were placed on the HUAC blacklist – included *My Pal Gus*, *Rhapsody*, *The Opposite Sex* and the evergreen comedy *Teacher's Pet*, for which they were Oscar-nominated. They even co-wrote the Italian swashbuckler *Swordsman of Siena* in 1962. Going it alone, she moved into the world of TV movies (producing as well as writing) and was president of the Academy of Motion Picture Arts and Sciences from 1979-83.

❧ Another blacklisted screenwriter, **Richard Collins** (*Riot in Cell Block 11*), died in February at 98. Other US writers who died in 2013 included **Tom Jankiewicz** (January, 49), **Gerry Day** (February, 91), **Don Payne** (March, 48), **Mickey Rose** (77) and **Michael France** (51), both in April, **Don Nelson** (86) and **Gary Brandner** (80), both in September, and **William Harrison** (October, 79). **TS Cook** (65) and **Mike Gray** (77), Oscar-nominated writers of the 1978 thriller *The China Syndrome*, died in January and April respectively. Writer-director

Gary David Goldberg died at 68 in June and Canadian comic screenwriter **PJ Torokvei** at 62 in July.

JIM KELLY

Born: *5 May 1946, Paris, Kentucky, USA.*
Died: *29 June 2013, San Diego, California, USA.*
In 1972 karate champion Jim Kelly was Calvin Lockhart's martial arts instructor on *Melinda* and the following year he went to Hong Kong to star opposite Bruce Lee and John Saxon in the cult Kung Fu smash *Enter the Dragon*. In the brief but memorable Blaxploitation career that resulted, he was *Black Belt Jones* in 1974 (reprising the role in *Hot Potato* a year later) and played the eponymous *Black Samurai* in 1976. In between, he formed a combustible triad with former football heroes Jim Brown and Fred Williamson in *Three the Hard Way*, *Take a Hard Ride* and *One Down, Two to Go*. In 1978 he took *Death Dimension* as his cue to retire, becoming a tennis pro instead.

❧ Heavyweight boxer **Ken Norton**, who starred in the mid-'70s Deep South potboilers *Mandingo* and *Drum*, died in September, aged 70. **Bruce Baron**, American star of Asian ninja potboilers in the 1980s, died at 63 in November.

JEAN KENT

Born: *29 June 1921, London, England.*
Died: *30 November 2013, Bury St Edmunds, Suffolk, England.*
"I have two favourite roles, one grim and one gay," wrote Jean Kent in this annual's 1949 edition, conceding that the froth of *Trottie True* just had the edge over the hard-hitting *Good-Time Girl*. Either way, she brought a startling degree of sex appeal to post-war British cinema, together with a certain flinty quality that set her well apart from the competition. She made her first Gainsborough picture, *It's That Man Again*, in 1942 and broke through two years later in *Fanny by Gaslight*. Thereafter she co-starred with Stewart Granger in *Caravan* and *The Magic Bow*, Michael Redgrave in *The Man Within* and

Jean Kent

Wojciech Kilar

The Browning Version, and in 1950 was outstandingly good as *The Woman in Question*. Post-heyday film roles included *The Prince and the Showgirl*, *Grip of the Strangler* and (her last, in 1975) *Shout at the Devil*.

❧ Other British actresses who died in 2013 included **Daphne Anderson** (90) and **Sophiya Haque** (41), both in January, **Elspet Gray** (February, 83), **Pat Keen** (March, 79), **Katherine Woodville** (74), **Pat Ashton** (82) and **Diane Clare** (74), all in June, **Anna Wing** (July, 98) and, in September, **Olga Lowe** (93), **Barbara Hicks** (89) and **Annette Kerr** (93).

JOHN KERR

Born: *15 November 1931, New York City, New York, USA.*
Died: *2 February 2013, Pasadena, California, USA.*
Harvard graduate John Kerr lost no time in conquering Broadway, winning a Tony award aged 22 for the controversial *Tea and Sympathy*. Vincente Minnelli then provided him with his film debut, as a psychiatric patient in *The Cobweb* (1955), prior to retaining him in the sanitised film version of *Tea and Sympathy*. Having starred opposite Leslie Caron in *Gaby*, by 1957 Kerr was playing a major role in *South Pacific* and sharing a 'best newcomer' Golden Globe with Paul Newman and Anthony Perkins. Nowadays, however, he's probably best remembered as the sour-faced avenger in Roger Corman's second Poe film, *Pit and the Pendulum* (1961). Regularly called upon in later years to play lawyers on TV, he had by then become a successful attorney in real life.

❧ **Steve Forrest**, star of the 1954 Poe adaptation *Phantom of the Rue Morgue* and the mid-'60s British TV series *The Baron*, died in May, aged 87. Other

US actors with cult films to their credit included **Jonathan Winters** (*The Loved One*; April, 87), **Jay Robinson** (Caligula in *The Robe*; September, 83) and, in November, **Tony Musante** (*The Bird with the Crystal Plumage*; 77). **Vic Lundin** (83) and **Paul Mantee** (82), co-stars in 1964 of Byron Haskin's *Robinson Crusoe on Mars*, died in June and November respectively.

WOJCIECH KILAR

Born: *17 July 1932, Lviv, Poland.*
Died: *29 December 2013, Katowice, Poland.*
Though chiefly preoccupied by chamber and symphonic compositions, this Polish composer had been working on film scores – nearly 100 already – for over 30 years when his superbly ominous music for the Francis Coppola version of *Dracula* brought him international attention in 1992. At home he'd collaborated with directors like Andrzej Wajda, Krzysztof Kieslowski and Krzysztof Zanussi – especially prolifically with the latter, starting with *Family Life* in 1970 and ending with Kilar's last feature, *Revisited*, in 2009. Triggered by *Dracula*, there followed several other English-language pictures, notably Jane Campion's *The Portrait of a Lady*, James Gray's *We Own the Night* and three for fellow Pole Roman Polanski – *Death and the Maiden*, *The Ninth Gate* and *The Pianist*. The last of these won him a César, one of many such accolades he received during his career.

❧ **Armando Trovajoli**, celebrated composer of well over 200 Italian film scores, died at 95 in February. Other composers who died in 2013 included Canada's **Normand Corbeil** (in January, aged 56), India's **K Raghavan** (October, 99) and Japan's **Toshiaki Tsushima** (November, 77).

BERNADETTE LAFONT

Born: *28 October 1938, Nîmes, Gard, France.*
Died: *25 July 2013, Nîmes, Gard, France.*
Bernadette Lafont became an earthily provocative touchstone for France's Nouvelle Vague in François

Bernadette Lafont

José Larraz

Truffaut's second film, the 1957 short *Les Mistons*, and several of Claude Chabrol's early features, among them *Le Beau Serge* and *Les Bonnes femmes*. After a brief lull she returned, more maturely confrontational, in Nelly Kaplan's *La Fiancée du pirate* (A Very Curious Girl, 1969), Moshé Mizrahi's *Sophie's Ways* (1970), Truffaut's *A Gorgeous Bird Like Me* (1972) and Jean Eustache's *The Mother and the Whore* (1973). Later, there was a César for Claude Miller's *L'Éffrontée* in 1985 and a few reunions with Chabrol, notably *Masques* (1986). Prolific in both film and TV in later years, she received a Lifetime Achievement César in 2003 and the Légion d'honneur in 2009. Her penultimate film, *Paulette* (2012), was not only a star vehicle but also a huge hit.

ALFREDO LANDA

Born: *3 March 1933, Pamplona, Navarra, Spain.*
Died: *9 May 2013, Madrid, Spain.*
Several performers have had 'esque' attached to their surnames but Alfredo Landa may be unique in lending his name to an entire subgenre. Having first gained attention in the classic 1962 heist comedy *Robbery at Three O'clock*, he later became the cheerfully impish Everyman figure at the centre of numerous Landismo films – vulgar but chaste sex comedies not unlike Britain's Carry On pictures, albeit transferred to the fading Franco regime. One of the first, *No desearás al vecino del quinto* (1970), was an unprecedented box-office smash, taking nearly 180 million pesetas. After the Landismo period he metamorphosed into a powerful dramatic actor in 1980s titles like *El crack*, *The Holy Innocents* (for which he won Best Actor at Cannes), *The Enchanted Forest* (for which he received a Goya) and *Sinatra*. An honorary Goya followed in 2008.

❖ Other Spanish performers who died in 2013 included **Anna Lizaran** (in January, aged 68), **Fernando Guillén** (also January, 80), **María Asquerino** (February, 87), **José Sancho** (March, 68), **Mariví Bilbao** (April, 83), **Amparo Soler Leal** (October, 80), **Amparo Rivelles** (November, 88) and **Elvira Quintillá** (December, 85). Musical comedy stars **Manolo Escobar** (82) and **Lolita Sevilla** (78) died in October and December respectively.

JOSÉ LARRAZ

Born: *[exact date unknown] 1929, Barcelona, Spain.*
Died: *3 September 2013, Málaga, Andalucía, Spain.*
This refined Spaniard first gained fame as a brilliant comic-book artist in Paris, then as a highly imaginative purveyor of British exploitation films. Encouraged by Josef von Sternberg, whom he met in 1968, he relocated to England and crafted a crepuscular eroticism all his own in small-scale titles like *Whirlpool*, *Deviation* and *Scream and Die!* His most famous films, *Symptoms* and *Vampyres*, were shot over a six-month period in 1973/74. The former was a creepy mood piece and (to the consternation of snobbish UK critics) an official British entry at Cannes; the latter was a daringly frank and bloody sex-horror that has acquired a major latterday cult. Back in Spain, his remaining films, including a comedy with Alfredo Landa [qv], were more formulaic, though his 1985 mini-series biopic *Goya* was both a critical and commercial success.

TOM LAUGHLIN

Born: *10 August 1931, Minneapolis, Minnesota, USA.*
Died: *12 December 2013, Thousand Oaks, California, USA.*
Having appeared in a few 1950s films – among them *Tea and Sympathy*, *Gidget*, *Tall Story* and the lead in Robert Altman's *The Delinquents* – Tom Laughlin was director-star of the biker movie *The Born Losers* in 1967, introducing his iconic Billy Jack character. This half-Navajo Vietnam vet subsequently became a major countercultural icon when given his very own film, *Billy Jack*, in 1971. The same mixture of hapkido action and fuzzy philosophising recurred in *The Trial of Billy Jack* (1974), after which Laughlin made a non-Billy Jack period Western, *The Master Gunfighter*, and the barely released 1977 folly *Billy Jack Goes to Washington*. Thanks to Laughlin's revolutionary idea of saturation booking, the second and third Billy Jack films are credited with inventing the modern blockbuster before *Jaws*.

GEORGES LAUTNER

Born: *24 January 1926, Nice, France.*
Died: *22 November 2013, Paris, France.*
Writer-director Georges Lautner turned out roughly

Bigas Luna

Elmore Leonard

a film a year (sometimes more) for well over three decades, from *La Môme aux boutons* in 1958 to *L'Inconnu dans la maison* in 1992. His populist touch – fostered by regular collaborations with screenwriter Michel Audiard – first manifested itself in three early '60s comedy-thrillers starring Paul Meurisse as capricious secret agent 'Monocle'. Films like *Les Tontons flingueurs*, *Galia*, *Pasha*, *Flic Story*, *Pas de problème!*, *Cop or Hood*, *Le Professionel* and *Happy Easter* were expertly crafted showcases for such major stars as Lino Ventura, Bernard Blier, Mireille Darc, Jean Gabin, Alain Delon, Miou-Miou, Jean-Paul Belmondo and Sophie Marceau, while his intriguing psychedelic noir *The Road to Salina* (1969) boasted Rita Hayworth. Rather belatedly, in 2012 he was honoured at Cannes with a screening of his 1964 film *Les Barbouzes* (The Great Spy Chase).

❧ Other French directors who died in 2013 included Patrice Chéreau and Édouard Molinaro [both qv], **Jacques Dupont** (in March, aged 91) and **Denys de la Patellière** (July, 92). **Daniel Duval**, also an actor, died in October at 68, and screenwriter **Jean-Marc Roberts** in March, aged 58.

ELMORE LEONARD
Born: *11 October 1925, New Orleans, Louisiana, USA.*
Died: *20 August 2013, Bloomfield Township, Michigan, USA.*
Before his enthronement as grand master of the hard-boiled, blackly humorous crime novel, Elmore Leonard started out writing Westerns, and the first three screen versions of his work – *The Tall T* (1956), *3:10 to Yuma* (1957) and *Hombre* (1966) – all qualify as classics of that genre. As a screenwriter, from 1969 to 1989 he notched up *The Moonshine War*, *Joe Kidd*, *Mr Majestyk*, *Stick*, *52 Pick-Up*, *The Rosary Murders* and *Cat Chaser*. Adaptations by others began in 1969/70 with *The Big Bounce* and *Valdez is Coming* but only gathered momentum with the success of *Get Shorty* in 1995. There followed *Touch*, *Jackie Brown* (Leonard's favourite), *Out of Sight*, *Be Cool*, remakes of *The Big*

Bounce and *3:10 to Yuma*, *Killshot*, *Freaky Deaky* and (in 2013) *Life of Crime*. And there will almost certainly be plenty of posthumous additions.

❧ Best-selling American novelist **Tom Clancy**, whose books sired such films as *The Hunt for Red October* and *Patriot Games*, died in October, aged 66.

PATRICIA LOVELL
Born: *[exact date unknown] 1929, Sydney, New South Wales, Australia.*
Died: *26 January 2013, Sydney, New South Wales, Australia.*
Patricia Lovell only produced half a dozen feature films, but two of them remain classics, one an atmospheric masterwork that kick-started the boom in Australian production and the other a blockbuster that consolidated it internationally. Her 15-year tenure as 'Miss Pat', glamorous stooge to the television marionette Mr Squiggle, wasn't quite over when her first film, Peter Weir's *Picnic at Hanging Rock*, began shooting in February 1975. Next she handled two Ken Hannam films, *Break of Day* and *Summerfield*, prior to reuniting with Weir for Australia's then most expensive film, *Gallipoli*. She followed the film's international success in 1981 with *Monkey Grip* and, in 1986, the TV movie *The Perfectionist*. She became a Member of the Order of Australia the same year, published her autobiography, *No Picnic*, in 1995 and in 2004 received an honorary award from the AFI.

❧ Other Australian film personalities who died in 2013 included actors **Bille Brown** (61) and **Penne Hackforth-Jones** (69), in January and May respectively. Directors **Jonathan Dawson** (77) and **Chris Kennedy** (64) both died in August, and multi-award-winning sound editor **Andrew Plain** (60) in December. Australian actor **Bruce Beeby** (91) and New Zealand's **Walter Brown** (86), both of whom appeared in numerous British second features, died in October.

BIGAS LUNA
Born: *19 March 1946, Barcelona, Spain.*
Died: *6 April 2013, La Riera de Gaià, Tarragonès, Spain.*
Starting as a painter and interior designer, Bigas Luna only ventured into filmmaking on the collapse of

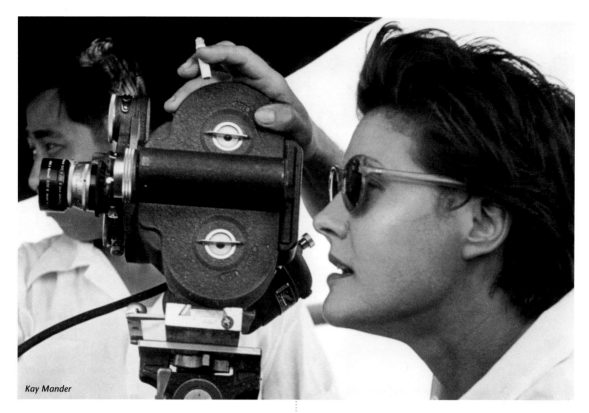

Kay Mander

Spanish censorship. His 1978 film *Bilbao* gave notice of the explicit sexual fetishism that was to become his forte, but after the spiritual thriller *Reborn* (1981, his only English-language film) and the Pirandellian horror *Anguish* (1987) he retired, only to be coaxed back for *The Ages of Lulu* in 1990. There followed the Iberian trilogy (1992-94) that made his name internationally (and likewise launched Penélope Cruz and Javier Bardem). *Jamón jamón*, *Golden Balls* and *The Tit and the Moon* displayed the surrealist influence of his friend Salvador Dalí but deconstructed Spanish machismo in an outrageous, slyly subversive, lushly realised style all Luna's own. His remaining films included *The Chambermaid on the Titanic*, *Volavérunt* and lastly (in 2010) *Di Di Hollywood*.

KAY MANDER

Born: *28 September 1915, Hull, East Yorkshire, England.*
Died: *29 December 2013, Castle Douglas, Dumfries and Galloway, Scotland.*
Passionately devoted to social issues and consistently innovative in chronicling them, Kay Mander was a crucial figure in Britain's documentary movement. *Highland Doctor*, which she directed for Paul Rotha Productions in 1943, pioneered the drama-documentary mode; two years later the similarly groundbreaking *Homes for the People* was made by her own company, Basic Films, on behalf of the Labour Party, and by 1950 her French-language documentary *La Famille Martin* had won a BAFTA. Having directed a fiction feature, *The Kid from Canada*, for the Children's Film Foundation in 1957, she found further opportunities lacking and instead became continuity supervisor on such major films as *From Russia with Love*, *Fahrenheit 451*, *That'll Be the Day* and *Tommy*. In 2000 she was herself the subject of a documentary, *One Continuous Take*.

RICHARD MATHESON

Born: *20 February 1926, Allendale, New Jersey, USA.*
Died: *23 June 2013, Calabasas, California, USA.*
This grand master of horror and science fiction was first published in 1950 and hit cinema screens seven years later, via the screenplay (based on his own novel) for *The Incredible Shrinking Man*. He moved on to the two major brands of 1960s horror, adapting *House of Usher*, *Pit and the Pendulum* and *The Raven* for AIP plus *Fanatic* and *The Devil Rides Out* for Hammer. His own work sired such films as *The Omega Man*, *The Legend of Hell House*, *Someone is Bleeding* (for Georges Lautner, qv), *Somewhere in Time* and, more recently, *What Dreams May Come*, *Stir of Echoes*, *I Am Legend*,

Richard Matheson

Mariangela Melato

Éduoard Molinaro

The Box and *Real Steel*. On top of all this, he was the author of such classic 1970s TV movies as *Duel*, *The Night Stalker* and *Trilogy of Terror*. A formidable CV by any standards.

MARIANGELA MELATO

Born: *19 September 1941, Milan, Italy.*
Died: *11 January 2013, Rome, Italy.*
This fascinating, multi-award-winning actress maintained a distinguished stage career alongside a film CV boasting collaborations with Vittorio De Sica (*We'll Call Him Andrew*), Claude Chabrol (*Nada*), Mario Monicelli (*Caro Michele*) and Luigi Comencini (*Il gatto*), plus two Elio Petri titles, *The Working Class Goes to Heaven* and *Todo modo*. But it was a 1971-74 trio of provocative Lina Wertmüller films – *The Seduction of Mimi*, *Love and Anarchy* and *Swept Away*, all co-starring Giancarlo Giannini – that sealed her international reputation. At the turn of the 1980s she made *Flash Gordon* in Britain and *So Fine* in Hollywood, and latterly she appeared in *Il petomane*, *The Good Soldier*, *Dancers* and *Mortacci*. There were also reunions with Giannini (*My Darling My Dearest*, 1981), Wertmüller (*Summer Night*, 1986) and Monicelli (*Dirty Linen*, 1998).

ÉDOUARD MOLINARO

Born: *13 May 1928, Bordeaux, Gironde, France.*
Died: *7 December 2013, Paris, France.*
This "artisan indispensable du cinéma français" (to quote *Télérama*) began in style, achieving international distribution with his first feature, the 1957 Jeanne Moreau vehicle *Le Dos au mur*. After several further thrillers and the Brigitte Bardot showcase *Une Ravissante idiote* (1963), he hit his comic stride with the late '60s duo *Oscar* and *Hibernatus* (both starring Louis de Funès), then made the classic farce *L'Emmerdeur* (A Pain in the A***) in 1973. Having directed Christopher Lee in the engaging pastiche *Dracula Père et Fils* (1976), he received two Oscar nominations for the smash hit *La Cage aux folles* (1978), rapidly turning out a sequel and a single Hollywood venture, *Just the Way You Are* (1984). Amid much TV, his final features included the costume pictures *Le Souper* (1992) and *Beaumarchais l'insolent* (1996).

SARA MONTIEL

Born: *10 March 1928, Campo de Criptana, Spain.*
Died: *8 April 2013, Madrid, Spain.*
En route to becoming one of Spain's most legendary film stars, Sara Montiel made her debut in *Te quiero para mí* in 1944, four years later starring in *Locura de amor* opposite Aurora Bautista (see last year's In Memoriam). Thereafter, a successful stint in Mexican films provided her springboard to Hollywood, where (billed as Sarita Montiel) she was cast alongside Gary Cooper in *Vera Cruz*, Joan Fontaine [qv] in *Serenade* and Rod Steiger in *Run of the Arrow*, as well as briefly marrying *Serenade* director Anthony Mann. On returning to Spain in 1957 she became a bona-fide phenomenon via award-winning performances in *El último cuplé* (The Last Torch Song) and *La violetera* (The Violet Seller), subsequently alternating exotic screen vehicles like *Mi último tango* and *La bella Lola* with an equally stratospheric recording career.

❧ Four other key players from Mexico's Golden Age died in 2013 – **Lilia del Valle** (in January, aged

Michael D Moore

Milo O'Shea

84), **Joaquín Cordero** (89) and Cuban-born **Carmen Montejo** (87), both in March, and former Miss Mexico **Ana Bertha Lepe** (79) in October.

MICHAEL D MOORE

Born: *14 October 1914, Vancouver, British Columbia, Canada.*
Died: *4 March 2013, Malibu, California, USA.*
Mickey Moore, as he was billed in silent pictures, numbered Tod Browning, Maurice Tourneur and Cecil B DeMille among his directors and Mary Pickford, Blanche Sweet, Gloria Swanson and Mary Miles Minter among his leading ladies. Having finished his acting career on a pre-teen high in DeMille's 1927 Biblical epic *King of Kings*, he returned initially as a prop man, then became a prolific assistant and second unit director on the likes of *When Worlds Collide*, *The War of the Worlds* and *The Carpetbaggers*. He was also fully fledged director on such 1960s titles as *Paradise Hawaiian Style* and *The Fastest Guitar Alive*. Later second unit credits included *Patton, The Man Who Would Be King, Raiders of the Lost Ark* and *Never Say Never Again*. He retired, aged 85, after completing work on *102 Dalmatians* in 2000.

❧ Among other American filmmakers who died in 2013 were designers **R Gilbert Clayton** (90) and **Garrett Lewis** (77), both in January, poster artist **Mitchell Hooks** (89) and Disney editor **Norman R Palmer** (95), both in March, three-time Oscar-winning sound editor **Charles L Campbell** (June, 82), Oscar and BAFTA-nominated editor **Frank Morriss** (July, 85) and choreographer **Marc Breaux** (November, 89).

HAL NEEDHAM

Born: *6 March 1931, Memphis, Tennessee, USA.*
Died: *25 October 2013, Los Angeles, California, USA.*
"I'll never win an Academy Award," Hal Needham

once quipped, "but I'll be a rich son of a bitch." In fact, he subsequently won two – for a camera car/ crane design in 1987 and an honorary Oscar just eight months before his death. As Hollywood's ace stunt man of the 1960s, he became a firm friend of Burt Reynolds, and it was through him that Needham made his directorial debut with the 1977 smash *Smokey and the Bandit*. Other rumbustious Reynolds assignments included *Hooper, The Cannonball Run* and *Stroker Ace*, together with *Smokey* and *Cannonball* sequels, while non-Reynolds titles included *The Villain, Megaforce* and *Rad*. His credo: "When people see one of my movies, I want to get their adrenalin flowing. If I don't, then I haven't done my job."

❧ **David R Ellis**, another stunt man turned director (*Final Destination 2, Snakes on a Plane*), died in January, aged 60. **Ted Post**, who directed Clint Eastwood in *Hang 'Em High* and *Magnum Force*, died at 95 in August. Other American directors – all with a few features to their names amid plenty of TV – included **Jack Shea** (April, 84), **William A Graham** (September, 87), **Jonathan Kaufer** (October, 58) and **Jeff Pollack** (December, 54). **Del Tenney**, maverick producer-director of the 1960s cult curios *The Horror of Party Beach* and *The Curse of the Living Corpse*, died at 83 in February.

MILO O'SHEA

Born: *2 June 1926, Dublin, Republic of Ireland.*
Died: *2 April 2013, New York City, New York, USA.*
On stage in Dublin from age 12, Milo O'Shea had small

roles in British comedies like *Mrs Gibbons' Boys* and *Carry On Cabby* before scoring a remarkable late-1960s hat-trick – playing Leopold Bloom in the controversial *Ulysses*, Friar Laurence in *Romeo and Juliet* and the insane Durand Durand in *Barbarella*. Soon afterwards he starred in the BBC sitcom *Me Mammy*, then another bunch of diverting film roles – *The Adding Machine*, *Loot*, *The Love Ban*, *Theatre of Blood* – preceded his move to America in 1976. As well as winning a Tony on Broadway and doing masses of TV, he found time for several US films, from *The Verdict* to *The Purple Rose of Cairo* and *The Dream Team*. Appropriately, several of his final engagements – notably *The Butcher Boy* and *Puckoon* – returned him to Ireland.

❖ Other Irish actors who died in 2013 included Peter O'Toole [qv], **Helena Carroll** (in March, aged 84), **Sean Caffrey** (April, 73) and **Gerard Murphy** (August, 64).

NAGISA ŌSHIMA

Born: *31 March 1932, Tamano, Okayama Prefecture, Japan.*
Died: *15 January 2013, Fujisawa, Kanagawa Prefecture, Japan.*
Nagisa Ōshima was the cinematic provocateur who wrote and directed the taboo-busting *Ai no corrida* (Empire of the Senses, 1976). Acquitted on a charge of obscenity, he followed it with the milder supernatural drama *Ai no borei* (Empire of Passion, 1978), for which he won Best Director at Cannes. When his early New Wave polemic *Night and Fog in Japan* (1960) was suppressed by its Shōchiku sponsors, he went independent and crafted a long series of radical statements, among them *Pleasures of the Flesh*, *Violence at Noon*, *Diary of a Shinjuku Thief*, *Death by Hanging*, *Three Resurrected Drunkards* and *Boy*. After his 'Empire' duo, he made *Merry Christmas Mr Lawrence* in 1982 and went into eclipse three years later with *Max mon amour*. He made a powerful comeback, however, with his last film, *Gohatto* (Taboo, 1999).

❖ Japanese actors who died in 2013 included **Isao Natsuyagi** (May, 73), **Kei Suma** (December, 78) and **Rentarō Mikuni** – star of Kon Ichikawa's *The Burmese Harp* and Masaki Kobayashi's *Kwaidan* – in May, aged 90.

Nagisa Ōshima

Peter O'Toole

PETER O'TOOLE

Born: *2 August 1932, Connemara, Republic of Ireland.*
Died: *14 December 2013, London, England.*
This swaggering, mercurial, larger-than-life thespian was a throwback to an earlier age. Emerging from the RSC, he won world stardom as *Lawrence of Arabia* in 1962, following it with a long string of 1960s vehicles – *Becket*, *Lord Jim*, *What's New Pussycat?*, *How to Steal a Million*, *The Night of the Generals*, *The Lion in Winter* and *Goodbye, Mr Chips*. Subsequently, titles like *Murphy's War*, *Under Milk Wood*, *Man of La Mancha*, *Man Friday* and *The Stunt Man* were interleaved with two signature roles – the lordly Jesus freak of *The Ruling Class* (released in 1972) and, ten years later, the capricious matinée idol of *My Favorite Year*. Starting with *The Last Emperor* in 1987, there were several rewarding autumnal moments, notably his fêted performance as an elderly actor-laddie in *Venus* (2006). Oscar-nominated eight times, he won an honorary Oscar in 2003.

ELEANOR PARKER

Born: *26 June 1922, Cedarville, Ohio, USA.*
Died: *9 December 2013, Palm Springs, California, USA.*
The textbook definition of a class act, Eleanor Parker was a protean performer aptly hailed as 'The Woman of a Thousand Faces'. Her electrifying display as a triple personality in *Lizzie* (1957) was a case in point, but her three Oscar nominations came earlier in the decade, for *Caged*, *Detective Story* and *Interrupted Melody*. She'd established herself back in the 1940s in such films as *Between Two Worlds*, *The Very Thought of You*, *Pride of the Marines*, *Of Human Bondage* (redefining the old Bette Davis part), *The Voice of the Turtle* and *The Woman in White*. Later credits ranged from

Eleanor Parker

Rossana Podestà

Scaramouche, The Naked Jungle and *The Man with the Golden Arm* to *Home from the Hill, The Sound of Music, An American Dream* and – her last notable feature prior to plenty of TV – the 1969 thriller *Eye of the Cat.*

ROSSANA PODESTÀ

Born: *20 June 1934, Tripoli, Libya.*
Died: *10 December 2013, Rome, Italy.*
Rossana Podestà started her film career aged 16 and from 1953-55 played 'Rossana' in the Mexican film *La Red*, Nausicaa in *Ulysses* opposite Kirk Douglas, and the massively publicised title role in Robert Wise's multi-national epic *Helen of Troy*. There were a couple of American films thereafter – *Santiago* and *Raw Wind in Eden* (with Esther Williams, qv) – but she was otherwise occupied with spirited peplum extravaganzas like *Fury of the Pagans* and *Sodom and Gomorrah*. Her filmmaker husband, Marco Vicario, then starred her in the gruesome early giallo *La vergine di Norimberga*, the hit caper movie *7 uomini d'oro* and the '70s sex comedies *Intimacy, Homo Eroticus* and *The Sensuous Sicilian*. She made her final film, Giuseppe Bertolucci's *Segreti segreti* (also starring Mariangela Melato, qv), in 1984.

PERRETTE PRADIER

Born: *17 April 1938, Hanoi, Vietnam.*
Died: *16 January 2013, Rueil-Malmaison, France.*
Having made her screen debut in 1959 in Robert Hossein's *Les Scélérats*, Perrette Pradier won a 'most promising newcomer' award for *Au voleur!* (Stop Thief). Almost at once she was cast as Constance Bonacieux in Bernard Borderie's two-film adaptation of *The Three Musketeers*, later working with Julien Duvivier (*La Chambre ardente*), André Hunebelle (*OSS 117*) and opposite Fernandel in *Blague dans le coin*. She was also showcased in a couple of French-shot Hollywood films, Fred Zinnemann's *Behold a Pale Horse* (1964) and John Guillermin's *House of Cards* (1968). Later in her career

she became famous as 'la reine du doublage', providing French voices for, among others, Julie Andrews, Diane Keaton, Kathleen Turner, Faye Dunaway, Margot Kidder, Jane Fonda and Jacqueline Bisset.

◆ **Georges Descrières**, who played Athos in Borderie's *Musketeers* films and was a 2004 recipient of the Légion d'honneur, died at 83 in October. Other French players who died in 2013 included **David Dewaele** (in February, aged 36), **Valérie Benguigui** (September, 47), **Pierre Massimi** (October, 78) and, in December, **Catherine Bégin** (74) and **Mado Maurin** (98). Critic, actress, TV presenter and screenwriter **France Roche** also died in December, aged 92.

RUTH PRAWER JHABVALA

Born: *7 May 1927, Cologne, Prussia, Germany.*
Died: *3 April 2013, New York City, New York, USA.*
A brilliant novelist and short story writer, Ruth Prawer fled Nazi Germany in 1939, settling first in England and then (with her husband Cyrus Jhabvala) in India. In 1961 director James Ivory and producer Ismail Merchant asked her to adapt her early novel *The Householder* into a film; further Merchant-Ivory collaborations included *Shakespeare-Wallah, Bombay Talkie* and *Autobiography of a Princess*. In the 1980s the trio turned to meticulously elegant literary adaptations such as *Quartet, The Bostonians* and *A Room with a View*; the last won her an Oscar, while *Heat and Dust* brought her a BAFTA to accompany the Booker won by her original novel. Another Oscar followed in 1992 for *Howard's End* plus, a year later, a third nomination for *The Remains of the Day*. Her final screenplays included *Jefferson in Paris, Surviving Picasso* and *The Golden Bowl*.

Elías Querejeta

Dale Robertson

ELÍAS QUEREJETA

Born: *27 October 1934, Hernani, Gipuzkoa, Spain.*
Died: *9 June 2013, Madrid, Spain.*
A soccer pro during the 1950s, Elías Querejeta put something of the same fleet-footedness to good use when reinventing himself as a film producer, cleverly dodging state censorship and revolutionising the prestige of Spanish cinema as democracy arrived. Writing several of his films and involving himself in every aspect of production, he was as much an auteur as his directors, leading to seismic bust-ups with Victor Erice and Wim Wenders. But, starting with Carlos Saura's *La caza* (1965), his influence was profound. His 12 other Saura collaborations included *Peppermint Frappé*, *La prima Angélica*, *Cría cuervos* and *Mama Turns 100*, and in the meantime he produced a timeless classic in Erice's *The Spirit of the Beehive*. Director protégés included Jaime Chávarri and Montxo Armendáriz, and his last major hit was Fernando Léon de Aranoa's *Mondays in the Sun* in 2002.

DALE ROBERTSON

Born: *14 July 1923, Harrah, Oklahoma, USA.*
Died: *27 February 2013, San Diego, California, USA.*
In the 'Rising Stars' section of this annual's 1952 edition, Dale Robertson was described as a "six-foot-and-more, broad-shouldered youngster with the kind of smile which makes girls go ooooohhh!" Though best known for the 1950s/60s TV shows *Tales of Wells Fargo* and *Iron Horse*, he'd previously had a good run in big screen Westerns, starting as Jesse James in *Fighting Man of the Plains* (1949). Thereafter he was a stoic star presence in such 1950s horse operas as *Return of the Texan*, *The Silver Whip*, *Sitting Bull* and *Hell Canyon Outlaws*, mixing these with occasional musicals like *Call Me Mister*, *Golden Girl* and *The Farmer Takes a Wife*. His last film of note, the British production *Coast of Skeletons*, appeared in 1965.

EDDIE ROMERO

Born: *7 July 1924, Dumaguete, Philippines.*
Died: *28 May 2013, Quezon City, Philippines.*
Outside the Philippines, writer-producer-director Eddie Romero was best known for fusing lush local colour with over-the-top mutant mayhem in such late '60s/early '70s grindhouse standbys as *Brides of Blood*, *Mad Doctor of Blood Island*, *Beast of Blood* and *Beast of the Yellow Night*, as well as showcasing Pam Grier in both *The Twilight People* and *Black Mama White Mama*. At home, however, he was venerated as a cinema pioneer and for anatomising specifically Filipino themes in war films like *Cavalry Command*, *Lost Battalion*, *Intramuros* and *Manila Open City*, together with historical dramas like *Gamito Kami Noon … Paano Kayo Ngayon?*, *Banta ng Kahapon* and *Aguila*. He was also executive producer of Francis Coppola's Filipino-shot *Apocalypse Now*. Having started winning awards in 1951, he was named a National Artist of the Philippines in 2003.

❧ Romero's fellow Filipino writer-director **Danny L Zialcita** died at 73 in March. **Bella Flores**, veteran villainess of Filipino cinema, died in May, aged 84.

RICHARD C SARAFIAN

Born: *28 April 1930, New York City, New York, USA.*
Died: *18 September 2013, Santa Monica, California, USA.*
"The beauty of *Vanishing Point* was that I met the challenge to physicalise speed," noted Richard Sarafian of his most famous work. Made in 1970, this trippy road movie captured the countercultural moment and remains a major cult. Prior to it, Sarafian had been Robert Altman's assistant, directed plenty of TV, made his feature debut on the streets of New York City with *Andy* (1964), then turned out the British films *Run Wild, Run Free* and *Fragment of Fear*. After it, his evocative flair for rugged location work was indulged in the early '70s Westerns *Man in the Wilderness* and

The Man who Loved Cat Dancing. But then he lost momentum, removing his name from his final film, *Solar Crisis* (1990). Latterly, he had acting roles in such 1990s titles as *Bugsy, Bound, Bulworth* and *Blue Streak*.

ALAN SHARP

Born: *12 January 1934, Alyth, Perth and Kinross, Scotland.*
Died: *8 February 2013, Los Angeles, California, USA.*
This Scottish novelist had had a few plays produced in TV drama strands like *The Wednesday Play* and *ITV Playhouse* when he decamped at the turn of the 1970s to the USA. There he got a half-dozen of his expertly contrived screenplays produced in rapid succession; the results, often grimly fatalistic in tone and all released between 1971 and 1977, were *The Last Run, The Hired Hand, Ulzana's Raid, Billy Two Hats, Night Moves* and *Damnation Alley*. Apart from Sam Peckinpah's *The Osterman Weekend* (1983) and, two years later, *Little Treasure* (which Sharp directed himself), he was otherwise preoccupied with television until lured back to the cinema for the Scottish epic *Rob Roy* (1995) and the eccentric Lord Dunsany adaptation *Dean Spanley* (2008). Sadly, a projected biopic of Robert Burns went unrealised.

❖ British screenwriters **Snoo Wilson** (*Shadey, Eichmann*) and **Jon Manchip White** (*The Camp on Blood Island, Crack in the World*) both died in July, aged 64 and 89 respectively.

PATTY SHEPARD

Born: *1 October 1945, Greenville, South Carolina, USA.*
Died: *3 January 2013, Madrid, Spain.*
Just as Italian cinema exploited the deathly eroticism of Merseyside's Barbara Steele, so Spanish filmmakers

Mel Smith

found her icily alluring counterpart in South Carolina's Patty Shepard. Domiciled in Madrid from the age of 18, she moved from modelling into a 20-year film career, working for Jesús Franco [qv] at one end of it (*Lucky el intrépido*, 1967) and José Larraz [qv] at the other (*Edge of the Axe*, 1988). In between she was a fixture in Euro-Westerns (*The Man Called Noon*), Italian gialli (*My Dear Killer*), crazy comedies (*Watch Out We're Mad*), cerebral chillers (*The Glass Ceiling*) and lurid Iberian horrors like *Hannah Queen of the Vampires, El monte de las brujas* and as a memorably spooky Blood Countess in *La noche de Walpurgis*.

MEL SMITH

Born: *3 December 1952, London, England.*
Died: *19 July 2013, London, England.*
Mel Smith was an indispensable feature of the influential TV comedy hits *Not the Nine O'clock News* and *Alas Smith and Jones*; also with Griff Rhys Jones, he set up the production company TalkBack in 1982, selling it for many millions 18 years later. As an actor, his big screen credits included *Bullshot, Morons from Outer Space, Restless Natives, The Princess Bride, Wilt, Brain Donors* and *Twelfth Night* (as Toby Belch). Starting in 1988, he also directed several films. *The Tall Guy* was an engaging debut, *Radioland Murders* a misfiring Hollywood detour, and *Bean* a massive success; showcasing his old telly co-star Rowan Atkinson, it made over $250 million in 1997. His remaining films, *High Heels and Low Lifes* (2001) and *Blackball* (2003), couldn't compete.

Patty Shepard

Luciano Vincenzoni

Audrey Totter

GILBERT TAYLOR

Born: *21 April 1914, Bushey Heath, Hertfordshire, England.*
Died: *23 August 2013, Newport, Isle of Wight, England.*
Honoured by the British Society of Cinematographers in
2001 and by its American equivalent five years later, Gil
Taylor began his film career at Gainsborough Studios in
1929. Initially an assistant to the likes of Freddie Young
and Günther Krampf, he graduated to fully fledged
cinematographer in the late 1940s on the Boulting
Brothers pictures *The Guinea Pig* and *Seven Days to Noon*.
His innovative lighting techniques were soon much in
demand, with multiple assignments for J Lee Thompson
(among them *Yield to the Night, Woman in a Dressing
Gown, Ice Cold in Alex*), Richard Lester (*It's Trad Dad!*,
A Hard Day's Night) and Polanski (*Repulsion, Cul-de-Sac,
Macbeth*), plus one apiece for Kubrick (*Dr Strangelove*)
and Hitchcock (*Frenzy*). He also lent visual distinction
to the 1970s mega-hits *The Omen* and *Star Wars*.

❖ Russian cinematographer **Vadim Yusov**, fêted for his
collaborations with Andrei Tarkovsky (*Andrei Rublev,
Solaris*), died in August at 84. Mexico's **Rafael Corkidi**,
best known for photographing Alejandro Jodorowsky's
El Topo and *The Holy Mountain* but also a writer-director
in his own right, died in September, aged 83. 'Direct
Cinema' pioneer **Michel Brault** also died in September,
aged 85; as well as photographing *Mon Oncle Antoine*
(frequently cited as Canada's best ever film), he also
wrote and directed the Palme d'Or winner *Les Ordres*.

AUDREY TOTTER

Born: *20 December 1917, Joliet, Illinois, USA.*
Died: *12 December 2013, Los Angeles, California, USA.*
After a lengthy apprenticeship in radio drama,
Audrey Totter was perfect casting for the 1945 film
Bewitched, in which she provided the 'other' voice
of schizophrenic Phyllis Thaxter (see last year's In
Memoriam). In the flesh she had a rather brittle,
hardbitten, cold-eyed quality that ideally suited the
equivocal 'dames' of film noir, a type that followed
her from *The Postman Always Rings Twice* and *Lady
in the Lake* through *The Unsuspected, High Wall, Alias
Nick Beal* and *Tension*, with an interesting variation as
Robert Ryan's concerned wife in *The Set-Up*. ("The bad
girls were so much fun to play," she recalled in 1999.)
Released from a six-year MGM contract, she appeared
in 1950s potboilers like *FBI Girl* and *Women's Prison*
prior to spending 30 years mainly in TV.

❖ Other nonagenarian US performers who died in 2013
included Deanna Durbin, Eleanor Parker and Esther
Williams [all qv], **Allan Arbus** (in April, aged 95), **Jean
Stapleton** (May, 90), **Harry Lewis** (93) and **Maxine Stuart**
(94), both in June, **Michael Ansara** (July, 91), **Roger
McGee** (91) and **Virginia Vincent** (95), both in October,
and **Mickey Knox** (November, 91). **Elliott Reid**, male lead
opposite Marilyn Monroe and Jane Russell in *Gentlemen
Prefer Blondes*, died at 93 in June, and **Irene Kane**,
female lead in Kubrick's *Killer's Kiss*, at 90 in October.

LUCIANO VINCENZONI

Born: *7 March 1926, Treviso, Italy.*
Died: *22 September 2013, Rome, Italy.*
It rankled with him, but Luciano Vincenzoni – the
celebrated 'Script Doctor' of post-war Italian cinema
– was best known abroad as the dryly witty co-writer
of Sergio Leone's iconic mid-1960s Westerns *For a Few
Dollars More* and *The Good, the Bad and the Ugly*. He
would have preferred to be remembered for scripting
Mario Monicelli's *La grande guerra* (1959), for his award-
winning collaborations with Pietro Germi (*Seduced and
Abandoned*, 1964; *Signore & signori*, 1967) or for Elio
Petri's refined 1968 chiller *A Quiet Place in the Country*.
He began his career in 1954 with *Hanno rubato un tram*

Michael Winner

Esther Williams

(They've Stolen a Streetcar) and ended by providing the story for Giuseppe Tornatore's *Malèna* in 2000. Other films included *Death Rides a Horse*, *Tough Guys*, *Orca*, *Il conte Tacchia*, *Raw Deal* and uncredited work on *Avanti!* for Billy Wilder.

❧ Two-time David winner **Nino Baragli**, who edited *The Good, the Bad and the Ugly* among more than 200 other films, died at 87 in May. Cinematographer **Luigi Kuveiller**, whose credits ranged from Wilder's *Avanti!* to Dario Argento's *Deep Red*, died at 85 in January. Among Italian screenwriters, **Vincenzo Cerami**, an Oscar nominee and David winner for Roberto Benigni's *Life is Beautiful*, died at 72 in July. **Alberto Bevilacqua**, co-writer of, among others, Mario Bava's *Planet of the Vampires*, died at 79 in September.

PAUL WALKER

Born: *12 September 1973, Glendale, California, USA.*
Died: *30 November 2013, Valencia, California, USA.*
Paul Walker moved all the way from Pampers commercials as an infant to the giddy heights of the phenomenally lucrative *Fast and Furious* franchise. His first film role, aged 12, was in *Monster in the Closet*; after much TV he broke through with the 1997 Disney comedy *Meet the Deedles*. Teen hits like *Pleasantville*, *Varsity Blues*, *She's All That* and *The Skulls*, plus the grim psycho thriller *Roadkill*, propelled him out of the 1990s and towards *The Fast and the Furious*, which teamed him with Vin Diesel in 2000 and sired six further blockbusters, with Walker reappearing in all but one. His other films included *Into the Blue*, *Running Scared*, *Flags of Our Fathers*, *The Lazarus Project* and *Hours*. He died in a car crash.

ESTHER WILLIAMS

Born: *8 August 1921, Inglewood, California, USA.*
Died: *6 June 2013, Los Angeles, California, USA.*
Cheated of Olympic glory by the advent of World War II, champion swimmer Esther Williams instead gained world fame in a field she had pretty much all to herself – the big screen Technicolor 'aqua-spectacular'. After an MGM test run in *Andy Hardy's Double Life* in 1942, her first big hit, a couple of years later, was appropriately entitled *Bathing Beauty*. For a good decade thereafter, she was a major box-office draw in such lavish musical divertissements as *Thrill of a Romance*, *Easy to Wed*, *Fiesta*, *This Time for Keeps*, *On an Island with You*, *Take Me Out to the Ball Game*, *Neptune's Daughter*, *Pagan Love Song*, *Texas Carnival*, *Skirts Ahoy!*, *Dangerous When Wet* and *Easy to Love*. Another apposite title: her 1999 autobiography was named after her 1952 hit *Million Dollar Mermaid*.

MICHAEL WINNER

Born: *30 October 1935, London, England.*
Died: *21 January 2013, London, England.*
Moving from a cigar-chewing, censor-baiting provocateur to waspish restaurant critic and ad campaign star, Michael Winner was one of those rare directors who become celebrities in their own right. Beginning with the literally threadbare nudie-cutie *Some Like It Cool* and pop musical *Play It Cool*, he soon graduated to a 1963-67 hot streak represented by *West 11*, *The System*, *You Must Be Joking!*, *The Jokers* and *I'll Never Forget What's 'is Name*. The youthful British bravado of these engaging films was succeeded by the 1970s Hollywood gloss of grisly potboilers like *The Mechanic*, *The Stone Killer*, *Death Wish* and *The Sentinel*. Winner signed his name to two nasty *Death Wish* sequels in the 1980s, following these with such disparate latterday oddities as *A Chorus of Disapproval*, *Dirty Weekend* and (his last, in 1998) the aptly titled *Parting Shots*.

Noel Harrison

Lucyna Winnicka

Other film personalities who died during the period under review included:

Oscar-winning audio innovators **Stefan Kudelski** (from Poland) and **Ray Dolby** (from the USA) died in January and September, aged 83 and 80 respectively. Five-time Oscar winner **Petro Vlahos**, whose pioneering work in blue/green-screen compositing began with *Ben-Hur* and *The Birds*, died at 96 in February.

Also from the USA: **John Brascia** (May, 80), who danced with Cyd Charisse in *Meet Me in Las Vegas* and wrote *The Baltimore Bullet*, and 95-year-old **AC Lyles** (September), the veteran Paramount producer behind numerous Westerns. Other US producers included **Robert Relyea** (March, 82), **Daniel H Blatt** (October, 76), **Hilton A Green** (assistant director on *Psycho* and producer of its 1980s sequels; October, 84), **Marty Hornstein** (December, 81) and New Zealand-born **Lloyd Phillips** (*Twelve Monkeys*, *Inglourious Basterds*; January, 63). In July and August, **Cory Monteith** (Canadian-born star of TV's *Glee*) and fellow actor **Lee Thompson Young** died at the tragically early ages of 31 and 29 respectively.

Warhol Superstars **Taylor Mead** (88) and **Louis Waldon** (78), both

of whom appeared in *Lonesome Cowboys* and other Factory products, died in May and December respectively. Actor and porn mogul **Fred J Lincoln** died at 75 in January and porn star **Harry Reems** at 65 in March.

From the UK: veteran disc jockey **David Jacobs** (September, 87), who played himself in several British pop films, and **Noel Harrison** (October, 79), who starred with Hayley Mills and Oliver Reed in *Take a Girl Like You* and whose recording of 'The Windmills of Your Mind' was popularised by the 1968 film *The Thomas Crown Affair*. Nigerian actor-playwright **Yemi Ajibade** (January, 83) made his career in Britain, as did Sri Lankan-born **David Spenser** (July, 79).

From mainland Europe: Spanish costume designer and winner of six Goya awards **Javier Artiñano** (July, 71) and **Lucyna Winnicka**, iconic Polish star of *Night Train* and *Mother Joan of the Angels* (January, 84). Also, Czech actress **Jiřina Jirásková** (January, 81), Finnish actor **Matti Ranin** (November, 87) and Danish actors

Peter Steen (February, 77), **Holger Juul Hansen** (March, 88) and **Ole Ernst** (September, 73). Norwegian actress **Eva Bergh** – whose sole foray into English-language cinema paired her with John Mills in *The Long Memory* – died aged 86 in February. Dutch actor-director **Kees Brusse**, who not only starred in *The Silent Raid* but also assisted its director Paul Rotha, died at 80 in December.

Armenian actor **Sos Sargsyan**, who featured in Tarkovsky's *Solaris*, died aged 83 in September. Turkish actor **Tuncel Kurtiz** (77) died in September, as did 79-year-old Moroccan actor (and Claude Lelouch regular) **Amidou**. From Russia: actors **Andrei Panin** (50), **Valeriy Zolotukhin** (71), both in March, and **Yury Yakovlev** (85) in November.

Cuban producer **Camilo Vives** died at 70 in March and Argentina's Oscar-nominated screenwriter **Aída Bortnik** at 75 in April. Finally, from India: producers **Sudhakar Bokade** (July, 57) and **Tammareddy Krishna Murthy** (September, 93) plus multi-award-winning director **Rituparno Ghosh** (May, 49).

Afterword

by **Mansel Stimpson**

History repeats itself: at this time in 2013 I was not only surveying the year's releases to date but was also looking ahead to note some of the summer attractions that had not been screened when we went to press. Most of those upcoming features were blockbusters and so it is once again in 2014, for cinema seems in recent years to have settled into a summer pattern which does not change even though variety is in short supply. Thus, with the emphasis on spectacle be it ancient or modern (or, indeed, futuristic), we are given the latest instalments of current franchises or revivals of old ones, but with precious little among the general releases to appeal to audiences not drawn to those areas of cinema.

If last year we were awaiting *Star Trek Into Darkness*, this year it is *Transformers: Age of Extinction* and, whereas 2013 gave us *The Wolverine*, 2014 provides *X-Men: Days of Future Past*, although the latter comes with two

consolations, the return of director Bryan Singer and the presence of the admirable Jennifer Lawrence heading its starry cast. Instead of the return of Superman in *Man of Steel*, this year we have a whole range of Marvel Comics superheroes in *Guardians of the Galaxy*. As for Tom Cruise, *Oblivion* may not have been a highlight of summer 2013 but he is back in what one hopes will be a better action movie, *Edge of Tomorrow*. Meanwhile the expendables refuse to give up since August is set as the date for Stallone, Schwarzenegger and Statham to reassemble in *The Expendables 3*.

When it comes to the resurrection of much older hits we find that 2014 is rather more wide-ranging than last year. 2013 rebooted *The Lone Ranger* but 2014 offers *Godzilla*, *Hercules* and another return to a series that started out as long ago as 1968 – this time it's called *Dawn of the Planet of the Apes*. In other areas of popular cinema we have Disney turning once again to

The franchise continues: Nicholas Hoult, James McAvoy and Hugh Jackman in *X-Men: Days of Future Past*.

live action with *Maleficent*, while animation is represented not by *Despicable Me 2* as in 2013 but by *How To Train Your Dragon 2*. An altogether more modern trend is the American comedy that puts emphasis on actresses rather than actors and this continues with *Tammy*, which pairs Melissa McCarthy and Susan Sarandon. The odd one out here – on more than one level – is *Jersey Boys*. Despite the success of *Les Misérables*, musicals are still comparatively rare, but in any case the last director one would expect to be in charge is the man handling this one, Clint Eastwood.

As I write, the quality of all of the titles mentioned above remains unknown, but what of the 2014 releases I have seen? Early in the year a number of critics tried to persuade us that we were living through a new golden age of cinema, but I found it impossible to agree. That's not to say that the early months of the year lacked quality work altogether. The acclaim for *12 Years a Slave* was entirely deserved and it was encouraging that this unflinching view of slavery in 19th century America (cinema's best ever treatment of the subject) achieved commercial as well as critical success. If that was a triumph for its director Steve McQueen, *Her* similarly found Spike Jonze on great form in a wholly original piece, a kind of love story in a new technological age in which Joaquin Phoenix, cast against type, was admirable and in which Scarlett Johansson gave the best voice-only performance since Max von Sydow's in Lars von Trier's *Europa* (1991).

If less than perfect, the Coen brothers' *Inside Llewyn Davis* with its affectionate warmth and

Wes Anderson's *The Grand Budapest Hotel* with its stunning designs were rewarding and individual films. But, as against that, one had Martin Scorsese's *The Wolf of Wall Street* which relished exactly what it was supposed to be criticising, the appallingly macho *Lone Survivor* and, in *The Railway Man*, a film which, regardless of its basis in actuality, played around with the facts and existed in an unreal world of its own. Other titles were better but less distinguished than one had hoped. I have in mind here the film about the mistress of Charles Dickens, *The Invisible Woman*, so much less satisfying than Claire Tomalin's biography (although Joanna Scanlan was a wonderful Mrs Dickens), *Mandela: Long Walk to Freedom* (well acted but an Attenborough-style biopic not in the same class as Attenborough's own *Cry Freedom*) and *Dallas Buyers Club* (again well cast but not without clichés of gay cinema despite its initially homophobic hero).

As the year went on, disappointments mounted. Commercial cinema failed to come up with a smash hit on the scale of *The Best Exotic Marigold Hotel* and Chiwetel Ejiofor's follow-up to *12 Years a Slave*, *Half of a Yellow Sun*, was all the more dispiriting because the cast and its theme (the sufferings of the Nigerian people in the 1960s) deserved better writing and direction. There were also a whole series of foreign language films that seemed to promise quality but did not deliver. *Before the Winter Chill* had Kristin Scott Thomas and Daniel Auteuil but none of the believability of *Leaving* (2008); *A Thousand Times Good Night* had Juliette Binoche as a war photographer but was totally outclassed by Sebastian Junger's 2013 documentary tribute to the late Tim Hetherington *Which Way is the Front Line From Here?*; *Bright Days Ahead* with Fanny Ardant was superficial and *Chinese Puzzle* from Cédric Klepisch seemed certain to disappoint fans of Audrey Tautou, whose role in it is insubstantial. My personal sense of disappointment extended to the Indian hit *The Lunchbox*, but I would recommend it to all those who relish the improbable escapism offered by a film like *The Best Exotic Marigold Hotel*.

Grouping together so many titles that let me down may make me sound grumpy, so this may be the place to mention that I welcomed *The Book Thief* which, disdained by many critics, struck me as being a well-judged piece for teenagers possibly ignorant about Nazi Germany (the film's source is one of those books aimed at young adults) but also a film that would be appreciated by older audiences. As for a June release that I have seen, I would be delighted if Amma Asante's *Belle* became a big box-office success. Based on fact, it is an 18th century tale with a mulatto heroine (the splendid Gugu Mbatha-Row) set largely in Kenwood House, Hampstead. It has a great supporting cast of British artists and should appeal to lovers of TV's *Downton Abbey*, while also drawing others because within a popular framework it deals with issues of human rights connected to the slave trade. If only they had smuggled Judi Dench into the cast it would have been an automatic smash hit, but it deserves to be one in any case since this is popular cinema at something like its best.

For further works of quality one can turn to a whole series of documentaries: the soccer film about American Samoa's team *Next Goal Wins* which even delights those who don't think of the game as beautiful; the highly original piece about painting and copies, *Tim's Vermeer*; the biopic *I Am Divine*; Kirby Dick's telling study of sexual abuse in the American military, *The Invisible War*, and that wide-ranging study by Mark Cousins of how childhood has been portrayed in movies, *A Story of Children and Film*.

As in 2013 a number of established directors have with varying degrees of success given us new work: Claire Denis (*Bastards*), Xavier Dolan (*Tom at the Farm*), Asghar Farhadi (*The Past*), Terry Gilliam (*The Zero Theorem*), Joanna Hogg (*Exhibition*), Roman Polanski (*Venus in Fur*), Godfrey Reggio (*Visitors*) and, with what is possibly the year's most divisive film, *Under the Skin*, Jonathan Glazer. My own favourites in this context are Jim Jarmusch's unique take on vampire movies (*Only Lovers Left Alive*), Lukas Moodysson's return to form with the Swedish youth film *We Are The Best!* and, for its masterly design, *The Wind Rises* which is said by Hayao Miyazaki to be his last film. I have yet to see another last feature, Ken Loach's *Jimmy's Hall* (although in his case Loach has said that he may yet make more documentaries and he has not entirely ruled out the possibility of small-scale works with actors). As for Richard Linklater's *Boyhood*, it sounds fascinating, a film made over the years as the players aged – that being a device that worked well for Michael Winterbottom in *Everyday*.

In contrast to the limited range of the summer attractions, the first half of 2014 has offered works as diverse and original as *American Interior* (Gruff Rhys performing around the USA while investigating the route of an 18th century ancestor: a film that is often laugh-out-loud funny) and John Michael McDonagh's *Calvary* with its astonishing mix of black comedy, thriller and religious concerns. No less quirky and photographically the highlight of the year to date

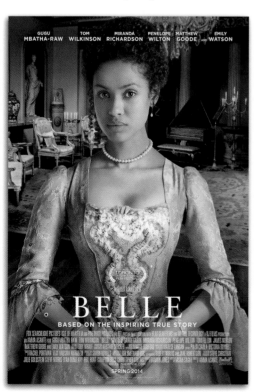

Left:
Gugu Mbatha-Raw at Kenwood House in *Belle*.

Below:
The Wind Rises, possibly Hayao Miyazaki's last film.

A series of provocations: the first part of Lars von Trier's *Nymphomaniac*.

is the Icelandic movie *Of Horses and Men* from Benedikt Erlingsson, while in Danis Tanović's *An Epsiode in the Life of an Iron Picker* we have a drama involving social issues in Bosnia as re-enacted by the real-life participants.

A true story of a very different kind has come to the screen in John Curran's *Tracks*. Here Mia Wasikowska portrays Robyn Davidson who made an adventurous trek across Western Australia with camels in 1977: her performance is wonderful. So too is that by Tom Hardy who holds the screen alone in Steven Knight's gripping drama *Locke*, and there is equal originality to be found in the Slovenian film *Silent Sonata*, a somewhat Felliniesque piece with a circus providing a

Australia with camels: Mia Wasikowska in John Curran's *Tracks*.

peaceful setting in a war-torn world (the real novelty here is that there is no dialogue whatever, no spoken word of any kind). Meanwhile Jia Zhang-ke's *A Touch of Sin* unexpectedly looks at violence in China and *Blue Ruin*, an American thriller by Jeremy Saulnier, proves to be the best Coen brothers film not actually made by them. Also American and powerful is Ryan Coogler's *Fruitvale Station*, a controlled but deeply felt portrayal of events during one day in the Bay Area leading to a killing.

There are plenty of other titles that deserve mention but for which there is no space. However, a word is required on the present state of censorship in this country given that 2014 included a remarkable week in January which emphasised how standards have changed. Two films, Alain Guiraudie's gay cruising drama *Stranger by the Lake* and Lars von Trier's two-part *Nymphomaniac*, were press shown within days of one another and both contained scenes so sexually explicit that even critics felt compelled to remark on it. As it happens both films were works of some quality, especially *Nymphomaniac* which in all kinds of ways was based on the notion that offering the audience a series of provocations can make for effective cinema. And so it proved for, while in total the work lasts four hours in the version released here, not for a moment are there any longueurs. Some may approve of the freedom allowed here and others may believe that the censors are not doing their job, but what these two films proved conclusively in the absence of protests from the public is that Mary Whitehouse is long dead.

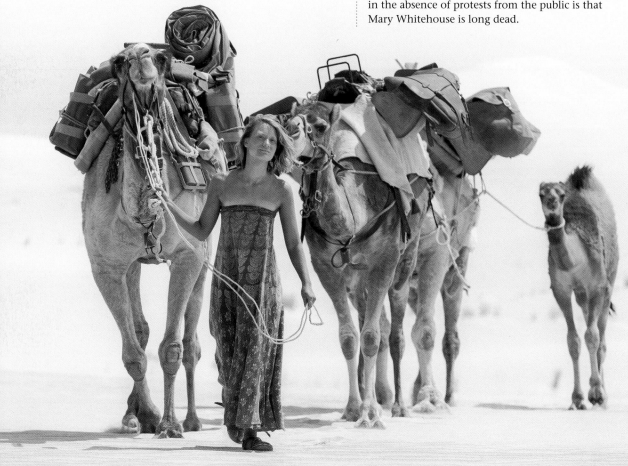